THE LIFE AND DEATH OF
AN IDEAL

The
Life and Death
of an Ideal

FRANCE
IN THE CLASSICAL AGE

Albert Guérard

W. H. ALLEN
LONDON
1957

944.03
G 929 l

62320

PRINTED IN GREAT BRITAIN BY
BILLING AND SONS LIMITED, GUILDFORD AND LONDON

A Madame et Monsieur Paul Bouju
qui ont su faire aimer à tant
d'Américains la douceur de France

CONTENTS

CONTENTS

x

BOOK III: THE EIGHTEENTH CENTURY

INTRODUCTION

INTRODUCTION

THE CLASSICAL AGE: "ONE FAITH, ONE LAW, ONE KING"

I. Self-Determination of Historical Periods. Living Interest of the Classical Age.

II. Other Names for the Period: Modern Times? The Ancient Régime? The Revolution is a part of the Classical Age.

III. The Spiritual Unity of the Classical Age: Rationalism, Autocracy, Reverence for Antiquity.

IV. Sub-periods: (a) The Renaissance. (b) The Religious Wars. (c) The Restoration of Order (Henry IV, Richelieu). (d) The Splendour of Louis XIV. (e) Decadence and Transition. (f) The Regency and the Pompadour Era. (g) The Return to Nature and the Eve of the Revolution. (h) The Revolution and the Empire.

V. Complexity and Inner Contradictions of the Classical Age: (a) Survivals of Medievalism; (b) gradual shift of emphasis from Tradition to Reason.

The Story of an Ideal and of an Effort.

I

WHAT is the Classical Age? Periods do not follow each other in orderly succession, like Kings and Presidents. Historians may argue indefinitely about the birth, accession to power, dethronement and demise of that phantom sovereign, "the Spirit of the Age." The germs of our most modern ideas can be found in the middle ages, and the quaintest medieval notions survive in our midst. We are fairly safe, however, in applying to periods, even more than to nations, the Wilsonian doctrine of self-determination. Consciousness is the one irrefutable test of existence. For three centuries, the French lived consciously under the classical dispensation. The state of mind that it implied had a definite beginning and a definite end. There was a moment when France said with Rabelais: "At last we are out of Gothic night!"; and a moment when she said with Victor Hugo: "The Lord be

3

praised! We are delivered from the Greeks and the Romans!" Granted that both attitudes revealed some injustice, much ignorance and more illusion: still, even a delusion is a force, and therefore a fact, in the realm of ideas. The Classical Spirit was a conscious factor in French culture. It is the evolution of that factor that we shall attempt to trace in this book.

In English-speaking countries, the French Classical Age is no longer considered as of commanding importance. We know that French doctrines and French models did affect, profoundly, our art, our literature, and our philosophy. But we also know that against such a domination there was a sharp and successful revolt. The dictatorship of Boileau is as dead as the autocracy of the Stuarts, or the claims of King George III to his American colonies. Not only are we emancipated: but the tables were actually turned; France eagerly submitted to the influence of Shakespeare, "Ossian," Walter Scott, and Byron. To the "modernist," French Classicism was nothing but a prolonged mistake; the true classical mind, not satisfied with an ideal at second hand, prefers to go back to the fountain and origin of the faith, Greece and Rome. If some of us are interested in the Classical Age at all, it is for Romantic reasons: not because Classicism has the words of eternal life, but because it possesses the majesty of death and the poetry of ruins. When the crumbling and leprous statues in the gardens of Versailles were cleaned up and restored as Louis XIV would have wanted them, that act of piety was denounced by some as Vandalism. Delicate souls enjoy the subtle odour of decay, as of autumnal leaves, left behind by those centuries of abundant and almost coarse vitality. Because their pastels are faded, we forget that their faces were rubicund.

Such will not be our attitude. We shall not study the Classical Age because it is dead, but because it is alive. It is said that History is past Politics: a definition which we find perfectly acceptable, inasmuch as Politics deals —or meddles—with every possible aspect of life. It is no less obvious that Politics is living History. But we shall

go farther and say that History is living Politics. Interest in death is decadent, not scientific. Let the dead
bury their dead! It is only when the facts of the past
have some bearing upon our own life, something in common with our own experience, that they are intelligible at
all. History can not carry us into the irrevocable past:
what it does is to reveal how much of the past survives in
the present.

In France, at any rate, the Classical Spirit is a live
issue: and France herself is a live issue for us. We can
not quite understand Raymond Poincaré without Charles
Maurras, Jacques Bainville and Louis Bertrand. They
may differ on many points, but they are steeped in the
same tradition. The ghosts of Richelieu and Hugues de
Lionne hovered over the Paris Peace Conference. The
spirit of Versailles affected the treaty of 1919. France
to-day is a fascinating battlefield between the seventeenth
century and the twenty-first. Louis XIV is stormed, captured and re-captured like a line of trenches on the
Chemin-des-Dames. Hardly had Louis Bertrand stamped
the majestic medal of the Grand Monarch but Félix
Gaiffe must show us its disreputable obverse.[1] Such partisanship, no doubt, is alien to the serenity of academic
history: but academic history is a frigid idol.

In that battle between past and future, we need hardly
state where we stand. A writer may often conceal his
convictions, but seldom his sympathies. Impartiality is
indispensable in establishing material facts. When it
comes to the selection of facts, which must needs be based
upon the appreciation of their significance, perfect inanity alone could attain to impartiality. The most conscientious judge on the bench can not lay aside his "prejudices," for they are embodied in the Code. All that can
be expected of him is that he shall disregard personal interest, animosity and caprice. To such a modest degree
of pragmatic impartiality, the present writer has some
reasonable claims. He has lived away from France for

[1] Louis Bertrand, *Louis XIV*, Paris, Arthème Fayard, 1923. Félix
Gaiffe, *L'Envers du Grand Siècle*, Paris, Albin Michel, 1924.

nearly a quarter of a century. For all these years, he has been teaching the history of French culture—a sobering process, under which juvenile radicalism could hardly survive; his many personal friends in France, whilst they belong to all creeds and parties, are mostly found on the conservative side. So he is able to enjoy Messrs. Maurras, Bainville, Dimier, Bertrand, without taking them too seriously; and to chuckle over *Penguin Island*, without being led into anarchism.

II

In many works on French History—for instance in Michelet's, still the greatest of them all—the times we call "Classical" are named "Modern," whilst the "Contemporary" period is made to begin with the Revolution. For men of Michelet's generation, the ashes of the Revolution were still warm: for us the great upheaval belongs to the past as completely as Louis XIV himself. The word "modern" in connection with the Bourbon monarchy seems to us a misnomer. It certainly fails to express the aspirations and the principles of the time. The eighteenth century, in some respects, may have been consciously modern: the sixteenth and the seventeenth were not. Progress, in those days, meant first of all a return to antiquity; in art, literature, and philosophy, a return to the standards of Greece and Rome; in religion, a return to the faith and practices of the Apostolic Age. Calvin, Boileau, Bossuet, would spurn the name Modernist as indignantly as our staunchest Fundamentalists to-day.

The term *Ancient Régime* is also in common use. Unfortunately, it is so elastic as to be almost meaningless. In Taine's *Origins of Contemporary France*, the Ancient Régime is made to include, legitimately enough, all that preceded the Revolution: it extends as far back as the inception of feudal and ecclesiastical privileges. There is much to be commended in such a division. The Dark Ages can hardly be called a "régime" at all; and the Ancient Régime, from the end of the tenth century to the end of the eighteenth, thus coincides with the rule of the

Capetian dynasty. On the other hand, M. Funck-Brentano, in his scholarly, paradoxical and popular study
L'Ancien Régime,[1] restricts the term to the state of
France on the eve of the Revolution; more definitely, to
the last few years of the reign of Louis XV, for the great
events of 1789 were already casting their shadow over the
fifteen years that preceded them. The time is fast coming
when the Second Empire will rightly be called "l'ancien
régime." A new order soon becomes ancient: the classical
ideal remains classical.

If we adopt the name "Classical Age," our story will
properly begin with the Revival of Learning, the rediscovery of Antiquity, which, originating in Italy, reached
France early in the sixteenth century. Its first manifestation is Humanism: and to the present day, "classical
studies" and "the humanities" are still held to be synonymous; the notion of "modern humanities" seems to many
a contradiction in terms. Thus our starting point is
clearly defined. But when would the Classical Age termi-
nate? If we use as our basis the cultural notion of Classicism, the period would extend until the time when the
Classical School was definitely superseded. Although the
germs of Romanticism are clearly to be found in Rousseau in 1750, and its manifestations were unmistakable in
Chateaubriand at the very dawn of the nineteenth century, it was not until two decades later, with Lamartine,
Vigny, Hugo, that the school assumed conscious existence.
In art as well as in literature, the Revolution is wholly
and austerely classical, and so is the Empire. There is
no coincidence between the purely political Revolution
and the cultural Revolution. As for the industrial Revolution, in germ under Louis XVI, but frustrated, it had
to wait, in France, until the eighteen-forties, and bore its
fruit under Napoleon III.

This leads us to consider the Revolution as the last
phase of the Classical epoch, rather than as the opening
of a new era. This contention may seem a paradox, if

[1] Frantz Funck-Brentano: *L'Ancien Régime*, Paris, Arthème Fayard,
1926.

not an absurdity. But it is by this time a paradox so
hoary, and supported by such sober political philosophers
that it has become venerable. De Tocqueville established
the continuity of political principles and methods from
the Ancient Régime to the Revolution; Albert Sorel made
the same demonstration in the domain of foreign affairs;
Louis Madelin adopted the same view in his Political History of France from 1515 to 1804. For Taine, the disease which killed the Ancient Régime and determined the
Revolution was none other but "the Classical Spirit," the
Philosophy of the Enlightenment. The Revolution came
to fulfil, not to destroy; the Convention rushed to completion the work of Richelieu; and Napoleon actually was
what Louis XIV had dreamt to be.

III

These three centuries, from Marignano to Waterloo,
richly varied as they were, offered a striking unity of
spirit. The very center of that unity is to be found in
RATIONALISM: the Classical Age was throughout
what it called itself towards its close, the *Age of Reason.*
Not that the Middle Ages had not used reason, or at least
reasoning, to such an excess that scholasticism has remained a by-word. But reason then was not supreme.
Even in philosophy, she was the handmaid of revelation;
in political and social life, she was hampered at every turn
by reverence for "custom." Not that later ages, including our own, have totally abandoned reason as their
guide: but, with Romanticism, reason was subordinated
to imagination and passion; with Realism, to observation
and experimentation. Even among French Radicals to-
day, nothing appears inevitably true on the mere plea
that it is logical.

The supremacy of Reason is characteristic of the whole
period. It was Reason that Rabelais and Montaigne
wanted to train in their educational schemes; even Montaigne's scepticism is a manifestation of rationalism:
Reason alone is capable of gauging its own infirmity. It

was Reason that Calvin used so masterfully in his controversies. Descartes, Molière, Boileau, urge us to honour, to obey, and even to love Reason:

> Aimez donc la raison: que toujours vos écrits
> Empruntent d'elle seule et leur lustre et leur prix.

Reason for them was synonymous with Nature and with
Truth. The ardent mystic Pascal teaches: "All the dignity of man rests upon his thought. Let us therefore
learn how to think correctly: such is the foundation of
moral life." The eighteenth century was a feast, and at
times a carnival, of reason; towards its close, we find
Reason formally enthroned on a revolutionary altar. The
supreme soldier, Napoleon, bowed to the same goddess:
above all his victories, he prized his Civil Code: Law
brought at last into harmony with Reason.

The second character common to these three centuries
is the growth of ABSOLUTISM, going hand in hand
with the growth of national consciousness. The France
of Louis XI was still a quivering mass of feudal princi-
palities caught in the royal net: some of them still restive,
and eager to break their bonds. Throughout the Classical Age, the net tightens and resistance ceases. The
nobles lose their feudal powers, retaining naught but
empty titles and obnoxious privileges; the cities lose the
substance of their charters; the provinces have to give up
much of their autonomy. This evolution is one of the
triumphs of Rationalism: order is conceived as unity and
clarity, for truth is single and logic is simple. The result
is an enormous growth of the central power, both in extent and in depth.

In the process, France was created: not a vague geographical expression and a sentimental aspiration merely,
like the *Douce France* of the *Chansons de Geste;* not as
"the French Section of the Catholic International"; but
as a nation, that is to say as a person, symbolized by her
King. Louis XIV was absolute because he was "France";
he might very naturally have said: *"L'Etat, c'est moi."*

Of this national absolutism, the monarchy was the sign and the instrument, rather than the essence. The Royalist historians are undeniably right in claiming that the Kings made the Nation, and that Royalism, therefore, is "integral Nationalism." But, as the nation grew to consciousness, the Kings became the servants of the entity their race had created. Under Henry IV and again at the time of the Fronde, the enlightened middle class and the masses rallied round the monarchy, chose it as their leader against the forces of disruption: a king thus supported became indeed sovereign "by the grace of God *and* the will of the people." It will readily be seen that in this also the Revolution continued without a break the classical tradition. The instrument was found wanting, the symbol was discarded, but the facts which had given the monarchy the substance of its power remained. National unity, national absolutism were still the ideals of France under the Republic as they had been under the Valois and the Bourbons. Louis XIV, Robespierre, Napoleon, under different titles, were priests of the same cause.

The third principle which pervades the whole period, and which in a sense is the most distinctive, is CLASSICISM in art and literature. In its broadest meaning, Classicism is the spirit of discipline, as opposed to the spirit of individualism; specifically, however, it implies the deliberate imitation of Greco-Latin models. The Middle Ages had known some vestiges of antiquity, and held them in great veneration. Yet the medieval mind was never wholly guided by what survived of Pagan antiquity. The power of the Catholic Church, the force of immediate local custom, were greater than the dimly remembered prestige of ancient Rome. Saints counted for more than classical heroes; and when Achilles and Æneas appeared in medieval poems, it was in the guise of medieval knights or barons. Our age, on the other hand, may claim a fuller, a more accurate knowledge of antiquity than the Classical centuries could possess. But no *Ipse dixit* of Aristotle, no precept of Horace, no architectural orders of Vitruvius are accepted by us as unquestionable authorities. Interest and even reverence may remain: the cult of the antique has perished utterly. Now that cult was constant during the period which we are studying. Education was Latin, not French; and the statues of Louis XIV represent him clad as a Roman Emperor, or even nude like a Greek hero. The enthusiasm of the early sixteenth century for rediscovered antiquity is known to every schoolboy. Not so familiar, perhaps, is the fact that the last stage of the period saw a recrudescence of fervour for the antique. At the very moment when Romanticism was germinating, architecture, sculpture, painting, were becoming more severely classical. A description of the Greek world was a best seller on the eve of the Revolution. The Pantheon in Paris was more Greco-Roman than the edifices of the Renaissance; André Chénier is a better Hellenist than Ronsard. The age ended appropriately with a Neo-Roman Emperor: Napoleon pastiched in his columns and triumphal arches the monuments of his predecessors, Trajan and Septimus Severus.

The worship of Greece and Rome, however, did not exist apart from Rationalism. Certain Romanticists professed to admire "like a brute" every jot and tittle of the Shakespearian Scripture: but the Classicists, better balanced, revered antiquity only because antiquity was the embodiment of reason. Corneille bows to the rules of Aristotle, not, he says, because they are Aristotle's, but because they are reasonable. Just as the national and the monarchical spirits were long identical, so were rationalism and respect for antiquity one and the same. The age at its best believed in a sort of cultural bimetallism: between the gold standard of Reason and the silver standard of Antiquity, there existed such a definite and invariable relation that the two could be used interchangeably.

IV

Whilst insisting upon the essential unity of the Classical Age, we do not mean to ignore the picturesque, and at times profound, differences between generations. The background of Rabelais and that of Diderot are not of the same colouring; and Fontainebleau under Francis I was not Fontainebleau under Napoleon.

Apart from great revolutions in thought or in material conditions, we might expect national life to be continuous. The living tissue of the country is constantly renewed, and, strictly speaking, there is no such thing as a "generation." However, it is a fact that the flow of history is not even: it forms a series of pools and rapids. It takes some time for an ideal to be conceived and formulated, more time for it to be brought within the reach of men. Hardly does the ideal triumph but it "materializes": and disenchantment sets in. Its successor may not be ready: inertia often keeps a dying or even a dead sovereign on the throne long after its usefulness is past. The process, speaking in purely empirical fashion, takes roughly half a century: in that time, the leading personnel is completely renewed, and men forge to the front "who knew not Joseph." Of such secondary cycles, seven or eight may be discerned in the Classical Age.

The reign of Francis I, prolonged without any radical change by that of Henry II, forms the first. It is the jocund day of the Renaissance, and starts with a young, handsome, chivalrous, artistic King, the victor of Marignano, the friend of Lionardo, the builder of the new Louvre, the founder of the great humanistic school which still exists as the *Collège de France*. The contest with the House of Austria, under these two reigns, was exhausting and indecisive. France, on the whole, was the weaker, and stood constantly on the brink of disaster. But even that painful struggle had its glamour: it was the first diplomatic and military conflict with the whole of Europe for its theatre. The country knew internal peace, and, thanks to the economic transformation, a substantial measure of prosperity. The morning hopes faded; the brilliant young knight, under the curse of dissolute living, fell into early decay; the bitterness of religious strife was increasing beyond control. Yet the splendour of the promises, and a few substantial achievements, were long

remembered: a vision of learning and luxury, or elegance
and valour.

Then the religious wars, long looming, broke out with
fury. It was a protracted, confused, deadly squabble,
tragic without grandeur. Martyrs and heroes were not
lacking: but what history wafts to us is chiefly the acri-
monious pedantry of the theologians, shrill amid the bru-
talities of hired or fanatical cutthroats. Atrocities repaid
atrocities: des Adrets vied with Montluc. As in the dark-
est day of the Hundred Years War, princely families,
oblivious of king and country, were fighting for spoils;
and Guises and Condés, worse than Armagnacs and Burgundians, were using their creed as a cloak. Between
Huguenots and Catholic League, Catherine de' Medici,
mother of three degenerate kings, steered a panic-stricken
course, punctuating deceit with assassination. Lovers of
romance still relish the *haut goût* of that age, its Baude-
lairian blend of depravity and religious bigotry, of morbid refinement and frantic violence: Voltaire called that
nightmare "a silken robe smeared with blood." Out of
this chaos arose the scepticism of Montaigne, the mocking
common sense of the Parisian Bourgeoisie in the *Satire
Ménippée*, and at last, smiling and wary, firm and supple,
the opportunism of Henry IV. The Edict of Nantes was
a truce made acceptable through weariness rather than
through genuine tolerance.

France had seen anarchy, and recoiled: the seventeenth
century will extol, in reaction, the ideal of discipline, and
submit with eagerness to its very excesses. The first half
of the century marked in every field a conscious effort
towards order. Manners, language, literature, religion,
were tamed and purified, even though originality had to
be mutilated: Malherbe won the day against Régnier or
Théophile de Viau. In government, the same progress
was achieved, but not without cruel jerks: too much depended upon a few all-powerful individuals. Henry IV
had been a miracle of tactful firmness: his widow was
weak and muddle-headed. Under her favourites, the
store of gold, authority and goodwill left by the wise

king was frittered away, and it took the ruthless hand of
Richelieu to check the mad course towards renewed chaos.
Richelieu, with the taciturn support of Louis XIII, did
his work cruelly, wastefully, but thoroughly: so thoroughly that the foreign origin, the cowardice, the corruption of his successor Mazarin could endanger, but not
ruin it. Through civil war and European strife, Mazarin led young Louis XIV to safety, and left him in
possession of unquestioned power at home, of unrivalled
prestige abroad.

By 1661, the Classical Age had reached its summit: a
pacified, orderly, self-confident France, under a young
King eager for glory. For twenty-five years, the em-
blematic sun of the Grand Monarch shone with uninterrupted splendour; it shone on victories and conquests, on
gorgeous court functions, artistic achievements, literary
masterpieces. The portraits of that generation breathe
invincible calm: the whole reign was, not an adventure,
but a consummation. No revolt, no opposition, no discontent: at least none audible enough to mar the majesty
of that peace.

Michelet divides the reign of Louis XIV in medical
terms: before the fistula, after the fistula. More conventional historians place the turn of the tide in 1685, when
the Edict of Nantes was revoked. It was the logical consequence of absolutism and its first irretrievable mistake.
Arrogance and prodigality, long admired as tokens of
greatness, bore their fruit at last. Before the end of the
century, the great servants of the monarchy were succeeded by mere courtiers, the great classical writers had
died. In the chorus of praise, grown stale and thin, dis-
cordant murmurs could be heard. As late as 1697, Louis
XIV was still holding his own, *nec pluribus impar:* during the war of the Spanish succession, famine, bankruptcy and utter defeat faced the ageing King. Under
the weight of infirmities, sorrows and repentance, Louis
XIV, never irreligious, grew more narrowly devout. The
genuine conversion of the master was hypocritically followed by the Court. The closing years of that intermi-

nable reign are somber: they are not ignoble. Under the
bludgeoning of fate, the monarchy preserved its indomitable dignity.

The rabble feasted on the route of Louis XIV's funeral
train. All the restraints of the last thirty years were
thrown to the wind. Of this reaction, the Regent took
the lead and remains the symbol. "The Regency" means
elegant and corrupt cynicism. It stamped the whole eighteenth century indelibly: there were nobles after the pattern of Philip of Orleans down to the very end of the
Ancient Régime, including his descendant *Philippe-
Egalité*. At any rate, that spirit prevailed almost without a check until the middle of the century. Young Voltaire was filled with it, and the Patriarch of Ferney had
not abjured it altogether. The Regency shows it in exaggerated form: its more subdued aspect is better exemplified by Madame de Pompadour, and her name is
frequently attached to the whole period. It would be
unfair to see in the Regency and in the Pompadour era
nothing but delightful sophistication and light-hearted
immorality. No doubt it was a time of ethical chaos: the
old order, with Louis XIV, had ended in moral bankruptcy, no new creed had been evolved, and scoffing scepticism was the keynote. But wit and taste were not the
only redeeming features of the time. The Regent himself
was kindly and liberal; even the Marquise de Pompadour
was singularly refined and keen-minded. Science and
philosophy were in vogue in the best *salons*. Voltaire and
Montesquieu knew how to turn a madrigal, an epigram,
and even a tale of dainty riskiness: but they could also devote years to *The Spirit of Laws* and the *Essay on Manners*.

Long before its iconoclastic work was fully done, the
eighteenth century had grown weary of negation. Destructive wit and the quest of luxurious pleasure ceased
to be the sole ideals. The "enlightened mind" aspired to
turn into a "beautiful soul." Virtue and Cleverness
fought for the crown. Surfeited society craved for a return to nature; "simplicity" was the latest fad of minds

which were the reverse of primitive. Of this new turn of
the French spirit, the immense vogue of Rousseau was the
clearest symptom. But the delicate hedonism and flash-
ing irony of the Pompadour era had not disappeared.
Rousseau alone, among the leaders, broke openly with the
"Enlightenment," and brought upon his head as many
curses as blessings. On the eve of the Revolution, Society, although it was yearning for pastures green, was
still witty, with more than a suspicion of frivolity and
wickedness. Between the drawing-room and the countryside, it compromised on the comic-opera hamlet of Trianon. "Virtue" was not to be officially supreme in France
until the dictatorship of Robespierre: its reign is remembered as "The Terror."

The Revolution, which includes the Empire, was the
climax of rationalism, classicism and autocracy. The
ideal slowly elaborated through three centuries was at
last fulfilled: France was united, leveled, standardized
under a strong central government: in Europe, she was
supreme. In that tragic quarter of a century, the Revolution forms a complete cycle of its own. It went through
all the phases of ardent aspiration, desperate fanaticism,
cynical discouragement, threatened relapse into chaos,
and finally resignation to mere material efficiency. Ful-
fillment is another word for suicide: the classical synthesis was dead before 1815. The factors of the new age,
—Romanticism, the historical spirit, the industrial revolution—were obscurely at work. But the fight of shadow
against shadow, the ghost of the Revolution against the
ghost of the Ancient Régime, was to continue on the
political stage for several generations.

These pictures blend easily into one another. Yet the
connection between them is not always easy to trace.
The method constantly used by Jacques Bainville to "explain" the course of French history consists in linking
important events with the phrase: "*It was inevitable
that . . .*" This is convenient, but meaningless. Whatever actually happened *did* happen, irretrievably: whether
it was inevitable or not, we shall never know. Narrative

history is a series of biographical romances which, if they were not true, often would strain credibility. It is hard enough to follow the most "inevitable" of historical processes; when we have to deal with conflicts of processes, the difficulty increases in geometric ratio; when personal and purely accidental elements are introduced, reason might as well abdicate. There was no "reason" why the legitimate heir of a Catholic crown should be a Huguenot prince; no "reason" why that adventurous pretender should not be a coward or a fool like many of his cousins, instead of being a man of unusual valour and sagacity; no "reason" why a fanatic should not have killed him, instead of Henry III, in 1589; and so *ad infinitum*. Yet under the irrational surface of history, vast tendencies flow in fairly steady streams. They merge or clash, slacken or rush ahead: but they are constant enough, and sufficiently independent from minor accidents, to be amenable to some rough kind of law. For that reason, *they* are the proper study of the historian who is not merely a seeker after the picturesque: concrete details count only in so far as they reveal these streams.

V

Was there such a law to the evolution of the Classical Age? The simplest scheme that will give unity to these tendencies is the universal rhythm of Formation, Perfection, Decadence. This standard pattern was specifically applied by Ferdinand Brunetière to the history of classical French literature; and, in this case, it fits with particular nicety, with a sort of truly classical symmetry. The great decade that saw the supreme flowering of classical genius (1660–1670) is exactly half-way between Marignano and Waterloo. With this obvious division we have no fault to find. It is convenient, and, in the main, it is not in contradiction with the facts. But, in itself, it is too simple to be of much service. There were in the classical age inner contradictions which made it far less rational, far less classical than it sought to be. The ideal was definite enough: but French society was never able absolutely to conform to its own ideal.

The first of these inner conflicts was caused by the persistence of medieval elements. French culture turned its back, somewhat too contemptuously, upon the middle ages: yet much of the middle ages survived, and could not be harmonized with the new principles. Feudalism was dead: but its trappings, titles, privileges, its caste consciousness and pride, remained long after they had become baseless and absurd. Not only did feudal prejudices and abuses endure throughout even the "century of enlightenment," but, at its very close, there was a virulent revival of nobiliary claims, a last desperate fight for existence of a system which, for three centuries, had been a hollow shell. Under Louis XVI, it was more difficult for a commoner to rise in the army than it had been under Louis XIV, and it is doubtful whether Bossuet could have become a Bishop on the eve of the Revolution. It is this survival of the empty forms and petty annoyances of feudalism up to 1789 that compelled the Revolution to be iconoclastic, thus giving the impression of a break in French history.

The second cause of confusion was the discrepancy between the true nature of the monarchy and its form. The national character of the King's power was obscurely felt by many; but it was accurately gauged by very few. It was difficult to realize that the monarch at Versailles, a nobleman among noblemen, was essentially the foe of the nobility, and the born leader of the middle class. It took the unconventional genius of Saint-Simon and the pitiless penetration of his disenchantment to discover in the brilliant reign of the Grand Monarch the triumph of "a vile bourgeoisie." Here is a phenomenon which after Spengler, we might call *pseudo-morphism:* the true basis of the government was the middle class, but, in externals, the supremacy of the privileged orders was unquestioned. The same confusion existed in the domain of thought and faith: whilst humanism and rationalism were the guiding principles, medieval theology had never formally abdicated. So freedom of thought was constantly encouraged, and no less constantly repressed. In the sixteenth century as well as in the eighteenth, philosophers were alternately favoured and persecuted. The Valois court struck an alliance with the Protestants, and forthwith massacred them. Louis XIV personally protected Molière, whilst *Tartuffe* was prohibited through the influence of the devout faction. The warmest apologists of the French monarchy praise its *instinctive* wisdom, and the *unconscious* consistency of its policy. On the conscious plane, the Kings and the privileged orders were guided, at times by classical ideas, more frequently by medieval shadows. The result was that an age which prayed so fervently to Reason showed itself, in its actions, far more capricious and far more chaotic than our own. A nation lives at the same time on several historical planes: Utopias and ghosts freely mingle with living men.

The third inner contradiction is more special to the Classical Age. We have defined Classicism as a sort of bimetallism, a belief in the permanent harmony of two standards, Reason and Antiquity. Classicism had complete faith in the stability of this ideal: as a matter of fact, the balance between the two elements was constantly changing. At first, Reason accepted gratefully, enthusiastically, the guidance of the antique tradition: even the freest mind in the sixteenth century, Montaigne, expressed himself through a string of classical quotations. But, under such excellent training, Reason caught up with its teachers, and learned how to dispense with them. With Descartes, Reason affirmed its autonomy: nothing is to be accepted as true on authority, were it the authority of the Stagirite himself, but only if it be plainly evident to the enquiring mind. The revolutionary character of Cartesianism was not immediately realized, although Bossuet was keen-sighted enough to discern it. The conscious turning point was the Quarrel of the Ancients and the Moderns: Reason bowed to its tutors, courteously enough, but expressed the determination of proceeding without their further aid. In literature, this state of mind did not bear fruit for another hundred years: but in science, in religion, in politics, Reason was henceforth emancipated: nay, it began pouring upon its former associate, Tradition, a stream of contemptuous terms: abuses, prejudices, superstitions. Such is the hidden rhythm, the inner drama of the classical age: the dissociation and conflict of its component elements. We find at first Reason working in cheerful subordination to Tradition; then Reason emancipated, but still respectful; Reason defiant; Reason triumphant. Some would be tempted to add: Reason, like President Paul Deschanel, going mad on its accession to power.

There is therefore nothing static about that age of classic repose. The classical mind fought for spiritual peace, but never fully attained it. Classicism, even in the heyday of Louis XIV, was an ideal, not a spontaneous reality. Hence the element of strain, of which all students of the period must be conscious. That very strain was not without grandeur, for it was a splendid display of human will. In this sense, the heroes of Corneille are the truest representatives of the Classical spirit. It had also its faults, likewise exemplified by Corneille: it made for stiffness, artificiality, even theatricality. That effort was not fully successful, and, at the time of the Revolution, the French had grown impatient beyond measure with its prolonged failure. The failure is a matter of history no less than the effort: the continued chaos of local customs, weights and measures; the teeming superstitions, the irksome abuses, the manifold absurdities of the ancient régime are as much a part of the picture as the logic of Descartes, the common sense of Boileau, the elegance of Racine, the majestic serenity of Bossuet. But this multitudinous picture we can not attempt to paint. Our study will essentially be that of a great effort, earnest and sustained. It failed, as all forms of Fundamentalism are bound to fail, because it wanted to chain living forces to an immovable point in history. But it was successful enough to dazzle many generations, and to compel our respect even to-day.

BOOK I

THE SIXTEENTH CENTURY

CHAPTER I

I. Rabelais's conception of the Renaissance: rediscovery of antiquity. An injustice: the true Renaissance that of the eleventh century. "The Thirteenth, Greatest of Centuries." Bewilderment in the fourteenth and fifteenth.

II. Persistence of the Medieval tradition: most clearly exemplified in Renaissance architecture; also in Clement Marot and in certain aspects of Rabelais.

III. The great discoveries and the great inventions (compass, gunpowder, printing-press) not brought about by rediscovery of antiquity.

IV. The true Renaissance a psychological fact: revival of optimism, escape from fifteenth-century morbidity, the Triumph of Life. Typified by Rabelais, the emancipated monk.

V. Rabelais. Pantagruelism: "Live in joy." Hymn to Pantagruelion. The Abbey of Thélème. Naturism: true *Humanism* its highest form.

I

"FOR that time was darksome, obscured with clouds of ignorance, and savouring a little of the infelicity and calamity of the Goths, who had, wherever they set footing, destroyed all good literature; which, in my age, hath by divine goodness been restored into its former light and dignity. . . . Now it is that the minds of men are qualified with all manner of discipline, and the old sciences revived, which for many ages were extinct. Now it is, that the learned languages are to their pristine purity restored."[1]

These words, addressed by Gargantua to his son Pantagruel, express with all possible definiteness the very spirit of the Renaissance. It was a deliberate condemnation of "Gothic" barbarism; it was an eager return to the light of antiquity. Such it was felt to be at the time; such it remained in the minds of generation after generation,

[1] *Rabelais,* Book II, Ch. VIII, Urquhart's translation.

B

unchallenged for three centuries. This conception of the Renaissance can hardly be disputed without transgressing the limits of the paradoxical and venturing into the realm of wilful nonsense.

Yet the feeling has grown that the name *Renaissance* is at least an exaggeration, and implies an injustice. It is not without cause that Henry Osborn Taylor, for instance, in his two substantial volumes on the sixteenth century, sought to avoid altogether that question-begging term. The word "Gothic" has long been redeemed from opprobrium. From purely "barbaric," its meaning changed to "picturesque and romantic," as in the "Gothic" novel of the late eighteenth century; and, in the nineteenth, Victor Hugo, among others, restored the "Gothic" among the very summits of art. To this revaluation of the Gothic must correspond a reconsideration, and perhaps a devaluation, of the Renaissance. The term will remain, right or wrong, just as "America" will perpetuate the name of Amerigo Vespucci; but it needs to be reinterpreted. Rabelais and his contemporaries were not wholly mistaken: but they were ill-informed and unwittingly unfair. Perhaps indeed were they unfair to the best there was in them.

If the word Renaissance has any meaning, it applies much more literally to the eleventh century than to the sixteenth. The English language, more fortunate than the French, is able to mark a clear distinction between the "Dark Ages" and the "Middle Ages." The half-millennium that followed the fall of Rome was "Gothic" in the worst sense. The hordes of blond beasts had well-nigh extinguished civilization; nor could much be saved by the barbaric Church they had fashioned in their own image. Antique culture had disappeared almost as completely as Christian mansuetude. Without Byzantium and the Arabs, it seems as though the light might have gone out altogether. A few barbarians of genius, a Theodoric, a Brunhilda, a Dagobert, struggled fitfully against the night. But even the greatest of these, Charlemagne, failed to dispel the darkness. After him, two interminable centuries of hopeless chaos.

Yet, during these five hundred years, Western Europe
had served its long apprenticeship, painfully, obscurely,
but not in vain. No definite turning point can be assigned;
no cause for the change of heart can be found in any particular event or in the career of any one man. But, about
the year 1000, evidences of a new birth were not lacking.
The old legend that Christendom had awaited destruction
in the year 1000 still has symbolical value: it seems as
though the world, recovering from its terror, had embraced
life with a new vigour. Anarchy was everywhere slowly
yielding to some rough feudal order; the monks were reforming themselves and the Church. The glorious words
of Raoul Glaber can not be quoted too often: "The earth,
shaking off the rags of its antiquity, was covering itself
anew with a white mantle of churches." Within less than
a century, we find the evidences of restored confidence and
restless energy in the great movement of the first crusade;
in the rapid progress of Romanesque architecture from a
debased pastiche of the Byzantine to an art singularly
robust and original; in the transformation of that art
into primitive Gothic; in the growth of definite vernacular literatures; in the first faint adumbrations of national
organization and national feeling. Then was *our* world
born. The very dynasties which ruled in the eleventh century are still represented to-day, and our culture has
never known again such an eclipse as that of the Dark
Ages. Compared with this almost magic transformation,
the revival of the sixteenth century loses much of its significance.

This rapid evolution led to "the thirteenth, greatest
of centuries," to borrow from a Catholic historian a title
which may be disputable, but which is by no means absurd. Appropriately, the age closed with the vision of
Dante, a *Summa Poetica* to be placed by the side of the
Summa Theologica of St. Thomas Aquinas, and by the
side of those great poems and treatises in chiseled stone
and filtered light, the cathedrals of Paris and Chartres,
of Amiens and Rheims. But after that? Not darkness
again: only, in France at least, a strange, sickly twilight

in which both faith and reason nearly lost their way. The true "Middle Ages" ended even before the direct line of the Capetians.

For this arrested growth of the medieval spirit, many causes have been suggested. The economic interpreters of history have their theories, in which the Black Death plays an important part. So far as France is concerned, the Hundred Years War alone would seem to be sufficient reason. But the cultural life of the country was not yet fully identified with the fate of the national dynasty. Whilst the French king was in distress, whilst many of his provinces were devastated by his own bands as well as by those of the enemy's, other parts, under English or Burgundian rule, enjoyed long periods of comparative quiet; Bordeaux, in particular, was markedly prosperous. So the war is not an all-sufficient explanation.

It may be noted also that the three centers of civilization from which Northwestern Europe had most to learn were, in the fourteenth century, in full decline. The revived Greek Empire was but a puny shadow, fighting against impossible odds; the Arabs had lost leadership in the Eastern Mediterranean to the more barbaric Turks; and the Moors of Spain were slowly receding before the reconquering Christian tide. Still, Western Europe in the fourteenth century was no longer dependent upon cultural importations. The student of culture must seek for the trouble in the very heart of culture.

Medieval civilization was essentially a Christian civilization; Christianity had then two lights, the Pope of Rome and the University of Paris; and both lights had grown dim. The Papacy had been humbled and enfeebled by the sixty-seven years of its "Babylonian Captivity" at Avignon (1309-1376); its return to Rome was the signal for a long series of schisms. Two Popes, and even three, anathematized one another. Heresies were breaking out in Bohemia and in England; the Council proclaimed its superiority over the Pope, and the French King his own supremacy in the administration of the French Church. For a world which, with Dante, had so passionately yearned for unity, such anarchy seemed to portend spiritual death.

The division of the Church could be healed, and was healed; but the great theological school, the University of Paris, the fountain head of Christian philosophy, had lost its vitality beyond hopes of recovery. The task of formulating the data of revelation in the terms of Aristotelian logic had been performed once for all. Henceforth scholasticism could go no farther: it could only lose itself in the intricate maze of its own subtle absurdity. And from such a fate there was no appeal: the Masters of Unreason were entrenched in their double infallibility, as theologians and as logicians. So the beacon set on Mount St. Genevieve diffused palpable darkness; all the efforts of the Doctors were bent on discovering even the most timid ray of light, in order to extinguish it.

Rabelais was not wrong therefore in referring to the period from which France was just emerging as "darksome, obscured with clouds of ignorance." He was wrong in assuming that such darkness had prevailed ever since "the Goths" had put out the light of ancient culture. The modern world had evolved a light of its own, which was burning still. The eclipse that left the fourteenth and the fifteenth centuries so bewildered was neither complete nor permanent. The rudiments of the modern secular state existed, as early at least as the days of Philip the Fair; the keyword of modern science, *experimentation*, had been uttered by Roger Bacon; the sturdy common sense of the middle class had asserted itself in John of Meung's *Romance of the Rose*. Within the Church herself, not only radical reformers like Wyclif and Hus, but quiet spiritual influences like those of à Kempis and Gerson proved that literalism, scholasticism and clericalism had not completely stifled the life of the soul. No new revelation was therefore necessary: only the release of undiminished energies now tangled up and wasted in obscure conflict. And the Church had repeatedly proved that she possessed that power of self-rejuvenation: with the Cluniacs in the tenth century, with the Friars in the thirteenth. Had antiquity not been "rediscovered," as the phrase goes, the progress of the human mind would hardly have been delayed. That "rediscovery" was much rather a sign of renewed activity than its starting point.

II

It would be unsafe, therefore, to take the revival of classical learning as a center in our study of the sixteenth century. It was by no means purely incidental: but neither was it essential. Our impression of history is to a large extent derived from bookmen, who are inclined to exaggerate the importance of bookish knowledge and of purely literary fashions. The sixteenth century continues the fifteenth, not the third.

This is particularly clear in the art of the time, and most evident in architecture. Of the three elements which were then blended, the national tradition, the influence of Italy and the models of antiquity, the first was overwhelming, the second superficial, the third comparatively negligible. It is not in the sixteenth century, but late in the eighteenth, or under Napoleon, that we find in France actual pastiches of Greco-Roman monuments. Under Louis XII and Francis I, the antique and even the Italianate affected the details of ornamentation, not the structure of the edifices; and this decoration of foreign origin, whilst frequently superior to that of the Flamboyant period, did not compare in exquisite fancy and loving realism with the purely French carving of the twelfth and thirteenth centuries. Late Gothic and so-called Renaissance merge by imperceptible degrees, as in the Church of Brou, or in the steeples of Tours, with their graceful cupolas and lanterns. There are few more delightful pieces of architecture than these delicate hybrids. The style is represented everywhere in France, particularly in Burgundy, Normandy and in the Loire region. But the Parisian examples of it are naturally the best known, and they are also among the most charming. St. Eustache suffers from the vicinity of the vast utilitarian

sheds of the *Halles Centrales;* the eighteenth century
clapped on to its West front a morose and utterly commonplace façade; the early nineteenth saw fit to bob its
delicate central spire in order to make room for a sema-
phoric telegraph; and the niches of its portals were bereft of their statuettes. In spite of so much Vandalism,
the Church remains impressive without: within, the combination of majestic restraint and aerial fantasy is well-
nigh unique. In all essentials, it is purely Gothic; yet
the details reveal unmistakably the influence of Italy.
St. Etienne-du-Mont, on a smaller scale, is freer, quainter,
even more appealing; within a stone's throw, the huge
bare masses of Soufflot's Pantheon enable us to measure
the abyss between the spirit of the Renaissance and the
systematic imitation of Antiquity.

In secular architecture, we find the same characteristics: medieval buildings choose to adorn themselves with
the fashionable garments of Italy, but at the core, they
remain French and medieval. Already in the fifteenth
century, the great feudal castles had discarded some of
their forbidding military gear: in its inner court at least,
Pierrefonds is a palace rather than a fortress. Italians
may have supervised the works of some châteaux in the
Loire region: but these famed buildings are racy of the
soil and rooted in local history. They retain the high
roofs, the richly ornamented dormers, the huge decorative chimneys that give such spirited grace to their sky-
line: all the charm of Chambord is found *above* the point
where an Italian edifice would end. Their winding stairs
are still frequently housed in jutting turrets. They have
moats and machicolations, and round towers at the cor-
ners, as though they were still expecting a siege: just as
the kings and the great lords still donned, for their state
portraits, medieval armours embossed with classical
scenes. Azay-le-Rideau, Chenonceaux, Chambord belong
to the days "when knighthood was in flower"—the flower,
perversely enough, blooming long after the season of
fruitage was over. The City Hall in Paris is Parisian,
not classical, in its inspiration. Its sharp roof of slate

brought no foreign note into the serried mass of the medieval city; and its campanile was properly a belfry of
Northern France.

Architecture is the simplest as well as the grandest
symbol of a civilization, and therefore the most effective.
The spirit of St. Eustache and Chambord was no less
patent in literature. The greatest names in the first half
of the sixteenth century are Clement Marot and François
Rabelais: an ill-assorted pair of worthies, an elfish sprite
and a fleshly giant; but both continue without a break
the purely Gallic tradition.

Marot is a more fortunate Villon, a less aristocratic
Charles of Orleans. He liked to be called the French
Vergil, on the strength of a pun: for Vergil also was
called *Maro.* There is no closer tie between himself and
classical antiquity. Greek remained Greek to him, and
the Latin authors he enjoyed, Vergil and Ovid, had never
ceased to be favourites in the middle ages. He translated them, with prettiness rather than with vigour, but
he was not inspired by them. His true classics were those
of the last three centuries, the *Golden Legend, Launcelot,*
the *Romance of the Rose,* and Villon. In language
and versification, he attempted no reform: indeed he
verged deliberately on the archaic. He still loved the old
forms which du Bellay and Ronsard were so contemptuously to brush aside; rondel or ballad, he handles them
all, not with the supreme and secret power of Villon, but
with exquisite mastery. He likes to juggle with rhyme,
but his taste keeps him from rivalling the verbal acrobatics of his immediate predecessors. His merits, which
are not to be despised, have nothing to do with ancient
or modern Rome. The quiet humour, veiled in conscious
naïveté; the wit that wraps into a jest, with the same deft-
ness, a madrigal or an epigram; the courteous smile, ironical and caressing; the "elegant badinage" which appealed
even to the gruff pedagogue Boileau: all that is French
of the French, and not classical in the least.

Destiny has dealt curiously with this frail laureate of
courtly lore. Extolled beyond measure in his lifetime, he

ought by rights to have been permanently obscured by
the more substantial glory of Ronsard. But Ronsard fell
into unjust disrepute, and Marot was revealed again,
neat and nimble, with his quizzical smile. La Fontaine
elected him as one of his masters; Racine, Jean-Baptiste
Rousseau, Voltaire himself pastiched his epigrams; and
to the present day there is a slender rill of society verse
"in the Marotic style." A stranger whim of fate, as we
shall see, turned this graceful trifler into a half-hearted,
very unsubstantial Protestant: an odd companion for the
redoubtable Calvin! He essayed, on his thin medieval
pipe, to render the Oriental strangeness and the fierce
majesty of the Psalms. For French literature, it was a
disaster: his poor little version blocked the way to greater
things.

In his art, Rabelais also belongs to the middle ages.
He represents the popular tradition as Marot represented
the courtly—the second part of the *Romance of the Rose*
instead of the first, Meung against Lorris. He has the
prolixity of the old romancers, but with a torrential
abundance which was not in them. He continues on a
vaster scale the ironical, plebeian epic, *Reynard the Fox;*
he keeps up the vein of the macaronic sermons, the farces,
the *fableaux.* His framework is a story of giants from
the local folklore. When, in the apologue of the Wood-
cutter and his lost hatchet, he takes us to Olympus, his
Jupiter is a patriarchal French king, a Saint Louis under the Oak of Vincennes, a Louis XII, Father of the
People. Of classic measure he shows no trace; and his
scattered attempts at Ciceronian eloquence are dead
lumber.

III

"Printing likewise is now in use, so elegant and so
correct, that better can not be imagined, although it was
found out but in my time by divine inspiration, as by a
diabolical suggestion on the other side was the invention
of ordnance." Thus Gargantua, in that famous letter

to his son Pantagruel, which is the true battle hymn of
the Renaissance.[1] The age was marked by inventions
and discoveries, no less than by the revival of ancient
learning. These inventions Rabelais mentions paren-
thetically, as it were, and gives us to understand that
they were by-products of the true Renaissance, the restoration of the "learned tongues." This opinion is no
longer unchallenged. At the risk of being called a Beo-
tian, it may well be maintained that the inventions and
discoveries that marked the dawn of the classical era were
of vastly greater significance than all the treasure-troves
of archeology and philology. For the average man, even
for the well-educated man, the face of our world would
hardly be affected if the text of Vergil or even of Plato
had been established with less scrupulous care. On the
other hand, a world without the printing press and without America would be very different from the one we
know. We do not deny that it might actually be better
without these two disturbing factors: we are speaking in
terms of tangible facts, and not of values.

Nor can we admit that these new conquests in the material world were in any sense the result of revived scholarship. They were at most concomitant with it. The expansion of the physical universe beyond the limits of early
medieval thought, but also beyond those of ancient knowledge, had been under way for two centuries before the
time of Rabelais. Marco Polo had not been urged by
Plato or Aristotle. The mariner's compass, without
which maritime discovery on a grand scale was unthinkable, had obscurely come into use in the thirteenth century. The Portuguese and the Spaniards who ventured
into uncharted seas were impelled by the spirit of restless adventure that had filled the Normans and the Crusaders. Columbus thought of gold, of power, and of souls
to be saved: he was a Knight of the Cross, not a classicist.
The great epic of discovery was the sudden fruition of
slowly accumulating medieval efforts. It was soon to
transform political and economic conditions, and ulti-

[1] Book I, Ch. VIII.

mately to bring about a recasting of our theological conceptions: it was not a return to the confined Mediterranean world.

Gunpowder was in practical use in the early stages of the Hundred Years War. For good or evil, it contributed to the reshaping of civilization. It dealt a death blow to actual feudalism, allowing only the titles and trappings to remain a while longer. It made the Kings supreme, and for the ubiquitous, erratic warfare of bands and barons, it substituted dynastic conflicts, national ambitions, and the elusive balance of European power. But whether gunpowder was invented by the Devil, as Rabelais puts it, or by a monk, as tradition maintains, certain it is that its formula was not found in a classical manuscript.

Most potent of all was the invention of the printing press. It was destined to create, after many generations, a democracy of culture, the essential condition of political democracy. The connection between this tremendous instrument of the modern mind and the revival of classical philology is most shadowy. It was not at Constantinople or Rome that it was evolved, but in Germany. It was first used, not for Greek or Latin masterpieces, but for Bibles and works of piety. The restoration of ancient literatures was thus but one evidence among many of the quivering eagerness which filled the European mind.

IV

Our contention is that the sixteenth century continues the fifteenth; but with a difference. That difference is the true "Renaissance." It can not be defined in any material terms, not even in terms of learning. It was a *revival of optimism*. Perhaps the point will be made clearer if it is illustrated with a modern instance.

In the last decade of the nineteenth century, France was permeated with a spirit of self-depreciation and haunted with the idea of decadence. Anthropologists like Vacher de Lapouge, polymaths like Dr. Gustave Le

Bon, popular journalists like Demolins united in proclaiming the racial decay of their own people and seeking the *Causes of Anglo-Saxon Superiority.* The hopeless incapacity of the French in the colonial field was
taken for granted; it was admitted also that their political life could be nothing but a succession of malodorous
scandals. Alsace-Lorraine was more than half-forgotten:
not out of pacifist idealism, but out of lassitude and
despair. Poets adopted "Decadence" as their watchword.
The ironical nihilism of Renan, Anatole France and Jules
Lemaître corresponded with the dilettantism of critics like
Rémi de Gourmont, the erudite and naïve perversities of
Huysmans in *A Rebours,* or the truculent anarchism of
Laurent Tailhade.

Ten years later, long before the outbreak of the Great
War, we find, not one isolated prophet of a French Renaissance, but a whole chorus lustily singing *France Herself Again* and *The Reawakening of French Pride.* That
such confidence was not misplaced was made manifest by
France's attitude throughout the great ordeal, and
through the more searching ordeal of unaided reconstruction. What had taken place? Literally nothing. M.
Loubet and M. Fallières were Presidents instead of Carnot and Felix Faure. No new manuscript had been
brought from Constantinople: on the contrary, classical
studies had received a rather sharp blow in 1902. France
had been suffering from a psychological disease: without
the aid of any drug, surgical operation or systematic diet,
her robust constitution had enabled her to recover. The
details of such crises are fascinating to study; their
causes are not necessarily mysterious and not invariably
obscure; but they are infinitely complex. In such cases,
the surest way of misunderstanding history is to use a
single influence as an *Open Sesame.*

The fifteenth century had all the elements of greatness of the sixteenth—except confidence and joy. It was
the Triumph of Death. The Dance of Death was its
favourite theme; it saw the world as a gaudy charnel-
house. The poems of Villon, whether they sing of fears

or regrets, exhale an acrid, pungent odour of death. The
sixteenth century was the Triumph of Life.

Why such a change? Political circumstances explain
it to some extent, but they do not go very far. The long
nightmare of the Hundred Years War was over; during
the second half of the fifteenth century, France enjoyed
almost untroubled internal peace. A country with varied agricultural resources, a people of invincible, ant-
like tenacity, recuperate rapidly. Villon, darkened by
his personal experience, was already a little behind the
time in his tragic outlook on life. All this is true. Yet
material prosperity and political order do not invariably
breed optimism. The literature of the Second French
Empire was disenchanted; nor did the Bismarckian era
sound a triumphant note.

It would not help either to say that human nature
needs hope, that despair can not be permanent. A pessimistic philosophy may retain its hold for countless centuries. Buddhism remains unconquered.

Perhaps, in this particular case, the legend of the year
1000 may serve again as a symbolical illustration. According to the old story, the world was awaiting its doom
at the turn of the first millennium. Nothing happened:
and that very "nothing" brought the release. In the same
way, the late medieval world was filled with nameless an-
guish, because its spiritual stars had been obscured. But
no apocalyptic catastrophe occurred. France worked on,
and prospered, although Popes and Councils wrangled,
and the Sorbonne was in its dotage. These were no eternal stars then, only flickering lanterns carried by bewildered men. When this was realized, France burst out
laughing at her former guides and at her former fears.

The first condition of Rabelais's joy in life was his escape from the nether world of spiritual dread. His anti-
monachism and his anti-Sorbonnism are fundamental.
Not that they were wholly new: to poke fun at monks and
theologians had been a favourite theme throughout the
Age of Faith. But whilst *men* had been attacked, with a
fierceness that surprises the modern mind, spiritual au-

thorities were not directly challenged. With Rabelais,
they are not so much challenged as ignored. The medieval satirist, whilst he is jeering, turns round uneasily,
in mortal fear of the Devil; he is ready to fall on his
knees before the very friar he is deriding. Rabelais's
laughter is perfect freedom. He had later to compromise, to edulcorate his attacks, for he had no desire of
becoming a martyr. But if his pen was not wholly free,
his soul was tormented by no scruple and by no fear. And
it must be remembered that Rabelais is not a solitary
genius. He was a sociable, active, practical man, in close
touch with his times. His books were immediately and
widely popular, as he had meant them to be. He was protected, in his adventurous, semi-detached ecclesiastical career, by great lords and even by Princes of the Church.
He may be taken, therefore, as a symbol of the medieval
mind emancipated at last: emancipated, not through the
magic of ancient books, but simply because it had steadily grown, whilst its keepers had fallen into decay.

V

The keyword of Rabelais, the essence of Pantagruelism, is "Vivez joyeux"—Live in joy. He picked out for
his subject a merry old tale of giants: a happy choice,
for the human mind, released from its fetters, felt like a
young giant gambolling on a young earth. Rabelais's
heroes go through the world with Gargantuan and Pan-
tagruelic appetite for all good things: for tripes and sau-
sages, hams and cheeses, beeves and muttons roasted
whole, and washed down with torrents of wine; but also—
for he is a bibber and glutton only in jest and symbol—
they are craving for all experience and all knowledge,
for the Trivium and Quadrivium of old, and "all the lore
of the Cabbalists," for "Greek, Hebrew, Arabic, Chal-
dean and Latin," for "all sorts of herbs and flowers that
grow upon the ground," and "all the various metals that
are hid within the bowels of the earth"; as Rabelais is no
bookworm or pedant, his characters are eager for all

sports, games, pleasures and exercises, for swimming, riding, fencing and jousting; and at last, he makes them also hunger and thirst for righteousness, knowing full well that "science without conscience is but ruination of the soul."

This triumphant Pantagruelism inspires the chapters, full of quaint erudition, practical knowledge and poetic enthusiasm, which, at the end of the third book, he devotes to the praise of the blesséd herb Pantagruelion. Literally, Pantagruelion is mere hemp; symbolically, it is human industry. Capping the wildest achievements of his own times with wilder boast and prophecy, Rabelais first shows man, by virtue of this Pantagruelion, exploring the remotest regions of his globe, "so that Taproban hath seen the heaths of Lapland, and both the Javas, the Riphæan Mountains." Men "scoured the Atlantic Ocean, passed the tropics, pushed through the torrid zone, measured all the Zodiac, sported under the equinoctial, having both poles level with their horizon." Then, "all marine and terrestrial gods were on a sudden all afraid." What is to prevent Pantagruel and his children from discovering some still more potent herb, by means of which they shall scale the very heavens? Who knows but they may "contrive a way to pierce into the high aërian clouds, and shut and open as they please the sluices from whence proceed the floodgates of the rain . . . then, prosecuting their ethereal voyage, they may step into the lightning workhouse and shop . . . where, seizing on the magazine of heaven, they may discharge a bouncing peal or two of thundering ordnance for joy of their arrival at these new supernal places. . . . And we the Gods shall then not be able to resist the impetuosity of their intrusion, . . . whatever regions, domiciles or mansions of the spangled firmament they shall have a mind to see, to stay in, or to travel through for their recreation."[1]

The spirit of the great adventure, the onrush of man's endeavour, devouring space, annihilating time, yea,

---

[1] Book III, Ch. LI, Motteux's translation, condensed.

Bergson would add, perhaps conquering Death itself, has never been more gloriously expressed than in these pages of gigantic, gorgeous and lucid humour.

There is much solid truth in Rabelais's most daring flights of prophecy. His Abbey of Thélème seemed at one time as wild as the rest. It has proved to be, not Utopia, but anticipation. Thélème is not, as those unread in Pantagruelism might imagine, a refuge for the sensualist and the slothful; it is purely and simply an ideal Anglo-Saxon university. Generously endowed, richly housed, well-provided with libraries in all languages, coeducational, blending sport, social life and study, it is the perfect antithesis of the old Sorbonne, and the perfect prototype of, for instance, Stanford in California. And what is the oft-discussed motto "Fay ce que vouldras"—Do as you please, but the pithy statement of a policy for which we are seeking in vain a properly pedagogical name, "the elective system," "the independent study plan," and "students' self-government"? "Because, saith Rabelais in justification of his gentle anarchism, men that are free, well-born, well-bred, and conversant in honest companies, have naturally an instinct and spur that prompteth them unto virtuous actions, and withdraws them from vice, (an instinct) *which is called honour*." On our examination books, we read: "The Honour System is an institution in this University. Its existence and enforcement rest with every loyal student."

Thélème is truly a University, not an Abbey. Its ideal is not selfish reclusion: when the time comes, youths and maidens leave their Alma Mater; friendships formed at Thélème "increase to greater height in the state of matrimony"; and the Thélèmites bring to their struggling brothers without the walls a reflection at least of their serene vision.

No philosophical label will fit this Pantagruelism: it is like the clear cool water of the Divine Bottle, all things to all men, according to their nurture and fancy. Of all possible tags, materialism and sensualism would be the worst; rationalism is thin and cold; Pantheism sounds

well, but, unexplained, is mere sound. Naturism would
do better. Rabelais loves Nature in all her shapes and
moods, even the lowliest; and he hates only those who
struggle in vain against good Mother Nature, and who
worship the sullen idol *Antiphysis*. But Nature, for Rabelais, is Life; and life is the life of man. His philosophy is Humanism in the wider and deeper sense—the love,
respect and service of Man, in whom we are taught to see
the image of God.

Rabelais has in abundance faith, hope and charity;
and yet, for the Supernaturalist, he is the arch-heretic.
He believes in Man, as though fallen men were not totally depraved; he preaches joy, as though this world
were not a vale of tears, in preparation for a probable
eternity of torture. Not in his obscenities, which never
hurt a soul, but in his large indulgence for his fellow
men, do the orthodox detect his damning sin. Who
knows? The wedding guest at Cana, He who said: "The
Kingdom of God is *among* you," may be claimed as a Master by Rabelais as well as by Calvin.

CHAPTER II

THE RENAISSANCE: INFLUENCE OF ANTIQUITY AND ITALY

I. Two conceptions of *Humanism:* faith in human nature, study of Greco-Roman culture. *Latin:* a living language in the Middle Ages; Vergilian and Ciceronian standards turn Renaissance Latin into a dead language. Progress of the vernacular in the sixteenth century.

II. *Greek:* its revival; not due to the fall of Constantinople. Francis I and Budé; hostility of the Sorbonne. Great vogue of Greek among scholars. Slender results; French culture remains based on Latin.

III. Influence of *Italy* greater than direct influence of Greece or Rome. Current of anti-Italianism a proof of the strength of that influence. Was it due to the Italian Wars?

IV. Genuine superiority of Italian culture in the early sixteenth century; its causes. Persistence of Italian influence in the seventeenth century.

V. Alleged contributions of the Italo-Antique Renaissance to French culture: sense of *personality* and sense of *beauty*. Excessive *cult of form*. The leaders of the Pleiad, du Bellay and Ronsard, are genuine poets and go beyond formal humanism.

I

THE "new spirit" in the sixteenth century was not the sudden discovery of long-hidden wealth, alien to French tradition, brought over as if by a miracle from a foreign land or from remote ages. It was, as we have seen, a release of pent-up energies, a revival of self-confidence and pride. It transcended and conquered medievalism: but only by means of powers that had grown steadily throughout the Middle Ages. For this new spirit, the most apposite name might be *Pantagruelism*, the enormous, earnest and joyful love of life which filled Rabelais; and Pantagruelism—faith in man, the love of man—was essentially *Humanism*. If by "humanity" we mean with Cicero *caritas generi humani*, or if we find its clearest expression in the *Homo sum* of Terence, then a

42

man can be a humanist with little Latin and less Greek:
the best humanists are seldom found in college cloisters.

A more restricted signification, however, is attached to
the word. Already Aulus Gellius under the Antonines
asserted that "humanity" was not, as the vulgar might
believe, synonymous with "philanthropy" or love of one's
kind: it implied erudition and discipline in the arts,
"*quod . . . nos eruditionem institutionemque in bonas
artes dicimus.*"

In the sixteenth century, the two conceptions were
blended: Erasmus, Rabelais were humanists in both senses
of the term. If it had come to a choice, it is infinitely
probable that they would have clung to the spirit, and
given up the letter. A confused fight went on for generations between the two ideals of humanism, the humane
and the formal. As a matter of fact, it has not yet come
to a decision: to the present day, there are excellent
minds in France who can not divorce "the humanities"
from "the study of Greek and Latin."

The Middle Ages had never ceased to revere and cultivate Latin, and in that field no actual Renaissance was
necessary. About a hundred Roman writers were known
to medieval scholars—rather more than the average educated man could name to-day. Nor were they mere names
and titles. Ovid was the universal master in the Art of
Love. Vergil's was literally a name to conjure with; it
was not the premonition of a new classical dawn, but the
strength of tradition, that made Dante elect him as his
guide, master and lord. Only Tacitus and Lucretius
seem to have suffered a prolonged and almost complete
eclipse. No doubt the Renaissance brought with it a decided improvement in the quality of the Latin used by
scholars. But, in this respect again, the usual conception of a Renaissance is somewhat misleading. Medieval
Latin had not invariably been corrupt. The universal
progress of the eleventh and twelfth centuries had been
felt in that field also. The poems of Alanus de Insulis,
for instance, *De Planctu Naturæ* and *Anticlaudianus*, are
far from despicable. Scholasticism, with its pedantry,

and its uncouth technical terms, created later an impression of barbarousness, which was retrospectively and unjustly extended to the whole period.

The efforts of the great Italian humanists, from Petrarch in his *Africa* to Cardinal Bembo, had the unexpected effect of purifying Latin out of active existence. It was difficult enough for Latin to hold its own, in the increasing complexity of modern life, against the competition of the vernacular. A living Latin, true to its origins and to its principles, but free from pedantry, willing to grow with the times, making intelligibility, not classical elegance, its supreme goal, might have served the purpose. But with the handicap of artificial Vergilian and Ciceronian standards, Renaissance Latin, embalmed in its frigid perfection, became the dead imitation of a dead past. So we have to note the paradox that the century of the Renaissance marks, not the revival of Latin, but the beginning of its decadence. The Ordinance of Villers-Cotterets, in 1539, made French instead of Latin the official language of royal administration. The first purely scientific works to appear in the vernacular belong to the same period: Ambroise Paré and medicine, Ramus and dialectics (1555). Calvin's French version of his *Christian Institute* (1540) made even theology accessible in the vulgar tongue. The process continued, slowly, but unchecked: in the seventeenth century, French secured equality with Latin as the language of diplomacy.

II

The true revival of learning, therefore, was that which took place, not in Latin, but in Greek. In this field, everything had to be done: broadly speaking, the Middle Ages had been wholly ignorant of Greek. Even Aristotle, the revered Master, was not known in the original; some of his works reached the Western mind through Latin translations from the Arabic. The Homeric stories had currency chiefly in the debased form of Dares the Phrygian and Dyctis. Plato was barely a name. In this case, "Gothic night" had reigned for nearly a thousand years.

What caused the change? With the love of simplification which is almost a necessity of popular history, it was long ascribed to the fall of Constantinople in 1453, and to the exodus of Byzantine scholars, laden with the treasures of Greek antiquity. This stock explanation is dangerously superficial. It lends excessive importance, for one thing, to a handful of grammarians, some of whom were rather disreputable, and none of whom ranked extremely high in pure learning. It gives to mere texts an almost talismanic virtue. Seldom do political events like the capture of a city bring about changes in the realm of culture, unless culture itself be ready for the change. For instance, from 1204 to 1261, the Latins had held Constantinople. The result of their conquest was a brisk trade in relics, in which they were vitally interested, but not in manuscripts or in ideas, which they were not ready to appreciate. On the other hand, the veiled power of Greek thought and art was obscurely felt in Italy as early as the days of Petrarch. The Hellenic Renaissance therefore was an infiltration and a growth, not a sudden irruption.

Certain it is that the new learning was hailed with delight by the best minds in France, whilst the theologians of the old Sorbonne growled. These last of the schoolmen quickly detected the scent of heresy in studies which disturbed their habits of mechanical infallibility. The Reform movement within the Church seemed to go hand in hand with Humanism, and increased their misgivings. Francis I sided with the progressives: he earned their lasting gratitude, and, through them, a fame perhaps more brilliant than his intellect. As early as 1520, he promised Guillaume Budé, most influential of French scholars, the foundation of a new College, devoted principally to the three classical tongues, Latin, Greek and Hebrew. This proclaimed the emancipation of scholarship from the tyranny of scholasticism; and it was the first germ of the glorious *Collège de France*, still the

highest school in the land, because it is the freest. It was
not until 1529, however, that the scheme was at last realized, in very incomplete fashion, through the creation of
Royal Professorships in Greek, Hebrew and Mathematics. Provincial universities followed. Lyons in particular, the capital of Roman Gaul, the religious metrop-
olis of France, and a cosmopolitan center second only to
Paris, had a brilliant roll of scholarly translators, editors
and printers. Rabelais, then a doctor at the General
Hospital of Lyons, was a member of that learned crew;
and so was Etienne Dolet, who was to expiate his freedom of thought at the stake. As early as 1534, Rabelais
could assert that "without Greek, a man should be
ashamed to account himself a scholar." And Ronsard,
a young nobleman, went back to school to master the new
learning. The greatest French Hellenists were then
Turnèbe and Daurat. Henry Estienne, whose father
had produced a vast *Thesaurus Linguæ Latinæ* (1531–
36) gave in 1572 his *Thesaurus Linguæ Grecæ*, in some
respects still an unsurpassed monument.

Were the results commensurate with so much eagerness and so much diligence? Hardly. Budé, Turnèbe,
Daurat, Estienne, are honoured names: in the history of
French thought or of French literary expression, they
count for very little. Rabelais was a voracious reader:
the fruit of his classical studies is an erudition so palpable as to be frankly pedantic. But no style could be
more completely devoid of Attic measure: this great classical scholar is the most unclassical of French writers. In
his philosophy, we find his own robust personality, and
the optimistic naturalism of the early sixteenth century
rather than the echo of Greek systems. He is not an
orthodox Pyrrhonian, Stoic, Epicurean or Platonist: he
is a rationalist and an eclecticist.

The rediscovery of Platonism ought to have been the
chief contribution of the Greek Renaissance: but French
Neo-Platonism is singularly thin, not to say lifeless. If,
as it is alleged, Platonism increased the tendency of
French Classicism towards abstract generalizations, it was

a doubtful blessing; but this assertion is too vague to be
capable of proof. We find traces of Neo-Platonism in the
rather obscure poems of the Lyons school, particularly
in those of Maurice Scève; it inspired an admirable sonnet of du Bellay, *The Idea*, without which no French
anthology is complete; but that sonnet was borrowed
from the Italian, and can not be credited to the direct
influence of Greek. No doubt the poets of the Pleiad,
and particularly Ronsard and Baïf, loved to parade their
Greek learning. Ronsard warned his readers at the outset that "unless they were Greeks and Romans, this book
would be nought but a heavy load in their hands." He
revelled in accumulations of classical epithets:

> *O cuisse-né Bacchus, Mystique, Hyménéan,*
> *Carpime, Evaste, Agnien, Manique, Lénéan,*
> *Evie, Evoulien, Baladin, Solitaire . . .*

and regretted not to be able to say of the Valois dynasty:

> *Ocymore, dispotme, oligochronien.*

Such lines justify Boileau's jibe that "Ronsard's muse,
in French, spoke Greek and Latin"; they also account for
the long eclipse of his fame. A greater Ronsard has
gradually been rediscovered: but Ronsard the Hellenist
remains safely dead.

Two aspects only of Greek literature passed into
French at the time of the Renaissance: Alexandrian
poetry, through the Pleiad; and Plutarch, through
Amyot's translation. Neither is negligible: but it must
be confessed that both are minor developments. They do
not represent the main stream of Hellenism. In other
and larger fields, Roman supremacy remained unshaken.
Although the French have studied Greek for nearly four
centuries, they have never managed to learn it: yet there
is a curious conformity, a pre-established harmony, as it
were, between the Greek mind and the French. Throughout the Classical period, French lyrical poetry placed
itself under the invocation of Pindar, but followed Horace; the French epic, a sickly homunculus, patterned
itself after Vergil, and not directly after Homer; the

French tragedy was long influenced by Seneca rather
than by Sophocles; the French comedy by Plautus and
Terence, not Aristophanes. The model for orators was
not Demosthenes, but Cicero; and Livy was familiar to
all educated Frenchmen, whilst Thucydides was not. In
the long line of French classics, only two are singled out
because, to them, Greek was a fountain of living waters:
Racine and André Chénier. The sixteenth century felt
no doubt the freshness, the delicacy and the power of
Greek. But the tradition of a thousand years, the influence of the Catholic Church, the kinship with the popular tongue, worked irresistibly in favour of Latin. In
this again, the Renaissance failed to break away from the
Middle Ages.

III

More potent at first than the influence of antiquity
was that of modern Italy. The Renaissance, in its essential elements, was not "caused" by the revival of classical learning, or by the imitation of Italian models: but
in its literary, artistic and social manifestations, it was
deeply influenced by them. The *colour* of French culture, of aristocratic culture at any rate, was no longer
purely French: it was antique, and it was italianate: and
italianate much more than antique.

It has always been admitted that antiquity was revealed to France through Italy. But the impression
often prevails that the Italians acted merely as organs
of transmission: at best, curators of an incomparable museum, cataloguers of a unique library, self-effacing teachers of a civilization no longer their own; at worst, glib
and beggarly ciceroni through the mighty ruins of the
ancient world. This is a distorted view. The Italians
were admired and followed for their own sake, and deserved to be. Indeed, it may be claimed that the vogue
of antiquity was in France to a large extent a by-product
of Italian supremacy: "humanism" in the narrower sense
was in France but an Italian fashion, and never took the
same hold of the national mind as it did in its native
country. Respected as a Guillaume Budé was, he never

was admired, courted, petted, spoiled, as was the case with
some of the great Italian scholars.

We are aware that in thus placing the Italian influence above the antique, we are on dangerous ground, for
we are at odds with the contemporaries themselves. The
French in the sixteenth century took pride in acknowl-
edging their indebtedness to Greece and Rome; they were
reluctant to confess their obligation to living neighbours,
with whom they traded, intrigued and wrangled, and
who, it must be said, easily roused feelings of distrust
and even of contempt. Rafaello Piccoli suggests in-
geniously that if through some cataclysm Italy had perished altogether early in the sixteenth century, the world
would place her culture, without hesitation, on the same
level as those of Greece and ancient Rome, the third and
not the least of the great classical lights. But Italy survived, a chaos of petty states, a chessboard for diplo-
matists, a cockpit for mercenaries. Furthermore, the
Italians themselves upheld the prejudice in favour of antiquity. Of their own superiority over their neighbours,
they entertained very little doubt: like the Greeks of old,
and the Chinese until yesterday, they considered all foreigners as barbarians. But they did not—then—claim
equality with their ancient masters. It was much later
that "the century of Leo X" was placed on a level with
those of Pericles and Augustus. So the French were
hardly to blame if they adopted a historical perspective
which was universally accepted in the Peninsula.

The supremacy of the Italians in modern culture was
therefore not admitted in so many words. On the contrary, there is a strong current of anti-Italianism in the
literature of the time. Du Bellay, who devoted such magnificent sonnets to *The Antiquities of Rome*, denounced
without mercy, in his *Regrets*, the corruption of the
Papal Court. He thus made effective use of a satirical
contrast which was to become a favourite commonplace,
and which is still found, unconsciously, in the etchings of
Piranesi two centuries later: Italy is a land of awe-in-
spiring ruins, haunted by lizards and lazzaroni. Henry

Estienne, the great printer and Hellenist, gave much of
his energy to a veritable anti-Italian crusade. In his *Dialogues of the New Italianized French Language* (1578),
he protested against the invasion of Italian words, which
were turning French into a semi-Italian jargon, and
against all the manners, tastes and costumes of ultramontane origin. He was vigorously with "Celtophile" against
his opponent "Philausone." The defensive warfare of
Estienne, however, establishes the reality of the danger
that he was combating. Rabelais had poked fun at the
Limosin scholar, who "deambulated by the compites and
quadrivies of the inclyte urb vocitated Lutetia, and des-
pumated the Latial verbocintion";[1] but in spite of such
ludicrous extremes, in spite of the semi-humorous pedan-
tries of Ronsard, it was hardly to be feared that sixteenth
century France should become Latinized or Hellenized:
Italianism, on the other hand, was an actual menace.

If we look again at the French châteaux and churches
of the time, we shall notice that they are French with
Italian ornaments, and owe little directly to Greece and
Rome. If we pick up a book of poems, especially of
those which, like the best sonnets of Ronsard and du Bellay, have deserved to survive, we shall detect the influence of Petrarch rather than that of Pindar. Amyot
made the conventionalized heroes of Plutarch a part of
the French ideal for three centuries: but the court of the
Valois found its bible in *Il Cortegiano* by Baldassare Castiglione. Classical learning affected only the lesser half
of mankind: very few women became good Latinists,
hardly any studied Greek at all, but, in aristocratic circles, all ladies knew Italian.

In this case again, a cultural phenomenon is frequently
explained through a mere political accident. It happened that Charles VIII, a weak-minded megalomaniac,
had shadowy claims to the Kingdom of Naples; that his
successor, good King Louis XII, the Father of the People, had some pretensions to the Duchy of Milan. Thus
it was that the French blundered into Italy, discovered

[1] *Rabelais*, Book II, Ch. VI.

Italy, and brought back that infection known as the Renaissance.

The facts are not so simple, and the process was far less dramatic. We do not want to deny the influence of the military expeditions across the Alps: we feel, however, that in themselves, they would not have sufficed. The movement had started long before Charles VIII's erratic foray through the Peninsula. Italy was no *terra incognita*. Italian merchants and bankers were ubiquitous; they were particularly powerful in Lyons. The connection between the two countries was close enough for King Charles V to hear of a noted Italian physician and call him to his court. All ecclesiastics, since the end of the Great Schism, had turned their eyes Romeward again. Rome and the Santa Casa at Loretto were still the places chiefly sought by pilgrims. On the other hand, we note —with mild surprise—the lack of response to the charm of Italy among those warriors who were supposed to act as "foragers of culture." We have a delightful biography of Bayard, the Knight without Fear or Reproach, by a companion of his who signs: The Loyal Servant: the dazzling vision of Italy does not seem to have struck him in the least. Armies are almost perfect non-conductors of culture: such, at any rate, was the experience of the present writer in connection with the American Expeditionary Forces. However, this lack of response is noticeable, not merely in soldiers, but even with scholars and poets. The discovery of Italy was such a vast, slow, collective movement that the share of each individual therein was remarkably small. Both Rabelais and Marot went to Italy: we find no sign in them of a sudden flame of enthusiasm. Even in the works of Baïf, who was half-Italian, a visit to Italy left very little trace. The clearest note struck by du Bellay in Rome was homesickness for the gentleness of his native Anjou. We feel tempted to believe that, like the Terror of the Year 1000, like the discovery of Oriental civilization through the Crusades, like the diffusion of Greek learning as a result of the fall of Constantinople, the "revelation of Italy" in

1494 is such an exaggeration that it might almost be termed a legend.

Would it be unduly paradoxical to see in the Italian expeditions a sign of Italy's growing fascination for the French mind, rather than its origin? "The Genoese, Louis XI is reported to have said, give themselves to me; and I give them to the devil." Back of this sally lay a healthy tradition. The task of the Capetians, slowly defined in the course of centuries, was to "make" France by giving her her natural frontiers, the mountains and the sea. In the North East, where no such physical boundary existed, their goal was to unite under their scepter all populations of French speech, and to protect by as wide a zone as possible their capital Paris, so easy of access through the valley of the Oise. A few villages on the Somme were of much more vital value to France than a city, a duchy or even a kingdom beyond the Alps. This great truth Louis XI realized and his successors forgot. Why did they thus deviate from their traditional course? It was not merely an accident: even Charles VIII could hardly have embarked upon such an expedition, if his policy had not found support among his counselors. The magnet that drew him, and drew Louis XII after him, and Francis I after Louis XII, was the magic prestige of Italy. It was not until the reign of Henry II that the true French tradition was resumed: the conquest of Metz, Toul, Verdun, Calais, far outweighed the loss of precarious holdings in the peninsula. Cultural and political factors are constantly reacting upon one another. Political events, being more definite, are the first to be registered by history, and thus assume the dignity of "causes"; but the achievements and aspirations of culture are the necessary conditions of political activity. The words of Pascal, so true in the realm of the soul, can be applied in the domain of politics and culture: "You would not seek me, if you had not already found me." Thus it was that France *sought* Italy in 1494.

IV

Italy was no doubt an incomparable prize. Its evolution had been different from that of Northern Europe. It had almost skipped the Middle Ages. Gothic architecture in its purity is hardly represented in Italy. In Dante, the foremost representative of medieval thought, the light of antiquity still lingers; and immediately after Dante, we find the spirit of the Renaissance already embodied in Petrarch. The vestiges of antiquity were of course more numerous than in the North: but the greatness of Italy in the Trecento and Quattrocento was not enclosed in Roman ruins. There was a living people, which, from the crucible of innumerable invasions, had come out singularly alert and energetic. There was a form of civilization, the City-State, probably the one best adapted to the full development of the individual. Whilst in Northern France, the nobles lived in the morose isolation of their castles, in Italy they took part in the throbbing, tragic, exulting life of the cities. The Mediterranean was still the chief center of trade, and the Italians were still supreme as navigators, traders and bankers. Tradition, race, institutions and wealth, all contributed to the brilliancy of Italian culture. After the great thirteenth century, Italy had forged ahead whilst France had lost her way. So there was much in French art and thought, about 1494, that appeared senile, compared with the lusty maturity of the Italians.

France, however, had too great reserves of power ever to become a slavish imitator of Italy: the excesses denounced by Estienne were freaks. But Italianism was not a passing vogue. If, as we believe, it did not create, but only coloured, the French Renaissance, at least the dye was so deep that it lasted for generations. When the Italian wars were over, Italian queens, Catherine and Marie de' Medici, prolonged the influence of their nation. A Concini could become, nominally, and a Leonora Galigai actually, a power in the realm. French literature long obeyed the dictates of Italian fashions: Arcadian

with Sannazaro, it became euphuistic with Marino. Even
in the period when France recovered her full autonomy
and began in her turn to assert her supremacy, Italian
forces were everywhere traceable. Church architecture
conformed obediently to the models of the Roman Jesuits.
Richelieu himself was succeeded by an Italian, Mazarin,
who ruled the Queen and the kingdom. The restoration
of good manners after the long era of civil and religious
wars was directed by a woman who was partly Italian by
birth, and almost wholly in her upbringing, the Marquise
de Rambouillet. The French Academy was an imitation,
more successful than any of its models, of the many
academies that existed in the Peninsula: the very name
Academy is a last vestige of Italian Platonism. Even the
rules of French classical tragedy came, not from Aristotle
directly, but from Italian theorists. Almost up to our
own days, the French have found it hard to understand
Art unless it was presented to them in an Italian form:
the Louvre is still overstocked with the works of second-
rate Italian painters, and with their imitations. It is
hard therefore to fix a limit in time to such an action.
Perhaps the voyage of Bernini to Paris in 1665 may be
considered as marking the beginning of the end, or at
least the turn of the tide. The great architect and sculp-
tor, the last giant of Italian art, although a sophisticated
giant, was commissioned to design a façade for the new
Louvre. He was received like a sovereign, sent home
laden with honours and presents: but his scheme was discarded in favour of the severer colonnade of Perrault.
But, in many fields, the influence of Italy was very far
from spent, even then. Until the first half of the nineteenth century, no person of culture could be ignorant of
Italian. For Jean-Jacques Rousseau, French music was
still a joke, and the Italians were supreme. A last evidence
of this Italian superstition survives in the French School
of Rome. Not only archeologists, sculptors and architects,
but painters and even musicians are supposed to need the
atmosphere of the Eternal City in order to perfect themselves in their art. No other influence to which French

culture was submitted assumed so many forms and proved
so enduring. That of Spain in the seventeenth century
was brief and trivial in comparison. Its only rival is the
Anglomania of the eighteenth and nineteenth centuries:
in France, the Enlightenment, Romanticism and the Industrial Era borrowed freely and consciously their inspiration from England.

It is difficult to measure, and more difficult still to ap-
praise, such a vast and indefinite element as a foreign
influence. It is potent only if it mingles with the local
traditions: so it becomes most effective at the very point
where it loses its identity. The problem in this case is
made more complicated by the fact that Italianism and
the worship of antiquity were so inextricably mixed. We
do not know where Plato ends and Ficino begins, or where
Aristotle hands over his scepter to Scaliger, Castelvetro
or Patrizzi. It is therefore the contribution of the Italo-
Antique Renaissance *as a single whole* to French civilization that we shall attempt roughly to estimate.

V

The dauntless optimism, the spirit of adventure, the
strides in scientific progress, the greater freedom of
thought, the new manliness of tone, which characterized
the sixteenth century at its best, and which we summed
up in the name *Pantagruelism*, are not ascribable to the
Italian Renaissance. These traits are most clearly seen
in men who were very un-Italian in their qualities and in
their faults: Thomas More, Erasmus, Luther, Ulrich von
Hütten, Rabelais. Francis Bacon was the heir of that
spirit, and transmitted it to the Enlightenment and to
our own age.

Two claims are advanced on behalf of the Italo-Antique
Renaissance: it favoured the growth of personality, it
fostered the sense of beauty. This would imply that the
Middle Ages had been deficient in both respects. It seems
audacious to assert that individuality was subdued in the
centuries that produced Hildebrand, St. Bernard, Abe-

lard, St. Francis, St. Dominic, Dante, and so many others, as clear-cut, as compact with life, as any figures in history. Our perspective was at fault; the Middle Ages, long neglected, seemed far-off and vague. Knights, crusaders, monks, merchants, lost their identity, became interchangeable units in anonymous groups. But is not the same process taking place for the worthies of the Renaissance? Now that it has in its turn receded into the dim past, do not condottieri, courtiers, cardinals, artists and grammarians, merge into conventional types? The Italian Renaissance, it is true, brought forth a ruthless breed of supermen, of flamboyant egotists, whose ideals were Machiavelli's *Prince* and Castiglione's *Courtier:* of these Benvenuto Cellini and Cesare Borgia may serve as examples. Fortunately that kind of *virtú* failed to establish itself in France: it was revived only in the nineteenth century, as a Romantic ideal.

It is not certain either that the Renaissance created the modern sense of Beauty. No one could assert that the builders and decorators of the cathedrals, or the limners of miniatures, were indifferent to beauty, even to physical beauty, to bodily grace, to luxury, to elegance, to symmetry and dignity of design. The Gothic masters were not inspired children, but careful and conscious artists. No doubt the Renaissance poets prated abundantly about Beauty—with a Platonic capital B—; no doubt beauty was achieved by them, but a beauty which to us is less poignant, less compelling in its mystery, than that of their predecessors. The superiority of the Renaissance can be accepted only if art be identified with three elements: the supremacy of the nude, a certain obvious harmony of composition, and a wealth of classical reminiscences. In all three, the Middle Ages were decidedly inferior to the sixteenth century. But we are no longer sure that any of the three is absolutely essential.

What the Renaissance did emphasize was the worship of *form*, form as an ideal in itself, loved and cultivated for its own sake. The Middle Ages had been neither amorphous nor free from formalism: a ballad is no less rigid in structure than a sonnet, and late medieval literature indulged in veritable acrobatics of versification. There is little question, however, that *formal* beauty became a cult chiefly through the action of the Italian Renaissance. The result was what de Sanctis calls "indifference to contents." "It no longer matters whether one has anything to say, but only how it is to be said. The man of letters is not expected to have an opinion: this is not expected of him. Still less is it expected that he should live in conformity with the views which he expresses. His ideas come from without: his sole duty is to give them form. His imagination is a storehouse of phrases, maxims, 'beauties'; his ear is filled with harmonies and cadences, void of any meaning. Thus were born in Italy the men of letters and literary forms."[1]

This "indifference to contents," as Brunetière pointed out, clearly resembles some modern forms of *Art for Art's Sake*. Such a doctrine is bound ultimately to identify beauty with certain formulæ, and art with a particular technique. The notion persisted through the classical age. Even Pascal, who had so much to say, and who took it so tragically to heart, compared literature with a game of tennis: "the players are using the same ball: one places it better."

The formulæ with which the literary mind was filled were those of the Italo-Antique Renaissance. *Humanism* and *Classicism* were narrowed down to a set of Greco-Latin myths, stories, canons, rules, and "felicities of expression," the *Elegances* of Lorenzo Valla, for instance. Boileau, a good rationalist and a good Christian, still believed that in poetry he had to be an orthodox Pagan. From Life to Art, from Art to Form, from Form to Convention, the humanistic ideal gradually lost touch with reality. And, deliberately, it eschewed contact with the people. The *Homo sum et humani nihil a me alienum puto*, was construed to apply only to the small band of the initiated. The rest were warned off, debarred from understanding high literature: "they will have, instead

[1] F. de Sanctis, *Letteratura Italiana*, I, p. 288, Morano, Naples, 1913.

C

of a book, only a heavy burden in their hands." "Nothing," Ronsard again declared with sublime arrogance, "nothing pleases me, except what displeases the common herd." The Greco-Latin tradition became the shibboleth of a self-appointed elite.

We must hasten to say that this pedantic and snobbish element, obvious and freely proclaimed as it was, did not constitute the whole of French classicism, nor even its essential part. Life and reason reasserted their rights: the seventeenth century might do obeisance to the Greco-Roman fetish: but it was above all an age of sturdy realism and vigorous common sense.

Even the poets of the Pleiad, the purest representatives of "Humanism" in French literature, are not, fortunately, fully consistent, either in practice or in doctrine. Like Chambord, Chenonceaux or St. Etienne-du-Mont, they are hybrids. They imitate antiquity and Italy, no doubt—and the stricter the imitation the more lifeless the poem. But they are French noblemen first of all, and not ultramontane antiquarians. "Of all things I most detest pedantic learning," said du Bellay, who was none the less the companion-at-arms of that pedant, *"docte, doctieur et doctime Baïf."* Du Bellay and Ronsard were not wholly indifferent to contents. They were ardently devoted to their country, and especially to their native provinces, Anjou and Vendômois. If some of their lyrics are not free from scholarly mustiness, others are eternally fragrant, and fresh with dew. Both have a note of sweet melancholy at the contemplation of beauty, love and death. But Villon had handled before them that eternal theme; and the pretty descants of Ronsard on "falling rose petals" can hardly match the haunting refrain: "Where are the snows of yesteryear?"

The manifesto of the school, the *Defence and Illustration of the French Language*, by Joachim du Bellay (1549), is a very ambiguous piece of writing. It condemns, a little too sweepingly, the old French tradition, with the obsolete intricacy of its literary forms. It urges the poets to imitate the Ancients and the Italians, or

rather to plunder them: "Ransack again the treasures of
Rome, as your ancestors did of old (and this time, du
Bellay quaintly adds, there will be no geese at the Capitol
to give you away) ; pillage once more the temple at Del-
phos." But these lines ring with juvenile arrogance, not
with superstitious awe and submission. It is the *French*
language that Ronsard and du Bellay want to cultivate,
because it seems to them as noble a vehicle of thought
and feeling as the classical tongues. Their creed is a
confused blending of learning and spontaneity, of superstitious classicism and modernism. It is in the works of
du Bellay, the spokesman of the scholarly school in
poetry, that we find the most radical denunciation of
literal classicism: "Pondering oftentimes on the reason
why the men of this age are as a rule less learned in all
sciences and of less worth than the Ancients, among many
causes I find this one which I dare maintain is the principal: *the study of the Greek and Latin languages.* For,
if the time we consume in learning these languages were
devoted to the study of science, Nature has certainly not
grown so barren, but she would bring forth in our time
new Platos and new Aristotles."[1] It is the whole doctrine
of imitation that stands here condemned: and yet that
doctrine was the central tenet of the Renaissance. The
seventeenth century was to clarify much of that turbid
thought. The essential ambiguity, however, was not
wholly removed. The meaning of *humanism* kept hover-
ing between "erudition" and "faith in the human race."
This blessed ambiguity saved France from a new tyranny
as narrow as that of decadent scholasticism. The pedantic, literal conception of Humanism and Classicism prevailed in name only: it was able to hinder progress, but
could not wholly arrest it.

[1] J. du Bellay, *Defence and Illustration*, Book I, Chapter X.

CHAPTER III

THE MONARCHY OF THE KING'S PLEASURE

I. *The Royal Power.* Unquestioned supremacy of royal office at the end of middle ages. The last semi-independent provinces: Burgundy, Brittany. The last feudal rebel: Constable of Bourbon. Feudal nobles turned into courtiers. Franchises of provinces and cities devitalized.

Foundations of Royal Power: ownership, feudal suzerainty, Christian consecration, Roman tradition. Cæsarian Democracy: the absolute King also the first servant of the people.

II. *King and Court.* Francis I, the ideal Renaissance King. Brilliancy, charm. Alleged shallowness.

The Court: enormous increase. Migratory: Loire and Parisian Regions. Elegance, immorality and extravagance. One of the causes of financial chaos.

III. *Government and Administration.* Court, Privy Council, Grand Council, etc. Ambiguous character of Parliament. Growth of an hereditary bureaucracy.

I

THE early Capetians, with magnificent claims, possessed but very limited powers. Their title was recognized, in rather vague theory, from Flanders to Barcelona. In sober reality, they were barely "first among their peers," and Louis VI could be defied by a mere Sire of Montlhéry between his two royal cities of Paris and Orleans. From the accession of Hugh Capet in 987 to the death of Louis XII in 1515, the power of the kings, through many vicissitudes, had gained substance. When Francis I came to the throne, the conception of absolute monarchy had fully crystallized. It was manifest that France no longer was a loose congeries of fiefs: she was a nation, and she had a ruler.

The King was unquestionably supreme in his realm. The last great feudatories disappeared at that time. The most threatening had been the Dukes of Burgundy, vassals more splendid at times than their suzerains, and who

had not scrupled at uniting their forces with those of
England. The last Duke had visions of a renewed Lotha-
ringia or Austrasia, maintaining its independence between France and the Empire. He had held Louis XI a
prisoner. With the death of Charles the Bold, that danger vanished. Brittany, so long an almost sovereign
state, was personally united with France through the
marriages of the Duchess, Anne, with two successive
Kings. One great feudal power remained: in his own
right and through his wife, Charles of Bourbon, Constable of France, controlled large domains in the very
heart of the country. He was quasi-independent, and
Moulins was a veritable little capital. In Bourbon, the
double danger which these princely houses created was
clearly revealed: he could, at any moment, become the
center of an aristocratic coalition against the crown; and,
like the Burgundians, he could, without a qualm, nego-
tiate directly with the Emperor or with the English. So
strong did he seem that Francis I, well aware of his trea-
sonable intentions, did not dare to have him arrested: the
King was not yet absolutely sure of the loyalty of his
nobles. But France as a whole was already more monarchical than her aristocracy. The Constable's vassals
refused to follow him against the national sovereign.
Compelled to flee to the Emperor Charles V, he led an
army into Provence, hoping that at least a party or faction in France would rally to his standards. Again he
was disappointed. He perished in the siege of Rome, a
mere adventurer on a large scale, a prince without a land,
a Frenchman without a country, a Catholic excommunicated by the Pope. Popular imagination took pleasure
in contrasting his sinister fame with the pure glory of
Bayard.[1] Yet Bourbon was not so much a criminal as
an anachronism: he still called "transfer of allegiance"
what France had learned to call "treason."

We shall see that, nearly half a century later, two great

---

[1] Bayard, at the point of death, rebuking the Constable, is a favourite scene in popular imagery. Young Louis XIV erased the name
of Charles of Bourbon from a genealogical table, and substituted:
Bayard.

families, the Bourbons and the Guises (Lorraine),
brought France to the verge of ruin. But there was a
difference: they stood as leaders in factional strife rather
than as territorial lords; their object was to control the
king, but not to disrupt the monarchy; and their power
for evil was due, not to their feudal claims, but to exasperated religious passions. Under Richelieu and again
at the time of the Fronde, some great nobles rebelled, and
allied themselves with foreigners. The victory of the
monarchy was not therefore complete and secure in 1515;
but the unity and indivisibility of the kingdom had already become a cardinal principle of national policy. For
that reason, an Assembly refused to ratify the treaty of
Madrid: the dynasty and the people were one on this
point. The principle survived the dynasty: the Revolution proclaimed the Republic "one and indivisible."
Whoever, within or without, threatens that unity, is an
enemy of the State; and of that unity, the King is the
living symbol.

No other element could challenge the absolute supremacy of the crown. Feudalism, in the sixteenth century,
was only a survival: its decadence had begun fully two
hundred years before. The nobility preserved titles,
privileges, wealth and influence: but its actual power, its
sovereignty within definite limits, were gone beyond recall.
Everywhere the King's coinage displaced that of the local
lords. The administration of justice passed more and
more into the hands of royal officials. Two factors particularly hastened the decline of the feudal class. It was
an aristocracy of warriors, and in the Middle Ages, a
Baron in his castle, with a handful of men, could defy
a king. But artillery had changed the conditions of warfare. The knight's armour, and even the walls of his
keep, were not proof against cannon balls; the central
government alone was rich and well-organized enough to
take full advantage of the new armament. Gunpowder is
therefore acknowledged as a great instrument of centralization. Then the steady decline in the purchasing
power of money impoverished the nobility: for the dues

they collected from their tenants had been fixed generations before, and the invincible attachment of the rural
population to "ancient custom" made a readjustment impracticable. The nobles would either sink to the position
of rude country squires, hardly richer, or better educated,
than the peasants among whom they dwelt; or they had
to flock to the Court, and live on the King's bounty.
France was prosperous, the King was open-handed, and
the nobles became increasingly his dependents. Thus began the gilded servitude which, under Louis XIV, was
reduced to such a perfect system.

Just as the privileges of the nobility were left un-
touched in name and form, the franchises of the provinces
and cities were seldom suppressed outright or even curtailed: ancient France was no less averse than England
to any radical measure. But they became gradually mere
names and forms. There were still in many parts of the
country "States" or Assemblies; whilst they were not
wholly devoid of power, their meetings were chiefly social
occasions, when the Governor entertained royally the
nobles of the province. The turbulent communal spirit
vanished almost entirely. Both in royal towns and in
chartered cities, municipal honours were reserved to a
few substantial families, known for their devotion to the
king. The religious wars interrupted that process: for
a few troublous years, there were again little municipal
republics in the realm. But France recoiled from the
threat of national dissolution, and, in the seventeenth
century, the independent spirit of the local bourgeoisie
was hardly even a memory. Gradually, almost imperceptibly, all Frenchmen of whatever province or degree
were being turned into obedient subjects, all equal in submission before the majesty of the crown.

That power, materially so great, was rooted in many
traditions, which made it morally irresistible. Perhaps
its chief basis was *ownership:* France was essentially the
royal domain. It had started with the little duchy between Seine and Loire; it had grown slowly, through conflicts, marriages, heritages; the Capetians had shown the

same instinctive obstinacy which a French peasant displays in rounding off his father's farm. The doctrine that the king owned France was not based on abstractions, but on facts. The king·was the first of proprietors, and his hereditary rights were a model and a guarantee for all proprietary rights.

In so far as feudal notions still survived, the king was the ultimate suzerain, the apex of the ideal pyramid. He was also, and more emphatically, the Lord's anointed, like David and the royal line of Israel. The holy chrism used at his coronation imparted to him a sacred character. His touch cured "the King's Evil."[1] The glamour of this mystic origin was strengthened by the long alliance between the monarchy and the Church, an alliance which had begun with Clovis; by vague memories of Charlemagne, whom legend had turned into a Frenchman, a crusader and a saint; by the more substantial prestige of St. Louis.

Finally, the King was also the heir of Rome; the "legists," since the reign of Philip the Fair, had identified the principle of his rule with the Roman conception of the Sovereign and the State: the ruler is the incarnation of the state, and his will is law. On all these grounds the King's authority was absolute. Already Christine de Pisan, under Charles V, called that authority "imperial and pontifical." It was a commonplace that the French King was "Emperor in his Realm."[2]

This doctrine was practically unchallenged under Francis I. La Boétie's *Discourse on Voluntary Servitude*, which it is claimed he composed at the age of eighteen (ca. 1548), was an exercise of juvenile rhetoric in the ·antique manner, and devoid of genuine significance. Under the stress of the religious wars, the abso-

---

[1] A kind of scrofula.

[2] The tradition that the French Kings were descended from Francus, son of Hector, does not seem to have originated with the humanists of the sixteenth century. Naturally enough, it appealed to them, and Ronsard, as the laureate of France, made it the theme of his still-born epic *The Franciad*. Although a careful scholar like Henri Hauser mentions it on the same level as the Roman, the feudal and the ecclesiastical traditions, we have not found any evidence of its vitality.

lute power of the crown was brought into question. François Hotman, in his *Franco-Gallia* (1573), tried to establish that the French monarchy was a representative one, and subject to the authority of the law. Other views prevailed. Twentieth century minds were already thinking in the sixteenth century, just as sixteenth century minds are still active in the twentieth. But in both cases, history is bound to disregard minor currents.

More vital perhaps than any of these was what we might call the democratic, or better the Cæsarian, tradition: the king as leader and servant of the whole people; soldier, lawgiver, dispenser of justice. It was for such a king—for the *idea* of such a king—that Joan had fought and suffered death; it was this national character that had made Charles VII, mediocre and selfish as he was, the *Well-Served*, just as it was to make Louis XV the *Well-Beloved*. That tradition was Cæsarian, not constitutional. The germ of representative assemblies, akin to the English Parliament, existed in the States General: but they never enjoyed a normal growth. Whilst the monarchy was in desperate circumstances, through foreign invasions, civil wars, threatened bankruptcy, the minority of a king, the States were convened. They asserted their power on such occasions with a definiteness which, in the light of their ultimate failure, comes as a surprise. This was particularly the case in 1484, soon after the death of Louis XI. The Hundred Years War had given the States their best opportunities, and they were to have their chance again during the religious wars, from 1560 to 1593. This constant association with disaster made the very name of States General distasteful to the monarchy. Invariably, the selfishness of the privileged orders precluded the possibility of constitutional reforms; and the Third Estate realized that they had more to gain by supporting the King than in opposing him in conjunction with the Clergy and the Nobility. Francis I and Louis XIV, the early and the perfected types of absolute monarchy, never convened the States at all. After a last futile meeting in 1614, that unwieldy and disappointing institution remained in abeyance until 1789.

In the early sixteenth century, all these traditions united to give the monarchy incomparable prestige. Louis XII, not a great king by any means, had one of the finest titles that may be given to a ruler: the Father of the People. The country was bursting with eager activity; the French mind had sloughed off the pessimism and formalism of medieval decadence. It is at that unique moment that Francis I appeared.

II

The hereditary principle is a lottery. The distant cousin who succeeded Louis XII might have been a sickly child, a dullard, a morose old man: fate brought to the throne, at that golden hour of the young Renaissance, an ideal Renaissance prince. He was twenty years old, vigorous, radiantly handsome, a lover of chivalric valour: immediately upon his accession, at Marignano, he gave evidence of his prowess. Fond of luxury, even of display, he dazzled England and posterity with his Camp of the Cloth of Gold. But, in his prodigality, he was a connoisseur: he sought out Leonardo da Vinci and brought him over to France. He was a friend of scholars and poets, "honoured learned men equally with warriors," in the words of an old rhyme in his praise. He showered upon them fair words and at times substantial benefits. He sided with Budé against Béda, with humanism against the obscurantism of the Sorbonne. He was the Prince par excellence, the hero, the lover, the protector of arts and letters.

It is difficult to be the spoilt child of fortune without becoming—spoilt. Francis I is a disappointment: the young athlete of 1515 died at fifty-two, a tragically decayed charmer, gnawed by the Nemesis of his amorous pleasures. The knight of Marignano was to be, eleven years later, the luckless commander of Pavia and the captive of Madrid. The friend of humanism did not pre-

vent Louis de Berquin and Etienne Dolet from suffering
death; Marot, to whom he had shown favour, was exiled;
even his sister Marguerite was not free from persecution.
Historians do not agree in gauging his enigmatic personality. For Michelet, he is a scatterbrain young nobleman who turned into a soured, enfeebled rake; Bainville,
Madelin, are still impressed with the majesty of his bearing and with the soundness of his national policy. We
are not called upon to pass judgment upon him: the fact
that is significant for us, and which can not be denied, is
that he gave a new luster, and almost a new meaning, to
the kingly office. He was in many respects a prototype
of Louis XIV, with less sustained and self-assured perfection, but with the colour, the bravado, the dash of
Italian *virtú*, which make the Renaissance so much more
fascinating than the age of Boileau.

The Court also assumed new proportions and a new
tone. All Kings had held court: even Louis XI at Plessis-
lèz-Tours, even Charles VII in his evil days, when he
was mockingly known as the King of Bourges, had a
retinue and a ceremonial. A large household, brilliant
social functions, elaborate *étiquette*, were part of the state
in which a great nobleman was expected to live, and the
King of France could do no less. But, before 1515, there
was no radical difference between the royal court and that
of a high feudal lord. With the enhanced prestige of the
monarchy, a new standard of magnificence seemed to be
required. The nobles were conscious of the needed
change, and grumbled at the parsimony of Louis XII.
"I would rather be laughed at by courtiers for my nig-
gardliness than cursed by the people for my extravagance," answered the good king. After his death, a different ideal prevailed, and Francis I had no such scruples.
He was fond of pleasure and of admiration; so he surrounded himself, not with a few kinsmen, grand officers
and personal servants, but with hundreds of nobles great
and small. As every one of these nobles had a retinue
according to his station, the court became a little commonwealth of six and even ten thousand people.

To gather, house and entertain such a multitude even
in one permanent center would have been a costly undertaking. But the difficulty was increased by the migratory
habits of Francis I. Like his predecessors, he loved the
region of the Loire, the famed "Garden of France": he
added a wing to Blois and constructed Chambord. He
must also have a worthy and modern residence in his capital, and began rebuilding and enlarging the Louvre.
But he was not satisfied with these. Fontainebleau was
his favourite: the mighty hunter loved the great forest.
It is now a vast, chaotic and not very attractive pile of
buildings: but the interior decoration, entrusted to il
Primatice and Rosso well fulfilled his ideal of sensuous
splendour. Nor was this all: he had also a castle at
Neuilly, oddly called Madrid, as though he wanted to be
constantly reminded of his enforced residence in the
Spanish capital. Madrid, surrounded with open galleries
and decorated with brilliantly coloured terra cotta, was
destroyed at the time of the Revolution; St. Germain, on
the contrary, still another of his major country seats,
survives on the impressive bluff that dominates the me-
andering course of the Seine. When a new whim urged
the King from one castle to another, not only did the
whole court with its innumerable staff follow, but even the
furniture and the hangings. Thus the adventurous joy
of camping was combined with comfort and dazzling
luxury. These rapid changes may explain why the royal
residences of the Renaissance impress us as magnificent
rather than livable: they were mere stations in the eternal
quest for pleasure. Chambord, a dream palace in its
sylvan solitude, was nothing but a gigantic hunting
lodge; as a permanent residence, it was uninhabitable, and
its various illustrious owners have found it a white ele-
phant.

The life for which the art of the time had prepared
such a gorgeous setting could hardly be expected to be
ascetic. Very few French kings have even remotely ap-
proached the saintliness of Louis IX: Francis I was not
one of them. He indulged his immense appetite for en-

joyment, on a scale which even Italy could barely rival.
A court whither men are drawn by the lust of ambition
and pleasure is no favourable ground for the Christian
virtues; at any rate, the royal circle of Francis I was free
from gloomy hypocrisy. He did more than any other
sovereign to stamp magnificent immorality as the natural
privilege of the great. Here again, Louis XIV followed
him, and did so with such majestic assurance that no one
would call it effrontery. The kings of the classical age
must enjoy the liberties of their prototype Jupiter.

In comparison with his resplendent father, Henry II
was dull and even somber. Among the Valois kings, he
stands out as relatively moral. He neglected his wife,
Catherine de' Medici, for another woman; but to that
woman, Diana of Poictiers, much older than himself, he
remained abjectly devoted until his death. He placed his
idol on an altar which all artists adorned in eager rivalry:
effigies, emblems, ciphers, poems, innumerable mythological allusions, preserve the fame of the great Diana. We
find it hard to understand the infatuation of Henry II.
Physically, his divinity seems to have been vigorous rather
than charming; morally, she was narrow, imperious,
grasping, and could very easily be cruel. With the sons
of Henry II, and particularly with Henry III, the court
became increasingly a place of ill repute. The standards
of the time are well preserved for us in the writings of
Bourdeille, better known as Abbot of Brantôme—a very
secular Abbot, we must hasten to say. In his *Lives of
Great Captains* and *Illustrious Ladies*, deeds of blood and
deceit alternate with scandalous anecdotes, and never
evoke a flicker of indignation. In this limited sphere, the
Italo-Pagan Renaissance had achieved its object.

The cost of this continuous festival was naturally stu-
pendous, and the bourgeois caution of Louis XI and
Louis XII had to be flung to the wind. The King was
absolutely reckless, and "the King's pleasure" was law.
The country, in the first decades of the sixteenth century, was prosperous, the royal domain had vastly increased, and yet the monarchy was constantly in financial

distress. This was usual under the ancient régime: periods of good management, when debts were reduced, taxes lightened and a surplus accumulated, occurred perhaps two or three times in as many centuries, and never proved lasting. Chaos was the rule, order the exception. The absence of a regular budget, the prodigality of the Kings, the never-ending wars, were not alone responsible. The classical age did not, in the three centuries of its existence, evolve a fiscal system in harmony with its aspirations. Whilst the monarchy was becoming national, and assumed responsibilities on a national scale, the feudal principles still prevailed in finance. The clergy served the State with their prayers, the nobles with their swords, and to pay taxes in vile cash, like a commoner, would have seemed to them a degradation. A country in which nine-tenths of the real property belonged to the privileged orders and escaped taxation could not have a well balanced budget. Naturally matters were worse under a king who kept a court of unexampled splendour, and who embarked on wars on a continental scale. But, even for a good administrator, the task would have been practically hopeless. Sound finances were impossible in France until the night of August 4th, 1789, which put an end to feudal privileges. The shadow of one age was thus prolonged through the whole of the succeeding age; the absolute monarchy, with its ideal of order and stability, struggled through a perpetual crisis; and a situation which might well be termed impossible endured, paradoxically, for three centuries.

The men who handled the king's monies knew a little better than he how to take care of their interests. The ancient régime presented almost from beginning to end the scandalous contrast of an impoverished treasury with absurdly wealthy treasurers. Periodically, it was found necessary to teach these unfaithful stewards a lesson, and make them disgorge. In this also, the reign of Francis I is a first sketch of that of Louis XIV. Francis executed Semblançay as Louis was to punish Fouquet. In both cases, the sacrificed financier was the representative of a vicious system rather than a criminally dishonest man, and the severity of the sentence seemed excessive. In both cases also, the victim retained friends, and poets notably honoured themselves by their fidelity to a fallen power. Clement Marot, in an indignant epigram, praised the noble countenance of old Semblançay on his way to the gallows, and contrasted it with the hangdog look of his "infernal judge" Maillart; and La Fontaine wrote a touching elegy on the downfall of Fouquet.

III

In theory, the king ruled alone. In practice, he naturally had to employ innumerable agents, to delegate his power, and to seek advice. Francis I hated the routine of business as much as Philip II of Spain seems to have loved it. Louis XIV united traits of both, and knew how to balance his duties and his pleasures. But the king's authority remained entire: he could be influenced, but not openly thwarted. Those who ruled the state under him were his personal servants.

Barely emerging from feudalism, the absolute monarchy was still unorganized. There was no sharp distinction between the officers of the king's household, and those who administered the kingdom. Court, domain, nation, were not clearly separated: all belonged to the sovereign. The Grand Master of the Household, the Grand Chamberlain, the Grand Squire, the Constable, the Chancellor, had at the same time definite court duties, and indefinite political powers. According to the King's favor, any one of these—or even others, a Treasurer, an Admiral—might become the chief personage in the State. Chancellor Duprat, for instance, enjoyed great influence; during the ill-fated expedition that ended at Pavia, he governed the country under the regency of the Queen Mother, Louise of Savoy, and faced the crisis with great skill and determination: but other Chancellors remained obscure. Under Henry II, the Constable, Montmorency, was supreme. Absolutism in its purity, as represented by

Francis I, Louis XIV and Napoleon, is not compatible with the institution of a prime minister.

The Court, in feudal days, had a social and an administrative meaning: it was the assembly of the king's friends, companions and counsellors. The brilliant horde that Francis I dragged with him from one end of France to the other was of course purely social. Collectively, it might create an atmosphere that would influence the king: but it had no definite function. The different attributions of the primitive *Curia Regis* had passed to a series of Councils, which, however, were loosely organized and not strictly specialized. From the political point of view, the most important was the Privy Council, composed of permanent members, and of noblemen summoned intermittently by the King. But, although this body was absolutely in the hand of the sovereign, and had purely advisory powers, Francis I was afraid that it might acquire some degree of independence: important decisions were therefore discussed in a small, informal committee of the king's most trusted advisers, known as the Council of Affairs.

The Grand Council was a supreme Court of Justice, and one of the chief instruments of absolutism. For cases could be arbitrarily withdrawn from the regular jurisdiction, and submitted to the Grand Council, which was under the immediate influence of the King. This was called the right of "royal evocation."

The Grand Council was an obedient tool: the rôle of the Parliaments was much more ambiguous. The Parliament of Paris was by far the most important, and indeed the only one which was intimately associated with national history. The Parliament was purely and simply a court of justice, without any legislative power. It had no authority except as an agent of the crown: the claims that it was in some obscure fashion the heir of the Merovingian assemblies of the people seem purely fanciful. But one of its functions was to keep a record of the royal edicts and ordinances. In case some new legislation were contrary to the fundamental traditions of the monarchy,

the Parliament, before recording the new act, had the
right to call the King's attention upon the difficulty, or,
as it was termed, to offer a "remonstrance." This right,
which like most rights under the ancient régime, had
never been formally recognized, conferred upon the Parliament a vaguely political character, and a remote resemblance with the function of the Supreme Court of the
United States in safeguarding and interpreting the Constitution. In essentials, the Parliament was in agreement
with the King: it represented the legalistic, unifying,
national tendency against feudal chaos. In some cases,
however, it might stand for the monarchy even against
the king. It was deeply attached, for instance, to the
liberties of the Gallican Church, and fought bitterly
against the Concordate of 1516. The great absolutists,
Francis I and Louis XIV, distrusted the Parliament, and
curtailed its privileges. Under weak governments, on the
contrary, under Mazarin, under Louis XV and Louis
XVI, the Parliament would assert itself with great
vigour; its defiance repeatedly took the form of a judiciary strike, paralyzing the most important tribunals in
the land. Once it went to the extreme of actual rebellion.

The Parliament, like the States-General, is a melancholy Might-Have-Been. There is something very attractive about the idea of Tradition formally embodied in
an assembly of learned judges, appointed for life,
wealthy, and therefore independent; devoted to the State
and to the Church, yet no servile worshippers of the King
and of the Pope. And there was enough truth in that
ideal picture to make the figures of a few great Parlia-
mentarians very impressive indeed: the names of d'Aguesseau and Lamoignon are among the most honoured in
French history. Unfortunately, the Parliament had no
firm basis for its claims. Its opposition to the monarchy
was far from enlightened; and it developed, during the
classical age, all the faults of a narrow caste. The Revolution extinguished it unceremoniously; Napoleon found
no place for it in his reconstruction of France; and the
restored Bourbons had no thought of reviving it. There

is hardly any institution that lasted so long, played so active a part, and left so little regret.

The sixteenth century saw, not the inception, but the rapid growth, of an hereditary bureaucracy. This curious system might be called a new feudalism: here again a confusion was established between "property" and "authority." The practice arose out of the eternal financial troubles of the monarchy. The kings, whilst deprecating the purchase of an office as strongly as we condemn the buying of a senatorial seat, soon winked resignedly at the abuse. As they found it profitable, they would create new offices for the sole purpose of selling them. Occasionally, in a fit of capricious righteousness, these bought appointments were cancelled, which satisfied justice—and made it possible to sell them over again. The officials who had thus heavily invested in their charge considered it as their property and wanted to keep it in their family. The principle came to be practically recognized under Henry IV, and lasted till the end of the ancient régime. The king, source of all bounty, found it convenient to give away valuable offices to his friends, in the same fashion as he distributed ecclesiastical preferments. Hence the extraordinary multiplication of the official class. In a sense, this enhanced the power and prestige of the monarchy.

Why were the practical bourgeois of ancient France so eager to pay their good money for the privilege of serving the crown? First of all, the investment brought direct returns: with each function went fees to be collected; and it was admitted that judges should receive from both parties certain *douceurs* (not bribes!) known as "spices" (*épices*). But the possession of an office also gave a man a new standing in the community. The officials formed a new privileged order, a sort of bourgeois nobility, exempt from the most vexations and most onerous forms of taxation. So the sale of offices was really a spendthrift's expedient: whilst it brought ready cash to the treasury, it dried up future resources.

The growth of an hereditary official class qualified to

a considerable degree the absolutism of the French kings.
The management of the Kingdom, in its innumerable details, was entrusted to a special body of men, almost a
caste, and that caste developed some of the qualities of
specialists. The officials had long traditions of service,
and a sense of professional honour. The danger with
them was not so much incompetence and arbitrariness as
formalism and attachment to routine. The proliferation
of that bureaucracy paralyzed the king himself: finally,
it stifled the monarchy. There was enough intelligence
in the eighteenth century to recognize the need of reforms, and energy enough to undertake them. But the
mass of privileged persons was too compact: in addition
to the clergy and the nobility, survivors of the feudal
régime, there were the Parliaments to be taken into account, and the innumerable office-holders created by the
Kings themselves. Against their serried ranks, Maupeou,
Turgot, Necker, were powerless. A revolution was needed
to cure the evil.

. . . .

In principle, an autocracy, founded on actual power,
hallowed by the Church, identified with Law, in harmony
with the aspirations of the people; in practice, a series of
kings, of whom one only, Henry IV, was well above mediocrity, whilst several were profoundly despicable; a Court
of dazzling brilliancy, abysmal extravagance and loose
morality; a central government slowly taking shape, but
never completely extricating itself from chaos; a ubiquitous bureaucracy, more attached to its own privileges than
to the service of the country: such was the political régime
of the classical age. Thus it appeared immediately upon
the accession of Francis I; under Louis XIV, it was rationalized, made more efficient, and more magnificent still,
but not essentially altered; and it survived, incapable of
radical change, until the reign of Louis XVI. Are we
taking too gloomy a view of the ancient régime? We are
not blind to its elements of picturesque grandeur; especially do we believe that political forms, whilst not indif-

ferent, are not the most reliable standards by which a civilization may be appraised. At any rate, the Monarchy of the King's Pleasure was prevented by its inner contradictions from becoming consistently and irresistibly oppressive: it had the saving grace of absurdity. Perhaps we ought to be thankful if historians, four hundred years hence, have as good a word to say for our times.

CHAPTER IV

ECONOMIC AND SOCIAL CONDITIONS IN THE SIXTEENTH CENTURY

I. *The Economic Renaissance:* real, but not a revolution.

II. *Local Economy:* agriculture and essential industries: the economic unit is the *pays* (small district). A few larger, more highly organized industries: metallurgy, textile, printing.

III. *Persistence of Medieval System.* Guilds and corporations. Monopolistic tendencies. Hereditary class of masters. Brotherhoods and "Compagnonnages."

IV. *Influence of Monarchy:* arbiter between masters and men, producers and consumers. Creation of new masters by letters royal. Monarchy sides with the masters against the men.

V. *Economic Periods* in the sixteenth century: (a) up to 1525, prosperity; (b) 1525–1560, difficulties; (c) 1560–1593, Religious Wars, ruin.

VI. *Currency and Prices.* Rising prices, even before flow of precious metals from America. Influence of this factor on feudal nobility and on peasants. Working people: *real* wages probably not increasing.

I

THE Renaissance is one. Inventions, discoveries, the progress of national organization, Humanism, did not occur about the same time through a mere coincidence; neither was one actually caused by any of the others. All are manifestations of the same spirit: a revival of confidence and activity in every field. It was natural therefore that there should be also an economic Renaissance at the beginning of the sixteenth century.

This Renaissance was very real, and it was the essential background of all the rest. Art and even scholarship are luxuries. A famished country can not produce Pantagruel, Chambord or the *Thesaurus Linguæ Latinæ*. Without making a fetish of the "materialistic interpretation of history," we may note that great cultures have seldom, if ever, lacked the basis of economic prosperity.

Prosperity, however, is no guarantee that the highest culture will thrive.

The other aspects of the Renaissance, as we have seen, implied no sudden discovery and no radical change; they marked the resumption and acceleration of a progress which had grown slack, but which had never ceased altogether. Classical antiquity, Italy, the personality of Francis I, coloured but did not create the French Renaissance. Definite events and dates—1453, 1494, 1515—are not points of departure: they help us plot the curve, but the curve is continuous.

The same considerations apply in the economic realm. We might be tempted to ascribe the commercial Renaissance to a single, dramatic factor: the discovery of America, and the vast influx of precious metals from the mines of the new world. Here again, it seems that the "catastrophic" theory is misleading. The revival of prosperity had begun very definitely before the discovery of America. The profound changes due to the increased amount of money in circulation did not take place until the French Renaissance had reached its climax. The methods of production, the organization of commerce and labour that had prevailed during the last centuries of the middle ages survived, practically unaltered and almost unchallenged, until the reign of Louis XVI.

In culture, there was at least the illusion of change, which impressed the contemporaries. In government, the change was real, although it was not fully conscious: the balance had definitely shifted in favour of the monarchical principle, whilst the forms of feudalism lingered interminably. In the economic world, there was no essential change at all, either fancied or real, conscious or unconscious. Minor transformations were inevitable in the course of three hundred years: but they could not bear comparison with the "industrial revolution," which refashioned England, and then continental Europe, from the middle decades of the eighteenth century to the middle decades of the nineteenth.

II

France was still almost exclusively an agricultural country. Hardly any one, except perhaps, Jean Bodin, thought of a *world-economy*—an idea still alien to many minds in our own days. Very few more had a clear conception even of a *national economy*: this was reserved for the seventeenth century, and particularly for Colbert. The range of the economic system was not even regional or provincial: it was strictly local, and its unit was the *Pays*. The *pays* is a small natural and historical district, usually with no official boundaries, but with definite common interests and traditions. Morvan, Caux, Brie, Thiérache, Goëlle, Vexin, Valois, Vermandois, we could name at random scores of them, and there are literally hundreds. Modern geographers, like Vidal de la Blache, have paid great attention to these little worlds almost sufficient unto themselves, and often marked off by very noticeable differences in climate, production, architecture, dialect, the type and temper of their inhabitants. It was high time they should thus be thoroughly studied, for they are disappearing fast. Political centralization, roads and railways, industry on a large scale, world commerce, have made them obsolete. The capital of such a *pays*, the country town, the equivalent of our county seat, with its weekly market, its fairs a few times a year, its half-dozen shops and its three or four primitive industries, may appeal to us for its quaint and melancholy charm, but it is doomed. At best, it can only vegetate; and it is a question whether many of those that were destroyed during the Great War can ever truly live again.

In the sixteenth century, most of the produce that was not consumed on the farm never went farther than the nearest country town. The roads were much safer from brigandage than they had been in the Dark Ages or in the early Middle Ages: but they were none too safe, and far from comfortable. The era of great road building, the pride of the old monarchy, was to begin a little later. The rivers were obstructed with mills, dams, chains, nets, and especially with innumerable tolls. The Loire, for instance, the chief highway in what was at the time the leading region in France, was made almost impassable with vexatious obstacles. The kings issued edicts after edicts, abolishing the tolls and ordering the removal of obstructions: but as soon as the attention of the central power was diverted, the same abuses sprang up again. Custom barriers, high and capricious, separated almost every province from its neighbours. The great fairs of Champagne had been ruined by the Hundred Years War. It was safer to trade at home.

As the population, thinned by over a century of warfare and by the Black Death, was not excessive; as the soil was of good average fertility; as disastrous extremes of heat or cold, drouth or rain, are rare in France, the country lived safely and prosperously enough on that purely local basis. This gave ancient France her marvelous power of recuperation after national catastrophes, a power which she has not completely lost. An economic life based upon world trade is much richer, but much more sensitive, than one based on innumerable independent cells.[1]

Only a few places had a broader outlook. Beauce, for instance, had specialized in grain, and exported it, not to its capital Chartres only, but as far as Paris—fully fifty miles away. Seaports naturally had still larger connections: Bordeaux sent her wines far and wide, particularly to England. But these were exceptions.

Few industries had gone beyond the stage of the home craft. Metallurgy, naturally, required greater specialization and concentration. But even in this case, nothing

---

[1] The persistence of a local economy can be measured by the fact that, within the author's memory, the thin and sourish wines of Argenteuil and Suresnes still had a market in Paris. Thirty years ago, there were market gardens within the walls of the Capital; much of the supplies of the Halles Centrales was brought by horse-carts from farms within a twenty-mile radius. London was already drawing upon New Zealand, Canada, Argentina, the West Indies, China and Siberia for its breakfast table. The extreme conservatism of the French in economic matters is partly explained by this unbroken tradition of local self-sufficiency.

even remotely approaching the modern scale of production could be dreamt of. Pockets of iron ore were widely
distributed in France; the crude Catalan method was
used—furnaces do not seem to have been introduced until
the latter half of the century; and the only fuel in common use, wood, was ubiquitous. As the king owned a
large share of the forests, he was indirectly a partner in
all iron manufacture.

The royal cannon foundries, the largest and most elaborate of all metallurgical establishments, were among the
very few industries truly national in scope. The others
were of recent introduction, and not based on the local
tradition: for example, silk weaving and printing. Louis
XI had induced Italian silk-weavers to settle in Lyons,
and a flourishing branch of the trade was established at
Tours. In this case, the method, and at first the raw
material, came from abroad; the merchants, for a market,
had to look to the aristocracy throughout the land, and
even beyond the national boundaries; the local economy
was left behind. The concentration of many looms in
certain cities, which had already taken place in Flanders,
could hardly be said to constitute industry on the large
scale; for there was very little division of labour, and the
weavers worked, not in large factories, but in their own
houses. It is only recently that this primitive method has
been superseded in Lyons.

Printing was such a new-fangled, expensive and complicated business, that it was long concentrated in large
cities, particularly in Lyons and Paris. Francis I favoured it: but evidently he had not gauged its full power,
for, in a moment of reactionary panic, he was tempted to
decree its suppression. In these new trades, and in the
two great cities, we find the adumbration of the present
industrial régime. The long strikes of the printers in
Lyons (1539–41–44), are already curiously modern in
character.

III

With these few qualifications, it may be said that the medieval system still prevailed in commerce and industry. Whenever we touch upon medieval history—or upon the history of the classical age—the word *system* is likely to be misleading. The economic system, like feudalism itself, or medieval Christianity, was a mass of traditions, revealing certain tendencies, but full of gaps, flaws, conflicts and absurdities. The distinction between apprentice, journeyman or companion, and master, was pretty general. But the organization into guilds or "corporations" did not prevail in all cities, nor in all the trades of the same city. Lyons, for example, was freer in this respect than Paris. Even in Paris, the organized craftsmen had to fight constantly against the competition of isolated workers. Home industry and village industry could not very well be bound by the rigid rule of the "corporation."

The guild system is extremely attractive in theory; and, if it could be purged from its medieval faults, it might well be an ideal for our own days. But, in the sixteenth century, it had already lost its vital power. Instead of protecting the public against poor work, and the masters against unfair or wasteful competition, the guild had developed thoroughly selfish and monopolistic tendencies. These were manifested chiefly in two ways: the attempt to create a closed, hereditary aristocracy of masters, debarring the journeymen from legitimate advancement; and the endless, costly, frequently absurd and ludicrous conflicts between rival organizations.

The notion of privilege was firmly anchored in the medieval mind. Whilst feudalism was losing ground in the political world, something akin to the feudal spirit was at work among officials and among craftsmen. They also wanted to turn an opportunity for service into a proprietary right, and to transmit that right to their descendants. In theory, the craft system was democratic: any companion could become a master, "provided he knew the trade and had the wherewithal," *s'il sait le métier et s'il a de quoi.* In practice, the number of masters' patents was limited, and the dice were loaded in favour of the masters' sons. The aspirant had to present a "master-piece" as evidence of his proficiency: no one could reason-ably object to this requirement, of which our Doctor's Dissertation is a survival. But the masterpiece was used as an instrument of discrimination. The jurymen would require of a companion a very elaborate and costly piece of work—a coffer with silver hardware, in a case which has come to our knowledge. Even if the candidate re-tained possession of his masterpiece, he often found that it was purposely so useless that it could not be marketed, and the cost of producing it was a dead loss. In addi-tion, the banquets to the examining masters, as prescribed by custom, were made absurdly expensive. The masters' sons, on the contrary, were allowed to present a much simpler masterpiece, or even were excused altogether. The companions repeatedly protested against such injus-tice; they had resort to the Courts; they even appealed to the King. But on the whole, they made no headway.

This creation of a privileged class among the artisans has found modern apologists. They have conjured up the vision of an ideal world, in which, instead of abstract, dangerous and delusive "Rights of Man," each individual had concrete, definite, hereditary rights which were his lawful possession. Among such an aristocracy of labour, we would expect the stability and the professional ex-cellence that go with long tradition, and also a sense of *Noblesse Oblige.* Every man then knew his station, with all the privileges thereunto appertaining; a master crafts-man was as secure in his position as the king or the baron in their respective spheres. Such a régime would be per-fect indeed, but for two objections. The first is that all aristocracies tend to insist much more strongly upon their privileges than upon the duties which created and justi-fied these privileges. The second is that the basis of the system was exceedingly narrow. If we put together the clergy, the nobility, the officials, and the quasi-hereditary masters, we find only a minority of persons with a guaranteed status: all the rest of the population remained deprived of rights, either abstract or concrete. The fact that the benefits of privilege extended far beyond the two higher orders explains the long stability of the ancient régime. The clergy and the nobility would have scorned to recognize the kinship between their own principles, and those of the guild masters: yet there was a secret solidarity between them. Wide apart as they seemed, they were to stand and fall together. The abolition of the "corporations" was effected by the Revolution at the same time as the abolition of feudalism.

It is the very nature of privilege to be jealous and punctilious. So we find in the world of commerce and industry the equivalent of those long quarrels for precedence and points of etiquette that loomed so large in the eyes of the Duke and Peer Saint Simon. The corporations were contentious and quick to resent any infringement of their customary rights. There was an epic battle between the shoemakers and the cobblers. The cobblers could only mend old shoes, not make new ones. But the problem was: When is a new shoe technically an old shoe? And the cobblers secured the right of manufacturing practically new shoes, provided they used *inside* a piece of old leather. There was another Homeric fight between the *oyers-rôtisseurs*, or dealers in roast goose, and the *poulaillers*, or poulterers. The goosemen were wrong, for they were selling chicken as well as roast goose; but the *poulaillers* were not right, for they were only privileged to sell their fowl raw, and not cooked. The *rôtisseurs* won the day: but then they had to face the formidable hostility of the licensed cooks. And so *ad infinitum*: such lawsuits were transmitted from generation to generation, among the precious traditions of the craft. Corporations had their "hereditary foes" and their wars of revenge right up to the end of the ancient régime. In the course of time, they elaborated regulations and drew up distinctions which, for their minuteness and subtlety, would have done credit to a scholastic theologian.

The masters, who were deriving full benefit from association, were mortally afraid lest the companions should take advantage of the same method. The corporation, although it included the three degrees, masters, men and apprentices, was ruled entirely by the masters. The *Confrérie* or Brotherhood might be more democratic. The Confrérie was at times clearly distinct from the Corporation, at times almost identified with it. Essentially, it represented the religious and social side of the professional association; and, as members of the same trade usually lived in the same vicinity, it was a sort of neighbourhood league as well. It was placed under the patronage of some saint, whose festival was celebrated with procession and mass; frequently it built, or at least adorned, a special chapel in the parish church. In spite of its unimpeachable purpose, the brotherhood was suspected by the masters, and denounced by the clergy. It seems that banqueting had usurped an excessive share in its activities, and that religion served as a pretext for orgies. Repeatedly, in 1498, in 1533, and again by the great Ordinance of Villers-Cotterets in 1539, the brotherhoods were abolished. But it was not in the nature of absolutism to be obeyed, or even to be consistent: as early as 1541, the Drapers had been allowed to restore their brotherhood, and many others followed.

If a mixed association like the Brotherhood, under the control of the masters, incurred their suspicion, *a fortiori* a union entirely among journeymen, and a secret one to boot, would be severely under the ban. These unions, however, did exist. They were created for the special benefit of the itinerant workman, the companion on his "tour of France." They had their conventional names, their mysterious rites, their charities, their rough code of justice. They had their feuds also, for there were rival orders among them. They were called *Compagnonnages*. The compagnonnages made concerted action among journeymen possible, and in consequence were constantly persecuted. Still, they managed to survive the ancient régime and the corporations, and did not disappear until

the industrial revolution had brought with it a new type
of unions. At the end of the nineteenth century, the
present writer could still find some traces at least of their
quaint vocabulary among Parisian working men.

If we have exposed without indulgence the evils of the
corporative system, it is not that we are blind to the fine
qualities of the old craftsmen. The long apprenticeship,
the slow promotion, the elaborate masterpiece, the rigid
and minute regulations, the invincible aversion to change,
did not, as might be feared, lead to total stagnation, but
to stability and thoroughness. Not only pieces of furniture, jewelry, plate, brass and pewter ware, but even articles of clothing were made to last for generations. They
were created and they were handled with the loving reverence which is due to heirlooms. Such possessions are
not mere belongings of the family: they are part of the
family, and their accession ought to be entered at the
proper date in the family register. The result has been,
even in modest homes, a slow accumulation of honest and
beautiful things. A hundred years of democracy, and of
cheap, machine-made luxury, have not fully ruined these
treasures of old France. To this day, there are interiors
in the provinces which the richest collectors could hardly
match in their mellowed unity: for theirs is not the artificial unity of a single "period," fit for parvenus only: it
is the unity of organic growth. This is the redeeming
aspect of a world based upon privilege and tradition.

IV

The Kings did not attempt radically to alter the corporative system: at least not until the second half of the
eighteenth century. But they sought to permeate it with
their influence. They were the supreme arbiters among
their subjects—between public and corporations, between
rival corporations, between masters and men. This gave
them constant opportunities for intervention; each intervention meant an increase in the authority of the crown,
and usually also it implied an additional tax for the royal

treasury. For instance, in 1581, very reasonable regulations were issued, doing away with the scandalous abuses
of the banquets which the new masters had to provide on
their initiation: but, in compensation, the masters had to
be sworn in before a royal official, and for this service a
fee was charged. In spite of all regulations, the banqueting evil was not fully abated—but the royal dues continued to be collected all the same.

In the middle ages, the corporations were connected
with the feudal régime: it was the local lord (or the commune as the collective equivalent of a feudal lord) who
fixed the number of masters and issued patents to them.
Gradually, this privilege passed into the hands of the
King. The corporation, on the basis of their ancient statutes, enjoyed a large amount of autonomy. But the
King had the right of creating new masters at will, by
royal letters, and these masters were exempt from the
usual obligations of masterpiece, banquet and examination dues. This royal prerogative was naturally resented
and resisted by the corporations: had it been used indiscriminately, it would have ruined the whole system. This
the kings were not prepared to do. So the direct creation of masters had the effect of qualifying the traditional
régime without superseding it. In a sense, it acted as a
useful check on the narrow policy of the corporations
which, left to their own devices, would have created an
eternal monopoly in favour of a few families. But in
many cases, the kings were guided, in this domain also,
by their ever-recurring need for new resources. The new
creations were seldom gratuitous: the King—or the favourite to whom he delegated his power—pocketed the
fees. Thus, eight years after the marriage of his sister
Marguerite with the King of Navarre (1572–1580),
Henry III decided to celebrate the joyful event by em-
powering her to create two new masters of each craft in
all the cities that she had entered, or might enter in the
future. It was a handsome brotherly gift, which cost the
royal donor nothing at all.

This prerogative enabled the crown to favour the establishment of new trades, or to foster new processes in old trades. There is no doubt that, if the existing corporations had been listened to, they would have condemned every innovation as "contrary to good custom, and destructive of vested interests." It was thanks to the kings that the silk industry was introduced, and that glassware, mirrors, ceramics, could be perfected. Bernard Palissy, the heroic artisan, artist, scientist, writer and religious martyr, who discovered after a stubborn fight new methods of enameling earthenware, received a patent as "inventor of the rustic figuliness of the King and of the Constable." The intervention of the monarchy, on the whole, was an element of progress.

In the constant conflict between masters and men, the Kings, as a rule, placed their authority at the service of the masters. It is a tradition which even republican governments have not quite outlived: those in authority must stand together. The French monarchy never was truly democratic in its sympathies: it was at best "mesocratic," devoted to the interests of the middle class. So the crown agreed with the masters in condemning and punishing strikes and in attempting to suppress brotherhoods and *compagnonnages*. When several causes, particularly the influx of precious metals, brought about a sharp increase in the cost of living, the kings adopted the view that the trouble was due to the unreasonable pretensions of the working men; and, in a rising market, they strove to keep the wages down.

V

On the whole, the economic system of the sixteenth century is not in any sense modern, and can not even be called transitional: it is purely medieval. The great increase in activity was the result, not of a revolution, but of recuperation. It began immediately upon the close of the Hundred Years War. It was definitely noticeable under Louis XI, that is to say, before the discovery of America or the Italian expeditions. It was actually at

its height under Louis XII. Claude de Seyssel, a contemporary, is too much of a panegyrist to be taken literally: still, his glowing description of abundance and luxury under the good king, "Father of the People," is
confirmed by many other sources, French and foreign,
and particularly by Commynes, a shrewd man, and disenchanted.[1] Certain it is that Louis XII managed to
reduce the chief tax, or *taille:* such a measure is a fairly
sure sign of well-being, for tax reduction is least possible
when it is most needed, *i. e.,* in times of distress. This
brilliant prosperity continued under Francis I; the personal magnificence of the king and his court made it even
more evident. The Camp of the Cloth of Gold (1520)
has remained the symbol of that period of dazzling pro-
fusion. These good times, of course, were not the monopoly of France: they were even more striking in the
Netherlands and in the Hansa Towns. Unfortunately,
they were not to last.

We may consider the disaster of Pavia (1525) as the
beginning of a more difficult period. The boundless extravagance of the court, and the gigantic, interminable,
confused struggle with Charles V, drained the resources
of France at least as fast as they were produced. The
country stood the crisis of 1525 surprisingly well, and it
was attended by no economic catastrophe. But, from
1525 to 1560, it may be said that France barely managed
to hold her own. The French were rather slow in realizing that the "good days" were over. Each difficulty
seemed exceptional: the store of optimism accumulated
during the previous quarter of a century was not suddenly exhausted. However, disenchantment was slowly
growing: it is significant that Francis I, with all his authority and prestige, was abundantly lampooned and
caricatured.

The third period in the century, from 1560 to 1593, is
filled with the religious wars. Aimless, chaotic, ubiqui-

---

[1] This comparison between the reigns of Louis XI and Louis XII, by
Claude de Seyssel, oddly resembles, at times, a report from an American Boosters' Club.

tous warfare is far more destructive than great national campaigns: France, harried by bands of Huguenots and Leaguers, supported by Germans and Spaniards, was almost as thoroughly devastated as she had been during the Hundred Years War. The court of the last Valois was still displaying the most extravagant luxury: but it was like the rouge that grim old Montluc put on his cheeks to conceal the ravages of disease. Even in 1610, after the very fine efforts of Henry IV and of Sully, France had not fully recovered the prosperity that had been hers a hundred years before.

VI

We have reserved until the end the puzzling problem of money and prices. The controversies and confusion of ideas in Europe to-day might easily lead us to doubt the infallibility of experts in such matters; and it is hardly surprising that we should come to no very definite and convincing conclusion about the situation nearly four hundred years ago.

It seems quite clear that there was a sharp rise in prices, or, in other terms, a marked decline in the purchasing power of money; many contemporaries mention it, and unanimously complain about it. It is no less clear that hardly any one ascribed this phenomenon to what appears to us its obvious cause, namely the increased supply of gold and silver from the new world. Here again, Jean Bodin was clearer of sight than his generation. During the middle ages, the hoard of gold in Europe had increased very little; and, as much of it was immobilized in jewelry and in Church ornaments, the stock available for currency might well have been actually declining. Changes in price in that period were therefore not due to the amount of money in circulation, but to general prosperity or distress, and especially to the abundance or scarcity of labour. Under Louis XII, the population was increasing; the standard of living was rising even faster, and so prices were already mounting.

The mines of Mexico and Peru upset the fairly stable equilibrium of the money market. But America was not discovered until 1492; the first quarter of a century of the conquest was a period of preparation: it was not until 1520 that the new factor could be seriously felt. The silver mines of Potosi, which made Peru a by-word for fabulous wealth, were not discovered until 1545. It must be remembered also that the war between France and Spain, preventing a free flow of bullion between the two countries, retarded in France the effect of the American stream of precious metals. That obstacle was not fully lifted until 1559, when the peace of Cateau-Cambrésis was signed. This is enough to show that the true economic Renaissance, which took place chiefly between 1475 and 1525, was very little affected either by the American trade or by the increased quantity of gold and silver.

How did the mounting cost of living affect the community? It naturally hit hardest the classes with fixed resources expressed in units of money. The feudal nobility was dealt a severe blow: hence the impoverishment of the country noble, and the flocking of so many aristocrats to the court, where bounties, pensions, offices and other benefits were to be had. Many noblemen gladly sold portions of their estates to bourgeois, who, holding noble land, became gentlemen in their turn. The old fighting caste was thus disintegrated and diluted. Although real property remained in popular opinion the only substantial form of wealth, personal property assumed an importance that it did not possess in the Middle Ages.

Another result ought to have been an improvement in the condition of the peasants, who, as a rule, were no longer serfs. But, if the feudal burden had grown somewhat lighter, the load of royal taxation was increasing in proportion. However, these taxes were very easily collected during the first quarter of the century, which argues a fair degree of prosperity in the countryside. We need not mention again the disastrous effect of the religious wars: the peasants suffered even more than the inhabitants of walled cities.

When we come to the town population, we are non-plussed. D'Avenel, Levasseur and others have attempted to figure the value of *real* wages in the sixteenth century, in terms of the necessities of life, and in particular in terms of the cost of wheat. Their figures were bound to be approximations only, and they present many discrepancies in detail. They agree, however, in their general trend. Whilst nominal wages were soaring, to the great indignation of the masters, real wages were declining, to the sore distress of the workers. A journeyman was not so well off in the second half of the century as he had been in the first. However, the cost of prime necessities is not the sole test, except for those elements in the population who live close to the starvation line. We should have to examine whether there had been any shift *within* the budget of a workingman's family, and whether the comparative cost of semi-luxuries had increased or decreased. And especially, we should have to take psychological factors into consideration, and to ascertain whether one class *felt* itself better off or worse than before, in comparison with the other classes. The answer to these complex questions would be very uncertain even in the study of present-day conditions. When we deal with the Renaissance period, the difficulty is vastly greater. The splendour of court life, art and literature, the colourful pageantry of great wars, the sombre and intense drama of religious strife, have obscured for us the economic life of the sixteenth century.

CHAPTER V

THE REFORMATION

I. *Failure of Protestantism* in France: not due to "the Latin mind." Four alternatives, not two.

II. *Gallicanism:* Definition, origins. Strongly supported by Parliament. The Pragmatic Sanction of 1438 and the Concordat of 1516. The Church increasingly in the hand of the king.

III. *Pre-Reformation and Semi-Protestantism:* (a) the Humanists, Erasmus, Rabelais; (b) the group of Lefèvre of Etaples and Marguerite of Navarre.

IV. *Protestantism.* Luther. Calvin. The Reformation compared with the two aspects of Humanism. The starting point moral rather than theological. Stoic pride and fortitude of the Huguenots.

V. *Religious Wars.* Factional rather than religious: Guises *vs.* Bourbon-Condé-Navarre. Vacillating policy of the Valois. "Political" bourgeoisie rallies to Henry IV. Compromises of 1593 and 1598.

Philosophical result of the crisis: Montaigne's scepticism.

Political result: yearning for order and unity.

I

THE movement for religious reform filled the whole sixteenth century. In France, it was apparently defeated: the abjuration of Henry IV in 1593 and the Edict of Nantes in 1598 were the official acknowledgment of this failure. The Huguenot king was compelled to recognize that the overwhelming majority of his subjects had remained attached to Catholicism; and the very privileges which he granted to the Protestants emphasized the fact that the Reformers had to be protected through a kind of extra-territoriality, as though they were in France a foreign minority.

For this failure,—a fact which we may deplore but which we cannot deny,—many explanations have been offered. Protestantism, it is said, is essentially a Northern movement; Catholicism is more congenial to the "Latin mind." It is true that the "Latin" countries, Italy, Spain and France, have remained almost purely Catholic, whilst Northern Germany, Scandinavia and Great Britain turned Protestant. But the "Latin mind" is a myth. The identification of a Church with a particular race, while it is objectionable from the religious point of view, is extremely doubtful as a scientific fact. Calvin was a very typical Frenchman, and so were Coligny, Henry Estienne, Bernard Palissy, d'Aubigné, Sully. One of the most active centers of French Protestantism was—and remains—the South, covered with Roman ruins, preserving the physical type of the ancient Romans more purely than the Italians themselves, and keeping up through the Middle Ages the tradition of Roman law. The Scots and the Welsh are supposed to be "Celts" no less than the Irish and the Bretons: yet the former two are as determined in their Protestantism as the latter in their Catholicism. The population of Belgian Flanders is not different in race and speech from that of Holland: yet the Belgian Flemings are ardently Catholic, the Dutch in majority Protestant. The Southern and Western Germans (Austria, Bavaria, the Rhineland) have, on the whole, remained faithful to Rome: the other Germans have seceded. In countries of divided allegiance, like Alsace and Switzerland, the lines of religious cleavage do not agree with the political, racial or linguistic boundaries. The notion that the liberty-loving North rose in rebellion whilst the more timid South was content with its chains is fanciful almost to the point of absurdity. For no one would accuse the French of intellectual timidity, least of all in religious matters: we are inclined to rebuke them for their excessive "free-thought"; and large elements, in the North, changed their creed at the command of their masters with remarkable docility.

It has been repeatedly said that "there was not enough religion in France to make two." There is little wisdom in that epigram. The intensity of religious feeling on both sides was as great in France as anywhere. The earnestness, the mental vigour, the moral courage of the Huguenots are universally admitted. But French Catholicism also has many admirable names on its roll: not only those of administrators and orators, but those of mystics, saints and apostles. In the field of foreign missions, Catholic France has done more than her share, and honours the memory of many martyrs.

The fact is that the problem is much more complex than is usually believed. If we consider two elements only, we are bound to go astray. In every country, we can not understand the Reformation without a study of its relations with Humanism on the one hand, with the home policies and foreign policies of the Princes on the other. In France in particular, the conflict was not a single duel between Protestantism and Catholicism. There were four alternatives, not two, and a prolonged four-cornered fight took place between them. They were Roman Catholicism, Gallican Catholicism, Protestantism, and Free-Thought. Much that was achieved in other countries through the triumph of Protestantism was secured in France through what we may call the *classical synthesis*, or better the *classical compromise*, a *modus vivendi* between Rome, the Gallican tradition, and rationalism.

II

It is necessary therefore to understand the Gallican position as an essential element in the problem. The Church of France, whilst recognizing without question the primacy of the Roman Pontiff, had always maintained a large degree of practical autonomy. The king was not merely the administrator of secular power: he was also, as we have seen, endowed with a sacred character of his own. He was the Lord's Anointed; his coronation, hallowed by the perennial miracle of the Holy Chrism, was a special sacrament, a kind of ordination; his hands acquired the healing touch. He was not a mere lay ruler, but, like Constantine and Theodosius, a "Bishop from without," a "Bishop over Bishops." History had slowly strengthened these exalted claims. Although the Sor-

bonne was a Catholic, not a French, institution, it was
inevitable that the king of France should profit by its
prestige. At the moment when the Papacy and the Empire were weakening each other through their violent
conflict, the throne of France was occupied by a saint,
and Louis IX was the most revered personage in Christendom. His attitude to the Holy See was one of respectful
independence, and it is not surprising that a *Pragmatic
Sanction* should have been ascribed to him, in which he
was supposed to have proclaimed the principles of the
Gallican Church. This Pragmatic of 1269, in which Bossuet still believed, has long been proved to be apocryphal:
but legend, in this as in many other cases, had merely
hardened a tendency into a fact. When Philip the Fair
entered into conflict with the Pope, an assembly convened
at Notre Dame supported the national sovereign. During the "Babylonian Captivity" at Avignon, the Popes
were almost the retainers of the French Kings, and the
long schism that followed brought down the prestige of
the papacy to its lowest ebb. In the fifteenth century,
France was practically independent from Rome. The
Pragmatic Sanction of Bourges, in 1438, under Charles
VII, was an unequivocal statement of Gallican autonomy.

This policy of the monarchy was vigorously endorsed
by the Parliament. That body was like a lay clergy, almost fanatically devoted to a doctrine: the supremacy of
the State. This doctrine the Parliament would defend
even against the King. When Louis XI abolished the
Pragmatic of Bourges, the Parliament refused to register
his order. The conflict lasted throughout the reign; the
Parliament outlived the King, and the Pragmatic was
restored. It was with the greatest difficulties that Francis
I, autocratic though he was, secured the official registra-
tion of the Concordat which superseded the Pragmatic.
Up to the end of the ancient régime, the Parliament remained a pillar of Gallicanism—more consistently royalist in this respect than the Kings themselves.

The régime sanctioned by the Pragmatic of Bourges,
and dear to the clergy and the people of France, con-

tained elements of democracy as well as of national autonomy. The general councils were proclaimed superior to the Popes; and to the chapters of cathedrals, collegial churches and abbeys was recognized the right of electing clerics to vacant positions. Francis I needed, for his Italian policy, the support of the Pope; the Pope desired above all the suppression of the hated Pragmatic. The result was the compromise known as the Concordat of 1516. That instrument was to regulate the relations between the Church and the French State until the Revolution.

The chief point in the Concordat, from our point of view, is that it conferred upon the King the right of nominating a candidate to a vacant see, abbey or priory. The Pope alone could give the canonical "institution" or investiture: but, as he was not at liberty to withhold his confirmation, the royal nomination amounted to an appointment. If in theory, the Concordat recognized to the Pope a greater power than had been admitted under the Pragmatic Sanction, in practice the King, not the Pope, was supreme in the French Church.

The Concordat was far less simple than this summary indicates. Diplomatic compromises seldom are clear-cut and logical, and the ancient régime, so respectful of vested rights, seldom attempted sweeping changes, and never succeeded in carrying them out. Many benefices were conferred, not by the King, but by ecclesiastical, or even by lay, patrons; the Pope preserved direct powers in a number of cases; finally the right of capitular election was retained by certain abbeys, particularly by the wealthiest and most powerful of them all, Cluny and St. Denys. But the tendency of the Concordat was unmistakable. Gallicanism was actually strengthened by this treaty which was supposed to endanger it: but it was royal Gallicanism. The Church lost much of her independence, not as against Rome, but as against the King. France was self-governing within Catholic Christendom: the French Church was no longer fully self-governing within the monarchy. She ceased to be a sovereign body, and became merely an Order: a transformation somewhat similar to the one which was turning the independent feudal caste into a court nobility. As late as the separation of Church and State in 1905, these three factors entered into the problem: the Holy See, the secular Government, and the French Clergy. Without disloyalty to either temporal or spiritual power, the Church of France would have liked to manage her own affairs and especially to dispose of her own immense resources: in 1516 as in 1802, the two rulers came to an agreement to a large extent at the expense of the national clergy.

This great strengthening of the King's hands had far-reaching consequences. First of all, there was for the French King none of the inducements that tempted some German princes from the Catholic fold. The French Church was already his own; he disposed freely of her benefices to reward his friends and servants, including artists and poets whose ecclesiastical qualifications were of the most meager. Many a courtier, "inditing a sonnet, was dreaming of a bishopric." A reformation on Lutheran or Anglican lines, making him formally the ecclesiastical head of the nation, would neither greatly enhance his prestige, nor serve his material interests. Had the Pragmatic endured only a very few years longer, until the open rebellion of Luther and his excommunication, the history of France might have taken a totally different turn. As it was, when the crisis broke out, the monarchy was committed through self-interest as well as conviction to the defense of Catholicism. The vaguely liberal sympathies of Francis I, the influence of his gifted and loving sister, the necessities of his European policy, which made him the ally of Protestants and Turks, could not prevail against that fundamental fact.

Conversely, at a critical hour, the royal character of French Catholicism caused the masses of the French people to rally to its support: for "royal," in those days, was equivalent to "national." The balance was never equal between conservatives and reformers: the Protestants were from the first and in spite of themselves considered

as rebels against the State as well as against the Church.
The Catholicism of Ronsard in his *Discourses on the Evils
of the Time*, the hazy Catholicism of Montaigne, were
political, not theological creeds. These men—and most
men in France—were more interested in law and order,
as embodied in the monarchy, than they were in tran-
substantiation. This is confirmed by the fact that the
extreme Catholics, the Holy Leaguers, in sympathy with
Spain and in rebellion against their legitimate sovereign,
were later to be combated for the same reasons.

The large influence of the temporal power in the Royal
Gallican Church attenuated in a marked degree the conflict between orthodoxy and secular thought. The old
Sorbonne was not allowed freely to tyrannize over the
public mind: when its spokesman Béda went too far,
Francis I had him arrested. During the whole classical
period, the dangers of extreme clericalism were thus held
in check; and this made the development of independent
thought a possibility. It would have been difficult for
Spanish Catholicism, for instance, to produce a Descartes,
a Molière, not to mention a Voltaire. It is amusing to
note the number of semi-ecclesiastical personages—not
invariably edifying—in the political and cultural history
of the ancient régime. Their archetype was Rabelais,
that strange vagrant monk and priest, half-unfrocked
and in open rebellion against the Sorbonne; and the line
continues down to the society and philosophical *Abbés* of
the eighteenth century, the most respectable of whom was
probably the psychologist Condillac. In this respect
again, the Gallican Church was not unlike the Anglican:
Voltaire might very well have been an Abbé, just as Swift
became a Dean.

III

The urgent need for religious reform had been felt for
several generations before 1500. But, early in the sixteenth century, it took a definite turn. Medieval inhibi-
tions had grown weaker, on account of the long scandal
of the great schism; and the European mind had ex-

perienced a revival of self-confidence and energy. Humanism, in the larger sense, and the reforming spirit, combined to form a kind of early Protestantism, very different, however, from the open revolts led by Luther and Calvin.

It was an ambiguous movement, at the same time conservative and liberal, and therefore doomed to failure. Wisdom is with the moderates, but fanaticism alone arouses enthusiasm. The best representatives of that state of mind were Erasmus—who, as a good European, belongs to the history of French culture as well as to that of the Netherlands—and Rabelais. Both were determined critics of ecclesiastical abuses; both were particularly bitter against the massive pedantic ignorance of the theologians, and both sought in the new learning salvation from scholasticism. Both had transcended the region of dogmatic discussion, and had no desire to exchange one narrow orthodoxy for another. Both, for all their intellectual daring, were prudent, sensible and somewhat timid men: Rabelais was ready to maintain his opinions "to the fire—-exclusively," and that "exclusively" disqualified him as a leader. So they wielded little influence in the religious crisis. When the struggle became too bitter, Rabelais toned down his virulent attacks against the Sorbonne; he was very angry with Dolet for reprinting his book without these attenuations; he was most probably sincere, although a trifle over-emphatic, when he called Calvin "demoniacal." He had no more sympathy with *Papefigue* (Pope-scorner) than he had with *Papimane* (Pope-worshipper). The violent anti-Catholic tone of his posthumous Fifth Book is usually accepted as evidence that the work is to a large extent apocryphal. Rabelais is a thorough "naturalist" and "humanist": man to him is the end and the measure of all things. He has therefore no place in the history of orthodox supernatural religion.

A long step further on the way to the Reformation we find Lefèvre of Etaples and his school. Lefèvre believed in faith above works, in grace and not in human merits.

In this, he was at least as radically opposed to the "naturalists" like Rabelais as to the upholders of a superstitious ecclesiasticism. In Lefèvre all the essentials of Protestantism are to be found: against spurious authorities and corrupt traditions, he appealed to Christ alone, and to the pure doctrine of the apostles. A true Renaissance scholar, he wanted "a return to Antiquity," and the restoration of the original sacred texts, in the same spirit as Budé or Estienne attempted to give correct editions of the classics. He desired to clear the very sources of religious life from the age-long deposit of medieval legends; and he wanted also to make these living waters available to all men, through French translations of the Old and of the New Testaments. His thought was fully formed by 1508, before Luther could have any influence upon him; and he gathered round him a number of earnest men, Budé, Farel, Cop, Roussel.

He was in particular the spiritual center of the "group of Meaux," thus named because Briçonnet, a friend of Lefèvre, became Bishop of that see in 1516. In 1523, Lefèvre was made Briçonnet's Vicar General. This purely French and peaceful Reformation enjoyed the sympathy and active support of Marguerite d'Angoulême, sister of Francis I, and Queen of Navarre. It is odd that this gentle, scholarly and deeply religious princess should be chiefly remembered for her *Heptameron*, a pastiche of Boccaccio, in which themes and treatment are as risky as in the original, whilst the brilliancy of the Italian is wholly lacking. Clement Marot, the pretty court poet, belonged through some accident to this twilit school: his graceful levity, his superficial sensuous grace, hardly prepared him to be the translator of the Psalms, and to suffer persecution and exile for his faith.

Marguerite herself is an excellent example of the group. She had no desire for a violent rupture with ecclesiastical authority: whatever changes were necessary should be effected quietly and from within. Her religious attitude would be recognized to-day as purely Protestant: it was a gentle mysticism seeking direct support in the promises of Scripture. But her theology was never clearly formulated, and she did not challenge the essential Catholic dogmas, or even the main points of Catholic discipline.

This moderate reformation, like the enlightened humanism of Erasmus and Rabelais, was destined to be swept aside. In theology, Lefèvre was soon left behind by Luther, and then by Calvin. Briçonnet, in his diocese, forbade the reading of Luther's works (1523), and, whilst not persecuting on his own authority, he did nothing to avert persecution. Perhaps the worst obstacle to the success of the school was that it insisted on piety and righteous living rather than upon dogma. Francis I might conceivably have accommodated himself with any doctrine: we can imagine him as a Landgrave of Hessen or as a Henry VIII. But the quiet and austere mysticism of the group of Meaux was out of harmony with the pleasure-loving spirit of the court. Thanks to Marguerite's protection and to his own moderation, Briconnet escaped censure and died in peace in 1534. Lefèvre found refuge in Marguerite's little court at Nérac, until his death in 1536 or '37. The school thus faded away without any tragic crisis: it shared the dismal fate of most half-revolutions.

IV

On October 31, 1517, Martin Luther nailed his ninety-five theses upon the door of the Court Church at Wittenberg; in 1518, Zwingli initiated his reform movement at Zürich. Their names and their activities were almost immediately known in France. Lefèvre and his friends were at first favourable. But when Luther was excommunicated in 1520, the French reformers were hopelessly divided. Some, like Clichtove, who had been among the most active lieutenants of Lefèvre, rallied to the strictest orthodoxy taught by the Sorbonne. The principal leaders, Lefèvre himself, Briçonnet, Marguerite, persisted in their gentle dream of a change of heart without any dogmatic upheaval. Many went over to the bolder doctrines from Germany, and complained that they were abandoned

and even persecuted by their former friends and masters.
About 1530, a Protestant party was already in existence,
and, between 1530 and 1536, we see the definite beginnings of a Protestant Church.

During these critical years, French Protestantism was
without a leader: Lefèvre and Briçonnet wanted to stop
on the hither side of heresy and schism. It was therefore
a ubiquitous, spontaneous growth. Not of learned origin:
artisans rushed where humanists feared to tread. It was
not until 1533 that Calvin sprang into prominence and
it was only two years later, with his *Christian Institute*,
that he assumed the spiritual guidance of the movement.

John Calvin (or Cauvin) was born at Noyon in 1509.
The influence of his father, agent for the clergy of the
diocese, had prepared for him an easy and profitable
career in the Church. At the age of twelve, he was nominally "in charge" of a chapel in the Cathedral: that is to
say, he pocketed the revenues attached to it. But he conscientiously prepared himself for his ecclesiastical duties.
He was a student in Paris (1523–27), at Orleans and
Bourges (1528–29), in Paris again (1529–33). The
Universities of Orleans and Bourges specialized in civil
and canon law. A long tradition ascribes to Normans and
Picards a peculiar aptitude and excessive fondness for
the law. Calvin's father had legal training; and Calvin
himself revealed in his thought the qualities of a jurist
even more than those of a philologist, a philosopher or a
mystic.

In November, 1533, the Rector of the University of
Paris, Cop, opened the session with a speech that had been
prepared for him by young Calvin. This speech was by
no means radical in its theology, nor was it defiant in
tone. The Blessed Virgin was solemnly invoked; divisions
were deprecated and the spirit of peace extolled. Yet it
was virulently denounced by the conservatives, and such
was the opposition that Cop and Calvin found it necessary to flee.

The King, however, was still reluctant to be forced into
the camp of the Sorbonne extremists. Thanks to this

hesitating policy, Calvin was able to return to Paris, whilst Béda, the most violent of the reactionaries, was exiled for the second time. But the neophyte zeal of the new faith left little room for compromise. Already in 1528, a statue of the Virgin had been desecrated in Paris, and that sacrilege had caused an explosion of Catholic passion. Of this angry mood, Louis de Berquin was the victim in 1529: accused of being in sympathy with Erasmus and Luther, he was, not the first martyr, but the first martyr of note. In October, 1534, placards posted in Paris and in the provinces violently attack.d the Mass as idolatrous. This lashed to fury the fanaticism, not of the Sorbonne only, but of the whole population. Terrible reprisals followed: hundreds of men were arrested, scores were taken to the gallows or to the stake: Clement Marot, a personal favourite of the King, had to run away. On January 21st, 1535, in solemn expiation for the blasphemies of the placards, a great procession was ordered in Paris. It was devoutly followed by the King, bareheaded, wax taper in hand. Now Francis I was committed: but even then, he still strove for peace. In 1535, he offered an amnesty, and was hoping against hope for reconciliation. More decisively, Calvin had taken his choice. He went again into exile, never to return.

Calvin sought refuge, first in Basel, then in Geneva (1536). Banished from the latter in 1538, he was recalled in 1541. Henceforth and until his death in 1564, he ruled the little republic with a rod of iron. His life and work at Geneva belong to general history rather than to the study of French civilization. Suffice it to say that Geneva became the Protestant Rome, the school of doctors, and the school of martyrs as well. Theodore de Bèze (Beza) was chief among the field agents of the new church. The French Protestants or Huguenots now had a head, an organization, a doctrine. Under persecution, which was severe during the last years of Francis I and pitiless under Henry II, their faith grew more definite and more ardent. Against this persecution there was as yet no organized resistance.

The Protestant Reformation was now complete, and we

may attempt to analyze its chief elements. It was obviously the fruit of the teeming activity and self-confidence of the time, like the revival of learning, the artistic Renaissance, the great inventions and the great discoveries. In this domain also, man wanted to be emancipated from what seemed the senile childishness of the old order. Luther, like Rabelais, felt that at last the human mind had emerged from "Gothic night." There was at the basis of the Reformation something of the joyous spirit that filled Pantagruel. It can be felt in Luther's table talk. It is admirably voiced by Ulrich von Hütten: "O Century! It is a joy to be alive!"—"The wind of freedom blows!" Unfortunately, this spirit did not prevail in French Protestantism. No wind of freedom blew where Calvin reigned; nor was it a joy to be alive.

The Reformation was akin also to the other side of the Renaissance, the narrower Humanism, the return to antiquity. Pantagruelism was looking forward, and was to inspire Bacon's great profession of scientific optimism: "The golden age is before us, not behind." On the other hand, classical scholarship, Vergilianism, Ciceronianism, the Aristotelian tyranny in logic, rhetoric and poetics, were forms of antiquarian superstition, text-worship, literalism, in a word bibliolatry. This element entered for a large part into the Reformation, and warped its course. Hitherto, the supreme authority in religion had been the living Church: she was the appointed guardian of a tradition anterior to the New Testament, and of which the Bible itself was only a part; she was the interpreter of a continuous revelation. Now, fifteen Christian centuries were declared dead, and ruled out of spiritual history in the same way as they were contemptuously brushed away from literary history. In this respect, Humanism and Reformation alike were reactionary. Worse: they not only wanted to put history back, they did not want it to resume its course. To the apostolic generation and to the writers of the Augustan age had been entrusted for the last time the immutable words of divine and human wisdom.

The Reformation took a very definite theological turn.

But its very essence was not theological: it was moral. The corruption of Christendom was flagrant: the Church herself set about to reform it, and succeeded to a large extent, as she had repeatedly done before. But this time, self-reformation came too late to avert a schism. At the point of departure, we find definite evils; the next step was an attack upon the powers that permitted such evils; the third, a denial of the traditions or doctrines that these powers invoked in their defence; the fourth only a consistent revised theology. The luxury of the Roman Court, the sale of indulgences, the existence of Purgatory, the worship of the saints were thus challenged in order. Ultimately, this led to the denial of Papal authority, and to the substitution of the Bible for the Church as the sole rule of faith. Puritanism therefore is not a by-product of the Reformation, but its starting point and its greatest glory. We do not mean that all Protestants were virtuous, and that they had a monopoly of virtue. Few Protestants could rival the devotion, the energetic asceticism, the thirst for martyrdom found in the annals of many religious orders. The Huguenots had not a few disreputable leaders, like Châtillon, Condé, or, on a lower plane, des Adrets. Henry of Navarre was no saint, even when he was their champion and their idol; and few Catholics were more dissolute than the nominally Protestant court of Charles II in the next century. Still, it was moral indignation and the love of right living rather than theology that made saints and martyrs. In France particularly, the necessities of a desperate struggle further deepened this original austerity. In their puritanism, the Huguenots were at odds not merely with the relaxed Catholics of the Valois court, they opposed also the indulgent naturalism of Pantagruel, which might so easily lead to self-indulgence; they hated even more the revived Paganism, the unmoral *virtú*, of the Italian humanists and artists. In this respect, the Renaissance and the Reformation diverged irremediably. Rabelais was a worshipper of Physis, Calvin the Pope of Antiphysis: for his cardinal dogma was the depravity of human nature.

The practices denounced by the Protestants as superstitions and abuses were called by the Catholics "pious
works." It was an easy temptation, in the heat of controversy, to condemn, not mechanical and soulless works
only, but all human works as utterly worthless. Since all
merit is denied to human activity, since human nature is
utterly corrupt, man can not be saved through his own
efforts, but exclusively through the grace of God. The
pitiless and irrefutable logic of Calvin did not shrink
from the last consequence: the unqualified denial of free
will. This faith which is so often praised as the triumph
of liberty in the modern world denies liberty at every
turn. There is no free thought in orthodox Calvinism:
the infallibility of Scripture allows of none; neither is
there any freedom of action. Yet out of this doctrine of
enslavement did rise some of the strongest characters in
history. The creed itself would lead to a somber and passive fatalism: what saved the Huguenots was their attitude of rebellion. To break away from ancestral faith,
to defy spiritual and secular authority, to court persecution and martyrdom required daring and vigorous souls.
When the new faith became safe and honourable; when
people called themselves Calvinists out of respect for tradition and conformity; when Protestantism no longer
voiced the spirit of protest, the salt of the earth lost its
savour.

V

It was not until the reign of the weak child Francis II
that the conflict between the two Churches blazed into
civil war. Some Protestant leaders had hoped to remove
the sickly young king from the influence of the queen's
uncles, the Guises, and to bring him under their own. It
was the ill-concerted and ill-fated conspiracy of Amboise.
From that moment (1560) to the abjuration of Henry IV
(1593), France knew no peace.

For this horrible welter, in which the country nearly
perished, the conflicting creeds were only partly to blame.
No doubt, throughout the land, Catholics and Protestants

fought cruelly for their faith; both sides persecuted and
committed atrocities wherever they had the upper hand.
But these wars soon became chiefly political. They should
be named the wars of the Guises rather than the wars of
religion.

At first, the chief rival of the Guises was a Catholic, the
Constable of France, Montmorency. The three nephews
of Montmorency, Admiral de Coligny, d'Andelot, and
Cardinal de Châtillon, became later the leaders of the
Huguenots. They united forces with the Bourbon-Condé-
Navarre connection; and the struggle between the two
groups recalled the reckless fury of the feud between
Armagnacs and Burgundians during the Hundred Years
War. The Huguenots sought support from abroad: the
Netherlands, the German Protestants, Elizabeth. The
Guises allied themselves with Spain.

Between the two raging parties, the monarchy was
helpless. Under the three degenerate sons of Henry II—
Francis II, Charles IX and Henry III—their mother,
Catherine de' Medici was, if not the actual ruler, at least
a constant and trusted counsellor. Her policy shifted be-
wilderingly: at times she attempted to annihilate the
Protestants, as in the night of St. Bartholomew (1572);
at other times, she flattered them, granted them amnesties
and privileges, used them to check the overbearing power
of the ultra-Catholic Guises. Some recent historians have
praised the fitful, disingenuous and cruel methods of
Catherine as masterly. It seems that the middle course,
advocated by the Chancellor, Michel de l'Hospital, could
have been followed without these unaccountable and tragic
jerks.

The confused details of the struggle fortunately do not
belong to our field. The murder of Guise at Blois, by
order of the King (December, 1588), led to the assassination of Henry III in July, 1589. Distracted France
found herself with her capital in the hands of a fanatical
religious demagogy, an odd alliance of monks and aristocrats with the rabble. The legitimate King, Henry of
Navarre, detested as a heretic, was a mere adventurer,

wandering gallantly enough through his recreant kingdom at the head of a small army of his partisans.

The excess of evil led to a solution which determined the
course of French history for the next two hundred years.
The monarchy, weak as it had become, remained the only
possible center of authority in a divided nation. To the
legitimate king, heretic though he was, rallied all the
moderate and patriotic elements, all those who were not
Huguenots first of all, and not Holy Leaguers, but
Frenchmen, and lovers of order and peace. This spirit
found expression in the clever *Satire Ménippée*, the work
of a few witty and sensible *bourgeois*.

The great obstacle to national reconciliation was the
religion of Henry IV. France had not sold herself to the
bigoted Holy League; neither had she become Protestant;
she had remained moderately and firmly Gallican. Henry
IV declared that "Paris was well-worth a mass," and professed himself ready to "turn somersault." These cavalier
expressions show clearly enough that theology and mysticism had little share in the King's change of heart. But
the moderate royalists, or "Political Party," declared
themselves satisfied. Henry IV could at last enter his
capital, which as a Huguenot he had besieged in vain.
With his unique combination of military talent, diplomacy, genuine kindness and Gascon bluff, he defeated,
wheedled, bribed or otherwise won over his last enemies,
and pieced together his ruined kingdom. To his former
companions the Huguenots, he granted complete liberty
of conscience, and full equality before the law, with mixed
Courts as a guarantee of justice. Realizing that they
were a minority, and that the new régime was still precarious, he gave them also, temporarily, places of refuge,
with Protestant garrisons paid by the State. This was
the generous and statesmanlike Edict of Nantes (1598).

Monarchical unity appeared to the French mind as the
sole method of salvation: this was the political lesson
taught by thirty-three years of war. From the religious
point of view, the natural conclusion was the tolerant and
sceptical common sense which had finally guided Henry

IV and the "Political Party." The evils of fanaticism were patent: fanaticism therefore was the enemy. This second lesson was drawn, for all time, by the philosopher of the age, Montaigne. Are we not prizing our own opinions too highly when we "roast people alive" because they do not agree with us? Is not the record of human beliefs a chaos of contradictions and absurdities? (*Apology for Raymond de Sebonde*.) What do I know? Man is so fluctuating and diverse! All this, after so many trenchant affirmations supported by fire and sword, was wisdom indeed, and wisdom that remains useful and true. But it was a modest, a negative, almost a despairing kind of wisdom: the weary soberness that comes after an orgy. Montaigne is human, humane, sensible, congenial, delightful: but a trifle selfish, unpoetical, and not heroic in the least. The splendour of hope had faded, that we found in the hymn to the sacred herb Pantagruelion

France was now ready for an age of order almost at any price, of unity, of conformity. But the order had not been imposed by a tyrant: it had been deliberately chosen by common sense. Authority in harmony with reason: such was to be the keynote of the new century.

BOOK II

THE SEVENTEENTH CENTURY

CHAPTER I

THE RESTORATION OF AUTHORITY: HENRY IV, RICHELIEU, MAZARIN

I. The growth of absolutism clear through the centuries, but with eclipses. Weakness of Henry IV's position in 1593: nobles, cities, Huguenots still ready to rebel.

II. Henry IV's method: diplomacy, kindness, conscious use of his popularity. Autocracy by persuasion. Reconstruction: ably seconded by Sully. Foreign policy: the "Grand Design"?

III. Relapse into chaos after Henry IV's death. Richelieu, Louis XIII's constant support. Ruthless temper and method of Richelieu: contrast with Henry IV.

IV. Richelieu's Policy: against the Huguenots, against the nobles, against the House of Austria. Clear change from semi-feudal to bureaucratic monarchy. Richelieu's failure as a financial administrator: constant difficulties.

V. The Regency of Anne of Austria. Mazarin. The Fronde. France ruined. Mazarin's ultimate triumph, at home and abroad.

I

IN the perspective of centuries, the growth of absolutism in France is unmistakable. It was a permanent tendency of the dynasty: even the weakest Capetians dreamed of being "emperors in their realm." And this tendency was usually aided, not resisted, by the common people: any departure from it, it was thought, would lead to disaster. Absolute monarchy alone represented unity and order against the anarchy of warring nobles; alone it could serve as a rallying point against the ambitions of foreign powers—England in the middle ages, the House of Austria during the classical period. This is the very thread of French history. The dynasty had actually created the nation, by increasing the royal domain, and by making itself unquestionably supreme within the boundaries of the kingdom. Any falling away from this norm, through the fault of a worthless king, of selfish nobles, or of a demagogue like Etienne Marcel, was felt to be an

aberration and a crime. This thread leads us from Philip
the Fair to Francis I, from Francis I to Louis XIV, from
Louis XIV to Napoleon, in whom the immemorial aspirations of ancient France for unity, order and prestige were
magnificently fulfilled at last.

But it is only in the course of centuries that the trend
thus becomes manifest. The three Orders of ancient
France, and the Kings themselves, were not so clearly
conscious of the process as Charles Maurras and his school
are at present. Especially at the close of the religious
wars, men's minds were still in a state of extraordinary
confusion, and "classical order" was a remote ideal.
Through his abjuration, Henry IV became truly King of
France. He had the hearty support of the Moderates,
the "Third Party," the "Politiques." The Moderates, in
all probability, represented the majority: but that majority was voiceless and inert; among the active elements,
the Moderates were themselves a minority. It would be
a delusion to imagine the French unanimously falling on
their knees before their legitimate sovereign. Such harmony between ruler and country had existed in 1515; it
was to be found again, on the death of Mazarin, when
Louis XIV began his personal reign; the Consulate of
Napoleon Bonaparte offered another example of willing
submission to a national leader. Nothing of the sort occurred in 1593. Voltaire opens his Henriad with the
lines: "I sing the hero who reigned over France, both by
the right of conquest and by the right of his birth." But
when Henry IV was finally acknowledged, the actual conquest of his kingdom was still precarious and incomplete.
His hereditary title alone had not been sufficient to secure
the crown for him. He was by no means the heir of an
unchallenged tradition and the idol of the people: he did
not impose himself, he was compelled to compromise. Not
in theory perhaps, but undoubtedly in practice, his conversion to Catholicism was stringently imposed upon him.
It was not the white-plumed hero of Arques and Ivry that
triumphed, but the supple, canny, resourceful diplomatist. These humble beginnings of Henry's reign im-

mensely increase the brilliancy of his ultimate success. A
conquest it was, but a personal conquest, through cunning
and through service, through charm and through kindness. No doubt he was carried on a tide of public opinion: but the stream was so uncertain at first, so full of
treacherous eddies, that the skill of the pilot appears little
short of miraculous.

The leaders of the contending parties, and particularly
those of the Holy Catholic League, had entrenched themselves in the government of provinces and cities; below
them, local tyrants were attempting to create a new petty
feudalism. In a ruined kingdom, Henry had to find enormous sums in order to bribe his former enemies. One
after the other they "sold out" to him, for cash and honours. Brissac surrendered Paris for 480,000 livres; Vitry
gave up Meaux for 169,000; Villars sold the fortresses of
Normandy for 4,000,000; Mayenne received 3,500,000
for Burgundy; Guise nearly 4,000,000 for Champagne.
Another Guise, Mercœur, in Brittany, had succeeded in
reviving the old local patriotism of the province; he hoped
to make himself hereditary Duke, perhaps independent
from France under the protection of Spain. He was the
last to give up, and the greediest: in 1598, he exacted
more than 4,000,000. Poetic justice was rudely set at
naught: the great nobles who had caused such untold misery retired unpunished, their coffers bulging with gold;
and their daughters married into the royal family.

Even after they had given up their claim to feudal independence, the nobles remained unmanageable. The discipline which Francis I had been able to maintain had
been ruined through a whole generation of anarchy. No
majesty did hedge round a King whom all had known as
an enemy, a hated heretic, an adventurer. His officers,
if they attempted to enforce his edicts, were derided, or
forcibly resisted: in making their peace with a successful
rival, such men as Mercœur, Epernon, Soissons, had no
thought of submitting to the common law. The contagion of this spirit affected even the King's personal
friends. Biron, whom he had made a Duke and Peer,

Marshal of France, Governor of Burgundy, plotted against him with Savoy and Spain, and planned for his assassination. Forgiven once by Henry, he betrayed him again, and was beheaded in 1602. Not only did Joinville and Bouillon conspire with Spain, but also one of his favourites, Henriette d'Entraigues, and her family. Under Francis I, Bourbon had been an anachronism, a monstrous exception: under Henry IV, the King was not sure even of his closest friends.

The cities followed the example of the nobles: they too refused to surrender unconditionally. Lyons, Meaux, Orleans, stipulated that the King should maintain within their walls only a limited garrison, or none at all: with the result that Amiens, ill-guarded by its militia, was surprised by the Spaniards in 1597. The Huguenots were restive: they formed an organized republic within the State. With them also, it was necessary to compromise: the Edict of Nantes gave them more than their religious liberty. They secured guarantees which were contrary to the unity of the kingdom: they were allowed to protect themselves, because the King was aware that he could not adequately protect them.

II

In presence of such difficulties, a weakling would have been annihilated; well-meaning obstinacy, calling itself strength of mind, would have led to a renewal of the civil war; even an upright and vigorous prince might easily have succumbed. Fortunately, Henry IV possessed a unique blend of human and statesmanlike qualities. "Step by step" was his watchword. The nation trusted him, but at first trusted him only a little: it was his talent to make that little fructify. Naturally subtle and supple, with the exterior and the manners of a bluff man-at-arms, and trained to patience in the school of adversity, he knew how to yield, when resistance was not worth the candle. Sully, his companion, hated the thought of squandering all that good money on worthless traitors: "If we fight for it, said

Henry, it will cost us ten times more." But he yielded
without creating the impression of weakness: he yielded
because he could afford not to yield. He was conscious
of his military talents, of his growing popularity, of the
strength of his royal title. So he allowed himself to be
plundered so gracefully, with such cordial dignity, that
in giving way he made it plain that he was conferring a
favour. He was willing to liquidate the situation at a
heavy cost, provided the settlement was final. "Good-bye!"
he gaily cried to the Spanish troops as they were leaving
Paris. "Commend me to your master; but do not come
back again!" They did not come back: whatever gains
he made, great or small, he managed to hold. Bribery
usually breeds more bribery: but the great lords whom he
had paid found that they had been bought, and bought
once for all. "Paris was not built in one day," was another of his favourite sayings. He did not fully tame his
nobility: but each year their tone was a trifle lower. They
were feeling the iron hand.

No prince ever put more diplomacy at the service of
authority. It was not purely cleverness on his part: he
was a kind man, and hated to hurt. The opening words
of a speech to the Assembly of Notables convened at
Rouen in 1596 are an excellent example of his method:
"I did not call you, as my predecessors did, merely to have
you endorse my decisions; I brought you together to hear
your counsels, to believe them, to follow them, in a word
to place myself entirely in your hands. . . ." Is this a
complete surrender? Henry does not mean it so, and does
not want his words to be so misinterpreted. So he adds:
"Such a desire is not customary with Kings, grey-beards,
and conquerors." Naturally, the Notables advised and
granted everything that he wanted. "My predecessors,"
he said to his Parliament, "were afraid of you, and did not
love you. I love you, and I fear you not." When he
forced the Edict of Nantes down their throats, he used
the same unexampled mixture of familiarity, persuasion
and authority. "I am working for peace: those who wish
to hinder my Edict want war. You will be very ungrate-

ful if you cause me this trouble. . . . I am the King now: as King do I speak, and mean to be obeyed." Was his tone a little too peremptory? He hastens to correct the impression: "Grant to my entreaties that which you would refuse to menaces. You will not do it for my sake, but for your own, and in the interest of peace." The Parliament of Paris yielded; the other Courts followed, with some reluctance. On the 1st of January, 1600, the Edict was the law of the whole land.

Henry IV was popular, and knew that his popularity was an asset: he cultivated it for the good of the kingdom. Like Napoleon, he collaborated actively, consciously, to the growth of his own legend—a legend more amiable and considerably truer than Napoleon's. He was not insincere: he played a part, but that part was himself. He was expected to be gay, impulsive, familiar: he did not have to wear a mask, he had only to show the public that side of his nature that the public wanted to see. Franklin, during his stay in Paris, exploited his own personage with exactly the same kind of shrewdness: calculating, yet not deceitful. Roosevelt also carefully and honestly lived up to the type that he had made famous. These men were not histrionic. Henry IV had played, and was still playing, too desperate a game, with the welfare of the country as the stake, not to use his popularity for all it was worth. Of no other ruler are there so many friendly anecdotes reported, so many wise and kindly sayings, at times homely and folklike, at other times more flamboyant, with a touch of bravado, a romantic waving of the white plume. His very weaknesses served him: he was le Vert Galant, the ardent but not too exclusive lover. His affair with Gabrielle d'Estrées, with its mysterious and tragic end, rather endeared him to the Gallic heart; and he was easily forgiven when, in late middle life, the most powerful king in Christendom, he pursued at the same time his "Grand Design" for the reorganization of Europe, and the charming little Princess of Condé.

Thus was authority gently, almost imperceptibly restored. It was autocracy by persuasion—with the stick

in reserve: "*Bâton porte paix.*" But the wearing down
of opposition was the lesser part of his task: the problem
was to use his authority for the public good. Especially
after internal and external peace had been established in
1598, Henry IV did bend all his efforts to the restoration
of his ruined land. He found in Maximilian de Béthune,
Duke of Sully, an ideal collaborator. Sully could be an
able general, a treasurer of unexampled efficiency, a promoter of agriculture and public works. The highways
were improved by him, and lined with trees which the
peasants long called by one of his names, "Rosny." Regular relays of horses for the use of the public were organized. The first French canal with locks was begun between the Seine and the Loire (canal of Briare); the
Southern Canal between the Mediterranean and the Ga-
ronne was planned. Henry believed with Sully that
"ploughed field and pasture land were the two fountains
of life for France": he read assiduously the famous treatise of Oliver de Serres, *Théâtre d'Agriculture.* But,
broader-minded than Sully, he also favoured industry,
foreign trade, luxury. He planted mulberry trees, so
that France could produce her own silk; he displayed
with great pride silk stockings of French manufacture;
he started the tapestry works of the Gobelins. No doubt
the ruins of forty years were not repaired in one day.
The "boiled fowl," *la poule au pot*, that he wanted to see
on every peasant's table of a Sunday, remained a pious
wish. But prosperity did return, in an appreciable measure. For a wonder, the *taille*, the chief tax on the commoners, was lightened. Sully, whilst relieving the burden
of the people, filled his arsenal with ordnance, and his
vaults with a war chest, enormous at the time, of 20,000,-
000 livres. As in the days of St. Louis, the prestige of
the French King went far beyond the frontiers of his
country. He was still in his prime, and his work far from
completed, when he perished under the knife of a fanatic,
Ravaillac.

His death leaves unsolved the fascinating riddle of his
foreign policy. He was about to embark on a great en-

terprise. Would he have worked in European affairs as
great and as beneficial a transformation as he had already
achieved in his own kingdom? He had sound principles,
and Sully, at any rate, ascribed to him grandiose projects. Long before Napoleon III—that ill-fated forerunner of ill-fated Woodrow Wilson—he had clearly expressed the "Doctrine of Nationalities": let all Spaniards
be ruled by the King of Spain, all French-speaking people by the King of France. That ideal was singularly
more practical than the dreams of Italian conquest which
had haunted four kings for three-quarters of a century;
it was much more feasible than the notion of the 'historic'
and 'natural' frontier of the Rhine, which had already
taken hold of French imagination. His great Peace Plan
may have existed only in Sully's mind. It was nobly conceived: but even if it had been practicable, it would not
have led to permanent peace, for, like Napoleon's scheme
of European organization, it implied the supremacy of
France. It may be that both his doctrine of nationalities
and his Grand Design were only *Gasconnades:* he was
essentially an opportunist. Certain it is that he was pre-
paring for war with many trumps in his hand. He had
money, and a kingdom at peace. He had an army, and,
for the first time, almost a national army. He was a good
commander, who had not only won the brilliant skirmishes
of Arques and Ivry, but who had manœuvered without
loss of prestige against the most famous general of the
time, the Duke of Parma. He had good lieutenants, the
chief of whom came from his trusted Huguenots. He
died, and all his plans went for naught.

III

Here the spasmodic character of monarchical institutions appeared again with sinister clearness. "The King
is dead: long live the King!" does not tell the whole story
when a child of nine succeeds a Henry IV. The Parliament, only too glad to assume political powers, entrusted
the regency, "according to custom," to the Queen Mother,

Marie de' Medici. The Regent was an ignorant, weak-minded and lethargic woman, very much under the influence of her compatriots, Concini and his wife Leonora Galigai. These foreign adventurers, who had at least the merit of discovering Richelieu, became the actual rulers of France, to the great disgust of the French nobility.

The dangerous policy of bribing malcontents was resorted to again: but it had required the tact, the firmness, the personal authority, the reserve strength of Henry IV to make it a success. Under a weak ruler, each dole served only to whet the appetite of the aristocracy. "The days of kings are over: the days of princes have come," they arrogantly proclaimed. Jealous of Concini, they rebelled against the Regent, giving as their justification the very prodigalities by which they had profited. To cover their mutiny with a semblance of legality, they clamoured for the States General. These were convened in 1614. The utter selfishness, not only of the two privileged orders, but also of the Third Estate, was again manifest, as well as their irremediable disunion. This abortive assembly was dismissed, not to meet again for one hundred and seventy-five years.

In 1617, a bold plot, with the complicity of the King, destroyed Concini. The Marshal d'Ancre, as he was now called, was shot down as he was entering the Louvre, and no one rose to avenge him. This marked also the end of the Queen Mother's ascendancy. But it meant only the substitution of one worthless favourite for another: d'Albert de Luynes, who had amused the boy King with his skill in falconry, misruled in his stead until December, 1621.

It took three more years for the "appointed man" to make himself supreme. Armand de Richelieu, Bishop of Luçon and Cardinal, had served Marie de' Medici and worked under Concini. He had somehow offended the King: "At last, Luçon, I am free from your tyranny!" Louis XIII angrily cried when the Italian Marshal had fallen. Yet Richelieu was to conquer the King, and to keep his favour for eighteen years. Marie de' Medici her-

E

self, who had turned against her protégé, was unable to
shake her son's confidence in him: when the quarrel became too bitter, it was the King's mother who was forced
into lifelong exile. The young Queen, Anne of Austria, and
the King's brother, Gaston of Orleans, were humbled and
made powerless. As for the great nobles who rose against
Richelieu, exile, imprisonment and death were their reward: Montmorency, "first baron of the realm," went to
the scaffold. The contemporaries, knowing the King's
original aversion for Richelieu, and noting that he had
become wax in his minister's hand, could account for the
change only through some kind of magic. If only the
spell could be broken, the King would be himself again!
But the spell lasted as long as the Cardinal lived. Once
only did it look as though the Minister's power were
shaken and already his many enemies were rejoicing: but
the King once more rallied to Richelieu's support, and the
episode remains known as "the Day of Dupes" (Nov. 10,
1630).

Historians, romancers, dramatists, have long taken it
for granted that Louis XIII, known to be timid, even
morose in his manners, was weak of mind and weak of
will. His constant support of his great minister admits
of a more natural explanation. Weaklings are capricious, and may be violent in their caprices: Charles IX
ordered the massacre on the night of St. Bartholomew.
After all, the King was the King, and heard it repeated
on every side. Richelieu, a son of the lower nobility, had
no formidable faction in the State to shield him from
disaster. A prince of the Church could not have been
shot as unceremoniously as a Florentine adventurer like
Concini: but, had the King given a nod, there would have
been no lack of great lords ready to arrest the Cardinal,
and lead him to Vincennes or to the Bastille. *Not to give
that nod* required on the part of the King constant vigi-
lance and energy. His voluntary servitude was a triumph
of the will. Louis XIII must have understood Richelieu.
He placed the interest of the monarchy above his own
pride; and his handsome, melancholy figure, half-effaced

in the background of his own reign, acquires thereby a strange and somber nobility.

Richelieu, at the beginning of his ministry, expounded his plans to Louis XIII; and, at the close, he summed them up in his *Political Testament*. The impression was created that, in the words of Mignet, this man "never did anything but what he intended to do." If this were the case, he would be unique in history. On closer inquiry, the claim appears palpably exaggerated. Richelieu, although not a born opportunist like Henry IV, was frequently compelled to compromise. He was no revolutionist: he respected the traditions of ancient France. He had no thought of suppressing at once, if ever, all the privileges and abuses that hampered the exercise of royal authority. He paved the way for Napoleon: but he was no Napoleon. Yet, though he had no radical doctrine in mind, and though he had to feel his way in the accomplishment of his purpose, the purpose was unmistakable: to make the King's power absolute in France and supreme in Europe. The policy of Richelieu is not a system: it is a tendency; but it is a tendency with the intensity of a passion.

And it was served by an energy which grew more ruthless at every step. We must guard against the legends that cumber history: but they are seldom without foundation, and our duty is to account for them, not merely to explain them away. It was not Alfred de Vigny (in *Cinq-Mars*) or Victor Hugo (in *Marion Delorme*) who invented the redoubtable character of the red robed tyrant, served by such instruments as Laffemas and Laubardemont. Richelieu himself fearlessly proclaimed that clemency was a weakness, and that weakness was a crime. He was not cruel: he was too great to find pleasure in the sufferings of others. But the sentiments, the rights, the liberty, the life of his victims counted for nothing in his eyes when *la Raison d'Etat*, the "reason of state," had spoken. He gave currency to that sinister phrase: place Richelieu's *Raison d'Etat* at the service of Rousseau's *Social Contract*, and the result will be Robespierre.

No contrast could be more striking than that between those two great servants of the same cause, Henry IV and Richelieu. The first wanted to be loved; the second, to be feared. A difference in temperament, no doubt, and, at the bottom, perhaps a mere physiological difference: for, in spite of premature infirmities, Henry IV knew the joy of animal well-being; whilst, in spite of his commanding presence, Richelieu was constantly fighting for health. A difference in the times of their activities: Henry IV was compelled by the weakness of his original position to use persuasion as well as force; his work was not wholly undone after his death, and the minister of his son could speak more imperiously. Perhaps it was, most of all, a difference in stations. For Richelieu, of comparatively modest origin, a son of the provincial nobility allied with the *bourgeoisie*, the State, far above the great lords, was a sort of formidable idol, to be served by methods of terror. For Henry IV, and for lesser men like Francis I and Louis XIV, the State was no Leviathan, but something accessible and personal,—their own domain, their family, *themselves*,—and therefore something more human. Few hereditary kings are as ruthless as usurpers and ministers. The beautiful fiction that the King was the father of his people had its saving grace, and that grace could not be imparted to Armand de Richelieu.

IV

The policy of Richelieu can not be more adequately summed up than in his own terms, which every child in France learns by heart like a magic formula: to suppress the political privileges of the Protestants, to reduce the nobles to strict obedience, to humble the House of Austria. In the first of these aims he was unqualifiedly successful. The situation created by the Edict of Nantes was a provisional compromise, and Henry IV himself considered it only as such. It was inconceivable that, in a unitary state, a portion of the population should have its own fortresses, its own army, its own diplomacy, with the possibility of using them all against the national sovereign. The combination of sectarian autonomy with feudal ambitions and lawlessness, which had nearly destroyed France, could appear again; and it did reappear with such a leader as the Duke of Rohan. The situation, tolerable under Henry IV, thanks to his moderation and to his personal prestige, had been made worse by the weakness and violence of his successors. The feeble and abortive campaign of De Luynes against the Protestant stronghold of Montauban had exasperated and emboldened the Huguenots. Richelieu addressed himself to the task with his incomparable determination. The obduracy of the defenders of La Rochelle found its match in the relentlessness of the besiegers (1627–28). The heroic little city, the sea capital of the Huguenot Commonwealth, was starved into surrender; the mountain fastnesses of the Cévennes were subjugated; Rohan went into exile; Montauban, the chief inland fortress, was overawed, and the rebellion was ended, at Alais in 1629, not by a negotiated peace, but by an *Edict of Grace*.

Richelieu, Cardinal though he was, hardly seems an ecclesiastical character at all; cuirass and helmet seem to fit his haughty mien better than a cassock; yet he was a sincere, an ardent Catholic, and heresy to him was an abomination. But he respected the work of Henry the Great; he wanted immediate peace in the realm; his foreign policy made him the enemy of the great Catholic powers, Spain and Austria, and therefore the natural ally of the Protestants. So he used moderation. The Edict of Nantes, in all its religious and civil stipulations, was confirmed; and the Cardinal could faithfully promise to the Huguenots that "now they had submitted to the common rule of all subjects, whose safety could depend only on the graciousness and good faith of their prince, His Majesty would be pleased to assure them that, as subjects, he made no difference between them and the Catholics." Richelieu kept his word. The ruin of the Protestants as an armed power was followed by no persecution, by no abridgment of their rights. Huguenots were employed by the State; Rohan, three years after Alais, was in command of a royal army; even Guiton, the Mayor of La Rochelle and the soul of its defence, became a naval officer in the Cardinal's service.

The subjugation of the great could not thus be achieved in a single campaign. Richelieu, as we have seen, repressed without pity all conspiracies directed against him, whether the culprit be "the first baron in the land," Montmorency, or a mere upstart, a boyish favourite of the king, like Cinq-Mars. He enforced with his customary rigour the edict against duelling—an evil which Henry IV himself had sought in vain to abate. Bouteville, another Montmorency, who had openly defied the law, was executed. In this warfare on one of the most cherished traditions of the nobility, Richelieu was not wholly successful: duelling survives in attenuated form to the present day; but he asserted his authority. It was at least a symbolical gesture: the nobles knew their master. Symbolical also was his order that all fortified castles not on the frontier should be dismantled. The loss in picturesqueness was great; and it was doubtful whether a medieval fortress could have long resisted the king's ordnance. But the peasants everywhere heartily joined in the leveling work: the proudest crown was torn from feudalism; it was a foretaste of the fall of the Bastille. Some of the highest positions in the State, traditionally reserved to the greatest of the nobles, and which conferred excessive prestige on their incumbents, were done away with. The Grand Constable, permanent head of the army, thus disappeared; the Grand Admiral was also suppressed, the duties of his charge being assumed by Richelieu himself under a new title.

One of the chief dangers he had to guard against was the power of the provincial governors. These, belonging to the highest nobility, constantly aspired to hereditary tenure and semi-independence. The long-delayed, reluctant and costly submission of Mercœur in Brittany, the rebellion of Montmorency in Languedoc, were only outstanding examples of this peril. Richelieu took care to shift the governors about, so that they would not take root in their provinces, and so that the King's supremacy should be unchallenged. In order further to reduce the Governors' power, he sent into the provinces administrators or *Intendants*, middle class officials entirely in his devotion, and responsible to himself alone, and he gave them very extensive attributions. Ultimately, this institution was to transform France altogether from a semifeudal kingdom into a centralized bureaucracy: the prefects of Napoleon are the heirs of the *Intendants*. Here again, however, Richelieu was no radical. He did not invent this method, which had been used occasionally by Henry IV and even by Francis I; and he did not apply it constantly and universally. His *Intendants* were frequently akin to the *Missi Dominici* of Charlemagne: royal inspectors on temporary missions, rather than executive officials in permanent residence. This much may be safely asserted: that the institution made decisive progress under him.

The struggle with the House of Austria was not carried to a triumphant close under Richelieu himself. He had at first to be content with indirect intervention in the Thirty Years War: Gustavus-Adolphus was supported by his subsidies. When France herself joined the fray, she was not immediately successful: in 1636, the Spaniards advanced as far as Corbie in Picardy, and the capital was in a panic. It was not until after the Cardinal's death that the French won their first decisive victory, at Rocroy (1643), against the renowned veterans of Castile. The downfall of Spain, the helplessness of the Empire, were due to internal causes rather than to the blow dealt by the French armies. Still, the policy of the Cardinal, continued by Mazarin, is invariably credited with the triumph that was sealed in 1648 by the treaties of Westphalia. It was he who made the supremacy of Louis XIV in Europe a possibility; and even to-day, the diplomacy of Richelieu remains a prestigious and perilous model for those statesmen who, like G. Hanotaux, know a great deal too much history.

This is the tale of the Cardinal's successes: it is impressive. The story of his failures is hardly less striking. His magnificent game on the chessboard of Europe was expensive, and he was no financier. He was very fond of prodigal display in his own household, and he was royally lavish in the service of His Majesty. He was too conservative, and too much engrossed with other problems, boldly to tackle the essential evils of the ancient régime: absurd privileges in taxation, faulty methods of collection, absence of a definite budget. He was ignorant in economic matters; and because he signed grandiose charters for trading companies, conceding the exploitation of a continent to a few men without experience and without capital, he thought he had done enough for the prosperity of France. As a matter of fact, this glorious minister was in constant financial distress; and although the middle class suffered, the burden fell most heavily upon the common people. The Cardinal, ruthless with the great, was not tender with the poor. There were repeated insurrections, due, not to disloyalty, but to sheer despair; and they were repressed, as the rebellions of the nobles had been, with the usual iron hand. If the comparatively short and superficial crisis of the Fronde left France utterly ruined, it was because the country, at the death of Richelieu, was already nearing exhaustion. The glory and order that Richelieu brought to the kingdom were dearly purchased; and the verdict of the French might well be an endorsement of Corneille's homely verse:

> Qu'on parle mal ou bien du fameux Cardinal,
> Ma prose ni mes vers n'en diront jamais rien.
> *Il m'a fait trop de bien pour en dire du mal,*
> *Il m'a fait trop de mal pour en dire du bien.*

V

Louis XIII survived his minister by a few months only (December 4, 1642–May 14, 1643). Once more a minority, once more a regency, with an untrained foreign queen in control. But Anne of Austria, the mother of Louis

XIV, "hated work and loved Mazarin"; and that Italian adventurer, soldier, diplomatist and cardinal, ruled France for eighteen years.

The first open revolt against him was led by the magistrates of the Parliament of Paris, supported by the populace; it lasted only from 1648 to 1649. But the nobles had been drawn into the conflict, and their old unruly spirit flared up again. Of the many disturbances which had afflicted France, this, known as the *Fronde*, was the most chaotic. The leaders had no guiding principle: they detested Mazarin, and they were not wrong in condemning his corrupt and expensive rule; but they had no substitute to offer. So we find them changing side according to the caprices of fortune and the whim of their ambition. Now Condé, the victor of Rocroy, was with the crown, and now he was allied with Spain; and it so happened that his great rival Turenne, shifting also, was generally on the other side. An element of romance made the conflict even more erratic: noble ladies, Madame de Chevreuse, Madame de Longueville, Mademoiselle de Montpensier, cast themselves into heroic parts, and were blindly followed hither and thither by their adorers. Victor Cousin, the eclectic philosopher, two centuries later, fell in love with them collectively, and devoted to these charming rebels a series of fascinating biographical studies. To make confusion worse confounded, a born agitator, Paul de Gondi, Bishop Coadjutor of Paris, was constantly brewing mischief. With incomparable verve and a genius for intrigue, he plotted indefatigably for a variety of purposes: to oust Mazarin and succeed him; to be confirmed as Bishop of Paris; to secure the Cardinal's hat, as he finally did under the name of Cardinal de Retz. His *Memoirs* are among the most vivid productions of the classical age: but they fully confirm the verdict of his time as to his political incapacity.

The whole affair lasted five years (1648–1653), and was called the *Fronde* (the Sling) in derision, as though it had been a game for children. But France lay in ruins. Mazarin, supple, diplomatic, as humble in his demeanour

as Richelieu had been haughty, yielding to the storm,
kept out of sight—and out of danger. But he had not
relaxed his hold on the Regent. He did not conquer his
enemies: he allowed them to wear themselves out. He represented, however unworthily, the monarchical principle,
that is to say national interest, order, internal peace. So
this man, who had been so bitterly hated and so justly
despised, finally returned in triumph. To his death, he
displayed his power and his semi-regal state as insolently
as Richelieu. He had amassed, in the distress of the
country, a fabulous, a scandalous fortune. A deplorable
administrator, but a great diplomatist, he was largely
responsible for the treaties of Westphalia (1648) and the
Peace of the Pyrenees (1659). In 1661, he left France
to Louis XIV, with the nobility thoroughly tamed, and
even servile; the Parliaments hopelessly discredited; the
people putting their whole trust in a strong royal government; and the French monarchy without a peer in
Europe. That such a consummation should have come
through a Mazarin is one of History's most exquisite
ironies.

CHAPTER II

THE RESTORATION OF ORDER IN LITERATURE AND SOCIETY

I. The Classical Compromise: authority, tradition, reason. The sixteenth century an age of literary confusion: "At last came Malherbe!"—Guez de Balzac—Vaugelas—The Three Unities in the Drama.

II. Restoration of Urbanity in Society. The Hotel de Rambouillet—Woman Triumphant—Mademoiselle de Scudéry: the "Map of Tenderness"; excesses of "Preciosity."

III. The Academy. Richelieu—Membership—Programme—The Dictionary—*Sentiments on the Cid*—Chapelain.

IV. The first half of the seventeenth century not tame—Survivors of the Renaissance: d'Aubigné—Independents: Régnier, Cyrano, Théophile and the "Libertines"—The Romantic influence of Spain—The Burlesque School: Scarron—Worship of will power, conscious heroism, glory.

V. Rationalism. From Montaigne to Descartes—Descartes as a representative of the "classical compromise": his Provisional Code. His essential thought: disregard of tradition; radicalism.

I

FROM the accession of Henry IV to the death of Mazarin, we have noted the constant craving for national *order*. The lawlessness of the religious factions on both sides, the irresponsible selfishness of the nobles, even the usurpation of political power by the Parliament, had repeatedly brought disaster upon the kingdom. Authority must prevail: firm, but smiling and persuasive with Henry IV, somber and pitiless with Richelieu; even a Mazarin was in the end universally accepted and obeyed, because he stood for the sole permanent authority, that of the King.

But, great as was this craving for order, it did not lead to sudden and abject submission. Order, in medieval and Renaissance France, had been an aspiration rather than a possession: so the worship of order was perhaps less fanatical than in our own days, when we have enjoyed it for so long that we know what we have to lose. The theoretical absolutism of the Kings, until 1661, was not of the dictatorial nature which we find in many governments of post-war Europe. Authority did not rest solely on tradition: the idea of pure legitimacy had been obscured during the years when the hereditary claimant to the throne was rejected by the majority of the people. Neither could it be based exclusively on force: to make force the supreme arbiter was to invite civil war. The authority that the French desired had to harmonize all these elements; in order to be irresistible, it must have on its side tradition, power and *reason*. Henry IV was the perfect embodiment of this ideal: legitimacy, persuasion, and "*le bâton qui porte paix*," the big stick. Even after 1661, French absolutism was not the result of superstitious reverence for the past, and still less the child of servile fear: it was felt to be, above all, *practical* and *reasonable*.

Now, exactly the same process was taking place in literature and society. The monarchical spirit and the classical spirit are the fruit of the same compromise; both reached their point of maturity with the personal rule of Louis XIV. We have traced the development of the former from 1589 to 1661: we shall now consider the latter during the same period.

The literature of the French Renaissance leaves with the reader a sense of splendid confusion. Rabelais had matchless vitality: but he never was able completely to fuse his own personality, his medieval heritage, and his enormous new learning. The poets of the Pleiad had what Rabelais lacked: a definite sense of beauty; but it was too often obscured by their antiquarian pedantry, or by their unbalanced ambition. Montaigne, at the end of the period, had learnt modesty: but his wisdom was only the smiling acceptance of chaos; it created an impression of laxity, and even of fatigue.

Enfin Malherbe vint! The desire for reasonable dis-

cipline found its incarnation in this petty gentleman from
Normandy, and Boileau was not wrong in hailing him as
the true founder of modern Classicism. There is little in
Malherbe that is attractive. His private life was as immoral as that of Henry IV: but in addition he was pedantic and surly. As a poet, he lacked facility and imagination: he left a thin volume of verse, and many of his
pieces were written to order. He is chiefly famous for a
Consolation to Du Périer on his Daughter's Death, which
reached the father years after his bereavement, and com-
forted him with the thought that, great or lowly, we are
all doomed to die. Yet, with this scant equipment, Malherbe won the day. He won it because the Pleiad had
already lost it. In condemning Ronsard he was kicking
a dead lion. Nor were Ronsard's disciples better able to
hold their own. Tasso and Goethe admired du Bartas,
the author of an epic on Creation, *The Week:* but no
French critic has ever taken his confused grandeur, or
grandiosity, very seriously. Agrippa d'Aubigné, the
Huguenot, was a belated representative of the Renaissance, when he brought out, in 1616, his *Tragics,* a passionate, lyrical and satirical epic of the Religious Wars:
d'Aubigné was ignored for two centuries, and even today,
is barely mentioned in text books which devote a whole
chapter to Malherbe. Mathurin Régnier, the satirist,
with all his verve and picturesqueness, could not prevail
against "the tyrant of words and syllables." The days
of flamboyant fancy were over. Common sense was king,
and caprice was sedition.

The success of Malherbe makes it clear that neo-classicism was not identical with humanism. The ancients
never ceased to be revered: but French literature had become autonomous. Malherbe put an end to the attempt
at enriching the language from above and from without.
His norm was usage, not learning. He went so far as to
say: the usage of the porters on the Hay Wharf in Paris.
The scholars had gone too far; the speech of the Court
was spoilt by Italian and Gascon influences; it was salutary then for literature, not to "go to the people"—Mal-

herbe was not such a democrat!—but to draw from the
people. Poetry should not be esoteric, but natural and
national. This implied no lowering of standards: Malherbe taught the value of hard work and discipline, even
in the use of the plainest language. These virtues, moral
rather than poetic, served him well: with his modicum of
talent, he conquered authority, and lasting fame. He
handled nothing but commonplaces, and did nothing to
conceal their obviousness: but, a few times in his career,
he gave them a plenitude, an infallible adequacy of expression, which are quietly and indestructibly supreme.
France still repeats:

> Elle était de ce monde où les plus belles choses
>   Ont le pire destin;
> Et, rose, elle a vécu ce que vivent les roses,
>   L'espace d'un matin.[1]

What Malherbe did for French versification, Guez de
Balzac achieved a little later for French prose. He too
had very little to say, and said it in faultless form. His
treatises, *The Prince, The Christian Socrates*, and his
letters, may often seem pompously inane. But his sen-
tences form a stately procession, not, like Rabelais, a
joyous riot, or like Montaigne's, a capricious and lazy
sauntering. His style is oratorical, Ciceronian in the very
worst sense of the term; but it is French, not Latin, in
vocabulary and construction. He was the professor of
rhetoric of a generation which produced and enjoyed
Bossuet.

With these two stylists is linked the grammarian, Vaugelas. He likewise sought order, clearness, dignity; and
he sought them, not in borrowings from antiquity, not in
abstract rules, but in the harmony of usage and common
sense. His *Remarks on the French Language* acquired
such authority that "*parler Vaugelas*" was synonymous
with "*parler correctement*."

---

[1] It was not merely an affectation that prompted Paul Valéry to use
Malherbian forms for some of his most abstruse poems. Subtle and
condensed as he is, Valéry is an intellectualist, a rationalist, and therefore a distant heir of Malherbe and Boileau.

The same battle was fought, and won by the same side, in the dramatic field. The medieval drama had disappeared: the performance of the Mysteries and Miracles had actually been prohibited by law in 1548; it was feared that their free and rather crude realism might be a cause of scandal at a time of bitter religious division. The tragedies inspired by the doctrines of the Pleiad, like Jodelle's *Cleopatra*, were lifeless pastiches of Seneca's rhetorical plays. The tragi-comedy, frequently imported from Spain, was full of extravagance. The cultured public was sighing for simplicity, reasonableness, *order*. For these, the so-called Aristotelian rules seemed to provide the needed foundation. Mairet's *Sophonisba*, in 1634, was the first *regular* tragedy. In 1636–37, the dazzling triumph of Corneille's *Cid* was the occasion of a complex literary quarrel, in which the question of the three unities was the most definite element. It is obvious that this epic drama, still very close to its Spanish origins, could hardly be compressed within the limits of a single place and a single day. The public had hailed the play with enthusiasm, and it seemed as though Corneille could have made a victorious plea for greater freedom. But even a masterpiece, and a popular masterpiece at that, can not change the trend of evolution. Corneille felt it, and did not dare to challenge the new discipline. He argued, with the subtlety of a pettifogging Norman lawyer, that his play was regular "within the meaning of the act"; that the action took place in a single city; that Rodrigue's betrothal, his first duel, his impromptu victory over the Moors, his second duel, and his reconciliation with the fiancée whose father he had just killed, did not occupy, if you counted carefully, much more than twenty-four hours. This lame defence was an acknowledgment of the rules. Henceforth, Corneille applied them meticulously, although not without a visible effort. To Racine, they were nature itself; and it took the Romantic revolt to dislodge them—partly—from the French stage.

There are moments when rules are resented, and moments when they are welcome, simply because they are rules. The French wanted, in literature as in politics, neither tyranny nor lawlessness, but liberty under law: obedience to reason is perfect freedom. Here again, the worship of the past played only a subordinate part. It was not the humanistic superstition, the *Ipse dixit* of antiquity, that moved Corneille: it was common sense. The fact that Aristotle and modern common sense were in agreement was reassuring; if they had differed, which would Corneille have followed? He told us unequivocally in his *Discourse on the Three Unities:* "Many protest against this rule which they call a tyrannical one; and they would be right, if it were founded only upon Aristotle's authority; it is the *natural reason* upon which it is based that compels our acceptance." Even Abbé d'Aubignac, most pedantic of hidebound classical critics, professed the supremacy of *natural judgment.* We see in Corneille's case the definite establishment of that "cultural bimetallism" which is so characteristic of the classical age at its point of perfection. Authority reposes upon two standards: tradition and reason. Between the two, there is an unchangeable relation: not "sixteen to one," as in W. J. Bryan's bimetallism, but absolute parity. So there is no conflict, and both are equally valid. If, however, conflict were possible—a sacrilegious hypothesis!—then reason must prevail.

II

The call for decency and order was felt in polite society also. The Valois Court had been a model of elegant corruption: through the wars, elegance was ruined, but corruption was not cured. The needed reform did not originate with the King: the social leadership of the royal circle went through a long eclipse. Henry IV, with all his endearing qualities, retained on the throne the manners of a Gascon captain; the tone of his conversation and of his letters is frequently that of the barrack-room. He practiced polygamy without the cloak of stateliness that Louis XIV managed to throw over his vices. Louis XIII was taciturn; Richelieu was too formidable a figure to take the lead in social entertainment. So the scepter was picked up, and held for nearly half a century, by a private person, the Marquise de Rambouillet.

Catherine de Vivonne, who, at the age of twelve (1600) had married the Marquis de Rambouillet, was much influenced by Italy. Her mother was connected with the greatest Italian families, her father had been Ambassador at Rome, and she spoke Italian as fluently as French. Italy, although already in decadence, had a much longer and stronger tradition of social refinement than France. The young Marquise found the court of good King Henry insufferably coarse. She excused herself from attendance as much as she could, and, by 1613, she had already established her own *salon*. In 1618, she had her Paris residence rebuilt on her own plans, and her room, the famous Blue Room of Arthénice (anagram of Catherine) became the very center of refined society and literature. Malherbe would tone down his gruffness for her benefit, and, as long as he lived, remained the official poet of the Hôtel de Rambouillet. Racan, Balzac, Vaugelas, Chapelain, were among the literary lights. There, almost for the first time, poets and nobles met on a footing of social equality—an equality somewhat conventional and precarious, but none the less welcome. Voiture, the great favourite, the recognized "little king" (*rey chiquito*) of this select circle, was the son of a rich wine merchant. And especially, it was at the Hôtel de Rambouillet that women, or rather ladies, resumed the direction of literary taste. On the whole, sixteenth century literature was essentially masculine, in Montaigne as well as in Rabelais —and we might add in the *Heptameron* of Marguerite of Navarre. Henceforth, even philosophy will have to be made intelligible to the queens of society: their absolute rule ended only with the Revolution.

Without undue gallantry, it may be said that their influence, on the whole, was salutary. Madame de Rambouillet and the other great ladies of the time had no less common sense, and far more delicacy, than the average man of their class. Madame de Sévigné, for instance, was vastly superior in seriousness, as well as in charm and virtue, to her clever and wicked cousin Bussy-Rabutin. The "monstrous regiment of women," in French literature, caused very little loss in profundity; there was a very definite gain in clearness, in urbanity, in freedom from pedantry.

The heyday of the Hôtel was from 1630 to the outbreak of the Fronde. Then the greatest, both in society and in literature, considered it a supreme honour to be received by the incomparable Arthénice. La Rochefoucauld, St. Evremond, were 'among those present'; Corneille, awkward and tongue-tied in company, appeared in the Blue Room. He even read to Madame de Rambouillet and her guests his *Polyeucte*, which, by the way, was icily received. It is said that Bossuet, an infant prodigy, was asked to deliver a sermon at 11 o'clock in the evening: so that the official wag of the group, Voiture, could comment that "he had never heard any one preach so early, nor so late."

The crisis of the Fronde dealt the Hôtel a severe blow. The Marquise was ageing, although she preserved far beyond middle life her majestic beauty. Julie, her eldest daughter and chief helpmeet, had, after interminable delays, "rewarded the flame" of her patient suitor Montausier; Voiture, the incomparable organizer of cultured pastime, died in 1648. Already Mademoiselle de Scudéry had become a rival to be reckoned with. The Marquise died in 1665: Louis XIV was to be her true successor.

Even with the great Marquise and with her daughter Julie, the dangers of excessive refinement could be felt. The exquisite nothings of Voiture were overpraised. Society fought earnestly about the respective merits of two sonnets, *Urania*, by Voiture, and *Job*, by Benserade, without realizing that both were elaborately vapid. Purism was creating a new pedantry, hardly less offensive for being fashionably scented. These evils ran to an extreme in the group of Mademoiselle de Scudéry. It was she who concocted those ten-volume society romances, *Great*

Cyrus, Clelia, in which all the notables of the set were depicted in historical or allegorical garb. It was she also who devised the clever map of the Country of Tenderness, wherein, through a series of symbolical villages, you might progress from *New-Friendship* either to *Tenderness-on-Inclination,* or to *Tenderness-on-Respect,* unless, missing your way, you fell into the *Lake of Indifference* or the *Sea of Enmity.* To this mixture of sentimental subtlety, affectation in style and excessive purism in vocabulary the term Preciosity was attached, and Molière did yeoman's work when, at the very outset of his Parisian career, he laughed *Les Précieuses Ridicules* into lasting disrepute. Still, there was in the classical age a blend of delicacy and dignity which would hardly have come into existence without the *Précieuses.* Madame de Lafayette and Madame de Sévigné were among them: this alone justifies them in the eyes of posterity.

III

About 1629, a number of gentlemen were in the habit of gathering to discuss, informally, some question of language or literature. They agreed to meet at the home of one of them, Conrart, because of its central location.

The freedom and privacy of these reunions were among their chief attractions. So the members of the group were none too well pleased when, in 1634, Richelieu suggested that they should form themselves into an Academy, under his exalted protection. The Cardinal's desire was law, and the Academy, with the unassuming name of *Académie Française,* came into being. It received its letters patent from the King in 1635. Through the absurd fear that the new body might turn into a rival, the Parliament refused to register these letters until 1637.

The Academy was composed at first of modest gentlemen belonging to the middle class or the lower nobility. But, long before the end of the ancient régime, prelates, great lords and even princes considered it an honour to be admitted to membership. Even in our democratic

days, the Academy would not be complete without a
sprinkling of dukes, bishops, marshals, ambassadors, great
lawyers and conservative statesmen. It is an epitome of
good society, the most exclusive of clubs, the last refuge
of polite conversation, a permanent and better organized
Hôtel de Rambouillet. But ladies, who rule the Salons,
are barred out of the Academy. They have taken their
revenge by making Academicians, since they could not
be Academicians themselves. Academic electioneering has
been a favourite sport with Paris hostesses, at least from
the days of Madame de Lambert in the early eighteenth
century to the days of Madame de Caillavet in the late
nineteenth.

Not all the original members were writers. Conrart, in
a sense the true founder of the Academy, for he was its
first host and its first secretary, published nothing: he is
perhaps the only man who ever won a place in literary
history on the strength of his obstinate and prudent
silence, held up as an example by Boileau. The term
"Immortals," which came early into use, was not meant
ironically: but neither was it of much consequence. It
was a commonplace that poets distributed immortality
with a very liberal hand, and without forgetting themselves. The jibe of Rostand in *Cyrano de Bergerac* was
true even under Richelieu, and remains true to-day:

> *Porchères, Colomby, Bourseys, Bourdon, Arbaud:*
> *Tous ces noms dont pas un ne mourra, que c'est beau!*

The purpose of the French Academy never was primarily to reward literary excellence. Genius does very
well without academic honours: in the seventeenth century, Pascal and Molière, in the eighteenth Rousseau and
Diderot, in the nineteenth Balzac and Michelet, occupied
the mythical "forty-first armchair," which is the French
way of saying that they never were Academicians at all.
The Academy is meant to represent, in the realm of language and literature, that *authority based upon tradition
and reason*, which we find in every other manifestation of

the classical age. Genius achieves authority, but, in doing so, ignores tradition and reason—or rather it creates a tradition and a reason of its own.

The Academy was expected to act in a legislative and judicial capacity. On its programme were a historical dictionary of literary usage, a standard grammar, authoritative treatises on rhetoric and poetics. It was also planned that words should be divided into castes—those reserved for the *sublime* or lofty style, those belonging to the undistinguished or *mediocre*, and those to be branded as *low*. None of these schemes matured. All that the Academy managed to do was to compose a Dictionary of current usage. Vaugelas had been the soul of the undertaking: after his death in 1650, the work dragged on interminably, and the first edition did not appear until 1694. Both Furetière and Richelet had stolen a march on the slow moving Academicians: one determined specialist, as Littré was to show again in the nineteenth century, can outstrip a club of forty amateurs.

In its critical or judicial function, the Academy was even less fortunate. The first task that was imposed upon it by Richelieu was an examination of Corneille's *Cid*. There is little doubt that the imperious minister wanted the play to be formally condemned; and when he appointed special courts or commissions to judge his enemies, the fate of these was sealed in advance. The Academy, which he had captured, but not created, showed more independence. The *Sentiments* or Opinions on the *Cid*, which it finally published, kept a pretty fair balance between the enthusiasm of the public, the scruples of the theorists, and the curious hostility of the Cardinal. To Richelieu's praise be it said that he did not suppress the play, as he might so easily have done: Napoleon, in similar cases, did not hesitate. But Richelieu had a decent regard for the opinion of mankind, and, in a literary quarrel, used only literary weapons. Although the compromise arrived at was honorable for all parties, the task had not been a congenial one; and, from that time, the Academy refrained from expressing its official and col-

lective opinion in matters of literature, except through
the awarding of innocuous prizes.

The man who had drawn up the *Sentiments* for the
Academy—and for Richelieu—was Chapelain, who, for
many years, was an informal Secretary of State for Literature. He had conquered authority chiefly through his
virtues of common sense, kindness and dependability, virtues to which his critic Boileau paid unstinted tribute.
He strengthened his claims with a vast epic on Joan of
Arc, *La Pucelle*, an ill-fated title, for Voltaire also was
to make it a by-word. For some twenty years, Chapelain
was "about to publish" his *Pucelle:* when it came out at
last, its leaden weight dragged the poet into oblivion.
He is chiefly remembered at present as Boileau's victim:
he should perhaps be known rather as Boileau's predecessor and prototype, not exactly the Dictator of Parnassus,
but its chief police officer. In his hands was the list of
royal pensions to be distributed among writers, with his
own name at the head. This control of princely favours
gave him a prestige that the satires of Boileau and even
the overpowering tediousness of *La Pucelle* could not quite
destroy.

IV

Our constant repetition of the shibboleths "authority,
order, tradition, common sense," has inevitably produced
an impression of tameness and even of dullness; and this
impression is not altogether wrong. The classical age
proper, the Grand Century, is fundamentally *bourgeois*,
and *bourgeois* culture tends to foster the virtue of unimpeachable moderation which, in our own days, is so admirably exemplified in Major Henri Bordeaux.

The leading tendency, however, does not sum up a
whole period. It usually encounters resistances which are
more fascinating than conformities; the tendency itself
is an indication of the forces that it had to combat.

The first two generations of the seventeenth century
were finally tamed: Condé, Turenne, turned into loyal

officers and faultless courtiers; Retz, La Rochefoucauld,
survived their wild days by many a quiet year. But they
were not naturally tame. So in literature: by the side of
Malherbe, Balzac, Vaugelas, Chapelain and the Academy,
we find a teeming mass of writers, full of verve, fancies
and rebellions.   D'Aubigné hardly belongs here: he was
rather a younger member of the Pleiad, straggling nearly
half a century behind. Mathurin Régnier was probably
the most gifted, and the one whose works have best held
their own: Boileau and Molière were indebted to him.
Cyrano de Bergerac, thanks to Théophile Gautier and
especially to Edmond Rostand, is the one whose personality—a nose, a plume, a rapier—stands out most pic-
turesquely. With Cyrano should be mentioned his fellow
"libertines"—in the classical sense of free-thinkers: St.
Amand the glutton, Théophile de Viau, a true lyric poet,
who was sentenced to death for his impiety, and whom
Corneille preferred to Malherbe and Racan. In *Précieux*
circles, common sense was not invariably victorious. The
Marquise de Rambouillet admired *il cavaliere* Marini,
whose long poem *Adone* was a perpetual coruscation of
conceits. The pseudo-Arcadian sentimental romance of
Honoré d'Urfé, *Astrée*, can hardly be called a triumph of
classical reason; the many-tomed lucubrations of Madeleine de Scudéry, like the poems and tragedies of her
brother George, were full of romantic extravagance.
   The influence of Spain at that time retarded the development of true classicism. The political power of
Spain was waning: but it was still impressive. In the
cultural domain, "trade follows the flag" at times with
a long delay: thus it was not under Louis XIV, at the
height of her actual power, that France dominated most
exclusively European civilization, but under Louis XV,
when her political prestige was at its lowest ebb. The
Spain of the period deserved to be studied: it was the
Spain of *el Siglo de Oro*, the Golden Century, the age of
Cervantes, Alarcón, Guillen de Castro, Lope, Calderòn,
and also, alas! the age of Gòngora and his *estilo culto*.
We need hardly point out the Spanish element in Cor-

neille, and even in Molière; in lesser men like Rotrou, it was even more pronounced. It was not limited to the choice of subjects—*Le Cid, Le Menteur, don Sanche d'Aragon, don Juan;* or to the favour enjoyed by certain forms, like the tragi-comedy and the cloak-and-sword drama; it revealed itself in a spirit of haughtiness and defiance, of grave punctilious courtesy, of hypersensitive honour, of flamboyant daring and braggadocio, which is very far from classic reasonableness.

Then there was the ransom to be paid for the excesses of preciosity: the counter-excesses in the form of burlesque and coarse realism. The craze for the burlesque became a veritable disease, especially at the time of the Fronde, that burlesque epic. Its greatest exponent was Scarron, the first husband of Françoise d'Aubigné who, as Madame de Maintenon, became the morganatic queen of Louis XIV. That predecessor of the Grand Monarch was a cripple, indomitably laughing away poverty and disease. He travestied the *Æneid,* wrote spirited farces, and showed himself a master of picaresque realism in his story of strolling players, *Le Roman Comique.*

If we examine more closely that period, we find that its ideal was not dull conformity, but will-power. When we think of Richelieu, we are not impressed by his intelligence, however vast and keen it may have been; still less by his "sweet reasonableness" or by his Christian virtues. He was not sensible and not saintly, but *heroic:* and the will alone creates heroes.

The grandeur of Corneille's personages has no other foundation. Corneille is not invariably the poet of duty, or even the poet of reason. He admires his own *Medea,* his *Cleopatra* (in *Rodogune*), who are criminals, hardly less than his *Nicomède* or his *Polyeucte.* No doubt—and in this the classical hero differs radically from the *Sturm-und-Drang* rebel or the Byronic blasphemer—the chief triumph of the will is found, not in vain explosions, but in self-conquest. Not the indulgence of passion, but the subordination of passion to reason, is the Cornelian ideal, the finest achievement of unconquerable will. "All her

passions, said Mademoiselle de Scudéry about Madame de
Rambouillet, are subjected to her reason." A little later,
the heroine of Madame de Lafayette's novel, the *Princess
of Clèves*, also sacrificed passion to reason; and Corneille
repeatedly proclaimed the same message:

> *Et sur mes passions ma raison souveraine. . . .*

But it is not a sacrifice to a conventional, abstract or
alien ideal: the victory over self is the highest triumph
of self, self-realization, and not self-effacement. It is accompanied with that exulting joy that Corneille calls "*la
gloire.*" Better be a "glorious criminal"—and what other
term will fit Condé at certain stages of his career?—than
an inglorious conformist. But "glorious conformity,"
self-will in the service of a cause greater than self, that is
perfection indeed. Such are the patriotism of Horace,
the statesmanlike clemency of Augustus (*Cinna*), the
Christian zeal of Polyeucte. And such was the ideal of
Corneille's contemporaries. The Jansenists, as we shall
see, and Pascal the greatest of them, were Christian stoics
without Christian humility; heroes of the will who denied
the freedom of the will; glorying in self-discipline and
rejecting imposed order; and that is why they were persecuted by the representatives of conformity and compromise, the Jesuits and the King.

V

We have so far used indiscriminately the words "common sense" and "reason." The distinction between the
two is one which it has never been easy, nor even safe, to
establish.

Montaigne's lesson—if the word is not too pedagogical
for his rambling *causeries*—was that neither common
sense nor reason existed in this world. Opinions once
widely held seem ludicrous to-day; and, as Pascal, his disciple in many ways, was to say, a mere geographical accident alters the validity of our views: "truth on this side
of the Pyrenees, error on the other side." If Montaigne

is essentially "reasonable," it is only in the sense of "moderate." To be sure, without confessing it, he thought that his own "good sense" was not quite "common"; and whilst he doubted all creeds ("excepting, of course, our Holy Religion, Catholic, Apostolic and Roman"), and all philosophies, even scepticism, he believed pretty firmly in Michel de Montaigne. But a systematic rationalist he was certainly not.

Montaigne's Pyrrhonism was the result of despair, the devastation left in the wake of theological and civil conflict. With Charron, the intellect, still warily, resumes its march. Charron no longer doubts his own doubt: he demonstrates it. This may be an inconsistency: but it satisfied the age of Henry IV. In Charron's *Wisdom*, orthodoxy, scepticism and rationalism lived in good accord, probably because not one of them was strong enough to put up a good fight.

The compromise philosophy that goes with the restoration of order could not be better expressed than in the words of Descartes. Here are the "three or four maxims" of his code of morals:

"The first was to obey the laws and customs of my country, adhering firmly to the faith in which, by the grace of God, I had been educated from my childhood, and regulating my conduct in every other matter according to the most moderate opinions, and the farthest removed from extremes, which should happen to be adopted in practice with general consent of the most judicious of those among whom I might be living." (Orthodoxy; moderation; conformity.)

"My second maxim was to be as firm and resolute in my actions as I was able, and not to adhere less steadfastly to the most doubtful opinions, when once adopted, than if they had been highly certain." (Consistency.)

"My third maxim was to endeavour always to conquer myself rather than Fortune, and change my desires rather than the order of the world." (Self-discipline, modesty, resignation.)

These are the three all-sufficient commandments of the

good citizen, and, if Descartes had observed them faithfully, he might have been a model of bourgeois wisdom, another Conrart.

But Descartes was not, except in sheer self-defence, the harmless and passive supporter of law and order that he professed to be. There was a touch of the adventurer in that mathematician who, for the fun of the thing, became a soldier of fortune during the Thirty Years War. So this code of comfortable sanity, with him, is purely provisional. When he described for us these low levels of 'safety in conformity,' he had already started thinking for himself—dangerously.

His point of departure was Montaigne's: no knowledge, imparted from without, can be certain. Every man believes that he is endowed with "good sense": this is "humanism" in its literal sense, and with a vengeance: man is the test and the measure of all things. And the first precept of the Cartesian *Method*, which sums up the whole of his revolution, is: "Never to accept anything for true which I did not clearly and evidently know to be such." And when can we say that we *know?* We know "what is presented to (our) mind so clearly and distinctly as to exclude all ground of doubt." Doubt therefore is not a sin, as it is in the eyes of theologians; and not a luxurious end in itself, as with Montaigne: it is an indispensable instrument in the testing of truth. If you would be a sure Fundamentalist, delve until you reach bed-rock; doubt until you can doubt no more.

And so Descartes doubts all sciences, the evidence of his senses, the whole external world: may not all this be a dream? He could, like Montaigne, doubt this or that particular doubt: he can not doubt the fact that he is doubting. He doubts, therefore he thinks; he thinks, therefore he is. With this axiom as a foundation, and with "evidence beyond the possibility of a doubt" as his criterion, he will reconstruct the universe. And a strange job he makes of it.

There is no poetic rapture, no eloquence, no obscurity, and therefore no "profundity" in the *Discourse on*

Method. But, in its homely garb, this philosophy is a unique lesson in honesty and courage. We may reach conclusions radically different from those of Descartes: but the first principle of the Method still stands. A man who accepts as true something which he does *not* know clearly and evidently to be such may be a poet, a theologian or a politician: but he is no scientist and no philosopher. Those who consider that first precept as a mere truism have not earnestly tried to apply it.

Descartes was not the prophet, but the product, of the classical spirit. He came long after Malherbe, and at the same time as Richelieu, Corneille, the Academy. He "rationalized" that spirit: the supremacy of thought, the firm use of the will, the contempt for external nature, the craving for clarity and order, all this is Cartesianism, and it is also Classicism.

But there is much in Cartesianism that goes beyond the Classical Compromise defined at the beginning of this chapter. Bossuet almost alone was clear-sighted enough to discern this. There may be compromise in the practical code of Descartes: there is none in his inmost thought. It is radicalism pure and simple. In him, and through him, the balance between "tradition" and "reason" is completely ruined. For Descartes, methodical reason is supreme, tradition counts for naught. Aristotle and Plato, St. Paul and St. Augustine, the Pope, the King and the Parliament in unison could not make him accept a thing for true, unless he clearly and evidently knew it to be such. It is radical democracy in thought: not democracy in the sense of mob-rule, but democracy as the denial of privileges, as a challenge to vested interests and constituted authorities in the realm of the intellect. "If I write in French," he says towards the end, "and not in Latin, it is because I expect that those who *make use of their unprejudiced reason* will be better judges of my opinions than those who give heed to the writings of the ancients only." The whole Enlightenment is here in germ.

The implications of this little book were not clearly

seen for at least fifty years. The Age of Louis XIV professed Cartesian Rationalism: but in fact it was still guided by the Classical Compromise. The "bimetallism" we have described was nominally unchanged, and even, until 1687, not seriously challenged: but one of its standards was slowly losing substance.

CHAPTER III

LOUIS XIV: PERSONALITY, COURT, GOVERNMENT

I. The Conception of Kingship. Perfection of Absolute Monarchy. Divine Right. Louis XIV's consciousness of his own grandeur. Pride tempered by classical moderation and common sense. No radical even in absolutism. Love of his function. Hard-working.

II. Physical Portrait: robustness. Love of pleasure. *The Life Enchanted:* stately without stiffness. His love affairs. Magnificence and glory his besetting sins.

III. Louis XIV's attitude towards the Court nobility: diffidence and generosity. Provincial nobility ignored and sacrificed. Nobility becomes frankly parasitical.

IV. Policy with the Third Estate: privileges of provinces, cities, Parliaments checked but not abolished. His instruments: the bureaucracy, the *Intendants*. The great ministerial clans. Mediocrity of the second generation. Unity of style: *magnificent order*.

I

In 1661, on the death of Mazarin, Louis XIV took in his own hands the reins of government. Henceforth and for fifty-four years, he was to be his own prime minister. He was more than "the State": he was "France." This is the point of perfection of absolute monarchy; after so many false starts and relapses, the King and the Kingdom were at last in complete harmony. The contemporaries, for a whole generation, worshipped the Grand Monarch. The tragic eclipse during his last few years was not final: the Royal Sun shone again for posterity. In the age of Enlightenment, Voltaire the iconoclast forgot his irony when he wrote *The Century of Louis XIV*. For a romantic democratic historian like Michelet, Louis XIV had little appeal: but in our own days, men as different as Ernest Lavisse, Jacques Bainville, Louis Madelin and Louis Bertrand studied him with sympathy, with passionate interest, with reverence. There is a famous tripartite cartoon by Thackeray, in which we see first *Ludovicus Rex:* a reduction of Hyacinthe Rigaud's magnificent portrait of the King; next comes *Rex*, the mere paraphernalia of royalty, the ample folds of the mantle, the monumental periwig; and finally *Ludovicus*, a wizened old man. This clever satire strikes us at present as deficient in historical sense. The essential character of Louis XIV is that in him it was impossible to dissociate *Ludovicus* from *Rex*. Every inch a King, and every moment a King.

His function to him was truly sacerdotal. The tradition which, as we have so often seen, linked the French monarchy with the Church, was for Louis XIV a living reality. The purely secular and somewhat flippant attitude of Henry IV ("Paris is well worth a mass") had been conveniently forgotten: the grandson of the Bearnese was the heir of Saint Louis, Charlemagne and Clovis, the Lord's Anointed. Louis was by no means a religious bigot: certainly not at least in the early years of his reign, when he took Molière and his *Tartuffe* under his special protection; but he was sincerely pious. His mother, a Spaniard, Anne of Austria, was an ardent Catholic: he heard mass every day, and told innumerable beads. He felt the hand of Providence guiding him in a particular way: his birth had been a special answer to prayer after many years of a barren union, he was "the child of the miracle," the gift of God, *Dieudonné*. The old Roman theories propounded by the legal officers of the crown, the universal craving for authority as the condition of order, the genuine and reasonable piety of the age, converged and united in the doctrine of Monarchy by Divine Right. This doctrine was accepted with a literalness which we find it hard to comprehend: it is significant that it was best formulated by Bossuet, not a fanatic, not a courtier, but a robust, sensible representative of the substantial middle class. Much that on the surface appears ludicrous and even monstrous in the worship of the King's majesty becomes intelligible when this universal belief in Divine Right is realized. If in the Chapel of Versailles, the courtiers turned their backs on

the altar when the King appeared, there was at least a
shadow of excuse for their undeniable servility: they were
bowing, not merely to a power of the flesh, but to the
vicar of God.

In this universal conspiracy in favour of absolutism, it
would have been only too easy for a young man's head
to be turned. Louis XIV was not protected against such
a danger by a powerful intellect or by a solid education.
St. Simon, who, in his final portrait of Louis XIV, attempts to be equitable, insists upon the ordinary quality
of his mind; Lavisse endorses the verdict of the savage
memorialist, and the protests of Louis XIV's most ardent
apologists are, on this point, so guarded as not to carry
much conviction. Few people, among his enemies, denied
him the title of a great king; fewer still, among his admirers, would dare to call him a great man. That Louis
XIV was absurdly filled with the idea of his own grandeur
is only too evident: he lived in a cloud of incense, and
court etiquette became the liturgy of a cult of which he
was both the high priest and the object. Yet there must
have been in him a saving grace, that guarded him from
the ultimate follies of omnipotence. That saving grace
was the fundamental virtue of classicism, common sense.
Francis I was capricious; even Napoleon, with all his
robust grasp of realities, could be visionary and unaccountable—in a word a Romanticist: Louis XIV seldom
lost his sense of *measure*. This is an ancient French trait
which classicism brought to full fruition, but which far
antedates classicism: in the medieval epic, the lack of it,
démesure, is considered as the *hamartia*, the inner flaw,
which proves the undoing of heroes. Louis XIV earnestly
believed that the source of his authority was divine; he
must have nodded approval when Bossuet repeated, in
scriptural language: "O Kings! Ye are like gods!" But
when provincial monks dedicated to him a thesis in which
he was compared with God himself, "in such a manner as to show that God was only the copy," Louis XIV,
on the advice of Bossuet, had it suppressed. Madame de
Sévigné, who reported the incident, comments sagely:

"Trop est trop"—too much *is* too much. It is this innate feeling that *trop est trop* which almost invariably preserved Louis XIV from irreparable mischief.

He had a quality rarer and more precious than brilliancy: a sense of his own limitations. He dabbled in poetry and loved praise: but he played a delightful and cruel joke, as good as a scene in Molière, on a foolish old courtier, Marshal de Gramont, who had shown himself ready to extol or damn a madrigal on the slightest hint of the sovereign. *He listened to reason:* he who, for more than half a century, decided alone, never decided on the spur of the moment, and never without consultation. He could keep his own counsel: but he had no secret from his advisers, as was the anarchistic practice of Louis XV and Napoleon III. He, the source of all authority, recognized superiorities. When he asked Boileau: "Who is the greatest writer under my reign?" and Boileau replied: "Sire, Molière," his answer was: "I did not think so; (he liked Molière, but thought of him only as a clever entertainer), *but you know better about those things than I do*," a confession which could hardly have been wrenched, on almost any subject, from Napoleon I, Adolphe Thiers, or William II.

Even what has been called the mediocrity of the King's mind, his lack of philosophical training, his love for details, from court gossip to minute military reviews, served him in good stead. It preserved him from the danger which was first to alter and then to destroy the ancient régime: the intellectual radicalism which was in germ in Descartes's philosophy. In that age which is so often described as Cartesian, Louis XIV was not affected by "rationalism" in the least. He too would have said that "reasoning drives reason away," *reason* for him being moderation, application, common sense. Descartes, in theory at least, wanted to clear the ground and start anew on a logical plan: Colbert dallied to some extent with such a Jacobin ideal, but Louis XIV not at all. He might have attempted a royal revolution, clarifying, simplifying, rationalizing the chaos of ancient France: he worked indeed in that direction, but he advanced with very cautious step. He curbed the powers that limited his own: he did not suppress them altogether. We shall see how closely, how jealously he watched the nobility: but he respected its privileges. He tamed his Parliaments: but the Parliaments survived, ready to resume their embarrassing opposition under the next king. The Revocation of the Edict of Nantes, his worst mistake, was indeed a revolutionary measure; but he thought he had prepared it with suitable caution, with twenty years of peaceful approaches; and he sincerely believed that the work was practically complete. He shrank from the idea of a *tabula rasa*. Better than Descartes, better than Colbert, he represented the classical compromise: authority founded both upon tradition and upon reason. The mental timidity, the sluggishness perhaps, that checked him, were closely akin to instinctive wisdom. They did not altogether save France from adventures: but in the end, they made the difference between disaster and irremediable catastrophe.

Louis XIV loved what he himself called "the business of being a king," *le métier de roi*. And that business, for him, was not limited to state functions. For these his fondness never waned: but business to him was also plain "business." He did not turn himself into an accountant or scribe, the first bureaucrat in the realm, like Philip II poring over his papers in the gloom of the Escorial. But he had adopted definite hours for his work in cabinet or council, and he never relaxed his self-discipline. In council, he was not dictatorial and he was not indifferent; he listened to reports, encouraged argument, and decided. During the last period of his ministerial autocracy, Cardinal Mazarin had made the Council a farce: he held it whilst he was being shaved, or playing with his pet monkey. Later, Louis XV was for a time dignified, impenetrable; but, under that mask of majesty, his mind was absent. On the contrary, the seriousness and the zest with which Louis XIV attended to the business of the State never flagged.

II

Thanks to the perfect congruency between the epoch, the function and the man, Louis XIV kept up the elaborate ritual of his court life, and the manifold duties of government, without being fatigued and without being bored. He was served by a vigorous physique. He was of middle height, and robust; not alert, not vivacious, as Henry IV, crippled though he was with rheumatism, remained to the end, but a trifle heavy. Compared with his father, the slender, clear-cut Louis XIII, he was almost coarse. The famous Bourbon nose undeniably has character: only the staunchest legitimists will find it beautiful. A slight droop in the full lower lip revealed his descent from Charles V. He was a voracious eater, in spite of stomach troubles tormenting him from early youth. He loved all physical exercises, was for a long time strangely devoted to the dance, remained until late a good horseman, and was not unequal to the fatigues of a campaign. But he was not an active military leader: he decided that "his grandeur attached him to the shore," as Boileau diplomatically put it. His visits to the front, his directing the final assault of a fortress, were only magnificent parades.

There was nothing gloomy about his constant stateliness: Louis XIV was the reverse of an Oriental despot, an Ahasuerus before whom even his favourite trembled. Ernest Lavisse insists upon the un-French elements in Louis XIV's character: his punctiliousness, his gravity, his elaborate courtesy came from beyond the Pyrenees. Few kings, adds the Republican historian, were truly French: a sly dig at those "nationalists" who combine the hatred of foreigners with their loyalty to the dynasty. In spite of such an authority, the "Frenchness"—not the "Frenchiness"—of Louis XIV seems to us undeniable. It is true that Henry IV, with his gay Gascon sallies, with his relapses into soldierlike coarseness, with the easy familiarity that he affected (playing upon it like a virtuoso

on a finely tuned instrument) is and ever was much nearer
the heart of the French people. There is nothing about
Louis XIV of the folk-like quality found in Louis XII
and even in Louis IX. The only legend which has that
flavour, the one that represents him sharing his supper
with Molière as a lesson to supercilious courtiers, may
have some symbolical truth, but is out of keeping with the
whole tenor of the King's life. Louis XIV never was,
never attempted to be, "popular." But he achieved the
miracle of remaining for half a century erect without
stiffness. He came to power a very young man, eager to
rule, eager to work, and eager to play. If he gave a few
hours every day to ceremonial, and many more to serious business, he had time to spare for every form of
amusement. In 1664, he gave at Versailles, then still a
minor royal residence, a series of entertainments called
The Pleasures of the Enchanted Isle, in which Molière
had a leading part. The title was a programme. A hard
worker, Louis wanted also his full share of enjoyment:
his hunger in that line was no less voracious than his
royal appetite at table. Work and play, he wanted his
life to be "the Life Enchanted."

Hunting, dancing,—he took part in ballets, attired in
mythological costumes, when he was no longer a youth,—
card playing, filled the many hours which he did not devote to state affairs. With his love of order, he saw to
it that his palace was not turned into a sharpers' den:
noble gamblers whose invariable luck became suspicious
were expelled without mercy. Not only did he preserve
de ency, but he established a standard of elegance, which
has remained unexcelled. It is not every sovereign, de-
sirous of "having a good time," who can be served by a
Molière or even by a Lulli. No doubt these pleasures, on
a truly Louis-Quatorze scale, would sit a little heavily on
modern shoulders: the tunic-clad girl of to-day would feel
crushed by the monuments of whalebone and brocade that
adorned the all-too-substantial charms of Madame de
Montespan. But the contemporaries bore the burden with
a smile. Madame de Sévigné was not in constant at-

tendance at Court; among her friends were men upon
whom the King had frowned—Retz, La Rochefoucauld,
Fouquet himself; she was of a free and sprightly dispo-
sition: yet, whenever she mentions the King, she conveys
an impression of perfect naturalness. Napoleon's courtiers felt that they were in the lion's den: Louis XIV was
a French gentleman entertaining gentlemen. His tremendous pride created no obstacle: he knew so intuitively
his own position and everybody else's that, himself at ease,
he made almost every one feel at ease.

One side of his nature is so universally familiar that a
mere allusion will suffice: his appetite for pleasure expressed itself in innumerable love affairs. By the side of
the official favourites, there were many fancies of a season or even of a day, which have been called "the small
change of adultery." He had a private door opened into
the apartments of the maids-of-honour; and he took it
very ill when the Mistress-of-the-Robe had the door walled
up. His great *liaisons* he flaunted with Jove-like cynicism; and he found a Molière to condone his Pagan philosophy.[1] There is in French history a long line of royal
mistresses, Agnès Sorel, Diane de Poitiers, Gabrielle
d'Estrées, down to Madame de Pompadour and Madame
Du Barry: all that can be said of Louis XIV is that, even
in his vices, he had "the grand style" so dear to Matthew
Arnold. The touching La Vallière, who loved him truly
and became a nun; Fontanges, best remembered for her
head-gear; and especially his true mate in magnificence
and imperiousness, Madame de Montespan: all are figures dear to historical romance. There is nothing more
dramatic in the life of the great king than the moment
when an investigation of the ubiquitous poisonings in
high society brought out the complicity of Madame de
Montespan. At any rate, the king's *amours* did not interfere with his policy. Madame de Maintenon, the pious
companion of his old age, belongs to a different period;

[1] *"Un partage avec Jupiter*
N'a rien du tout qui déshonore."
Amphytrion.

the *bourgeois* decency of his secret marriage with her
bears no resemblance to the scarlet splendour of his maturity. She was, not one of his sins, but part of his repentance, and perhaps his penance.

In other respects also, Louis XIV's boundless pride carried him beyond his classical sense of measure. France,—
at least the elements in France that were articulate,—
wanted a "great reign"; and Louis wanted to be a "great
king." Both had their desire: but in pursuing greatness,
it was difficult to draw the line between solid achievement
and display. There is much in the period that is grandiose rather than grand, and pompous rather than noble,
like many tirades in Corneille's tragedies. Louis loved
magnificence and he loved *glory:* on his death bed, he re-
pented, and warned his successor against these two temp-
tations.

Louis Bertrand, more royalist than the King, refuses
to follow Louis XIV in his retractation. Why be ashamed
of Versailles, and of all those wars in which France, by
herself, appeared "not unequal to many," *nec pluribus
impar?* As was said of Napoleon, "the cost is forgotten,
and the glory is remembered." It seems to us that Louis
Bertrand is here defending the classical age with the fer-
vid imagination of a romanticist. We are grateful to
Louis XIV for works of solid and useful magnificence,
such as highways, canals and royal manufactures; and
for works of sheer beauty also, for palaces and city em-
bellishments which added much to the patrimony of
France without imposing upon her a crushing burden.
The Place des Victoires, the Place Vendôme, the Colonnade of the Louvre, the Invalides, the triumphal arches
of the St. Martin and St. Denis gates, bear his imprint,
although they were not all due to his initiative. But, in
this as in theology, *trop est trop*. The Aqueduct of
Maintenon, which cost millions of money and thousands
of lives before it had to be abandoned, was an extravagant
blunder; and the charm of Versailles is actually impaired,
not enhanced, by the very immensity of the structure.
Louis fell, and some of his recent admirers are falling

after him, into what we call the American delusion of con-
founding size with grandeur. To a civilized mind, the
Parthenon is more impressive than the Pyramids, the
Sainte-Chapelle than the Trocadero, and the Venus of
Milo than the Statue of Liberty. It may be cheap democratic sentimentality to think of the blood and tears with
which the stones of Versailles were cemented: but it is not
the acme of refinement to gloat over the fact that the garden elevation is five hundred and eighty meters long, and
is adorned with nearly four hundred windows.

In the same way, we see little to rejoice in the majestic procession of wars, each deliberately brought about by
the King's gluttonous craving for glory. War of Devolution (1667–68), War of Holland (1672–78), War of
the Augsburg League (1689–1697), War of the Spanish
Succession (1701–14), they fill twenty-eight years out
of a half century. They look well in the pictures of Van
der Meulen: but the victories of Alexander, as painted by
Lebrun, would have done just as well. Boileau himself,
staunch royalist though he was, denounced in plain terms
the madness of this constant quest for glory. We shall
see in what a state of exhaustion and somber discontent
all this "magnificence" left the kingdom.

In the case of Louis XIV as in the case of Napoleon,
only wilful blindness will lead us to admire the whole
reign as one block, whilst the contemporaries themselves
were conscious of differences. The temper of France in
1700 no longer was that of 1661. It is an even more dangerous fallacy to admire the "glory" and lightly to dismiss the hatred, the ruin, the humiliation which are its
inevitable Nemesis. Autocracy never is safe or sane: all
that can be said is that an autocracy based on the "classical compromise" is somewhat safer than one which reposes solely on the divine right of individual genius.

III

When we think of Louis XIV, we have two pictures in
mind. The first might be an actual scene: the King at

Versailles, surrounded by his gorgeous courtiers: a nobleman himself, the head of their caste, their master no
doubt, but living their life and thinking their thoughts.
The other is a composite, an ideal vision, such as official
artists love to paint on the walls of State palaces: the
"Century of Louis XIV" and its makers. In the center,
the King again; but by his side, Bossuet, his ecclesiastical
right arm; Colbert, his regent in economic and administrative affairs; Louvois, de Lionne, who prepared his
armies and his diplomatic campaigns; Vauban, who cui-
rassed his kingdom with fortresses; Boileau, the Dictator
of Parnassus, and his friends Molière and Racine; Lulli,
his musician; Le Brun, the autocrat of fine arts; Man-
sard, Lenôtre, architects in stone or in living foliage; all
the representatives of that classical spirit which was focussed in his person; all bourgeois to a man, and some
very modest bourgeois.[1] Of the great servants of the
régime, only the military officers, and chief among them
Turenne and Condé, belonged to the nobility. In social
life, Louis was the prince of the nobles; in practical work,
he was the executive head of the bourgeoisie. The Court
was the ornament of his reign; the middle class the instrument of his rule. St. Simon was conscious of this contradiction: he denounced the age as one of "vile bourgeoisie," and his paradox is now universally accepted as
the sober truth. It is not certain that Louis XIV himself was conscious of the fact: he was not given to rationalizing.

[1] Nothing further will be said about this harmony between the different manifestations of the classical spirit. As a general idea, it has been
a truism from the very first; and a detailed demonstration of the obvious would require a whole volume. The students of French literature
will do well to familiarize themselves with the life and manners of the
time, through Memoirs, letters, pictures and prints: having done so,
they should pass resolutely beyond, from *civilization* to *literature*. It
can not be said too often that "environment and time" *explain* Racine,
but explain also Pradon, his dull-witted competitor; what they utterly
fail to explain is why Pradon is not Racine. It is important indeed to
ascertain the share of the Louis Quatorze Style in the art of the great
classics, in order to discount that share, and reach their elemental
genius. Had Taine used his own method in that direction, he would
have insisted, not on the obvious contrast between Shakespeare and
Racine, but upon their strange and profound kinship.

There was therefore a great mixture of motives in his treatment of the nobility. The Fronde had filled him with diffidence; his hasty flight to St. Germain, in his childhood, had remained impressed upon his memory, and Mazarin had taken good care to drive the lesson home. After the terrible discipline enforced by Richelieu, rebellion had broken out again: in every noble, Louis suspected a potential *frondeur*. In Louis's desire to have his nobility constantly under his eyes, we may read a policy of distrust. The Court nobles were his hostages, Versailles was their gilded cage. When he reduced them to magnificent servility, he may have remembered that from the same caste had arisen, not so very long before, men who had defied the crown. If this was in his mind, then he was reading aright the history of his race, which had ever found in the aristocracy its bitterest enemies.

But Louis XIV, we must repeat, was not a philosophical historian, a crowned Charles Maurras. It is quite possible that his pride alone dictated his policy. During the Great War, we have come across generals who thought their staff was never large enough for impressiveness; and Louis XIV, in whose mind as in whose features there was a noticeable element of commonness, may have wanted a large Court for the same reason that a modern hostess enjoys large receptions. We must never forget that it was not contemporary America that created the ideal: "the biggest in the world." The Pharaohs came long before.

Two contradictory facts are equally evident: the first is that Louis XIV carefully refrained from entrusting power to great aristocrats; the second is that he treated his courtiers, not only with generosity, but with consideration, with genuine kindness, with affability. None of the cruel contempt which Napoleon showed at times for his titled lackeys is perceptible in Louis XIV: he respected himself in his associates. A gentleman was raising money among his friends in order to purchase a great office, and was finding it a difficult task: "Why did you not count *me* among your friends?" said the King; and he gave him the needed sum. This offers us, we believe, a true picture of Louis XIV: not a suspicious tyrant, but a delicately generous host. If he kept from the nobles all sources of real power, he did not curtail their honorific and fiscal privileges, and he showered upon them honours and liberalities. Titles and sinecures were theirs, a constant round of festivities was provided for them, and presents without stint. If Louis XIV was the jailer of his nobility, no one could wish for a kindlier one.

It was not fear that urged the courtiers to Versailles, but hope. Nothing happened to the man who chose to stay on his estates: he was ignored, he was forgotten, he ceased to exist. No place or pension would ever come to him or to his kin. He had shut himself out of the Earthly Paradise. The provincial nobility, as depicted by Molière or Madame de Sévigné, is grotesque; and a man upon whom the King did not smile sank to the level of the Sotenville, Pourceaugnac and d'Escarbagnas. "Sire," said M. de Vardes, who, after a period of exile, had been reinstated, "when one is unfortunate enough to be kept away from your presence, one is worse than miserable, one is ridiculous." And he wept tears of joy, because the gates of the Enchanted Life were opening again.

This double policy,—friendliness and diffidence, all favours, no actual power,—was ultimately to ruin the nobility and the monarchy with it. Privileges accompanied with responsibilities have some justification: the privileges of social parasites will inevitably become intolerable. And the King, living among his nobles, became their prisoner in his turn. They formed a screen between him and his people. He too became, with Louis XV, a parasite, an absentee landlord, the chief and the worst of the hated privilege-holders. Louis XVI wanted to love his people, and his people craved to love him: but the aristocratic ring had grown too strong, and could not be broken. Louis XIV achieved the paradox of creating the most brilliant court in history, and the most useless. The result still dazzles the world: but it was an absurdity.

IV

The policy of Louis XIV with the privileged Third Estate was not radically different from his policy with the nobility: it may be defined as *conservative and friendly diffidence*. "Trust no Frenchman," Mazarin had said; and Louis did not trust the organized bourgeoisie any more than he did the aristocracy. Any right that did not have its origins in his person was a danger; but no right founded on tradition could be lightly swept aside.

The States General, of course, were not convened. The Assemblies of Notables, a safer substitute used by former autocrats, Francis I, Henry IV, Richelieu, were also given up. The privileges of the provinces and cities were whittled down whenever occasion offered. No revolutionary step was taken, and on the whole, these privileges, slightly reduced in some cases, survived: but the King took good care that they should be purely nominal. The cities continued to elect their officials, with all customary forms and amid traditional festivities: but they "freely" elected the men he had been pleased to designate. The Provincial States, in the parts of the country that had retained that institution, "freely" voted the supplies that he had indicated. Externally, very little was changed in the régime of ancient France: the monarchy was using, half-consciously, a process of imperceptible suffocation.

Nothing better illustrates the method of Louis XIV than his attitude towards the Parliaments. These judicial bodies, styling themselves Sovereign Courts, were a thorn in his flesh: sovereignty as he understood it could not be divided. They had assumed a right of censorship over legislation, that is to say over the expression of his royal will. They had, especially in Church affairs, a tradition of their own. They had resisted many kings, and once led an open rebellion. As the judges had bought their places, and had made them practically hereditary within their small caste, they were to a large extent independent from his authority. Yet Louis did not suppress the Parliaments and replace them with a new system of royal courts, as Maupeou did in the eighteenth century; he did not abolish the venality of offices, which, long tolerated, had been officially recognized and organized under Henry IV[1]; he did not even formally withhold the right of offering "respectful remonstrances." But, without altering the institution, he effectively silenced all opposition. A scene which occurred under Mazarin, in 1655, has been unduly emphasized and turned into a sort of legend: the young King, hunting at Vincennes, was informed that the Parliament was deliberating on edicts previously registered in his presence; he rushed to the city, entered the hall of deliberation, booted, spurred and whip in hand, gave his orders in curt scornful words, and rushed back to the hunt. This act of juvenile insolence is not in true Louis XIV style. But, in 1665, as he felt there were still a few sparks of independence in the Parliament, he summoned it, ready, as he said, "to give an unmistakable demonstration, either of the total submission of that body, or of the just severity of my punishment." The Court listened to the King's orders without a word. Then, one of the leaders rose and departed in silence. The others followed, one by one. Consternation could be read on all their faces. Henceforth, the Parliament gave no more trouble.

Louis placed his reliance not on the middle class as a class, but on men of the middle class, who were his instruments, his creatures, and whom he could dismiss at will. Ancient France was a tangled mass of privileges: without destroying them, Louis established everywhere, as a growing substitute, the authority of his agents. Thus the centralized bureaucratic state developed *within* the loose federation of petty sovereignties based on immemorial custom. It was not a revolution, but a dissolving picture;

[1] In 1604, the right of practically all office-holders to consider their charge as their property was recognized; in compensation, a tax, equal to one-sixtieth of the assessed value of the charge, was imposed upon them. This expedient had been suggested to Sully by a financier, Paulet, to whom the collection of the new tax was farmed out for nine years: hence its name *la Paulette*. Several efforts were made to change these conditions: one of them was among the causes of the Fronde. But the Paulette was not suppressed until 1790.

and, once again, it is not certain that Louis had definitely in view the transformation of the old régime. The local lord still preserved his ancestral right to administer justice: but all important cases and all appeals went to the King's jurisdiction. Provinces and fortresses still had their noble governors; but they were appointed for a limited period—frequently not more than three years. They were not expected to reside (the "exile" which M. de Vardes[1] had taken so much to heart had been the obligation of staying in his government, Aigues-Mortes); and all the actual work was performed by permanent officials. All the gilded sinecures at Court went to noblemen: but all the important executive functions were entrusted to a new administrative class, of bourgeois origin, and selected by the King.

The two chief instruments of government were the *Intendants* and the Secretaries of State or Ministers. We have seen that the institution of Intendants, occasionally used by Henry IV and even by Francis I, had been greatly developed by Richelieu. But even under Richelieu, they were inspectors on special missions rather than permanent executives. With Louis XIV, the system became definite. By the side of the Governors—mere figureheads,—and of the Provincial States—a mere historical show wherever they still existed—the Intendants had all the substance of power. Through them, the King was informed and could act. They were the prototypes of Napoleon's prefects, who survive to-day.

At the head were the ministers: men who owed everything to the King, who were responsible to him only, and who were jealous, for his sake and for their own, of every authority that did not emanate exclusively from him. They belonged to the middle class: indeed, the greatest of them, Colbert, was the son of a cloth merchant. They were different from that "nobility of the gown" which, although of bourgeois origin, had become semi-independent. Frequently, this difference reached the point of antagonism.

[1] *Cf.* p. 162.

The first ministerial team with which Louis XIV governed had been picked out by Mazarin; and the selection reveals the practical genius of that adventurer. The chief of them was Colbert, a sort of universal "Minister of the Interior," whom we shall meet again in studying the economic conditions of the time; Michel Le Tellier; his son Louvois, the great war administrator, and, as such, often suspected of being the evil counselor of the King; Hugues de Lionne, not a constructive genius in diplomacy, but a perfect instrument. These men identified their fortunes with the King, who rewarded them right royally. They were not disinterested, but they were honest. They secured the downfall of Fouquet, the Superintendent of Finances, who, like Mazarin, had managed to grow fabulously rich in a famished kingdom. They were ruthless with great and small alike: Louvois was "a bear"; Colbert, "the North Pole"; and they, like their master, were systematic and indefatigable workers. Under their vigorous impulsion, the huge state machine, still incomplete and hampered by all the survivals of feudal chaos, moved heavily and steadily, and accomplished its work.

The bureaucratic State, however, was destined to reach its perfection in Prussia, or in the France of Napoleon, and not under Louis XIV. After twenty years of "glory," Louis XIV was naturally confirmed in a sense of his own infallibility. His rule was all sufficient: what was needed in a minister was not initiative, but docility. So the second generation of the King's servants, the one he picked out for himself, was vastly inferior to the first. It may be symbolized in Chamillart, who cumulated the crushing heritage of Colbert and Louvois: Chamillart, an excellent man who played a very good game of billiards—but, of course, not quite so good as the King's. Napoleon ruled fifteen years and Louis XIV fifty-four: but already in Napoleon was felt the inevitable tendency of the autocrat: assured that no will is needed or wanted except his own, he is inclined to prefer smooth mediocrities.

Then, in a state so entirely based upon the hereditary principle, that principle was bound to assert itself among

the new administrative class. The ancient régime thought
in terms of families or dynasties rather than in terms of
individual merit. What we brand as nepotism was then
legitimate and praiseworthy. Le Tellier and Colbert were
the heads of rival clans, for whose members positions had
to be found. Colbert, in particular, established a magnificent connection, which received high-sounding titles
and intermarried with the old aristocracy. So by the side
of the nobility of the sword, by the side of the younger
and lower nobility of the gown, we find a third but most
aggressive ministerial nobility. Even Napoleon could
not resist the same temptation: dynasties of Bonapartist
officials were created, which were beginning to restrict his
choice, and to nullify his motto: a career freely open to
all talents.

The régime of Louis XIV therefore can not be defined
in simple terms. It was a theocracy; it was an autocracy.
It was the rule of "reason," not strictly according to Descartes; it was the rule of tradition, which the King might
seek to limit, but never refused to acknowledge. It had
the Court as a splendid, overgrown and useless flower, and
the bureaucracy as a robust stem. The unity of the period, admirably represented by its King, was a unity of
style, and not of governmental doctrines. The age of
Louis XIV consciously sought grandeur and order. That
it occasionally fell into the grandiose and the monotonous
was a danger inseparable from the attempt; but on the
whole, it achieved its aim as no epoch had done since the
days of Augustus.

CHAPTER IV

I. The anti-economic prejudice in the classical age. Not limited to nobility and clergy. Not wholly extinct.

II. Survival of the medieval system: guilds and crafts. Periods of economic recuperation (Henry IV), hardship (Richelieu), ruin (the Fronde).

III. Colbert. Fall of Fouquet. All-embracing activity of Colbert (1661–1683). Various aspects of Colbertism. Clearing up of the past. Ruthless efficiency.

IV. Colbert (II). Attempted reorganization of economic life. His great ordinances and codes. "Mercantilism" and protection.

V. Colbert (III). Active paternalism. State-fostered colonial companies. Royal manufactures. Subsidies, etc.

VI. Conclusion: Economic failure of the Grand Reign.

I

THE economic and social history of the sixteenth century is, as we have noted, still extremely incomplete. Our knowledge of these aspects of life in the seventeenth century is not much more satisfactory. Ernest Lavisse complained that "we are better acquainted with French society in the middle ages, with Roman society, with the society of ancient Egypt, than we are with French society in the seventeenth century, which remains obscure behind the grand stage scenery of Versailles. Such a state of affairs is evidently absurd." These words were printed in 1906. Nearly twenty years later, Henri Sée, in his *Evolution Commerciale et Industrielle de la France sous l'Ancien Régime*, without professing the same degree of agnosticism, recognizes that in certain important portions of the field, "everything remains to be done." The great Colonial Companies and the Royal Manufacturers, illuminated by some rays of the monarchical sun, are fairly well known. But the methods, the difficulties, the rewards of home trade and local industry, on the other hand, remain exceedingly vague.

"I can doubt everything," says Descartes, "except my own doubt." In the same way, our uncertainty about economic conditions in the seventeenth century is our only certainty; and this negative result, indirectly, has much to teach. It implies, for one thing, that for the men of the time, economic affairs were not worth recording and discussing, that they were beneath the notice of history. Every Frenchman, and the King himself, had to think about money matters: but these material concerns were considered as degrading necessities. The whole trend of thought was un-economic, or even anti-economic. There were already in the seventeenth century, as there had been in antiquity, in the middle ages, at the time of the Renaissance, communities in which economic considerations were recognized as vital. Of these, the Dutch Republic is the best example, and no two countries could stand in sharper contrast than this commercial commonwealth and the monarchy of Louis XIV. In France, the first Orders, the Clergy and the Nobility, scorned toil and trade. A cleric prayed, and a noble fought, for the realm, and that was enough. A gentleman might accept a pension, a bounty, a sinecure, a profitable privilege, a toll levied on the industry of others: but he would lose caste if he personally engaged in any gainful occupation. The only exceptions were certain forms of oversea trade, which had some of the glamour of adventure and conquest, and certain new industries, like glass blowing, which the Kings specially wanted to foster. That invincible prejudice of the upper classes is too well known for us to dwell upon it. More striking still, and more perilous, was the attitude of the *bourgeoisie*. The Third Estate espoused the ideal of aristocratic parasitism. If a craftsman or a shopkeeper rose to be a manufacturer or a merchant on a fairly large scale, his one dream was to give up his business as soon as possible, and to set up as a gentleman.

He would purchase an "office" from the King, an estate
from some impoverished noble; he would secure for his
children access to the "nobility of the gown," and try to
marry his daughter to a Count or Marquis whose scut-
cheon needed regilding. The ridicule poured by Molière
on these "would-be gentlemen," Arnolphe in *The School
for Wives*, the immortal Monsieur Jourdain, the ill-
starred Georges Dandin, is a healthy sign of change. It
was not a new social phenomenon that Molière was reg-
istering, but a new feeling. A bourgeois himself, an outspoken critic of the supercilious, sophisticated and idle
aristocracy, he was not condemning healthy ambition in
the name of nobiliary snobbishness: he realized that a
bourgeois was humiliating himself by abandoning his tradition of honest work. At any rate, this is the way in
which it strikes a twentieth century reader: it is the privilege of a classic, and the surest token of his greatness,
that his message can ever be reinterpreted in modern
terms.

There was some change in the attitude of the bourgeoisie in the eighteenth century: the growth of a new
spirit was accelerated by English influences, and was well
expressed by Voltaire, Diderot and Sedaine.[1] But, even
after the Revolution, the ancient prejudice survived.
Monsieur Jourdain reappeared as Monsieur Poirier,
father-in-law of a Marquis, and nursing the hope of becoming, "by 1848," Baron Poirier and a Peer of the
Realm. There were innumerable Georges Dandins under
the Third Republic: some of them came from America. The financial crisis which attended and followed the
Great War may have dealt the anti-economic superstition its death-blow. The vast middle class of small *rentiers*, living modestly on the income of safe investments,
has been the chief victim of the revolution in prices. The
so-called "liberal" professions have also been hit very
hard. Only those who actually cooperate in production
or distribution can face without fear the changed circumstances; so there may emerge from financial chaos a

[1] Cf. particularly Sedaine's drama, *Le Philosophe sans le savoir*.

France in which it will no longer be a stigma of inferiority to be working for one's living.

If we bear this prejudice in mind, we shall no longer be astonished at the paucity and insignificance of documents about the actual life of the working and trading classes. It was an uninteresting, a vulgar subject, not fit for the grand taste of the time. When Madame de Sévigné once visited a forge, she must needs turn her ironworkers into Cyclopses and Vulcans, so as to make the description acceptable for polite ears.

II

The economic fabric of society remained the same as in the sixteenth century, which had inherited it from the middle ages. Industry and local trade, on the whole, were still conducted on a very limited scale. In certain regions, like Lyons, and in certain lines of business, the rigid system of the guilds and crafts had never fully prevailed. Where it did obtain, and notably in Paris, the tendencies we have previously noted were still at work. The crafts fought bitter battles for their privileges, against independent workmen and against rival crafts. The masters sought to turn the crafts into a closed hereditary oligarchy; with the aid of the Kings, they strove, and on the whole strove successfully, to keep wages down. They struggled against the journeymen's secret societies or *Compagnonnages;* and in that struggle, they enlisted the support not of the Kings only, but of the Church as well. The forms of initiation into these societies, which were of religious origin, now seemed to pious people a parody of the sacred ritual. In the middle of the century, a small band of devout persons, the Company of the Holy Sacrament, was extremely active in prosecuting the Compagnonnages on religious grounds.

On the whole, the crafts, as strongly organized as ever, were losing their vitality. Their influence in municipal affairs, which had been great and at times decisive, became a thing of the past when the direct power of the

king was substituted for that of the burgesses. The
monarchy had asserted, and was extending, its authority
over the crafts. Yet, hampered by its invincible respect
for tradition, it did not succeed in imposing a standard
organization upon all trades—the dream of Colbert,—or
in doing away with the guilds altogether—the ideal of
Turgot. As in the sixteenth century, the intervention
of the crown was at times an advantage to the general
public: but in most cases, it was dictated by financial considerations. The King created new Masters, and collected the fees; innumerable inspectors, supervisors,
gaugers, weighers and measurers were appointed; their
offices or commissions were sold out by the King, and the
office-holders had to be supported by additional dues. Not
infrequently, the trades bought themselves off from the
threatened encumbrance; the new offices were abolished as
soon as created; and the whole transaction appeared in
its true light: a time-honoured method of squeezing more
money out of the productive classes.

The seventeenth century was marked by no essential
change in the conditions of economic life. The fluctua-
tions in prosperity, apart from the recurrence of good
and bad seasons, were due chiefly to political causes. The
reign of Henry IV saw a remarkable effort towards national reconstruction. In restoring order, the King was
also contributing to material well-being. No doubt the
increase in public wealth, and the personal popularity
that would follow, were sought by the Bearnese as conditions of his own power: but there was more in his policy than enlightened selfishness. He was no saint, and no
philanthropist: but he had a kind heart, a quick power
of sympathy, and, living away from Courts, he had seen
at close range the tragic distress of the people. The
French understood that their welfare was a genuine con-
cern of their sovereign, and they loved him accordingly,
even for mere velleities and pious wishes. Sully, colder of
heart and narrower of mind, had this merit at least, that
he hated the wastefulness of courtiers; agriculture he
loved with a jealous passion. Under the good king and his

efficient minister, France had a breathing spell; and although the prosperity of the early sixteenth century was not fully restored, the times of Henry IV were remembered and regretted up to the end of the ancient régime.

Much ground was lost, not only under the feeble or corrupt advisers of Queen Marie, during the minority of Louis XIII, but even under Richelieu. The great Cardinal was no economist; his grandiose plans for the absolute authority of the King in France, and for the supremacy of France in Europe, left him no time for petty thoughts of production or trade. His glorious ministry—we might well say his reign—was exceedingly hard on the population; and his death was hailed with rejoicings, not only by the nobles whom he had curbed, but by all classes of society.

The worst was still to be. Under Mazarin, France reached again the depths of misery that she had known during the Hundred Years War and the Wars of Religion. The Fronde, that comic-opera adventure of aristocratic heroines and their beribboned admirers, had for its background scenes of devastation and horror. The tragic experience revealed to France a saint, the most accessible, the most practical, the most active of modern saints, Vincent de Paul: but even the miracles of his charity could not cope with the ruin of the kingdom. Meanwhile, Mazarin was piling up tremendous wealth, and Fouquet, the superintendent of finances, could give on his estate at Vaux a foretaste of the future splendours of Versailles. When Louis XIV came to power, the diplomatic and political position of France was more favourable than it had ever been: but, economically, the kingdom was in a dilapidated condition. Colbert's gloomy picture of the state of affairs, which he drew repeatedly and complacently for Louis XIV, is open to suspicion: he no doubt wanted to enhance the magnitude of his task and the genuine greatness of his achievements. But his testimony is confirmed by many others: it was hardly possible to exaggerate the evil. This evil Colbert mitigated, if he could not cure it. The solid magnificence of the Grand

Monarch would have been impossible without the administrative genius, the absolute devotion to his work, the coarse and harsh vigour of his great minister.

III

Colbert sprang directly from the commercial class: his father had been a clothier at Rheims, and the young man may have learned the principles of trade from him, and from his uncle, a rich merchant. Colbert's father, however, was a "bourgeois gentilhomme" like the rest: he had purchased a nominal office of King's Secretary as a first upward step in the social scale. The son entered the service of Mazarin, won the confidence of the wily Cardinal, and successfully managed for him his scandalously overgrown fortune. Mazarin "bequeathed Colbert to the King" as a faithful and able servant.

The fall of Fouquet, in 1661, gave free scope to Colbert's ambition. He took care that his predecessor should never be able to rise again: he prosecuted him with a rigour bordering on ferocity, and which was not purely inspired by virtuous indignation. There is no question, however, but the Superintendent had been a "grafter" in the grandest manner of the classical age. He had friends among the aristocracy (Madame de Sévigné was one); among poets (Lafontaine never shone to better advantage); and, what was more to the point, among his judges in Parliament. The powerful secret cabal of the devout, strangely enough, supported him. Colbert's exertions, therefore, were not superfluous: and the new régime needed such a magnificent victim, as a symbol of its determination and power. With Fouquet out of the way, the rise of Colbert was immediate, and his ascendancy complete. In 1661, he was already in charge of finances and of naval affairs; in 1664, he became Superintendent of Buildings, Fine Arts, Tapestries and Royal Manufactures; in the same year, Superintendent General of Commerce; in 1665, Comptroller General of Finances—a more brilliant title for the position he had been filling since

1661; in 1669, Secretary of State for the King's Household, and Secretary of the Navy. It may be said that
until his death in 1683, the whole economic system of
France was in his hand. Colbert believed that the la-
bourer is worthy of his hire, and set his own price very
high: not only did he secure for himself all the great
functions that were to his liking, but he showered on his
whole connection wealth and titles: the clan of the Col-
berts became a social power even among the highest aristocracy.

The name of Colbert is inseparable from the notion of
a *national economy:* he was the first statesman of note to
think in economic terms and on a national scale. We have
seen that in the sixteenth century and in the first part of
the seventeenth, the economic unit was not even the province, but the small natural district, the *pays:* Colbert saw
France as a whole. Sully had been a careful manager
of the King's resources: but he still thought of the King's
fortune as a large private estate, and his ideal did not go
far beyond hoarding a few millions in gold: Colbert identified France with the monarchy, and wanted to enrich
the whole country for the greater glory of the sovereign.

There are many different aspects of *Colbertism.* First
of all, it meant order, efficiency, economy, in the administration of public finances: in other terms, the exact reverse of what Fouquet and his associates had stood for.
Then, carrying the same truly classical notion of order
and discipline into the realm of production, Colbertism
meant organization, "rationalization," as the French now
call it, the suppression within the kingdom of obstacles
to economic development, and the coordination of efforts.
This sharply defined conception of France as a unit implied rivalry against other national units: defensive and
aggressive campaigns in the marts of the world, trade positions to be besieged and carried by storm like fortresses,
a bid for financial victory and supremacy. Colbertism
thus stands most clearly for that kind of patriotism—or
protectionism—which holds that our neighbours' gain
must of necessity be our loss. Finally the national state

and the economic state being one and the same, it is the government's duty not merely to defend industry and trade against foreign competition, but to regulate them, to supervise them, and actively to foster them by all conceivable means: hence the creation of great trading companies and of royal manufactures under the direct inspiration of the crown.

These various forms of Colbertism were unequally successful, because they were not equally supported by those chiefly interested—the King, the merchants, the nation at large. It was as a rigid administrator of finances that Colbert did his best work: in this, the King was heartily with him, and although his methods were frequently harsh and at times unscrupulous, France realized that he was working for the public good. It was necessary, first of all, to liquidate the ruinous anarchy of the Mazarin régime—that Mazarin whom Colbert himself had served so faithfully. The condemnation of Fouquet was a first lesson, a decisive reply to the arrogant motto: *Quo non ascendam?* A special Chamber of Justice failed to punish adequately the men who had plundered the State: but it brought about a general clearing up of accounts. More than four hundred financiers were compelled to disgorge: the King's domain grew with the proceeds of confiscation; and sources of royal income that had long been mortgaged were recovered.

Colbert seemed to consider the *rentiers* or holders of State funds as among the profiteers from whom the State had to recapture illegitimate profits. Such a state of mind is still current among revolutionists, but it seems strange in the practical minister of a conservative monarchy. The *rentiers*, no doubt, had sought to take advantage of the difficulties of the government, and had driven a hard bargain: Colbert wanted to get even with them. He never was so happy as when he could find some excuse for a partial bankruptcy; it was a personal victory for him when he managed to reduce either the interest or the capital of the *rentes*. The high hand may succeed, if it be also a strong hand: the *rentiers*, dismayed but re-

spectful, accepted the curtailment of their claims, almost
thankful that it was not worse.

A weak government may evade part of its debt: but it
takes a vigorous government to do so, and at the same
time to restore confidence. This Colbert achieved, partly,
through the introduction of business methods: almost for
the first time, the monarchy kept accounts like a business
firm. Perhaps Colbert's ledgers were impressive rather
than accurate: his successor complained that they were far
from clear, and not in strict agreement with the facts.
But successors are proverbially censorious: the very attempt, at any rate, was a step in the right direction.
Louis XIV knew, roughly, the state of his finances as very
few of his predecessors had done. This knowledge, however, does not seem to have seriously affected his management of affairs: Louis XIV was extravagant with his eyes
open, whilst Francis I had been extravagant with his eyes
closed. Colbert was there to provide for everything.

Through a better administration of the vast royal domain, through more careful methods of apportioning and
collecting the old-established taxes, Colbert succeeded in
greatly increasing the revenue of the King, without imposing upon the people an intolerable burden. He even
managed to reduce the *taille*, the most iniquitous of taxes,
in so far as it was paid almost exclusively by the peasants.
But this faint attempt at social justice brought very little
relief to the poorest classes. Colbert's fiscal work was
made up of efficiency in practical details, palliatives, ex-
pedients. The broad reforms that he dreamed of, and
which could have given a permanent foundation to the
finances of the monarchy, were beyond his reach.

IV

For he did dream of a reform, and even of a revolution.
He was a Cartesian at heart, a thorough-going rationalist, a lover of logic, simplicity, symmetry. The rich
confusion of local traditions, in trade, taxes, legislation,
weights and measures, appealed to him not at all. In his

eyes, they were simply causes of inefficiency. He would have liked to do away with internal custom barriers, with ubiquitous tolls, with the privileges of provinces, cities, classes and crafts. We could easily imagine him, at the time of the Revolution, hacking down all those survivals with the somber zeal of a Jacobin; and, under Napoleon, rebuilding on the space thus cleared a vast and well-proportioned edifice. There was in that servant of Mazarin and Louis XIV a radical as well as a time-server. The radical in him was defeated. There was no public opinion yet to support him: even a hundred years later, public opinion failed Turgot in his great struggle. And, in this respect, Louis XIV was not with Colbert. Louis, as we have seen, was not a Cartesian radical, but the classical compromise incarnate: a lover of order, yet respectful of tradition; not a worshipper of abstract reason, but "reasonable" only in that sense that excesses and sudden changes were distasteful to him. The grand scheme of Colbert for a total reconstruction of France's economic structure remained a series of mere indications and velleities.

But the failures and the velleities of a man like Colbert leave a deeper imprint on history than the achievements of lesser men. Colbert could not abolish the distinction between the old provinces,[1] the later acquisitions, not yet thoroughly assimilated, and such lands as the Three Bishoprics and Alsace, which were wholly outside the custom system of France. But he did consolidate a number of dues and simplified their collection. And he issued great ordinances, carefully prepared by specialists, which were veritable codes. The Ordinances on Commerce, in 1673, remained in force until the end of the ancient régime, and was to a large extent the basis of the Napoleonic Code of Commerce in 1807. His organization of the seafaring population of France, under the name of *Inscription Maritime*, survived almost unaltered up to the twentieth century. His General Edict on Streams and Forests

[1] Known in this respect as Territory of the Five Big Contracting Companies, *les cinq grosses fermes*.

(1669) was systematically and almost absurdly rigorous. The Colonial Code, or Black Code, appeared after his death, in 1685.

Although economic affairs were Colbert's chief interest and his special domain, his reforming zeal extended to the whole of legislation. It was he who urged the King to be "a new Justinian"; in this he had to encounter the hostility of the Parliament, that impregnable fortress of privilege and precedent. Pussort, Colbert's collaborator, in the Ordinance or Civil Code of 1667, could only secure a very partial modernization of procedure: in Boileau's terms, he only "pared the claws of Chicanery." Just as finances, under Colbert and after him, became a trifle more intelligible, legislation, thanks to him, was perceptibly less chaotic. It was not a victory, but it was a promise. Colbert's ideal was not to ripen for another hundred years. Colbert was not "ahead of his time": the need for reform was bitter enough in 1661. It was the Parliament, and the other representatives of privilege, who were behind the time; and the King, "reasonable" rather than far-sighted, supported him only half-heartedly.

Even the *mercantilism* of Colbert was in the grand style of the age. He wanted France to be united and organized for production, but his goal was not wealth and well-being for their own sake: it was power, majesty, magnificence. By means very different from those of Louvois, the war minister, he too desired to make his sovereign "the most glorious king in the world." In his mind, the dynasty, the state, the people were one, as clearly as they were one in the mind of Louis XIV himself. So economic life was inseparable from dynastic and national patriotism: it appeared to him in the double terms of strict subordination of the individual at home, and, beyond the nation's boundaries, "sacred egoism," pitiless war against all rivals. This does not seem so far removed from the ideal of Italian Fascism.

Colbert's conception of the world was a static one. In his opinion, population and natural resources were practically fixed quantities. There was therefore only a certain amount of trade possible, and a limited quantity of wealth in circulation. You had to fight for your share: in such a world, no one could grow rich except at the expense of his competitors. The fabulous prosperity of the Dutch was a theft against the rest of Europe. The indefinite expansion of riches through discoveries and new processes, the parallel multiplication of the tokens of wealth through credit, had no place in his system. He was haunted with the superstition of gold: to be rich, for a man or for a nation, was to hoard specie. To buy for cash from a foreigner was a defeat, a capitulation, almost an act of treason: Colbert rebuked traders from Marseilles, who were guilty of leaving French gold in the Levant. To sell abroad for cash, on the contrary, and add to one's hoard, was a victory. Colbert did not invent protection (with a lurking desire for the absolute prohibition of imports), nor the craving for cash payment. But with him, these tendencies became dogmas: more than dogmas, they were passions. There are few Frenchmen to-day, and possibly fewer Americans, who are not Colbertists at heart. Only two French sovereigns took decisive steps in the direction of freer trade: Louis XVI in 1786, Napoleon III in 1860: in both cases, the results of the experiment were doubtful; and, as was to be expected, the complaints were much louder than the praises.

It is easy enough to criticize the selfishness of these conceptions. Nationalism is not enough, as we all know; but it may be vindicated as a broadening of the horizon, compared with the parochialism of a purely local economy. When Colbert found it impossible to burst open the barriers between Burgundy, Franche-Comté and Alsace, he can hardly be blamed for not having clearly before his eyes a European custom union which, two centuries and a half after his time, is still a Utopia.

At any rate, he stood squarely, and almost alone, against the "anti-economic prejudice." This indefatigable worker hated and scorned all forms of idleness and parasitism. He chided one city after another as addicted to laziness: he was the national foreman who wanted to see every one busy. He had no use for courtiers, who heartily returned the compliment: few men were less popular than this great servant of France, and it is a tribute to Louis XIV's fine sense of his national responsibilities that, in spite of so much hostility, Colbert's position never was seriously threatened. He scorned those office-holders who had purchased sinecures and were levying tolls on the actual producers. He had little love or regard, as we have seen, for the *rentiers* who had lent their money to the state: at heart, they were slackers who wanted to play safe, and to work as little as possible. He sought to reduce the vast horde of judges and lawyers with their innumerable retainers: there again, there was flagrant waste and parasitism. Although he could not freely express himself, in a period of orthodoxy and even of clericalism, he lamented the excessive number of priests, nuns and monks. He would have liked to postpone the age of ordination till 27, in order to thin the plethoric ranks of the clergy. He envied Holland for being free from such "unproductive elements." He urged the King to grant some social recognition to merchants, to call the most notable of them into consultation, to order that, when they obeyed the summons, they be suitably accommodated, to grace their manufactures with a royal visit and a nod of approval.

V

His work was not limited to efficient administration, removal of obstacles, codification and regulation, protection: all these were passive measures, and he felt that it was the duty of the Government to lead. Under the guise of commercial legislation, he fostered or even imposed the methods which he thought best: his Ordinance on Dyes, for instance, was actually an exhaustive treatise on the processes of the trade. He created or developed great economic organisms,—trading companies, industrial combines, royal manufactures. Yet he did not boldly profess paternalism as a doctrine: he did at least lip service to the ideal of liberty. It may be that, if the upper classes had not been hampered by the anti-economic prejudice, Colbert, contenting himself with the supervision of commerce and industry, would have welcomed private initiative. But the French, very different from the Italians, the Dutch or the English, had to be coaxed or even coerced into the economic field. If Colbert's practices do not agree with some of his words, they are in perfect harmony with his temperament. He was energetic, he was autocratic, and under any circumstances, he could hardly have refrained from intervention.

Henry IV and Richelieu had already fostered colonization: but their efforts had been spasmodic. Colbert was more persistent and more practical. He founded great monopolistic Companies, with extensive privileges. The King himself subscribed to their capital, and urged or compelled his courtiers to do likewise: he gave them formal assurance that, in so doing, they would not lose caste. There was a Company of the East Indies, one of the West Indies, one of the North, one of the Levant, and many minor ones. Not one of them prospered: not one could compare with the Dutch companies. The spirit of monopoly and magnificence hindered economic progress. There was inefficiency at the top: most of these bodies were administered from Paris, and Paris, then as now, was indifferent to maritime trade. Colbertism, in that line, was a sore disappointment. Perhaps it was not as complete a failure as it seemed: the great development of the colonies and of oversea commerce in the eighteenth century may be partly due to the long and painful preparation under Colbert. He sowed, and did not reap: this much is certain. But we are not quite sure whether he sowed the right seed.

The State, under Colbert, took an active hand in industry. This intervention assumed different forms. There were a few Royal Manufactures, owned outright by the Government, working exclusively for the King, and even, like Les Gobelins, operated directly by his officials. The principal of these were naval establishments at Brest, Toulon, Rochefort, and workshops which supplied the royal palaces with their luxurious decoration. Of the latter, Beauvais and La Savonnerie are well known, but they are eclipsed by the glory of Les Gobelins. Les Gobelins were founded by Henry IV, that true forerunner of Colbert: but it was Colbert who made it a State institution, and expanded it into a great center of decorative art. To the weavers of tapestries, who had already made it famous, he added goldsmiths, engravers, lapidaries, cabinet makers. Le Brun was the Director, and imposed indefatigably upon the whole production his rather formal and pompous style.

In other cases, manufactures founded by the King and encouraged by him, but under private ownership and management, retained the right of stamping their products with the royal arms. Others simply enjoyed some privilege or benefit granted by the King: monopolies, subsidies, free loans, fiscal exemptions. Such inducements were offered, in particular, when the Government wanted to attract managers or artisans from abroad. Thus miners and brass founders from Sweden were tempted by sundry advantages to settle in France. Italians brought the art of crape making, and, from Venice, the plate glass and mirror industry, which still thrives at St. Gobain. Van Robais, a Dutch Protestant, was granted many favours, including the free exercise of his religion, for establishing at Abbeville a manufacture of fine cloth. Colbert did not believe in the golden rule: whilst trying to bribe foreign workmen to come to France, he was very indignant when French workmen planned to emigrate. Through this constant quest for trade secrets, through his conviction that nothing was done abroad which the French could not do just as well, Colbert mitigated the greatest danger of the old guild system and of his own paternalism, namely stagnation. With him, no trade could rest content with "the good old way" if a better way were found. The supremacy attained by France, under Louis XV, in the industries of luxury, a supremacy never wholly forfeited, owes much to that tireless, lynx-eyed, progressive taskmaster.

VI

The beginnings of capitalism and concentrated industry may be traced in seventeenth century France: but they are very faint. Even in some of the large combines, like the Manufacture of French Lace (*Point de France*), the actual work was still done in individual homes; only in rare cases—some big foundries and textile mills—do we find the use of machinery, with a number of hands in the same shop, and a definite division of labour. At any rate, the contemporaries were not conscious of any great change.

On the whole, Colbert's life work was not crowned with success. His efficient administration of finances made the splendour of the reign possible: but the inveterate prodigality of the court and the never-ending wars upset his cherished plans for economy. The great reforms he had in mind, the vast simplification of legislation, the bold reorganization of trade, remained woefully incomplete: the upholders of tradition were too keen in the defence of their vested interests, and the King was indifferent. The economic conquests he undertook were precarious; his trading companies were vegetating; even his royal manufactures failed to give him full satisfaction. France had not heeded "the offer of Colbert," as Ernest Lavisse calls it: the offer to enrich King and country through incessant, well-coordinated, forward-looking efforts. The antieconomic prejudice was almost unshaken: Louis XIV was glad to have a faithful steward in Colbert, but he had no thought of turning himself into a Dutch merchant on a grander scale.

Just after Colbert's death (1683), as soon as his roughly efficient hand had ceased to control the clumsy and intricate machine, decadence set in again. Other causes were at work: the Huguenots, the most industrious element in France, left the country in vast numbers, carrying to Holland, Brandenburg and England those trade secrets and traditions that Colbert cherished so jealously.

Disastrous wars absorbed an ever larger proportion of
ever decreasing resources. Bankruptcy once more was
threatening.

We know little of the life of the common people, artisans and peasants, but that little is somber. The local
rebellions that broke out repeatedly under Louis XIV
were not political in character, and were not organized:
they have left little trace in history. They are significant
only as the spontaneous uprising of blind despair. They
were repressed with a ferocity which made even Madame
de Sévigné blanch: and the charming Marquise was not
in the habit of wasting her sprightly kindliness on mere
rustics—and jabbering, half-savage Bretons at that! We
are so familiar with La Bruyère's picture of the peasant
—a picture etched with the tragic vigour of a Callot—
that we are apt to think of it as "mere literature": "One
sees in the countryside wild animals, males and females,
dark, livid, all burnt up by the sun, crouching on the
ground which they dig and stir with invincible obstinacy;
they have something like an articulate voice, and when
they rise on their feet, they reveal a human face: and in
fact, they are men. They retire at night into their lairs,
where they live on black bread, water and roots. . . ."
This sounds like the mouthings of a socialist agitator:
yet La Bruyère was as moderate as he was keen, and
modern research has not softened the lines of his description. Colbert, harsh as he was, and a bourgeois, did think
of the peasants, enquired about their comforts, and even
their amusements: but he could do very little for them.
This failure is the obverse, and the indictment, of the
splendid civilization that created Versailles.

G

CHAPTER V

RELIGION IN THE SEVENTEENTH CENTURY

I. The Golden Age of French Catholicism. *Gallicanism:* autonomy without schism. Declaration of 1682. Constant ambiguity of the King's position.

II. *Revival of Piety:* Louis XIII and Louis XIV both pious. Preparation for a Christian death the acme of *savoir-vivre*. Reform of religious orders; new creations. The Company of the Holy Sacrament.

III. *Jansenism:* Its significance. The Arnaulds, St. Cyran, Jansenius and his *Augustinus,* Pascal and his *Provinciales.* Christian Stoicism. Duel with the Jesuits. Persecution.

IV. *Quietism.* Madame Guyon and the Molinists. *Fénelon* and Bossuet.

V. *The Protestants.* Treated fairly by Henry IV, Richelieu, Mazarin, Colbert. Campaign of conversion: its success among the aristocracy; Turenne. Policy of strict construction. Open persecution after 1679. Revocation of the Edict of Nantes, 1685. Its Consequences.

VI. *Religious Free-Thought.* The "Libertines" persecuted. Underlying Paganism of the Classical Age: Molière. Pascal's counterblast: *Thoughts.*

I

THE seventeenth century is the golden age of French Catholicism. In the ecclesiastical field as in the political, a great effort was made to restore decency and discipline. There also, the classical synthesis, or compromise, prevailed: authority, without which order was then inconceivable, was based jointly upon tradition and upon reason. No reform can be imposed upon a large body of men without entailing much formalism and even some hypocrisy: but the fundamental sincerity, the earnestness, the practical activity of the seventeenth century in religious affairs can not be doubted. All classes were affected, kings, nobles and bourgeois. Old monastic orders were purified and revivified; new ones sprang into life; charity received a splendid impetus; Christian education was fostered in all its degrees; in historical research, in philosophy, in literature, religion played a leading part. The zeal of the French Catholics went far beyond the national frontiers, and was manifested in world-wide missions, from China to North America. Even the strange flame of mysticism was not lacking in that age of solid common sense and classical moderation: the century of Descartes is also that of Pascal—and of Marie Alacoque.

Yet, in this domain also, we shall find that the craving for discipline and for the majesty of peace was destined to remain unsatisfied: classicism is an ideal rather than an achievement. Spiritual life would abdicate none of its complexity: the sustained effort for unity ended in weariness. It was an exhausted Catholicism that was left to meet, in the eighteenth century, the onslaught of "Philosophy."

The revival of Catholicism after the great scourge of the Reformation was, of course, not limited to France. The Church as a whole organized herself for defence and counter-attack. As early as 1535, the Jesuits were created as "the militia of the Holy See"; and the Council of Trent slowly built up the doctrinal and disciplinary entrenchments which were never to be surrendered. But this militant movement had, very naturally, its center in Rome; it enhanced the prestige and strengthened the hands of the Papacy; and for that reason, it was not followed with unqualified enthusiasm by the French Catholics. The canons of the Council of Trent were not received in France without difficulty: the Parliament was irreconcilable in its opposition. The Jesuits were not welcome as the leaders of the new Catholic crusade: they were viewed with suspicion and dread, as the enemies of the ancient liberties of the Gallican Church. At first, accused of condoning and even encouraging regicide, they were under the bann; but even after they had brought

Henry IV over to their side, they were not universally trusted. Brilliantly successful as educators, they won the affection of their pupils—even of such a pupil as Voltaire! Yet public opinion, in the seventeenth century, in the eighteenth, in the nineteenth, was only too willing to believe the worst of a Jesuit. As confessors of the King, some of them wielded great influence: but they could do so only by giving up some of their ultramontanism, and by refraining from any overt attack on the prevailing Gallican tendency.

There was therefore in the mind of France, "eldest daughter of the Church," as in the counsels of the King's "Most Christian Majesty" a secret current of hostility against the Court of Rome. This fact complicates the study of all religious problems: for Gallicanism, a vexing issue in itself, could be injected into any other issue. And, to heighten confusion, Gallicanism was a spirit, a policy, a tradition, but hardly a doctrine that could be definitely formulated. The King, the clergy and the Parliament were all Gallicans: but they were not Gallicans quite in the same fashion. One thing only they had in common: they would have recoiled with the same horror before the natural consequence of their Gallicanism, namely the possibility of a schism.

It was in 1682 that such a possibility loomed most dangerously. Louis was at the height of his pride and power; the Pope, Innocent XI, was unyielding, as only saints can afford to be. The two autocracies, both partly spiritual and partly temporal, faced each other with angry defiance. The English Ambassador was prophesying that soon England and France would have the same kind of religion. Bossuet was the natural leader of the French Church and the spokesman of the King. It fell to his lot to draw up, for the Assembly of the Clergy, a declaration which was a challenging statement of the Gallican position. In matters temporal, the Pope was denied all power, direct or indirect, over the King. In matters spiritual, the General Council, not the Pope, was recognized as supreme. The rules, usages and statutes ad-

mitted by the realm and the Church of France were to
remain unshaken. The Parliament endorsed these propositions: they became the law of the land, and as such,
were ordered to be taught in all seminaries. They never
were officially repealed. Even the Revolution did not end
them: in 1802, Napoleon tagged them on, of his own authority, to his Concordat.

But the clergy, whilst loyally following the King, was
averse to a rupture with the Pope. Bossuet himself was
no radical: in his "keynote sermon" on *The Unity of the
Church*, he had performed a prodigy of equilibrium; his
one desire was for conciliation. The King, persecuting
the Protestants, had no thought of playing the part of
Henry VIII and launching a new Protestant Church.
Rome showed the patience of the eternal: the Declaration
of 1682, never accepted of course, not even tacitly, was
not formally condemned and annulled until nine years
later, when irritation had been allayed. In 1693, Bossuet, again at the command of Louis, drew up a retractation to be signed by those Bishops whom the King had
appointed, but to whom the Pope had denied his investiture. This compromise, which might be termed a royal
capitulation, ended the deadlock, but did not clear up the
ambiguity. Gallicanism remained officially condemned in
Rome, officially enforced in Paris. No one knew exactly
whether, at any moment, the King would stand by the
Holy Father or by his own Courts of Justice. And the
two parties, contending with mellifluous acrimony, were
officially on the best of terms. The French, and particularly the fine old families of the Parliamentary aristocracy, were within the army of Catholicism like the veterans of Napoleon, devoted grumblers.

II

There were sturdy virtues in Gallicanism: but their
manifestations were frequently disagreeable. It is a
great relief to turn from this confused wrangling to the
positive achievements of Catholicism. When the virus of

political contention was eliminated, in 1598, a new spirit of earnest piety prevailed. The Kings themselves were affected. No sovereign in the sixteenth century can be described as devout: but the term admirably applies to Louis XIII and to Louis XIV. Even Henry IV had to tone down his good-humoured scepticism. Probe his conscience we can not: but the man who had said: "Paris is well worth a mass" spoke and acted thereafter as though he had always been an obedient son of the Church. With Louis XIII, no hesitation is permissible: he was almost a monk on the throne, and read his *Hours* as sedulously as if he had been in a cloister. His Christian conception of kingship was manifested in his devotion to the memory of St. Louis, whose feast became a great Church holiday. In 1638, he placed his realm under the special protection of the Virgin. His death, according to Vincent de Paul, was that of a saint. Louis XIV, brought up by a Spanish princess, practiced his religion with meticulous care, even in those years when his mode of living was very different from the Christian ideal, even when he was protecting Molière and frowning upon the "Cabal of the Devout." The intense, almost bigoted Catholicism of his later years was not a totally new element, due to the influence of old age and Madame de Maintenon: it was the final victory of forces which had existed in him from the first. He was the descendant of Philip II of Spain as well as of Henry of Navarre: the shadow of the Escorial can be traced over the splendour of Versailles.

France did not, slavishly and hypocritically, follow the ageing King in his return to religious life: his conversion had been preceded by many others, in all ranks of society. Arnauld d'Andilly, a Court favourite, had retired to Port-Royal as early as 1646. The Prince de Conti, who had been something of a rake, became a rather unlovely bigot. But other conversions did not offer this objectionable feature. Not only did nominal Catholics become practicing Catholics: but their practices, as a rule, far from benumbing their spiritual life, made it richer. That change of heart, that deepening of inner experience, that immediacy of intercourse with the divine, which certain Protestant Churches claim as their monopoly, were of common occurrence in classical France. When the lovely Duchess de la Vallière retired to a convent as Sister Louise de la Miséricorde, she was not driven by worldly despair, she was obeying an inner call. In the case of Pascal, we find, not a single conversion, but a whole series of conversions, a vertiginous ascent which carried him at last to the throne of grace. It is significant that the two great tragic poets of the time, Corneille and Racine, should both withdraw from the stage and plan to devote themselves to the care of their souls. To prepare for a Christian death was then the flower of *savoir-vivre*.

"Can a faith which is not active be a sincere faith?" queries Corneille in *Polyeucte*. The faith of the seventeenth century was active. This activity revealed itself strikingly in the reformation of religious orders and the creation of new ones. The Carmelites were introduced from Spain. St. François de Sales, whose *Introduction to Devout Life* ranked at the time as a second *Imitation*, established the Sisters of the Visitation: his original intention was they should not be cloistered, but should go into the world and minister to the sick. This ideal was realized by St. Vincent de Paul. He was the universal hero of charity. Galley slaves, prisoners of the Barbary pirates, foundlings, victims of the Fronde, all engaged his ardent and practical zeal. He left, as a priceless legacy, the Sisters of Charity.

Others devoted themselves to education. Bérulle founded his Oratory (1611), which at first was to be a center of meditation and study rather than a congregation. The Oratory deeply influenced the whole intellectual life of France: Malebranche, who attempted to reconcile Christian orthodoxy with Cartesian rationalism, was an Oratorian. Olier, who created the Seminary of St. Sulpice, for so long a great light in the Catholic world, found inspiration and support in the Oratory, and so did many others. The "Little Schools" of Port-Royal, and, at the end of the century, the Institute of the Brothers of the

Christian Schools (St. Jean-Baptiste de la Salle), reveal the same spirit.

The reform of Port-Royal is part of that great revival of earnestness in the Catholic Church. That abbey had become hardly more than a pleasant country home for the large Arnauld connection, when the young Abbess, Mother Angélique (Arnauld) restored the austerity of its rule. The spirit of Christian stoicism which was to make Port-Royal famous, existed before the group was committed to the theology of Jansenius. Later we find the conversion of Rancé, a man of the world who, since 1636, had been the nominal Abbot of a decadent monastery in Normandy. This, in 1662, he sought to revivify. He found some of his monks hardened in their sloth, and simply pensioned them off. With the rest, and with a few recruits as ardent as himself, he started the order of Trappists, one of the most rigorously ascetic in modern Christendom.

In 1627, a Peer of the Realm, Henri de Lévis, Duke of Ventadour, was inspired with the idea of creating, among laymen as well as priests, a secret society for the promotion of Catholic interests. This group took the name of *Company of the Holy Sacrament of the Altar*. It was devoted to all good works of edification and charity: but it was also a combative organization, fighting anti-Christian abuses such as blasphemy and duelling. Although its motives were unimpeachable, the mystery with which it was surrounded, its underground methods, and a pertinacity which at times amounted to ruthlessness, made it extremely unpopular whenever its influence could be detected. It was vaguely known as "the Cabal of the Devout," and it seems clear that Molière had this group in mind when he wrote *Tartuffe*. The Company was too earnest not to be intolerant: its campaign against "libertinism" (by which free-thought was chiefly meant) did not stop short of persecution. Even the workingmen's Brotherhoods and *Compagnonnages* were attacked, for their harmless pseudo-religious ritual. The Jansenists, although their virtues could not be impugned, were not

spared. Drastic restrictions were urged in the liberties
still enjoyed by the Protestants, and it may be said that
the Cabal sighed for the repeal of the hated Edict of
Nantes. But it did not survive till that day of triumph:
unauthorized, distrusted by King and Church alike, it
was dissolved in 1666. The public performance of *Tartuffe* in 1669 showed that France would brook no Inquisi-
tion—neither that of the Dominicans, nor that of the
"Cabal." It must be remembered, in spite of these un-
pleasant features, that the Company was created with the
noblest purposes; and that St. Vincent de Paul, most
charitable of men, Bossuet, a model of robust sanity, were
among its members.

III

Jansenism is a minor heresy, unpopular and obscure;
the Jansenists a handful of austere and stiff-necked believers; yet our whole conception of France must be different because Port-Royal existed. Smiling scepticism,
the gospel of the average sensual man, or the love of
majestic and formal unity, do not make up the whole of
the French spirit: by the side of Montaigne and Bossuet,
there is Pascal. And Pascal was not isolated: he was the
spokesman of a group. And that group, small and defeated, enlisted widespread, profound and lasting sympathies. The Jansenist controversy stirred the French
soul to its depths and affected even the course of the
French Revolution.

In 1599, a great Parisian lawyer, Antoine Arnauld,
secured for his daughter Angélique the Abbey of Port-
Royal, near Paris. The new "Abbess" was then eight
years old. But the child was soon affected by the wave of
religious earnestness which was sweeping over France.
In 1608, she decided to reform her convent. The pleasant
laxity which had turned Port-Royal into a sort of country
seat for the Arnaulds came to an end. At first, the father
was indignant at this mere chit presuming to "reform"
without his authority and even against it. But Angélique

won the day. The large Arnauld connection (Antoine had twenty children) was permeated with the new spirit, and Port-Royal became a center of devout austerity. In 1626, the nuns moved from Port-Royal-in-the-Fields, which they found unhealthy, to Paris. The buildings thus vacated were turned over to "hermits" or "solitaries," men in harmony with the Port-Royal spirit, and who desired to lead a pious life without joining a regular order. Some of the nuns came back in 1648, and the Solitaries built for themselves modest quarters outside the convent walls. "Port-Royal" thus signifies both a convent, and a free group of men: the material bond between the two was the Arnauld family.

It was only in 1623 that the convent came under the influence of a strange and powerful personage, Du Vergier de Hauranne, Abbot of St. Cyran. The outside world, including Richelieu, revered and distrusted him. He was a saint, and he was a mystic: but mystics go their lonely and perilous way, and saints are not amenable to formal discipline. Among the small cluster of the Port-Royalists, St. Cyran was a director and a prophet. St. Cyran was keeping in touch with Cornelius Jansen or Jansenius, Bishop of Ypres (1585–1636), and through him the doctrine which was to be called Jansenism took hold of Port-Royal.

Jansenius disclaimed any originality: his posthumous book *Augustinus* (1640) purported to be a mere abstract of St. Augustine's teaching. The essential point was that man could be saved only through the grace of God, and that such grace need not be vouchsafed to all men. If we brush aside theological niceties, we may say that Jansenius taught predestination as definitely as Calvin. But he was strictly orthodox on two fundamental questions: his faith in the mystic authority of the Church, and his faith in the Eucharist, remained entire.

The nuns of Port-Royal were not abstract theologians; neither were the hermits. Even the influence of such a man as St. Cyran would not have made them accept so ardently a difficult doctrine, if it had not been in profound

harmony with their spirit; and that spirit was one of
Christian heroism. They were Stoics and Puritans
among Catholics. Jansenism is essentially a creation of
the moral will, not of the intellect. Repeatedly the same
tense and proud attitude, the same vigorous and somber
conception of life, seem to have demanded the same rigorous philosophy: Marcus Aurelius, Calvin, St. Cyran,
Taine, were souls that would thrive best in an atmosphere
of tonic despair. They never felt themselves so victori-
ously free from all human bondage as when they proclaimed themselves the slaves of some superhuman power,
Fate, Providence, or Scientific Law.[1]

Angélique's brother, named Antoine like his father,
and known to his contemporaries as "the great Arnauld,"
assumed the leadership of the French Jansenists: in open
battle, concealment or exile, he preserved it till his death
in 1692. In 1643 appeared his treatise on *Frequent
Communion:* a foe to religious laxity, Arnauld felt that
the Sacrament had been made too easy of access. A profound spiritual experience might be blurred by constant
repetition and turned into a mere "practice." In 1649,
the theological storm broke out. The University of Paris
condemned five propositions extracted from Jansenius;
and in 1653 Pope Innocent X confirmed the sentence.
Arnauld defended himself with the skill of a trained theologian brought up in a family of lawyers: without fac-
ing the main issue, he argued on formal points and technicalities. The propositions were not found *literally* in
Jansenius; and they did not have in his book the sense
which his enemies attached to them. Arnauld was condemned, and, in spite of Pascal's masterly pamphlets, the
Provincial Letters, he was deprived of his degree. This
was the signal for a persecution which, except for a lull of
ten years (1669–1679), was not to relent until the last
nuns were dispersed, the stones of their convent over-
turned, and the very graves of their friends desecrated.

The bitterness aroused by this quarrel is no mere *odium*

---

[1] Napoleon, the most obvious example of triumphant will power, was
also a fatalist, a believer in "Destiny" and "the Force of Things."

theologicum. It was not so much the beliefs of the Jansenists that excited hatred, as their attitude. After all, they were respectful sons of the Church, and they said nothing for which they could not adduce the authority of St. Paul or St. Augustine. But, in an age of submission, they were a reproach and a scandal.

The struggle assumed the form of a duel between Port-Royal and the Jesuits. Hostility against the Jesuits was a tradition with the Arnauld family: in 1594, Antoine, the father, had delivered a great speech against them, which has been called "the original sin" of the family. The "little schools" of Port-Royal, in which Racine was a student, were all too successful, and threatened the educational monopoly to which the Jesuits were aspiring. Especially was there, between the two parties, a radical difference in method. The Jesuits wanted to conquer the world, AD MAJOREM DEI GLORIAM, to be sure, but, if need be, by using the world's own weapons. They were all things to all men, respecting the caste system in India, ancestor worship in China, and the customs of polite society at the court of the French Kings. The Jansenists, on the other hand, were rigid, uncompromising, and contemned the world.

So Pascal, following the lead of Arnauld, soon brushed aside the doctrinal problem. He had gone far enough, however, to prove that irony could be applied to theological discussion—a lesson which Voltaire learnt only too well. The *Provincial Letters* remain especially as an onslaught, tremendously effective and not wholly ingenuous, against the Jesuits.

These Fathers provided him with deadly weapons against themselves. Pascal had only to quote from their own treatises, and they stood condemned. As trained confessors, they had to discuss fine points,—at times dangerously abnormal points—of psychology and ethics. As practical "directors of conscience," they had to recognize the discrepancy that frequently exists between intentions and results. They also were led to admit that, in doubtful issues of spiritual jurisprudence, the opinion of a reputable authority had at least some presumption of

"probability" in its favour. None of these admissions but
was defensible; in the hands of an unscrupulous director,
however, they might easily lead to the worst degree of
laxity. Under the names of "casuistry," "direction of
intention," and "probabilism," they were exposed and
denounced as though they had been part of a general
scheme for dominating the world by condoning its vices.
The Jesuits, in France at least, never quite effaced the
stigma; neither did they ever forgive Port-Royal.

The King, influenced by the Jesuits, was ill-disposed
towards the Jansenists. He had been taught by Mazarin
to hate them, for Mazarin considered them as the friends
and accomplices of the Fronde. Then, in those early
years of his personal rule, Louis XIV did not like Puritanism of any sort: we have seen that he discountenanced
the Company of the Holy Sacrament, whose orthodoxy
was above suspicion. Finally, he was offended by their
sturdy independence. These good Christians, the slaves
of God's will, but of no other, were too much the captains
of their souls, like their contemporaries the heroes of
Corneille. Moderate and respectful as they affected to
be, they made it plain that, in their inmost heart they
bowed to no outside authority, King or Pope. There was
something rebellious, almost republican, Miltonic or Sa-
tanic, about such proud self-reliance. Even if they had
been wholly right, they should not have stood so stiffly
erect when every knee was bended.

As early as 1656, immediately on the condemnation of
Arnauld, the Hermitage and the schools were broken up.
The nuns refused to sign a formula of retractation
(1661), and, from 1664 to 1669, they were under inter-
dict, whilst Arnauld had to remain in hiding. Through
Madame· de Longueville and Pope Clement IX, a truce
was arranged (1669), and Arnauld even reappeared at
Court. But, with the death of their protectress (1679),
persecution was resumed, and Arnauld had to flee. The
last act, scattering aged and indomitable nuns into different convents, and destroying the buildings of Port-
Royal, took place in 1709-1710.

But the spirit of Jansenism was not limited to the small

group that suffered for its sake. Racine, after a long quarrel with his masters, had been reconciled with them, and tenderly wrote their history. Madame de Sévigné adored Nicole, the gentlest of their moralists. Boileau, a most moderate man, not ascetic in the least, the reverse of a mystic, told a Jesuit that the *Provincial Letters* were the masterpieces of French prose, publicly rejoiced because "Arnauld, the great Arnauld" had given him a few words of praise, and wrote a noble epitaph for the exiled leader. The Parliamentary families were permeated with Jansenism: their sincere piety, and their Gallican dread of the Jesuits, strengthened each other. Among the clergy, even among the Bishops, the Jansenists found sympathizers: Noailles, who became Archbishop of Paris in 1695, was their friend.

So it was ever necessary to kill Jansenism anew. In 1713, at the urgent request of the King, the Pope issued the Bull *Unigenitus*, which condemned the sect, not on five propositions only, but on more than a hundred. But a notable part of the clergy, and the Parliament as a body, continued to resist. Opposition was not silenced even when, in 1730 only, the Bull had been declared the law of the land. Worse still, in open disregard of Papal and royal policies, miracles were performed on the tomb of a Jansenist. The suppression of the Jesuits in France, through the undying hostility of the Parliament (1762), was a belated revenge of Port-Royal.

IV

In comparison with the prolonged and intense drama of Jansenism, the quarrel about Quietism seems trifling. In Quietism as in Jansenism, the will of God is exalted at the expense of man's freedom. But Jansenism is a pessimistic and tonic Christian stoicism, whereas Quietism is optimistic, and therefore relaxing. God is good, God is love: let us rest our hopes in Him. Mystical tendencies —and Quietism was highly mystical—are combated by the Church, whose authority they make unnecessary: "the

inner way" needs no outer discipline. These tendencies
are offensive also to the active common sense of the practical man. Fénelon had been tempted by Madame Guyon,
a disciple of the Spaniard Molinos, into the by-paths of
Quietism. Against him, Bossuet was the doughty champion of ecclesiastical authority and plain, workaday morality. Fénelon, a nobleman, the incumbent of the
princely archbishopric of Cambrai, a favourite with
Rome, was more subtle and more seductive than Bossuet.
It was hard to get a great prelate condemned for trusting
overmuch in the love of God. Yet Bossuet was evidently
upholding the constant tradition of the Church, and he
triumphed (1695–1699).

V

In 1598, France was the only great nation to admit the
coexistence of different churches. Everywhere else, even
in England, the faith of the monarch was the law of the
land. Henry IV had become an excellent Catholic and
even a friend of the Jesuits: but he had not discarded his
Huguenot friends, and Sully, in particular, remained his
right arm. It is possible, however, that Henry IV himself might not have considered the political privileges
granted by the Edict of Nantes as permanent. These
privileges were justified, in order to reassure the weaker
party, at the close of a prolonged and pitiless struggle;
but it was hardly conceivable that a Protestant Commonwealth, with its army and its diplomacy, should be tolerated, under normal conditions, within the kingdom.
The Protestant uprisings under Louis XIII were semi-
feudal rather than purely religious in character. They
were a sign of the relapse into anarchy, from which Richelieu was to rescue the country. After the siege of La
Rochelle, the peace of Alais, or Edict of Grace, was not
vindictive, and confirmed the spiritual rights of the minority. Richelieu himself was not only a Prince of the
Church, but a devout Catholic: however, he felt in honour
bound to respect, in all essentials, the pledge given by

Henry IV. The fact that in his rivalry with the great Catholic powers, Spain and Austria, he had to rely upon Protestant allies, did not wholly determine his policy, but naturally inclined him towards toleration. There were Protestants at court, and in the highest ranks of the army. The Academy which the Cardinal founded had for its nucleus the group of friends that used to meet at the home of Conrart, and Conrart was a Protestant gentleman. During the Fronde, the Protestants were loyal as a whole to the royal cause, and they were rewarded by the Declaration of St. Germain, in 1652, which confirmed the Edict of Nantes. As they were less affected than the rest of the population by the anti-economic prejudice, as they kept in closer touch with England and Holland, they played an important part in the industrial and commercial development of France; and for that reason, they were treated with fairness and in certain cases even with favour by Colbert.

However, the revival of Catholic piety and the craving for unity in all things, so characteristic of the seventeenth century, were not favourable to the free expansion of Protestantism. The survival of heresy seemed a last vestige of ancient anarchy: but the end of that scandal was to be brought about by missions, and not by means of violence. The royal word had been pledged, and, however reluctantly, it would be kept. Thus Richelieu himself published a *Treatise for the Conversion of Those Separated from the Church.* And a vast system of propaganda was organized, in which bribery supplemented more spiritual weapons.

This humane method did bear fruit. The higher Huguenot aristocracy in particular gave way. Loménie, Lesdiguières, Rohan, La Trémoille, Sully, Coligny, all these great names followed the Bourbons and the Condés into the Catholic fold. A Catholic Estienne was the heir of the great dynasty of the Protestant printers. Agrippa d'Aubigné, the Huguenot fighter, courtier, memorialist and poet, had a granddaughter who, as Madame de Maintenon, was to be the greatest foe of the "so-called Re-

formed Religion." In 1668, Bossuet, who, at Metz and
in Paris, had done wonders in that work of conversion,
won what seemed to be the crowning victory in the campaign: Turenne, illustrious as a general and as a prince
of the highest degree, abjured Protestantism.

Less legitimate was the policy of "strict construction,"
which Louis XIV adopted as soon as he assumed personal
power, in 1661. The Edict was to be respected: but nothing more than the Edict, interpreted with the most phari-
saical literalness. Thus the rights of the Protestants were
whittled down, without any possible redress. Protestant
schools were closed, and more than a hundred churches
destroyed.

Especially after 1679, the process of hypocritical suppression turned into open persecution. It was at that
time that Louis XIV, always orthodox and even pious,
was "converted" and became intensely devout. He wanted
to atone for the scandals of his private life by extirpating
heresy. He was all the more anxious to give signal evidence of his religious fervour, as he was then engaged in
a political and fiscal struggle with the Papacy: he had to
reassure the French Church and his own conscience. Both
the Jansenists and the Huguenots paid the price. In
1682, methods of violence were frankly resorted to by the
Intendants, acting under royal orders. Quartering dra-
goons in the home of recalcitrant Huguenots began in
1684. By 1685, the outward manifestations of the "disease" had practically disappeared: officially, there were
no more Protestants, except a handful of perverse agita-
tors. And so, amid the acclaim of classical France and
Catholic Europe, the Edict of Nantes was revoked.

It was soon discovered that the legal transformation of
the Huguenots into "New Converts" had not settled the
matter. A vast exodus took place, amid the severest hard-
ships. A whole population of grave, educated bourgeois,
prosperous merchants, skilled artisans, left France. The
silk industry at Tours, for example, was entirely ruined,
whilst England, Holland, Brandenburg received with joy
these valuable recruits. French Huguenot names survive

among the Boers of South Africa, and among the most anti-French families of the Prussian aristocracy. The peasants of the Cévennes mountains rose up in arms, and could be quelled only through the skill, diplomatic as well as military, of Marshal Villars. Throughout the eighteenth century, the Protestants had no legal standing, and the clergy grumbled constantly at the precarious tolerance which enabled them to exist at all. When relief came, on the very eve of the Revolution, it was too late. The spirit of French Protestantism was never broken: but it had ceased to be in harmony with the spirit of the nation. After 1789, there have been great French Protestants who were also great patriots: but, as a vital influence in French culture, the Huguenots had ceased to count: they had ceased to count long before 1685. Catholicism did not profit by their defeat, any more than by the defeat of the Jansenists. The result was that free-thought became the sole force of opposition to oppressive bigotry: Louis XIV paved the way for the Encyclopædists.

VI

The seventeenth century was an age of orthodoxy, spontaneous, self-imposed or enforced. But the free spirit of the Renaissance had not been destroyed: it had only been driven underground. From Rabelais and Montaigne to Voltaire, the tradition is unbroken.

Throughout the period, we hear of the "Libertines." The word is purposely ambiguous. It had been used in the sixteenth century to denote a sect which Calvin combated with the utmost rigour. In the seventeenth, it could mean anything from reasonable freedom in thought and action, down to blatant atheism and debauchery. This wilful confusion is an old device, which still serves; but the orthodox were not solely responsible for it. They called freedom licentiousness: but debauchees, on the other hand, loved to cover their vices with the cloak of philosophical liberty. Men like Théophile de Viau—a genuine poet, for all his sins—and Des Barreaux, com-

bined loose living and a diseased fondness for obscene
writing with a rather crude audacity in religious matters.
The redoubtable courtesan Ninon de l'Enclos was a free-
thinker as well as a free-lover; and it is an odd coincidence
that in her extreme old age, she should have made a
trifling gift to the boy Voltaire. This confusion was confirmed in the early eighteenth century, by the example of
the dissolute scoffers who rallied round Vendôme at the
Temple, or round Philip, Duke of Orleans and Regent of
France. The connection between immorality and free-
thought is not an inevitable one. Many orthodox people
were no saints: Mazarin and Louis XIV himself are instances in point. The trial of Madame de Brinvilliers,
the famous poisoner, revealed abysses of wickedness under
the decorum of courtly and Christian life; even the King's
most intimate circle was not spared, and Madame de
Montespan, the royal favourite, was compromised in the
scandal. All these vices and crimes could not be ascribed
to free-thought: the elements of magic and devil-worship
that came to light were rather evidences of superstition,
that is to say of inverted orthodoxy. Still, branding independent thinkers as moral perverts was too convenient
a weapon to be easily given up. Jesuits, Parliament,
Company of the Holy Sacrament, divided on other points,
united in the campaign against Libertinism. Jansenists
and Huguenots nodded assent. "Blasphemers" were
scourged, branded, sent to the galleys, hanged, quartered
or burned. And a very mild form of theism might be
considered as "blasphemous." *The Anti-Bigot, or the
Deist's Quatrains* (1622) was mentioned with bated
breath as a horrific document: to-day, it seems harmless
enough, and impresses us only with its insufferable dul-
ness.[1]

Yet the orthodox were not wrong: what these poor
Quatrains taught in such trite and uninspiring fashion
was the arch-heresy, and worse than heresy, *Natural Religion*, which sweeps away the claims of tradition and of
revelation itself. Open infidelity was rare, and could eas-

[1] Text in F. Lachèvre, *Le Procès du Poète Théophile de Viau*, II, 105.

ily be kept in check: but, under a thin pretence of conformity, the Libertines in the wider sense, the *Esprits Forts* or Sceptics, were legion. Montaigne and Charron remained the breviaries of well-educated men; the universal reverence for Greco-Latin antiquity created a prejudice in favour of Pagan philosophy. Gassendi, a mathematician and a priest, revived the fame of Epicurus. Descartes, cautious in his practical life, was popularizing even among Churchmen the principle that "we should accept nothing as true, unless we know it clearly and evidently to be such." Molière was an admirable representative of Bourgeois common sense: and it may be said that there is in Molière not a trace of supernatural Christianity. His ideal,—moderation, sanity, honesty, courage —is that of the Pagan philosophers, and of the "average sensual man," the sensible man of the world, "l'honnête homme." *Tartuffe* attacked the hypocrites, whom no one would care to defend. But it was plain also, and it explains the hostility of very fine men who were not Tartuffes, that Molière had no sympathy for the puritanical, the ascetic, the mystic view of life. The religion expounded by his mouthpiece Cléante might be endorsed by Voltaire.

This duality of the Classical soul—Pagan rationalism on the one hand, the Christian tradition on the other— never worried Louis XIV, but was most tragically felt by Pascal. For Pascal was a genius and a saint, whilst Louis was neither. Pascal, a scientist, a man of the world, familiar with the literature of antiquity and with Montaigne, had in him all the elements and all the weapons of intellectual "libertinism." However, he escaped from the sphere in which Montaigne, Molière, Voltaire, were satisfied. Conversions in his family and among his friends, the cruel probe of physical suffering, mystic experiences —visions and miracles—restored his faith in supernatural religion. He was the most pitiless of logicians, and the most ardent of believers; and in his *Apology of the Christian Religion*, he was hoping to bring together these two extremes of his being. He left only a heap of sublime fragments. The mysteries, the contradictions, the abysses of human destiny—far beyond the reach of Cartesianism—he expressed with a grandeur and a quivering dread unique in religious literature. The absolute victory of faith, the personal union of the soul with God, he also voices in words of fire. But what of the bridge across the chasm, what of the attempted reconciliation between reason and historical Christianity? At one time—a counsel of despair—he tells us to stifle reason, to seek refuge in "practices" that will stupefy our intellect. At another time, he advises us to "bet on Christianity" rather than unbelief: for, if Christianity be false, the sacrifice of some paltry pleasures, in this world only, will have been small indeed; if Christianity be true, a whole eternity of bliss or torment is at stake. This again is not a solution, but an abdication. Pascal was too great blandly to accept the classical compromise. If he had lived, would he have achieved the synthesis of rationalism and tradition? Men to-day are still eagerly searching his scattered *Thoughts* as though they must reveal the word of the eternal enigma; but the one lesson which none of his readers can escape is: *"Chercher en gémissant"* ("Seek with groaning").

CHAPTER VI

TRANSITION: THE BREAKING DOWN OF THE CLASSICAL COMPROMISE. GROWTH OF THE CRITICAL SPIRIT

I

THE classical compromise, the combined standard of tradition and reason, found its golden age in "the century of Louis XIV": the King, Boileau, Bossuet, were its worthy representatives. That compromise, however, was not a final and magic formula, responsible for the grandeur of the period, and to which France even now should return. It was a precarious solution, a brief moment of almost miraculous equilibrium. Its illogical and transitory character was veiled by the brilliant achievements of the time. So long as the enchantment lasted, so long as all was order, glory, prosperity, magnificent success in art and literature, criticism was silenced, and the result was an impression of majestic unanimity. But such moments of unquestioning national self-confidence are brief as well as rare. The belief that Napoleon had created a new and permanent synthesis did not endure much more than a decade. The "century of Louis XIV" was not so short-lived: but it lasted barely twenty-five years.

The King himself was long unconscious of any decrease in his power or in his prestige. In 1679, the peace of Nymwegen had proved him *nec pluribus impar*, in accordance with his proud motto. From 1680 to 1683, his might was such that he could capture cities in time of peace, as was the case with Strasbourg, none daring to offer effective protest. In 1682, he had stood even against the Pope, and maintained his authority over the French Church. In 1683, when Colbert died, he felt no doubt that he could "direct" his successor just as successfully. In 1685, the Revocation of the Edict of Nantes was to be the most signal proof of his power, and set the seal to his glory. Wise after the event, we see pride hastening before a fall. The losses in personnel were irreparable, for despotism, under Louis XIV or under Napoleon, does not create a second generation of efficient public servants. The victories were dearly purchased, and left resentment behind. The economic difficulties were no longer concealed, but rather brought out more glaringly, by the brilliancy of Versailles. And soon discontent became articulate, and could not be silenced.

A new sharpness of tone is felt soon after 1685. La Rochefoucauld, the representative of the defated nobility, was disenchanted and even "disgruntled" as early at least as 1665: but he was attacking human nature in general rather than the régime. The acerbity of La Bruyère is different (*Characters*, 1688). To the King, he pays due tribute, and there is no reason to believe that he is not sincere. But the Court, "the Great," are made to feel his lash. Between them and "the people," if a choice had to be made, he would deliberately side with the witless masses. Of the peasants, reduced to brutish misery, he gave that famous description, quoted *ad nauseam*, which anticipated by two centuries Edwin Markham's *Man with the Hoe*.

The Protestants, persecuted at first hypocritically and then with open violence, might profess to be none the less loyal to King and country, might be studiously moderate for the sake of the hostages left behind: still, their sufferings would wrench from them cries of protest which were heard throughout Europe and reverberated in France. *The Sighs of Enslaved France* (1689), either by the great minister Pierre Jurieu, or by the obscurer transfuge Michel Levassor, denounced absolutism in terms of the utmost boldness.

Then we find Fénelon, who nursed as yet no personal grievance, penning his warning Letter to Louis XIV (ca. 1692), a letter so bold that its authenticity was doubted until the original MS. was found. Boisguilbert, in his *Details of France under Louis XIV* (1695), and in his *Factum of France* (1705), arraigned the whole system of government without attacking the person of the sovereign. It was repeatedly asserted that Racine, a devoted admirer of Louis XIV, ventured at last to offer criticism, and that the King's contemptuous rebuke hastened the poet's death. Vauban, the great military engineer, one of the most useful servants of the monarchy, a fine type of the sturdy middle class, submitted to the King, in MS., his *Royal Tithe*, a diagnosis and a remedy: both were ignored. When the Memoir appeared in book form (1707), it was immediately condemned and suppressed. The belief that "all was for the best under the best of Kings" was evidently shaken to its foundations; the whole philosophy of government which had prevailed unchallenged during the years of prosperity lost its glamour as disaster impended.

But this tells only part of the story. It explains why, to an age of assent, succeeded an age of iconoclasticism. The view was long accepted that the eighteenth century represented simply the decadence and corruption of the classical spirit; that the generations of the Regent, Madame de Pompadour and Madame Du Barry were simply too puny to don the heavy armour of their fathers and submit to their austere discipline. This is hardly fair: the new spirit was not wholly destructive. The classical equilibrium was destroyed, not by loss of faith exclusively, but chiefly by the growth of other elements of faith. The period of transition, between 1685 and 1715, reveals an inextricable confusion of motives. The old order had failed: hence the cynicism found in Lesage's *Turcaret* (1709), and in the first parts of his *Gil Blas*. But already mankind could confidently look beyond that outworn synthesis. When the notion of eternal stability was ruined, it was succeeded, not by a conviction of decadence, but by a belief in progress.

II

One of the essential elements in that belief was the Cartesian philosophy. Descartes himself accepted the classical compromise in his practical life, and even gave it a formula in his provisional rules of conduct. But his thought was radical, and left no place for the authority of tradition. Both Bossuet and Fénelon were aware of the danger. We can not sufficiently emphasize the fact that in seventeenth century French, that language of flawless clarity, the word *Reason* is ambiguous. It may be interpreted as rationalism, or as reasonableness. In the first case, its chief instrument is logic; in the second, its foundation is experience. Descartes did not believe in "the wisdom of prejudice"; he substituted for it faith in the power of our own thought to-day. If we use the proper method, we shall be able to outstrip our ancestors. The golden age is not behind us: Descartes is no less optimistic than Bacon. Not only is progress possible, but there are no limits that can be assigned to it in advance. In his cold and ponderous manner, Descartes voices the same spirit that breathed in Rabelais's hymn to the sacred herb Pantagruelion; and, no less bold than Bergson, although on totally different grounds, he too anticipates that man may conquer "even death." It matters little that Descartes's physiology should be crude, his physics fanciful, and his rationalism too closely modeled on the method of Euclid. What is vital in a philosopher is his philosophy, that is to say his general attitude; and Cartesianism, secretly at odds with the cautious, pragmatic, tradition-worship of the age, was essentially forward-looking and modern. Molière gave a homely and irrefutable version of that philosophy: "The ancients are the ancients, and we are the people of to-day."

The second factor was the growth of the scientific spir-

it. We shall not attempt to sketch the history of science
in the classical age, but only to trace its influence on the
general movement of thought. It was in the latter half
of the seventeenth century that this influence first became
noticeable; and gradually it won ground at the expense
of metaphysics and even of literature. The great writers
of the eighteenth century are devotees of science; and the
reign of Napoleon, the climax of the classical age, was
marked by the paucity and inanity of its philosophers, by
the vapidity of its official literary men, and, in striking
contrast, by the brilliancy of its scientists.

The scientific spirit existed in Rabelais, no doubt: but
it was hopelessly intermingled with erudition and with
pedantry. The *savant,* for many generations, was the
philological scholar rather than the scientist: the tyranny
of the past had not been shaken. Then the mathematician became the *savant* par excellence. The seventeenth
century was in some respects the golden age of mathematics, the age of Descartes, Fermat and Leibniz, leading
up to the grandest triumph of the mathematical mind in
Newton. Gradually, through astronomy and physics,
studies in which observation and experimentation were
combined with mathematical formulation, the sciences of
the concrete were reached and developed.

This transformation had far-reaching consequences.
First of all, it made possible the popularization of science.
To the many, the higher mathematics must remain a
sealed book. Even more than in the case of metaphysics,
the pioneer goes "voyaging through strange seas of
thought alone" or almost alone. Fermat, Newton, in our
own days Henri Poincaré and Einstein, are said to have
experienced that vertiginous solitude of the discoverer.
And the explorer must clothe the result of his abtruse
cogitations in hermetic formulæ. On the contrary, there
is an accessible, an attractive, a popular side even to astronomy; experiments in physics are positively entertaining: theirs is the easy charm of parlour tricks. The de-
scriptive sciences of nature are picturesque and give food
to elementary curiosity. When science passed from the

refined and icy realm of abstraction to our concrete every-
day world, it could become a society fad; and—this is the
serious aspect of what might seem frivolous amateurish-
ness—the scientific ideal could slowly permeate large and
influential elements. The eighteenth century is the age
of "reform," of "philosophy," of "science": and the three
were taken to be almost synonymous. "Enlightenment"
covered them all.

We notice the growth of science in Molière's pictures
of French society. As late as 1660, the *Précieuses* had
little intellectual interest except in literature: the most
serious might go as far as moral philosophy. In 1672,
the *"Learned Ladies"* have taken the place of the Précieuses. They are still devoted to literature: sonnets, bal-
lads, epigrams and madrigals are events in their lives;
they are still concerned with the purity of the French
language, and the scepter has not slipped from the dead
hand of Vaugelas; classical scholarship is still held in high
esteem, and Vadius is abundantly kissed by his fair admirers, because he knows more Greek than any man in
France. But there is a difference. The very fuss that is
made over that pedant proves that Greek had become a
rarity. The new element is *science:* astronomy and the
vortices of Descartes are favourite topics. There is in the
attic a telescope which frightens simple souls like Chry-
sale's; and Trissotin, poet, pedant, drawing-room lion
and fortune-hunter, uses as a conversational opening the
new comet which has barely missed colliding with our
globe. Fontenelle, as we shall see,—Fontenelle, of whom
Trissotin seems a prophetic caricature—was to be the
efficient liaison agent between science, letters and society;
and Voltaire, the universal monarch of wit, the epitome of
his age, translated Newton.

This popularisation of the scientific spirit strengthened
enormously what we must call "modernism." In the arts,
in literature, even in philosophy, it was easy enough to
preserve undefiled one's faith in the supremacy of the
Ancients. Mathematicians probably knew better: but
their influence was limited to a small circle. For the

average educated man, the foundations of mathematics
had been laid for all time by the Greeks, and Euclid was
as much of a fixed point as Aristotle, Homer or Moses.
But, in the natural sciences, an attitude of blind reverence could not be preserved without becoming grotesque.
Molière held up to immortal ridicule the medical profession of the age, with its idolatry of Aristotle, Hippocrates
and Galen. But nothing in Molière is quite so farcical as
the desperate resistance of the medical Fundamentalists
against the discovery of Harvey. That the blood should
circulate in defiance of tradition was a scandal which
threatened all established authorities. On this ground,
however, orthodoxy was defeated in advance. The earth
continued to revolve, and the blood to course through
veins and arteries, in spite of all the anathemas fulmi-
nated by Church and Faculty.

III

The Quarrel of the Ancients and the Moderns is, in
itself, an episode of mediocre interest. It did not even
have the attraction of novelty: for the controversy had
come up a number of times before 1687. The issue never
was well defined; the protagonists—Boileau not excepted
—were not men of the very first rank; and the debate was
inconclusive. But, as a symptom, the Quarrel remains
important. The significance of a battle is not measured
by that of the village from which its name is derived.
Valmy has no intrinsic claim to our notice; the contest
was half-hearted and desultory: yet Goethe said: "On this
day and in this place, a new era is opening for the world."
On January 27th 1687, at a meeting of the French
Academy, Charles Perrault read a poem entitled *The Century of Louis the Great*. Perrault was a very clever man,
who transcribed into courtly and slightly archaic prose
the folk tales of *Ma Mère l'Oie;* he was the brother of the
no less clever Claude, an indifferent medical man (if Boileau is to be trusted) who turned into a first-class architect. But, for all his cleverness, his was a pedestrian

Muse. Few documents notable in literary history are so
completely devoid of literary charm as his poem. "Noble
antiquity ever was venerable, but I never believed that it
was to be worshipped. I view the Ancients without bend-
ing my knees. Great they are, no doubt, yet men like
ourselves; and, without fear of injustice, we may compare the century of Louis with the fine century of Augustus. . . . Plato, whom our ancestors thought divine,
is beginning at times to seem tedious; every one knows the
disrepute into which the famous Aristotle has fallen: he is
even less safe a guide in physics than Herodotus in history." Poets were not spared: fearlessly driving his paradox to the uttermost, Perrault dared to criticize Homer
himself: "a vast and powerful genius," to be sure, but so
apt to wander into interminable digressions that "Horace
is indulgent when he says that Homer occasionally slum-
bers." On the other hand, what a splendid roster of great
names is offered by modern France! "Régnier, Maynard,
Gombauld, Malherbe, Godeau, Racan, Sarrazin, Voiture,
Molière, Rotrou, Tristan"—an oddly jumbled list, which
posterity has not fully endorsed.

Such blasphemies aroused Boileau's classical ire. "It
was reported to the God of Poetry," he said in an indignant epigram, "that Homer and Vergil had been called
frigid and barren.—Impossible! answered Apollo, his
wrath kindling; or it must have been in America ("Was it
among the Hurons, or the Topinambus?")—No: it was in
Paris.—In the insane asylum, then?—No: in the Louvre,
in the Academy!"

The Quarrel went on, dismally rather than merrily, and
above all in very desultory fashion, for something like
seven years. In 1694, thanks to the efforts of their dying
friend, the great Arnauld, there was a reconciliation between Boileau and Perrault; and, in 1700, Boileau wrote
to his former adversary a public letter, remarkably courteous and sensible, in which he recognized the superiority
of the Moderns in science, in many arts, and even in certain forms of literature. The crusty old critic was no
fool and no boor.

We know that the Quarrel had its prolonged echo in England, with Temple, Boyle, Bentley and Swift. Early in the eighteenth century, it cropped up again in France. Madame Dacier, who had given a faithful and complete prose rendering of Homer, fought with Lamotte, who had found it necessary, in his versified version, to abridge the poem. These champions were inferior both to Boileau and to Perrault; although Fénelon said his word, and much later Voltaire tried to give an epilogue to the controversy, this last stage is the least interesting.

The Quarrel, however, had a significance far beyond its merits. We have seen that the comparative failure of Louis XIV had weakened the respect for traditional authority, and released criticism: there is a spirit, outwardly modern, which is purely negative, and therefore barren. Perrault's thesis, on the contrary, was the result, not of discontent, but of excessive self-satisfaction and pride. It was the natural, although unexpected, conclusion of all the praises lavished upon Louis XIV and upon his epoch. For the first time, the Moderns, having served their full apprenticeship, dared to challenge the Ancients in all fields, confident that they could hold their own. It was the moment joyfully prophesied by Rabelais and by Du Bellay: antique lore had served its purpose, and true Humanism was now able to proceed unaided. Classicism in the narrower sense had failed to realize that such a moment was bound to come; indeed there are men living today who have not realized it yet, and who repeat to their goddess Antiquity: "To whom should we go? Thou hast the words of eternal life."

Unfortunately, the value of the whole episode, as a crisis in the growth of the modern spirit, was spoilt by the extraordinary mediocrity of the controversy. The issue remained clouded. In science, the Moderns had the better of the argument: but they hardly needed that academic squabble in order to clinch their victory, which never was seriously in doubt. In literature, the honours remained rather with the defenders of the Ancients; but their advantage, due to the weakness of their opponents, was not

fully convincing. Had the Quarrel not proved abortive,
we might imagine the eighteenth century evolving a form
as fresh and bold as its thought really was. On the contrary, an age of unexampled daring was too timid to
shake off the shackles of pseudo-classicism. Even Voltaire pinned his hopes of glory to his epic and to his
tragedies—the least Voltairian of his works. In certain
lines, the superstitious reverence for antiquity, instead of
dying out, experienced a recrudescence: Vitruvius was
more of a tyrant under Napoleon than he had been under
Louis XIV. The feeble and futile efforts of Perrault and
Lamotte discouraged the Modernists: we shall have to
wait another hundred years, and more, before Romanticism delivered France from the thrall of Greece and
Rome.

IV

Officially discountenanced, and even persecuted, "Libertinism," in the sense of free-thought, survived throughout the seventeenth century. But its different elements
were not equally capable of growth. Théophile de Viau
and even Cyrano de Bergerac were late survivors of the
anarchistic Renaissance, stragglers of a defeated army.
They perished, and left no posterity. They are curiosi-
ties in the history of thought, not channels of influence.
Molière, on the other hand, is not a systematic apostle of
free thought; he is not partisan, even in *Tartuffe;* he
hardly ever preaches (and when he does, he is not Molière) ; he represents, not a moment in evolution, but a
permanent trait, the eternal rebellion of common sense
against all pretences and all forms of bigotry—artistic or
religious. On a lower plane, the independence of Lafontaine was mostly indifference. He followed, not Nature,
but *his* nature, which was that of Harold Skimpole. This
is even truer of lesser men like Chapelle and Chaulieu.

But there were others through whom the true apostolic
succession of Free Thought can be traced, from Rabelais
and Montaigne to Voltaire and Diderot. We have already indicated that Pascal, paradoxically enough, the

tragic and mystic Pascal, had at one time his place in that line. And this is not merely because he was well acquainted with the arch-sceptic Montaigne, the "natural man" against whom he was forced to invoke supernatural aid; but chiefly because of the jaunty tone of *persiflage* in his early *Provincial Letters*. These pamphlets marked the secularization of theology; and it is hard for theology to thrive in a secular atmosphere. As soon as a gentleman wrote for gentlemen (without forgetting the ladies) about the deepest and most technical problems of religious philosophy, authority melted before the irony of common sense. Such was not by any means Pascal's intention, and his ridicule of theologians is but a minor aspect of his work. Yet we can not forget that Voltairianism, as a style in religious controversy, was actually practiced by Pascal: Voltaire, a pupil of the Jesuits and a hater of the Jansenists, showed scant gratitude to his great forerunner.

One of the clearest titles to fame of St. Evremond (1613–1703) is that he wrote, quite independently of Pascal, a brief pamphlet with all the wit and irony of the *Provincial Letters:* it is the delightful *Conversation of Marshal d'Hocquincourt and Father Canaye*. St. Evremond's was a strange destiny. Exiled in 1659 for his outspoken criticism of Mazarin's diplomacy, he settled in London, and lived there until his death in 1703. Exceedingly French, he found himself perfectly at home in the Frenchified atmosphere of the restored Stuart Court. He had his share in the Quarrel of the Ancients and the Moderns—naturally on the modern side; he was chiefly instrumental in starting the English phase of it. His *Reflections on the Romans* anticipated Montesquieu. He lived so long that his "libertinism," which at one time might have seemed antiquated, became prophetic of a new day. He was a man of the Louis XIII and Louis XV eras who, through a caprice of fate, managed to skip the grand "century of Louis XIV" altogether.

Pierre Bayle (1647–1706) was a Calvinist who, in 1669, was converted by the Jesuits, and, in 1670, reverted to his former faith. This back-sliding or "relapse," as the official phrase was, exposed him to banishment. In 1681, he settled in Rotterdam, where he taught and worked until his death in 1706. Even in that haven of religious freedom, he did not enjoy untroubled peace. Jurieu, the intellectual leader of the French Huguenots, attempted to silence him. Against Bossuet and his doctrine of authority, unity, permanency, Jurieu had argued for liberty and progress: but, with the critically and historically-minded Bayle, Jurieu was as dogmatic as Bossuet himself. Sainte-Beuve would like to drag the name of Madame Jurieu into the affair: but this very Sainte-Beuvian hypothesis is hardly necessary. Many are the Dissenters who can brook no dissent from their own dissent. Persecuted right and left, Bayle preserved his philosophical equanimity: his only vengeance was to add some curious and erudite note in an odd corner of his vast Dictionary.

Bayle was not a great writer: his style is usually indifferent and not seldom soggy. He was no philosopher in the constructive sense of the term, for he quietly ignored all doctrines, even Pyrrhonism, in the conduct of his thought. He was not a scientist, although he corresponded with all the scientists in Europe. He was interested only in history, and in certain aspects of history: but he was not even a historian, for he had no system, and therefore no sense of order and measure. His masterpiece, the *Critical Dictionary* (1696–97), is an unorganized mass of notes on Moreri's errors; and the best that he has to give is found, not in the text, but in small type at the foot of the page.

Yet Bayle is no mere Renaissance philologist, no emancipated Benedictine. He is critical curiosity incarnate. He wants to know: and when he has started on his quest, there is not a single prejudice that can stop him. "Errors are none the better for being old," he said. Such a spirit, in an age of vested authorities, made the quiet bookworm a rather disquieting and even formidable personage. No wonder the local Huguenot Pope, Jurieu, found him little

H

to his liking. Bayle, no doubt, had a lurking fondness for paradox: otherwise he would hardly have started on his critical career. And his experience as a critic confirmed him in the belief that a paradox, matched against a prejudice, had at least an even chance of proving true. He was not by nature iconoclastic: only he had no reverence for idols. You can tell an idol, experimentally, by the fact that it can be shattered; but you never know until you try.

It is obvious that in all these respects he was the spiritual father of Voltaire, and of a great multitude of eighteenth century "philosophers." He has other Voltairian traits: irreverent irony, not so sharp as his great pupil's, yet keen enough; and a marked fondness for spicy details. As in the case of Voltaire, this last ingredient was added partly in order to whet the appetite of the reading public; but it also represents the author's own taste, which our purer age thinks none of the best. For the whole eighteenth century, his vast collection of facts was a model and an arsenal: there is much of the Bayle spirit in the *Encyclopædia* of Diderot and in the *Philosophical Dictionary* of Voltaire. Enemies of Voltaire, and in particular Emile Faguet, have attempted to exalt Bayle at the expense of his more famous successor. Voltaire is less meticulous as a critical historian, and his partisanship is much more flagrant; in his private life as well as in his open campaigns, his temper was much less serene. Yet it would be rather unkind to Bayle to insist upon a comparison.

Anatole France took conscious pride in claiming kinship with Bayle. He himself was described by Jules Lemaître as "an ironical Benedictine"—a phrase which aptly describes the compiler of the *Critical Dictionary*. Sylvestre Bonnard, Lucien Bergeret, Brotteaux des Islettes, and especially Jérôme Coignard, all those blandly sceptical booklovers who are avatars of Anatole himself, have their prototype in the Rotterdam refugee.

V

Both St. Evremond and Bayle were exiles: so it may be questioned whether they were truly representative of their time and country. Fontenelle, on the contrary, lived and throve in Paris, accumulated official honours, and was a universal favourite. He was a cool and deliberate time-server: yet not insincere, for he was far too clever to need the clumsy device of insincerity. He served at the same time his personal advancement, his own convictions, and the society in which he lived. His success, therefore, is much more symptomatic, in the history of culture, than the isolated efforts of far greater men.

He was born in 1657. The nephew of Pierre and Thomas Corneille, he attempted tragedy as a matter of course, and failed; he tried his hand at bucolic poetry and novel writing, and fared even worse. He at last found his way as a "polygraph," a universal utility man, a clearing-house or exchange counter for all forms of knowledge. He was not exactly all things to all men: he remained Fontenelle, a quiet but very distinct personality. But he was a man of letters among scientists and a scientist among men of letters; a philosopher in a drawing-room, a man of the world in the study. The miraculous skill with which he husbanded his steady but none too abundant intellectual resources is shown by the fact that he became a useful and honoured member of the French Academy, the Academy of Sciences, and the Academy of Inscriptions. The same wise economy enabled him, with a frame that was not strikingly robust, to live within a month of a hundred years, quietly active almost to the last. Many of his biographers hold it up against him: it seems as though a man could not become a healthy centenarian without a strong element of selfishness in his nature. In this, and in many other respects, we may be too hard on Fontenelle. There are extenuating circumstances for his excessive longevity.

Fontenelle represented an ideal which had been growing throughout the classical age: not the many-sided, intense *virtuoso* of the Italian Renaissance, and not the self-mutilating ascetic; not the thoughtless man of pleasure and not the narrowly practical man of action: but "the scholar and the gentleman," the all-round man suggested by Montaigne, the *"honnête homme"* of the seventeenth century, whose chief care is, in all things, to eschew pedantry; an intelligent amateur in every form of activity, a specialist only in the complex art of living. For the average man, this is not such a bad gospel. It was for such men that Fontenelle wrote, and such a man was he.

He is called in French *"un vulgarisateur,"* in English a popularizer. Both terms are inadequate. Fontenelle is never vulgar, nor even popular. He does not address the masses, any more than Voltaire did after him, any more than Henri Poincaré in his "popular" *Science and Hypothesis*. Like Montaigne, like Descartes, like Pascal, he submits the work of the specialists to the test of refined common sense. His work presupposes two conditions, which are too often lacking in our "popular" scientific books. The writer must have had serious training in the subject that he is expounding: and although Fontenelle was not a creative scientist, he could hold his own in intelligent discussion with the specialists. And there must be as a background an open and fairly large aristocracy of the intellect, which does not include the whole "general public," nor limits itself to the professional investigators. That "gentlemanly public" did exist at the end of the seventeenth century: Molière and Boileau referred to it as "the Court and the City." In the eighteenth century, it was to become, consciously, the chief influence in national life. Pessimists will have it that in the nineteenth century, it was swamped beyond any hope of return. Without such a public, we are exposed to constant and brutal clashes between Caliban and a caricature of Prospero: two forces almost equally blind, on the one hand uninformed, unthinking demagogy, on the other lop-sided learning. The people need enlightenment; but scholars and scientists need both practical sense and the human touch. What Fontenelle attempted to do was, not to "vulgarize," not to "popularize," but to "harmonize" and to "humanize."

Naturally, in the Quarrel of the Ancients and the Moderns, Fontenelle was on the side of Perrault: indeed he had anticipated Perrault in his ingenious *Dialogues of the Dead* (1683). In his *Conversations on the Plurality of Inhabited Worlds* (1686), he appears as the society savant, a more earnest Trissotin, teaching a fair Marquise the rudiments of astronomy interspersed with madrigals. The little book starts with a comparison between the charms of blondes and brunettes: but it contains, with a creditable amount of information which was not then so familiar as it is now, a surprising wealth of philosophy, the essentials of sound scientific thought, by which we might still profit. In his *History of Oracles* (1687), the abridgement of a Dutch treatise, we find the critical attitude of Bayle more clearly exemplified than in Bayle himself. Pagan oracles were held by the early Church to have some validity: they were not of God, but neither were they mere delusions or deceptions; they came from demons, who did possess genuine supernatural knowledge, albeit distorted and maleficent. Fontenelle proceeds, in all seriousness, to ruin the authority of Pagan oracles. He is killing the dead, and he knows it: but he is teaching us the use of instruments with which other corpses, which still bear the semblance of life, can be as neatly dissected.

Fontenelle's masterpieces are his biographical notices on scientists and scholars, mostly his fellow academicians. Without technicalities, he gives the gist of their work, and its import; without trying inquisitiveness, he conveys the tone of their private life, and their intimate character. Mr. Lytton Strachey has attempted to revive interest in these *Eulogies* of Academicians long forgotten; and if we owe in part to Fontenelle's example the delicate biographical art of Mr. Lytton Strachey, it is a debt which this generation should gratefully acknowledge.

In that maze of interests, social, literary, scientific, philosophical, Fontenelle was not without a guiding thread; and that thread was not purely and simply enlightened selfishness. He was no mere sceptic, any more than Bayle; he believed in reason, and in science as the earnest, painstaking service of reason. There is little flippancy in him, and no rashness. His doubt is honest, and not all-dissolving: he knows that he does not know, and he knows that, relatively and within definite limits, he does know. The eighteenth century is still constantly accused of "radicalism": but this was hardly true until Rousseau appeared on the scene, and Rousseau did not belong to that open aristocracy of culture which was so exactly represented by Fontenelle and Voltaire. "When it comes to new discoveries," he said at the close of his *Plurality of Worlds*, "we must not be overhasty in trusting our reason, much as we may be tempted to do so; true philosophers are like the elephants, who never take another step until they are sure of their footing."

Fontenelle was not the prophet, or even the guide, of his generation, but its secretary. In society as well as in the Academy of Sciences, he was the ideal secretary—accurate, industrious, open-minded, self-effacing. It was therefore the opinion of his time as well as his own that he registered when he wrote: "Authority has ceased to have more weight than reason."[1] Quiet words, but decisive. We may take them to heart yet.

Fontenelle was, in Arnoldian phrase, an apostle of "Sweetness and Light." The Arnoldian ideal has in it a touch of artificiality; in the case of Fontenelle, the 'sweetness' was thinned out and a trifle acidulous; the 'light' was steady, but far from dazzling, and gave no appreciable heat. Yet, after our orgies of Rousseauism, Romanticism and pure Scientism, we long at times for a quiet evening under the cool and distant stars; for well-bred voices discussing great themes without pedantry and without passion; for an Academy in the truest sense of the term, with Fontenelle as its Perpetual Secretary.

[1] Preface to the *History of the Academy of Sciences*.

BOOK III

THE EIGHTEENTH CENTURY

I. The rulers; the Regent: sudden reaction against régime of Louis XIV, Louis XV: education, character. The favourites: Madame de Pompadour, Madame du Barry. Acephalous Autocracy.

II. Aristocratic reaction: Fénelon as a forerunner, Boulainvilliers, St. Simon. The Parliaments. Ecclesiastical affairs: the Bull *Unigenitus,* the Jesuits.

III. Financial Difficulties. The banking and colonial schemes of Law; their collapse. The Financiers: their dissolving influence upon classical society.

IV. Eighteenth century France misrepresented by her government.

I

I T is an axiom with a flourishing school of political thinkers in France that monarchy means stability, and democracy means chaos. A dynasty has continuity of purpose: the irresponsible mob is swayed by incessant caprice. A crucial test of this theory came in 1715, when after seventy-two years of reign, Louis XIV left his throne to a child of five. The one principle of the new government was to reverse in all things the policies of its predecessor. The Regent was almost compelled, in self-defence, to adopt such an attitude. Louis XIV distrusted him; and, unable to deprive the first Prince of the Blood of the Regency, he had attempted to deprive him in advance of all actual power. The Regent therefore was first of all obliged to exorcize the ghost of the Grand Monarch, tyrannical beyond the tomb. The will of Louis XIV was set aside. The bastards whom he had raised to the rank of legitimate royal princes were shorn of their privileges. Whilst Louis XIV had waged an interminable and ruinous war against England in order to establish his grandson Philip V on the Spanish throne,

France, now in alliance with England, aided her in destroying the navy, the fortresses and the arsenals of Bourbon Spain. No "swing of the pendulum" in any democracy could have been more brutal.

This personal element, however, was not the sole cause of the reaction against the late régime: it merely gave it freer rein. The firm government of Louis XIV had been accepted, ev n with enthusiasm, so long as it had brought internal peace, a fair degree of prosperity, and glory abroad. But its oppressive and expensive character had long been felt. When financial ruin and military defeat had to be faced, the people still rallied to the King, who after all, was France. But the old love and confidence had vanished, and the funeral train of Louis was jeered and cursed at when it skirted Paris on its way to St. Denis. A radical change was expected on all sides. But there was the rub: *on all sides*. Many forms of discontent can easily be united in denunciation, only to start squabbling as soon as remedies are proposed. The result would have been perfect chaos, if the quiet energy of a hard-working, conservative people, and the momentum of the vast bureaucratic machine, had not kept the state fairly steady, in spite of its nominal rulers.

And never had rulers been more purely nominal. The Regent, Philip, Duke of Orleans, was lacking neither in intelligence nor in kindness. If he was a rake, at any rate he was for a long time an amiable one. He was too honest to pay hypocritical homage to virtue: thoroughly self-indulgent in practice, he did not profess or enforce rigorism for the benefit of others. In comparison with the gloomy bigotry of the Maintenon régime, his lazy "live and let live" policy assumed an air of philosophic humanity. But there can be no genuine goodness without strength of purpose. As his friend St. Simon reproached him, the Regent was *débonnaire* in the French sense of the term, that is to say weak, rather than genuinely kind. He was unsteady, ruined in mind and will as well as in body by the effects of his dissolute life. It was difficult to keep his attention focussed on the affairs of the state.

Resistance soon wearied him and wore out his best intentions. His boasted liberalism had no firm foundation, and the easy-going man could become high-handed, when he thought that brutality might save him some trouble. Even the amiability which was generally acknowledged by his contemporaries, and which, after a century and a half, still fascinated Alexandre Dumas and Michelet, did not stay with him to the end: there is no trace of it in the bloated and morose face we find in his last portrait.

In 1723, the King was declared of age: but he remained a figure-head. Twenty years later, on the death of his trusted tutor, Cardinal Fleury, his "personal reign" was said to begin: but time had brought neither knowledge nor energy. Even the desire to rule was lacking: Louis XV was destined to remain what he had been as a child: a bored spectator on the throne. Yet France longed to love her king. The handsome, timid little boy, so frail, surviving alone amid the ruins of his race, had appealed to the hearts of the people. As late as 1744, when, on his way to the front, he fell dangerously sick at Metz, thousands of masses were said for his recovery; he deserved then to be called Louis the Well-Beloved.

As a figure-head, he was not devoid of majesty and grace. He preserved, in public ceremonies, an air of Olympian aloofness, which was a kingly mask for his unkingly indifference. He was not a coward: once at least in his life, at Fontenoy, he displayed actual courage. He was not stupid. As a child, he had been taciturn, almost sullen, like Louis XIII; and, even in his young maturity, he remained diffident, ill at ease in the company of women; but the sisters de Nesle—three of them in succession—turned this royal boor into a courtly gentleman; and with his friends, he was pleasant, even witty. Madame de Pompadour retained her empire over him through her cleverness, her delicate taste and her social charm, rather than through mere physical attractiveness. He never was actively kind, but he was not cruel. A deplorable husband, even as royal husbands went in those days, he was an excellent father; with his daughters in particular, he

could be unaffected and cheerful. There was nothing
morbid or monstrous about him, as there was in Nero or
in the last three Valois. He was simply spoilt: but spoilt
unto rottenness.

The first heir of Louis XIV had been trained by Bossuet; the second by Fénelon; and neither lived to reign.
The education of Louis XV had been a masterpiece of a
different sort. Villeroy gave young Louis XV the sense
of his quasi-divine position, without an inkling of his
royal duties. Fleury, supple and gentle, made him a devout practicing Catholic, but did not succeed in making
him a Christian. Louis XV believed earnestly in Hell;
but he believed even more firmly that there would always
be a chaplain in attendance to save his soul on his death
bed. He acquired no discipline, no useful information,
not even an intelligent hobby. He loved hunting, and,
when he was tired of hunting, he would tie knots of rib-
bons or weave tapestry.

Alone on his artificial Olympus, untrained except to
laziness, prejudiced and unprincipled, timid at heart
whilst absurdly proud, superstitious and sceptical, he
yawned his life away. State business, which had engrossed his predecessor, bored him unutterably. In council, he hardly opened his mouth, and then only to reveal
the vacuity of his mind. He found more pleasure in petty
intrigues, even against his own ministers: he had his secret
police, his secret diplomacy. But even they failed to
amuse him for long. He could not take them seriously
enough to play the game. All his life was a pretence; he
himself was a pretence. He had flashes of Voltairian
irony, in which the utter futility of it all was revealed to
him. "Do not invest in royal securities," he advised one
of his business agents: "they say it is not safe"; and the
familiar cry of cynical despair: "After us, the deluge!"

What wonder that in this waste of dreary vanities, he
should clutch at pleasure, "the one thing as certain as
death"? Glorious Louis XIV had shown the way. The
Regent had freely flaunted his vices. The Court was even
less squeamish than the King: temptation was forced upon

him. It was the time when an honest German prince, persuaded that a Court Mistress was a necessary appurtenance of a royal establishment, appointed such a functionary, only to be seen walking sedately with her in a garden. The age found no fault with Louis XV on that score. Courtiers affected to admire the "constancy in inconstancy" that impelled him to take three sisters one after the other; and the one objection raised at first against Jeanne Antoinette Poisson, Dame d'Etioles and later Marquise de Pompadour, was that she, a mere bourgeoise, was poaching on the preserves of the nobility.

That remarkable woman was no figure-head, but a born ruler. Her career was a triumph of the will. She had been picked out and trained for it long before it seemed at all likely that she could ever meet the King; and she had consciously—we might say conscientiously—prepared herself for her dazzling destiny. Louis, as soon as he saw the young queen of financial society, was subjugated. But mere beauty would not have preserved his favour many months: she kept it for twenty years, until her death in 1764. Her daily existence was a combat: against the Church and the nobility, against possible rivals, against the eternal *taedium vitae* that was devouring the King; and she won so brilliantly that even the Queen finally accepted her, and made her a lady-in-waiting. In the chaos that reigned in France's diplomatic and military affairs, it is hard to tell whether the foreign policy that she advocated was worse than any possible alternative: it failed disastrously, and she had to bear the blame, before the contemporaries and before posterity. At home at any rate, her influence was fairly steadily on the liberal side. She protected Voltaire, like herself a parvenu of wit; and, according to S. Tallentyre, she even wanted to make him a Cardinal. She helped the *Encyclopædia*. She assisted in the discomfiture of the Jesuits —for which, in the hearts of certain French radicals, many of her sins will be forgiven. She deserved to give her name, not wholly in contumely, to a period in French culture, akin to the Regency, rather less immoral, fully as "enlightened," and more delicate in taste. An artist of some talent herself, a consummate actress of course, but also a musician, a painter, etcher, engraver, she was a generous and intelligent patroness. Her group,—her fatherly protector Tournehem, her brother Marigny,—officially directed French art for two generations: and the result of their guidance is not to be despised.

But the nature and the education of Louis XV were too vacuous to be satisfied with cultured hedonism. Even the marvelous resourcefulness of the Marquise de Pompadour failed to monopolize his interest. She had, willy nilly, to share the fate of legitimate queens and admit the existence of rivals; she even had to treat them with friendliness, as Marie Leczynska treated *her*. Legend has no doubt magnified the debauchery of Louis XV, and his private establishment of the Parc-aux-Cerfs was in all likelihood not quite so horrific as it has remained in popular imagination. But certain it is that advancing years did not moderate or refine the lust of the monarch.

Strangely enough, the Court, so hostile at first to Madame de Pompadour, a bourgeoise, welcomed without a qualm Marie Jeanne Bécu, Countess du Barry, a mere courtesan. We should not even mention that shameful and prolonged episode (1769–1774), if it did not throw such glaring light upon hereditary absolutism. The King, brought up in the belief that he could do no wrong, bereft by his very omnipotence from any vital interest, had become merely an old man seeking amusement and illusion. The Du Barry was pretty, vivacious, unconventional, refreshingly vulgar with odd reserves of native tact, madly prodigal but not sordidly grasping. At councils of state, she would sit on the arm of the royal chair, making faces at the ministers, and interfering in national affairs with the irresponsibility of a pet monkey. It is odd that her intervention was not wholly pernicious; as she was a mere instrument, she served at times a defensible cause, without an inkling of the real issue. If she brought about the dismissal of Choiseul, who had refused to acknowledge her, she helped the Triumvirate, d'Aiguillon, Maupeou and Terray; and it can at least be argued that these men were undertaking reforms which might have given the ancient régime a longer lease of life.

France thus offered for nearly sixty years the strange spectacle of an acephalous autocracy, a crown without a head. The absentee King, bored by etiquette as well as by business, was too ignorant to find any escape except in pleasure; and he finally accepted a priestess of pleasure from the gutter. Once he was teasing Choiseul about some love affair: "Be careful, Choiseul, your soul is in danger!" The minister dared to reply: "What about yours, Sire?"—"Oh!" the King answered, "my case is different: *I am the Lord's Anointed!*" The magnificent fallacy of Bossuet about the Divine Right of Kings needed such a *reductio ad absurdum*.

II

The government of Louis XIV had been an autocracy served by a bureaucracy: no other authority was tolerated. The nobility, the Parliaments, even the Church, exercised their powers only through a delegation of the King or by his permission: the King alone was the State. It was against this royal Cæsarism that the men of the Regency rebelled. It had been tyrannical, and men with sincere liberal velleities, like the Regent himself, were glad to see it at an end. But it had also been anti-aristocratic, and the old aristocracy raised its head again.

Of this odd mixture of nobiliary prejudices with a genuine desire for reform, Fénelon had been the illustrious forerunner. Salentum, in his pedagogical romance *Telemachus*, is a Utopia founded on the simple life and a rigid class system. The luxury of the great devours the substance of the people: in Salentum, the seven classes of freemen are distinguished by their costumes, and the one great incentive to luxury, which is the gratification of pride rather than that of the senses, immediately disappears. "Place in the first rank," says Minerva herself under the guise of Mentor, "those of the most ancient and brilliant lineage." Fénelon died before the King he had freely criticized: but the Regent had *Telemachus* printed, as a posthumous apology to the great apostle of Christian gentleness and aristocratic pride.

Boulainvilliers, who had long been inditing his curious politico-historical studies, addressed a Memoir to the Regent on the Regeneration of France. The basic theory of Boulainvilliers is the negation at the same time of popular government, and of absolute monarchy. It is an out-and-out defence of feudalism, the foundation of which he finds in the right of conquest. The hundred thousand descendants of the Franks alone form the dominant population. The King himself has no right to add to their number, or to curtail their privileges, which are as ancient and as venerable as his own prerogative. This bold doctrine rankled in the mind of the Third Estate. It made the nobility a class for ever closed, the oppressor, the enemy. In 1789, Siéyès, who defined the Third Estate as the very substance of the nation, said of the nobles: "Let them return to the German forests whence they came!"

But the most ardent and the most influential advocate of a nobiliary reaction was Saint-Simon. In the course of his long life, he never was able to get over the wonder of his being a Duke and Peer of the realm. Louis XIV did not appreciate him, and thought his stickling for etiquette absurd. Saint-Simon retaliated by despising and denouncing "that reign of vile bourgeoisie," in which a commoner like Colbert could hold the highest offices, wield more influence than a Prince of the Blood, and secure for his kin the most brilliant titles. Saint-Simon had placed his hope in Fénelon's pupil, the Duke of Burgundy; but that prince died too soon. The champion of the Dukes and Peers had his chance at last under his friend the Regent. He advocated the "Polysynodical System": the former ministers and secretaries of state were superseded by Councils, in which the higher nobility figured prominently, whilst the old officials were allowed to attend to the routine work. This cumbrous method did not function well, and was soon abandoned. But the attempted reaction left traces in French history. The incapacity of the aristocracy was exposed. The traditional alliance between King and bourgeoisie was for a while overshadowed and almost interrupted. Louis XV and Louis XVI were much more committed to the lost cause of the feudal aristocracy than Louis XIV had been. In 1789, as we shall see, it was almost impossible for Louis XVI to place himself where he rightly belonged, at the head of his people against the privileged orders. The reactionary dreams of Fénelon, Boulainvilliers, Saint-Simon, tolerated if not encouraged by the Regent, then bore their dangerous fruit.

The Parliaments had been curbed by Louis XIV, and reduced to their proper function, the administration of justice. But they had never given up their claim to be "sovereign courts," coordinate with the monarchy. They were confirmed in this exalted view of their office by the Regent, who needed them in order to annul the will of Louis XIV. They eagerly fell in with his plans; and, as a reward, the right of "remonstrating" was restored to them. Such an abridgement of absolutism might seem a conquest for liberty; and it would have been, if the Parliaments had represented anything beside themselves. As it was, they formed a small, selfish, reactionary caste; the restoration of their privileges was a victory for the spirit of privilege. Far from helping the cause of progress, the increased power of the Parliaments was, throughout the eighteenth century, one of the chief obstacles to reform. Their radical transformation by Chancellor Maupeou (1771–1774) would at least have given "enlightened despotism" a chance; but the death of Louis XV put an end to the brief experiment, which had been heartily endorsed by Voltaire and Turgot. Once more, a retrograde step was taken in the name of liberalism, and the Parliaments recovered their authority only to hasten the catastrophe through their constant and unintelligent opposition to change.

Nowhere is the chaotic character of the régime made

more manifest than in ecclesiastical affairs. Louis XIV
had one definite, consistent principle: unity. Accordingly, Huguenots and Jansenists had been outlawed. The
Regent, full of kindly intentions, thoroughly sceptical,
and detested by the religious bigots of the Maintenon
clique, was in favour of tolerance; and, under his rule,
Protestants and Jansenists could breathe. But, as in all
things, his velleities did not pass into law. The Edict of
Nantes was not restored; and, as early as 1724, the drastic
provisions of the Revocation were enforced again. It was
not until the very eve of the Revolution that the Protestants had some relief.

The Jansenist quarrel is a much more complicated
story. King and Pope had united in suppressing the
movement, which, by the Bull *Unigenitus*, in 1713, was
irrevocably condemned. The nuns of Port-Royal had
been dispersed, their convent pulled down, the very tombs
of their friends had been moved away. Yet the stubborn
spirit of the sect would not die. Jansenism still found
many sympathizers among the clergy and among the substantial middle class. The Parliament of Paris, in particular, was favourably inclined towards Jansenism, and
revelled in opposing both the King and the Pope. So,
within the ranks of the Catholics, an interminable and
obscure fight went on during the whole reign on the subject of the Bull. Sacraments were denied to dying Catholics who had not properly subscribed to the Bull; on the
other hand, the Parliament of Paris, as "guardian of the
canons" and defender of the liberties of the Gallican
Church, opposed legal procedure to theological weapons.
The attitude of the government was shifting. The Regent himself cared very little about the Bull *Unigenitus*
or any other; but his trusted counsellor, Dubois, longing
for a Cardinal's hat which the Pope alone could bestow,
wanted to please Rome by enforcing her policy. Under
the Duke of Bourbon and Cardinal Fleury, the government was against the Jansenists, but lacked determination
or power to end the troublesome agitation. The feverish
atmosphere created by this protracted quarrel favoured

a veritable epidemy of mysticism. In the age of Voltaire, the Jansenists proved the excellence of their cause by going into convulsions. The sick were healed at St. Médard's, on the tomb of Deacon Pâris, a Jansenist. The government saw fit to close the cemetery, and some wag put up the sign: "By order of the King: no divine miracle allowed here."

Back of the anti-Jansenist movement were the Jesuits, as in the days of Pascal. That great order was very widely distrusted and hated. In the eyes of the Gallicans, it represented Ultramontanism, the supremacy of Rome. Voltaire, one of their pupils, always kept a personal affection for his old masters, and preferred them to the gloomier Jansenists: still he saw in them the bulwark of a conservative, persecuting Church, and could not be expected to defend them. By an odd coalition of Gallicanism, Jansenism and Free Thought, under the ægis of Madame de Pompadour and through the instrumentality of Choiseul, the Jesuits were suppressed in France in 1761–62. They were treated without indulgence and even without fairness: their defence was not even heard. But the rigorous measures taken against them failed to rouse any sympathy in their favour; and, in 1773, the order was abolished throughout Christendom by Pope Clement XIV.

The scandal of this bitter fight favoured enormously the growth of unbelief. Voltairianism can hardly be understood without such a background. We may note that it was to a large extent under Gallican and Jansenist influences that the National Assembly voted the "Civil Constitution of the Clergy," one of the most disastrous mistakes of the Revolution.

III

In the history of France during the eighteenth century, two words recur with ominous regularity: deficit, bankruptcy. The remedies were obvious to every eye: economy and tax reform. But they were as impracticable as they were obvious: the anarchical levity that prevailed at the center of government made retrenchment unthinkable; and the classes best able to pay resented as an insult the curtailment of their fiscal privileges. The country was resourceful and thrifty; the eighteenth century was an age of economic expansion: so the catastrophe, ever impending, was averted for seventy-four years.

Under the Regency, a curious attempt was made to meet the situation by unprecedented means; and, to the present day, opinion is divided as to the merits of that wild adventure. Law, a Scottish banker, who had in vain propounded his "system" to Louis XIV, succeeded in securing the favour of the Regent. He created a private bank, which was extremely successful. He took over from one of the financial barons of the time, Crozat, the privilege of developing the Mississippi region. Then his bank became a Royal institution. His "Company of the Indies" absorbed all rivals, and monopolized the colonial trade of France. Finally, bank and company were amalgamated. Law had in addition the direction of the Mint and the farming of the taxes. By 1720, the foreign adventurer was officially Comptroller General of Finances; the management of the national debt was turned over to the wizard. Thanks to his undoubted genius, and to the uncompromising support of an erratic and absolute government, he had in his hand the whole economic fabric of France.

The expansion of credit through Law's banking activities was a new thing in France, and a particularly good thing in a country grown slack and self-diffident through many years of disaster. The prosperity that was suddenly whipped up did not wholly disappear when the scheme collapsed. The development of the colonies was a worthy enterprise, and it was undertaken with creditable energy. It was by no means an activity on paper: hundreds of ships were actually bought or built. But returns were bound to be slow, whilst hopes had run too high. The linking of three heterogeneous elements, a bank, a trading company, and the finances of the State, was overbold, and could succeed only through a miracle of luck and efficiency. The government yielded to the temptation of juggling with paper millions; the princes preyed upon the Company; the whole population caught the gambling fever from its leaders. The Rue Quincampoix served as an outdoor stock exchange, and saw the most sudden shifts of fortune. The scheme, too grandiose almost from the start, was inflated to absurd proportions. Had Law, who was honest as well as bold, remained in control, he might have saved the sound elements of his "system," and mitigated the ruins that would follow the bursting of the bubble. But his rivals saw their chance, and hounded him out of the country (Dec., 1720). The great lords, like the Duke of Bourbon, helped themselves by the cartful to all the cash available; and the brothers Pâris, Law's personal enemies, who were entrusted with the winding up of the affair, performed their task with ruthlessness.

The crisis revealed to the world at large the catastrophic power of speculation, and thus contributed to the demoralization of the age. It must be said, however, that the evils made manifest under the Regency were already in existence under Louis XIV. When we read Lesage's comedy *Turcaret*, we are struck by its Balzacian atmosphere and the modern tone of its satire. It could be entitled *Business is Business*, or *The Gold Digger*. Now *Turcaret* appeared in 1709. The rise of Samuel Bernard preceded the Regency; and Louis XIV, to use Saint-Simon's energetic expression, prostituted his majesty by showering courtesies on the financier. The ancient régime is frequently depicted as an age of social stability; every one knew his place, and progressed within his appointed sphere; no attempt was made to rise suddenly, as in our democracies, and to skip the intermediate steps. Such a perfect Salentum has never existed except in the imagination of Fénelon and Paul Bourget.[1] Successful financiers elbowed their way to the very front. They bought titles, and they bought noble connections. Great families were only too willing to "regild their 'scutcheons," as the say-

[1] Cf. *L'Etape.*

ing was, or, in cruder terms, to "manure their lands" with
the wealth of a successful commoner. The Count of Ev-
reux, of the princely family of Bouillon, married Mademoiselle Crozat; and the old Duchess called her daughter-
in-law "our little gold nugget."

Here as in all things, what the Regency did was to tear
aside a hypocritical veil. The eighteenth century did not
see again as insolent a parvenu as Fouquet, with his quasi-
regal scale of living and his *Quo non ascendam?* But the
princes of finance assumed a conspicuous place in society.
They had their handsome Hôtels or private residences in
the Faubourg-Saint-Honoré, their "Folies" in the sub-
urbs, their châteaux in the country. They patronized
magnificently art and literature. They were on friendly
terms with philosophers: the d'Epinays gave Rousseau a
home. Indeed they might be philosophers themselves, like
Helvetius. They were, in many different ways, a ferment
of dissolution for the régime. The people, who might
have preserved a while longer their reverence for a traditional aristocracy, took the habit of scoffing at riches and
titles the origins of which were only too well known; the
prestige of the ancient nobility suffered by contagion.
On the other hand, the old families borrowed no strength
from the new elements: they persisted in treating the
nouveaux riches with insufferable insolence, even whilst
accepting their money. This prevented a coalition of the
wealthy classes, old and new, which might have been a
factor of stability. There is more wounded vanity than
democratic feeling in the epigrams of Beaumarchais: and
Beaumarchais, forerunner of the Revolution, was an adventurer of finance.

IV

The Regent inaugurated, and Louis XV continued, an
era of incurable levity. Under this capricious régime,
there was licence without liberty, and violence without energy. It is never quite true even in a democracy, to say
that a people gets only the government it deserves:

France in the eighteenth century was vastly superior to her rulers. She was eager to respond to leadership: but leadership there was none. If left to herself, as under the lenitive rule of an old man, Cardinal Fleury, she laboured and prospered. Fortunately, a chaotic government, absolute though it may be in theory, is not all powerful even for evil: weakness has some of the advantages of tolerance. Whilst the home policy of the monarchy was offering the sorriest spectacle, and its foreign policy was even more lamentable, the civilization of France never was so brilliant, and never did her social prestige stand higher.

Yet there was something unwholesome in that brilliancy: the taint that was in the monarchy corrupted the whole of national life. Taste, charm and wit France possessed abundantly in those days, and already a curiosity for science, a philosophical daring which duller periods might envy. Yet it was not good that the Duke of Orleans should be able to help transmute "that rogue Dubois" into a Cardinal; that a wastrel like Louis XV should pose as "the Lord's Anointed"; that a Voltaire and a Choiseul should have to curry favour with Madame de Pompadour. It meant a devaluation of all values, many of which were sound still. France has not yet paid in full for the meretricious prestige won in the first half of the eighteenth century; not only has France suffered, but through France, the sane and generous ideas which she advocated, and which seemed contaminated with the Regency and Pompadour spirit. It was thanks to examples from above that Voltaire could write *La Pucelle*, and Diderot *Les Bijoux Indiscrets*.

France redeemed herself by her own efforts. In the second half of the century, we shall find a positive longing for simplicity and virtue; and, almost inevitably, that moral regeneration was accompanied by the most bitter contempt for Louis the Well-Beloved.

CHAPTER II

THE NEW SOVEREIGN: SOCIETY UNDER LOUIS XV

I. Public Opinion, Society, Conversation.
The newsmongers (*Nouvellistes*). The Gardens. The Cafés.
The Clubs. The Theatres.

II. The Salons: Madame de Lambert and the Academy. Madame de Tencin. Madame du Deffand.

III. The Salons: Mademoiselle de Lespinasse and d'Alembert. Madame Geoffrin. Madame d'Epinay. D'Holbach. Helvetius. Necker.

IV. Permeation of provincial France and Europe by the spirit of Parisian society. Voyages. Correspondences.
Influence of Society upon Art: decorative art. Moments and aspects: Watteau, Latour, Boucher.

I

Monarchy, under Louis XV, abdicated all leadership. The result, as we have seen, was disastrous confusion in diplomacy, war, government, ecclesiastical affairs. In art, literature and philosophy, the scepter passed to a new sovereign, public opinion. And that sovereign, amorphous, ubiquitous, irresponsible, made its power felt mainly through what is vaguely known as "Society."

The eighteenth century offers a clear demonstration that history is not just "past politics," if by politics we understand merely the official activities of public bodies. Politics, at that time, were beneath contempt; but the life of the country, which it is the task of history to record, had never been more intense. France managed to exist, to produce, to prosper, without institutions and without heroes. There was some one more powerful than the King, and wittier even than Voltaire: it was "Monsieur Tout-le-Monde," the collective mind.

With all our elected assemblies and our popular newspapers, it is hard enough at present to catch hold of the "phantom public." In the eighteenth century, these obvious modes of expression did not exist at all. The Parliaments might go beyond their judicial attributions and discuss political problems: but they had no mandate from the people. The Estates and Assemblies which survived in certain provinces had but a shadowy existence. The periodical press was in its infancy. The weekly *Gazette de France* founded by Theophrastus Renaudot in 1631 enjoyed a monopoly of political information: but so far as home affairs were concerned, it was the driest of court circulars. The *Mercure* was purely a literary review. Yet de Tocqueville, comparing ancient France and the France of Napoleon III, with its daily press, its Legislative Body, its plebiscites, was able to say: "France to-day is muffled, echoless: then it was vibrant. It was sufficient to raise one's voice to be heard afar."

The key to this paradox is "Society." Information was transmitted, opinions vented, measures suggested or opposed, ministers made or unmade, by word of mouth, or even by the suggestion of a smile and a shrug. "They say that man is a sociable animal: if this be true, the Frenchman is more of a man than all others; he is man *par excellence*." This ironical remark of Montesquieu's applied with full force to the Parisians of his time. Sociability was a smiling tyrant. When Rousseau decided to seek solitude, he created consternation among his acquaintances: he had committed the unpardonable sin, which only incipient madness could explain.

By "society" we should not understand in this case a definite and exclusive set. Society had no single center, and no recognized hierarchy. The Court was more numerous and more lavish than ever; but, uncontrolled by the King, it had become a mob, divided into shifting cliques which were warring for spoils. It could do much harm, but it could not lead. "Society" simply means conversation. Wherever people gathered informally and talked,—in a public garden, in the pit of a theatre, in a coffee house, in a club, in a drawing-room,—there a new cell of society came into being. Between a chance conjunction of idlers in the Palais-Royal Gardens, and the exclusive salon of Madame du Deffand, there was apparently an abyss: but between the most remote circles, there existed innumerable channels of communication. The rumour that originated among the newsmongers of *La Petite Provence* (a sheltered spot in the Tuileries Gardens) would be discussed the same evening in an aristocratic company; the song that amused the Pont-Neuf would at once proceed to the Faubourg St. Germain; and, conversely, an epigram whispered under a crystal chandelier would find its way, with mysterious swiftness, to the workshops of the Faubourg St. Antoine. Paris, high and low, was curiously cohesive in those days. In spite of social barriers, there existed a free-masonry of wit and public interest, which the Revolution, industry, science, democracy, have actually weakened and all but destroyed. It was that unorganized and invisible empire that was called Society.

Each of the public parks and promenades in Paris was a forum. Something of the kind survives in London, where Hyde Park, of a Sunday afternoon, offers such a picturesque collection of apostles,—cranks and fanatics, mystics and demagogues. But the usual method in the Paris of the ancient régime was conversation rather than oration. A subversive speaker may easily be jailed: a rumour plays hide-and-seek with the police. Each of these places had a specialty. At the Luxembourg, the favourite topic was literature; at the Tuileries, society gossip and foreign affairs; at the Palais-Royal, home politics; in the Cloister of the Cordeliers, destined to harbour one of the most radical clubs at the time of the Revolution, advanced opinions were expressed, according to police reports, as early as 1725. La Bruyère in his *Characters*, Montesquieu in his *Persian Letters*, Mercier in his *Tableau of Paris*, have sketched for us the physiognomy of the newsmonger or *nouvelliste*. There were *nouvellistes* of all kinds and degrees, from mere idlers and famished adventurers to respectable bourgeois, retired officers, priests and noblemen. Some, like "Bonhomme Métra" under Louis XVI, wielded a sort of recognized authority and were long remembered. Most of the "Philosophers" of the period, and later most of the revolutionary leaders, frequented these open-air clubs. The storming of the Bastille was decided among the *nouvellistes* of the Palais-Royal. The glimpses that we catch of these meetings make us realize the inadequacy of written documents, even for such a recent and well-known period as the eighteenth century. We feel that political consciousness grew to a large extent under the trees of the Paris gardens: yet these discussions could leave no definite records, and they form in history an element at the same time essential and imponderable.

Paris is not in "sunny France"—a phrase the irony of which was bitterly felt by our soldiers during the Great War; many months, in the capital, are bleak, and there is not one that may not be rainy. So the Parisians can not live out of doors as did the ancient Greeks and Romans. Impromptu clubs under cover were provided by the Cafés. The coffee house originated in the seventeenth century; but the eighteenth was its Augustan age. An Italian founded the *Procope:* as the Comédie Française was then located opposite, the house was long an active literary center. It was the Procope that introduced ices into France, a specialty in which it was later supplanted by Tortoni. Under the Second Empire (which now seems to us the Ancient Régime!), the Procope had an aftermath of influence and glory: radical students flocked to its rather dingy rooms, and listened to the vociferations of an unkempt young lawyer by the name of Léon Gambetta. At the *Régence*, the chief attraction was chess: but, for whatever purpose Parisians may congregate, talk will invariably be the best of the feast. Diderot and his crew of Encyclopædists were pillars of the cafés; and in Diderot's spirited sketch, *Rameau's Nephew*, we have what seems almost a stenographic report of the dazzling and cynical conversation in vogue at the cafés. A café was literally a *coffee* house in those days: with the substitution of beer and absinthe for "the beverage that Vergil lacked and Voltaire adored," a charming chapter in the history of French culture came to an end.

The organized Club is an English institution, and developed much later in Paris than in London. If its aim was social, it was felt to be an absurdity, a heresy: why deprive society of its *raison d'être* and chief ornament, woman? If it went into politics, it offered too easy a target to a suspicious police. From 1724, Abbé Alary gathered his friends, every Saturday from five to eight; as his apartment was on the mezzanine floor of President Hénault's palatial residence, the group was known as *Cercle de l'Entresol*. Abbé de St. Pierre, the lovable and Utopian reformer, who had denied to Louis XIV the title of Great, and proposed to organize "Perpetual Peace," was one of its chief oracles, and Montesquieu was a member. Cardinal Fleury, timorous rather than tyrannical, had the *Entresol* closed. Genuine political clubs were not to thrive in France until 1782, when, under English influences, one was founded by the Duke of Orleans. Immediately before the Revolution, they prospered exceedingly; and France, during the Terror, was actually subjected to the dictatorship of a club, the Jacobins.[1]

Public opinion, struggling for consciousness, found in the drama a powerful instrument. A theatre was an open club, and the most democratic there was. Not only did the common people have their own spectacles in the farces at the fair, particularly that of St. Laurent's; but they also thronged the *Théâtre Français*. A playhouse was an epitome of society: on the very stage, separated from the actors by a gilded railing, sat the young bloods of the aristocracy (this practice, so detrimental to stage illusion, was not abolished until 1759); in the boxes, the social elite, the nobility, the rich bourgeois; in the pit, all those —and they were innumerable in Paris—to whom the language of the classics was not a sealed book. The spectators in the pit were not seated. This uncomfortable custom made that part of the audience, thus jammed together, at the same time more responsive and more irresponsible. A joke, a jibe, a biting allusion, could be

[1] Free-Masonry, in its modern form also an importation from England, played to some extent the role of a liberal club. Cf. pp. 291-292.

hurled from the pit, and the offender, in the confusion of
laughter, applause or protest, would duck under the sea
of heads and elude the police. Thus the drama played to
some extent the part of our political meetings: allusions
were found even in Racine's *Athalie*.

The Regency went wild over the drama, which had been
frowned upon by Madame de Maintenon; and Voltaire,
who remained to his dying day the incarnation of the
Regency spirit, loved the stage in every capacity, as a
playwright, as an actor, as a spectator. He realized what
a unique opportunity for the propagation of ideas this
gathering of twelve or fifteen hundred people offered him;
and he deliberately turned the stage into a philosophical
pulpit. In his very first play, *Œdipus* (1718), he already
aims his shafts at the clergy: "Priests are not what the
foolish masses think: all their science reposes on our cre-
dulity." In *Zaïre* (1732), he preaches tolerance—or is it
indifference? "On the banks of the Ganges I should have
been a slave to false gods; in Paris a Christian; here I am
a Moslem." In *Mahomet*—a safe target—he denounces
the deceptions practiced by religious impostors, and the
fanaticism of their disciples (1742) ; in *Mérope,* he denies
the claims of an hereditary aristocracy: "He who serves
his country worthily needs no ancestors"; and he justifies
in advance the parvenu Emperor, the son of the Revolution: "The first king was but a fortunate soldier" (1745).
As he grew more absorbed in the philosophical struggle,
his plays became more openly propaganda tracts in the
form of versified dialogues.

Voltaire was not alone in using the stage for such a
purpose; even Marivaux, the delicate and sophisticated
analyst of love, is not averse to a "philosophical" touch
in the midst of his badinage. Nivelle de la Chaussée created that lamentable hybrid, the "lachrymose comedy":
but he made it a comedy with a purpose, the distant forerunner of the "problem play," and he denounced *The
Prejudice in Fashion* (1735) with the same earnestness
with which Brieux seeks to enlighten and uplift our contemporaries. Diderot's "middle-class tragedies," *The*

Natural Son (1757), *The Father of the Family* (1758),
were social manifestoes: not kings alone, but honest, hard-
working men, deserve to be glorified on the stage. The
same doctrine is preached, with much greater success, by
his modest disciple Sedaine, in *The Philosopher Without
Knowing It* (1765), an exaltation of the Third Estate a
quarter of a century before Siéyès. The wounded patriotism of France, betrayed by a preposterous government,
found vent in the success of *The Siege of Calais*, by Du
Belloy (1765). The drama is preeminently a social art:
Rousseau, in his rebellion against artificial society, did
not fail to reserve a very special curse for the stage; and
nothing did more to envenom the inevitable quarrel between him and Voltaire. But, in spite of Rousseau, the
drama retained its prestige and intensified its action up
to the very end of the ancient régime. The performance,
after long delays, of Beaumarchais's *Marriage of Figaro*
(1784) was a victory against the tottering world of privilege; and the tocsin that sounded so melodramatically in
M-J. Chénier's *Charles IX* or *The School for Kings*
(1789) was said to toll the knell of absolutism.

II

The Salon is not, therefore, the only Temple of Society; but it shows society in its perfection, and the eighteenth century saw the unquestioned reign of the Salon.
We do not forget the great part played by the Hôtel de
Rambouillet in refining manners and over-refining style;
Preciosity had its points when the Précieuses were such
as Madame de Lafayette and Madame de Sévigné; and
the famous Hôtel, which had sponsored the thin reputation of Voiture, was able also to acknowledge the glory
of Corneille. Still, the sphere of the seventeenth-century
Salon was limited. The greatest writers did not bow to
its power: indeed, with Molière, they might take a decided
stand against it. During the personal reign of Louis
XIV, after 1661, the Court, greatest of all Salons, threw
all the rest into the shade.

In the eighteenth century, on the contrary, the influence of the Salon is multiplied and intensified. The Court no longer is the sole center of social power: indeed, it becomes comparatively unimportant. There are minor courts, like those of the Duchess of Maine at Sceaux, or of the Grand Prior, Vendôme, at the Temple: but the charming business of "entertaining" was not the monopoly of princes. The nobility, high and low, nobility of the sword and nobility of the gown, did their share. The financiers had their Salons also: and as the hosts were wealthy far above the average of the older classes, freer from prejudices, compelled by limitations from above to extend their social circles into new realms, their gatherings were unusually rich in interest. We shall see how a mere bourgeoise, Madame Geoffrin, succeeded in becoming one of the social powers, not in Paris only, but in Europe.

The Salon is not a literary or a political institution: the pleasure of meeting congenial acquaintances is its essential aim: *Philosophy* is a by-product. Many of the Salons were not "philosophical" at all. A pleasing little curtain-raiser, *The Circle, or the Fashionable Evening*, by Poinsinet de Sivry, gives us the tone of these parties: we have heard more profound talk in Texas. Conversation was then truly "Art for Art's Sake": the subject mattered little, provided the proper tone of airy courtesy be maintained. If a secondary purpose existed, it was flirtation: the highly expert fencing of wits so well reported by Marivaux, in which, after a long assault, a conventional heart of red cloth stitched on your breast might be touched by a capped foil. Society did not allow itself to be infected with the pedantry of philosophy: it was philosophy that was tinged with what may be called the pedantry of society—a tone of artificial levity, a gesture of apology for every lapse into seriousness. It was this tone that Montesquieu adopted to perfection in his *Persian Letters;* and the habit so clung to him that even in his vast and solid masterpiece, *De L'Esprit des Lois* (On the Spirit of Laws), we too often find *De L'Esprit sur les Lois* (Witticisms about Laws).

Eighteenth-century literature, it has often been re-marked, is but "written conversation." Hence its accessi-bility, and also its apparent shallowness. Frequently that mask of smiling ease covered much earnestness and power: but posterity is pardonable in judging a period by the attitude it assumes. It is almost impossible to be fair with the age of Voltaire: so much of its activity was spent in conversations that have evaporated for ever. And even when records exist, they can not be fully adequate: con-versation is a constant give and take, and requires a par-ticular atmosphere. We can hardly understand the repu-tation of famous wits like Piron, Chamfort, Rivarol. Their best epigrams have no inner glow; they were jewels cut to catch and reverberate the light that was about them; the light is out and the sparkle is gone. We feel that we have only vestiges of the great ebullient force that was Diderot; and we can not sufficiently thank the Fates that kept Voltaire so long away from Paris, thus com-pelling him to write much of the wit and wisdom that otherwise he would merely have talked.

It was in the Salon of the Marquise de Lambert that the new type was first seen in its perfection. Born in 1647, the Marquise had lived through the great days of Louis XIV, when the traditions of the Hôtel de Rambouillet were still unforgotten. She was an energetic woman who, on her husband's death, had to fight, and fought success-fully, in order to keep in her hands the management of her estate. It was not until 1710 that her Salon was fairly launched; the waning prestige of the Court made that success possible; and she remained a power until she died, in 1733. Even through the worst days of the Regency, Madame de Lambert succeeded in preserving, in her gath-erings, a tone of scrupulous respectability. Card-play-ing, the sole purpose of many social circles, was rigor-ously banned from her drawing-rooms. On Tuesday, she entertained the aristocracy; on Wednesday, the men of letters; but, between the two sets, there were many chan-nels of communication.

The Academy was one. It had never been purely a learned body: in the eighteenth century, its social character was more clearly emphasized than ever before or since. The Academy itself was a Salon, or rather a club, where talented commoners, magistrates, noblemen could meet, in a dignified and friendly atmosphere, and on a footing of strict equality. A Duclos (1704–1772), a mere adventurer of letters, whose thin reputation had grown mainly in coffee houses and drawing-rooms, was able successfully to withstand the claims of a Prince de Clermont, a Marshal de Belle-Isle, who expected special privileges within the Academy in virtue of their rank. As women could not become Academicians, they took their revenge by making academicians—oftentimes far less worthy of the distinction than themselves. It was feminine favour that made Abbé de Bernis an Immortal at twenty-nine, just as it was his pretty verses on Madame de Pompadour's dimples that opened to him the highest positions in the state.[1] The Salon of Madame de Lambert was called the ante-chamber of the Academy; the name was afterwards applied to the little circle of Julie de Lespinasse; and the tradition of hostesses as powers behind the academic armchair has been preserved to our very day.

Fontenelle was an assiduous visitor of Madame de Lambert's, as well as an Academician—nay, a triple Academician. President Hénault (1685–1770) was a member of the same group. There is perhaps no better example of the Society spirit in the eighteenth century. Wealthy, brilliant, a leader of fashion, a master of wit, an epicure, the President made himself famous with his madrigals, his songs and his good dinners. But like his friend Voltaire, he had his serious side. He seems to have given some attention to the duties of his profession; and he wrote, among a number of legal, historical and even dramatic works, a *Chronological Epitome* which was one of the most successful books of the time. He adorned many Salons, including his own, as well as two Academies.

Madame de Lambert was eminently respectable: so was

---

[1] Bernis even became a Cardinal: but it was against the desire of his former protectress, Madame de Pompadour; and he redeemed the levity of his early career in the course of a long and honourable life.

Madame de Tencin, after her stormy and somewhat prolonged youth was over. A nun who grew weary of the
cloister, she was as resolute an adventuress as we find in
the chronicles of society. She was charming, and determined to make profitable use of her charms. The Regent
was one of her conquests: but, as he refused to mix up
love affairs and politics, she transferred her affections to
the all-powerful Dubois. She gambled successfully during the feverish days of Law's "System." She and her
brother, well assorted, played into each other's hands with
a touching sense of family loyalty: Tencin ultimately became a Cardinal. As an incident in her wild career, Madame de Tencin gave to the world Jean Le Rond, known
as d'Alembert, the mathematician and encyclopædist;
but, as she abandoned him at birth, the world and
d'Alembert very properly refrained from showing her
any gratitude. It is a redeeming point in Louis XV that
her very name "made his flesh creep," even at the time
when she numbered Pope Benedict XIV among her cor-
respondents. Yet she had become a gracious and thoughtful hostess, and early scandals were hushed into polite
oblivion. "A most excellent woman," said Chamfort after
a visit—"Yes," Abbé Trublet replied: "if she had to give
you poison, she would see to it that it was properly sweet-
ened." Fontenelle, the spoilt centenarian, regretted her:
"She always gave me my favourite dishes," he sighed at
the news of her death.

Like Madame de Tencin, Madame du Deffand had her
fling in the riotous days of the Regency. She too re-
formed, and, in 1739, opened her Salon, which immediately attained great prestige. President Hénault, the
universal favourite, was devoted to her, and visited her
every day. The aristocracy of all Europe sought admis-
sion into the charmed circle of her society. Madame du
Deffand was not one of your self-effacing hostesses: no
woman of the eighteenth century had a sharper wit. Her
epigrams and her letters would do credit to Voltaire himself: indeed, Voltaire respected her as an equal. She had
no spark, however, of the reforming zeal that burned in

the Patriarch; she remained, until her death in 1780, cool, aristocratic, somewhat cynical. For the enthusiasm and the Romantic eloquence of Rousseau, she had nothing but contempt. Sentiment, which she spurned, was destined to win a cruel revenge. When she was nearly seventy, and blind, she actually fell in love with Horace Walpole, a middle-aged worldling, not to say a fop. Walpole was too clever not to appreciate the keen intellect and the splendid social position of Madame du Deffand; but, mortally afraid of ridicule, he hardly knew how to acknowledge her strange and belated passion.

III

Madame du Deffand had a companion and assistant, Julie de Lespinasse, who, without birth, wealth or beauty, was fascinating. She proved such an attraction in Madame du Deffand's Salon that she felt able, and wanted, to rule a circle of her own. The most trusted friends of the house would meet in Julie's private apartment, before the Marquise was ready to receive them. When Madame du Deffand discovered this secret rivalry, a bitter quarrel broke out. Julie left her irate protectress, and, without resources, managed to set up a modest Salon. To Madame du Deffand's intense disgust, she was followed in her secession by many notable members of the group. The loss that was most sharply felt was that of d'Alembert, who had been a very special protégé of the Marquise's. Now d'Alembert became the chief ornament of Julie's upstart drawing-room, and made it the social headquarters of the Encyclopædists.

D'Alembert was in love with Julie, with more ardour than was to be expected from his cool, intellectual nature; but he believed that she was all intellect, and far above the common weaknesses of the heart. Neither the cloister, nor the Salon, neither mysticism nor "Enlightenment" can alter the essential traits of human nature: time was to reveal that the brilliant, philosophical Julie could love as ardently, as foolishly, as tragically, as any Romantic heroine: but, alas! not her devoted d'Alembert.

Madame Geoffrin, at fourteen, married a wealthy man-ufacturer of forty-eight, and, for seventeen years, seemed satisfied with her unassuming household. Then she began her social career, under the leadership of Madame de Tencin; and, with marvelous pertinacity, the modest bourgeoise succeeded in establishing the most brilliant and the most substantial social empire of the time. Monsieur Geoffrin, of course, was left far behind in that strenuous climb: when he died, the *habitués* learned for the first time who the plain gentleman was, who used to sit so silently at the lower end of the table. Madame Geoffrin could not be presented at the French Court: but she numbered Catherine of Russia and Gustavus III of Sweden among her friends; and the King of Poland, Stanislaus Ponia-towski, with many other celebrities in Europe, loved to call her "*Maman.*" She never was dazzlingly beautiful; she was not witty, like Madame du Deffand, nor magnetic, like Julie de Lespinasse. But she was tactful: she knew how to give rein to the boldest minds, yet to check them gently with her favourite phrase: "*Voilà qui est bien!*"—"That will do!"—when their paradoxes went beyond the limits of good taste; she was kind, in spite of her calculat-ing ambition; and she could afford to be open-handed. She had a special day for men of letters, and one for art-ists: she was among the first to discover the social possi-bilities of painters, sculptors and musicians. Boucher, La Tour, Van Loo, were among her friends; Rameau played on her *clavecin;* and, of course, she scooped the young prodigy Mozart when he came to Paris.

In all these Salons except Julie de Lespinasse's, the main purpose was social. Philosophers were welcome; they were even lionized, since philosophy was in fashion; but the hostesses did not fully commit themselves to their party. We have seen that Julie, on account of her friend-ship with d'Alembert, was more actively engaged in the great intellectual battle; Madame d'Epinay, through

Grimm and Diderot, was also identified with the Encyclopædist group. She was Rousseau's benefactress: personal
grievances, as well as divergences of opinion, turned them
into enemies. Her *Memoirs*, freely edited, and his *Confessions*, were documents in the long and bitter quarrel.

Baron d'Holbach (1723–1789) is better remembered
for the excellence of his dinners than for his materialistic
System of Nature (1770); he provided sumptuously for
such guests as Buffon, d'Alembert, Diderot, Helvetius,
Grimm, Raynal, Marmontel, Condillac, Turgot: he was
called the Philosopher's Butler, which is glory enough for
any German baron. Helvetius (1715–1771) was likewise
wealthy and hospitable. A tax-gatherer with a heart, a
plutocrat with a mind, he, like d'Holbach, contributed
a famous book (*On Intellect*), as well as lavish entertainment, to the philosophical campaign. Madame Helvetius
was a charming woman, who, after her husband's death,
kept up her connection with such men as Condillac, d'Holbach, Jefferson: it is said that both Franklin and Turgot
wanted to marry her. If she was fond of philosophers,
she was no less fond of animals, and her distinguished
friends found her house cluttered up with cats and dogs,
hens and birds. The last of the great "Philosophical"
salons was that of Necker; Madame Necker proved that
a devoted wife could also be a very successful hostess.
Young Germaine Necker, who was to be Madame de
Staël, was brought up in the exhilarating atmosphere of
Parisian society just before the Revolution. She yearned
incurably for that lost Paradise: to keep up the great
tradition of the liberal salon remained her dearest wish.
But the Revolution broke out; and when it ended, One
was in control, who could only command, not converse.

IV

All these salons were in Paris, whose social dictatorship
had become absolute, not in France only, but in Europe.

The provinces, however, were not somnolent. Beside the court of Stanislaus Leczynski at Nancy and at Luné-ville,[1] there were many little capitals, with their "States," a formal assembly which at least brought the notables together, with their Parliaments and with their Academies. It is significant that the award of a prize by the Academy of Dijon made Rousseau, hitherto a struggling musician, famous overnight: and the Academy of Dijon was only one of many. Social life needs peace and plenty; and, in spite of a chaotic government, in spite of disasters beyond the frontiers, France enjoyed internal tranquillity, whilst, in the cities at least, there was a surprizing degree of prosperity. Nantes and Bordeaux, for instance, show to the present day architectural traces of their wealth and taste under the reign of Louis XV. So there was in provincial France a rich and enlightened bourgeoisie, with that most precious of luxuries, intelligent leisure.

Between the capital and the provinces, there was frequent intercourse. Traveling was desperately slow according to modern standards—a fortnight from Paris to Marseilles—and, in the public coaches, woefully uncomfortable. But for the rich, who had their own uncrowded conveyances, the yearly trip to Paris might very well be a leisurely picnic. Alfred de Vigny, immediately after the era of railroads had opened, could very well sigh for the unhurried charm of the open road:

> *"On n'entendra jamais piaffer sur une route*
> *Le pied vif du cheval sur les pavés en feu:*
> *Adieu, voyages lents, bruits lointains qu'on écoute,*
> *Le rire du passant, les retards de l'essieu,*
> *Les détours imprévus des pentes variées,*
> *Un ami rencontré, les heures oubliées,*
> *L'espoir d'arriver tard dans un sauvage lieu."*

The automobile has restored some of the conditions

---

[1] The dethroned King of Poland, father of the Queen of France, had retained, by courtesy, his royal title, and been given for life the Duchy of Lorraine.

which Vigny was regretting: particularly "*les retards de l'essieu*" and "*les détours imprévus.*"

So, although the aristocracy was urbanized, and indeed excessively metropolitan, its members had not lost the habit of spending a few weeks on their country estates, and many a country gentleman came at least once a year to Paris. Buffon belonged to Montbard in Burgundy as well as to the capital; and Montesquieu, who lived mostly in his château at La Brède, was at home in the salons of Bordeaux as well as in those of the Parisian Faubourgs. As for Voltaire, he was ubiquitous, and wherever he was, at Cirey or at Lunéville, at Sans-Souci or at Ferney, he was the Ambassador of Paris, he was Paris.

Furthermore, these people corresponded enormously, correspondence supplying the needs now filled by the telegraph, the telephone, the picture postcard and the daily press. Even the friends who met nearly every day in the same salons exchanged notes in the intervening hours. Voltaire's correspondence is by far his masterpiece: but Voltaire was only the first among his peers. The formal literature of the eighteenth century, however intelligent and tasteful, is apt to strike us as second-rate: it is pseudo-classical, without the plenitude and majesty of the preceding age. But if we open a collection of letters, we are not among periwigged ghosts: we listen to courtly, cheerful, incisive voices; we catch the half-mocking curl of the lip, the keen, not unkindly glint of the eye, that La Tour was able to picture in his marvelous pastels.

Correspondence became, not merely a pleasure and a social duty, but a business. Noblemen, feeling themselves exiled in Austria, Poland or Sweden, craved for news from the Earthly Paradise on the banks of the Seine. Grimm, for instance, assisted by Diderot and Madame d'Epinay, conducted a professional "Correspondence" and had among his subscribers many foreign princes. The recipients were sworn to secrecy, and the collection of these letters was not published until 1812. Such secrecy had its perils. The correspondence trade might be plied by adventurers of a much coarser type than Grimm;

and it offered, in unscrupulous hands, admirable opportunities for slander and blackmail.

Art, under Louis XIV, had been overwhelmingly monarchical: there was no place in the sun except for Versailles or the Louvre. Under an absentee King, Society picked up the neglected scepter. The stiff majesty of the seventeenth century disappeared: a style was evolved which created a perfect framework for the intelligent pleasures of the salon. In this domain also, the reaction against the splendid rigidity of the previous reign went too far. Even architecture, the soberest of all the arts, had its moment of licence and almost of debauchery: all lines had to be twisted and broken into elaborate curves. But the most extreme examples of *Rocaille* or *Rococo* ornamentation were decency itself, compared with the riotous developments of the style in Germany and Italy. The influence of Madame de Pompadour, a woman of classical strength of will and bourgeois common sense, was decidedly on the side of a more temperate taste. The result, about the middle of the century, was an art which, for interior decoration, remains unrivalled. The French themselves have grown weary of the everlasting Louis XV drawing room; they have tried to escape from it into the less hackneyed regions of the exotic, the barbaric, the decadent, and the nondescript. But the Louis Quinze style, in its delicate cheerfulness, is an imperishable as the smile of Voltaire.

Curiously enough, the earliest and most perfect exponent of this eighteenth-century spirit, the most Parisian of painters, as it would seem, was a Fleming, Watteau (1684–1721); and he developed the delightful resources of his art in the gloom of Louis XIV's decline. There is no absurdity in this double paradox. The reaction which broke out in 1715 had been brewing for over a decade: Watteau was expressing, not the professed ideal of his time, but its secret longing. Flanders is a land of jollity and high colour: in Watteau, the exuberant animal life of Rubens is refined, subdued through Parisian influences, toned down by the national background of despair. Even during the Regency, Watteau never became coarse in his depiction of pleasure. His silken mincing puppets, whilst they dance or play the lute in dreamy gardens, or embark for the vaporous isle of Cytherea, "hardly seem to believe in their happiness":

> *Tout en chantant sur le mode mineur*
> *L'amour vainqueur et la vie opportune,*
> *Ils n'ont pas l'air de croire à leur bonheur,*
> *Et leur chanson se mêle au clair de lune. . . .*

His rivals and immediate successors, Lancret and Pater, were the graceful interpreters of the Regency spirit. Nattier, in his semi-mythological portraits, combined delightfully a remnant of classical formality with the frivolity of the prevailing mood. The brothers Van Loo were also great favourites. But the best representatives of the age were La Tour and Boucher. We have already alluded to La Tour's rich collection of pastel portraits, the best known of which are Voltaire's in his early maturity, and Madame de Pompadour's. Whoever is tempted to blaspheme the eighteenth century should look again at these eager, earnest, cheerful faces. If we could extract from La Tour's works a composite picture, we should entitle it: The Genius of Polite Society. Boucher reveals a more questionable aspect of the Pompadour era: with some injustice, it is rather better remembered than the intellectual keenness so well rendered by La Tour. Watteau's personages were embarking for the Isle of Love, lost in a silvery mist: those of Boucher have reached the end of their journey. There is nothing actually improper or even suggestive in his mythological or pastoral scenes, as there was in the works of many minor painters and engravers of the time: but his art is a frank deification of pleasure. The background of Boucher's pictures is frequently conventional; his drawing is not above reproach; there is about his soft and luminous goddesses

none of the wistful dreaminess that makes Watteau a
great poet of love: yet it would be pedantry or worse to
dismiss him with contempt. He stands for the extreme
maturity of unmitigated hedonism. Louis XV was to follow the creed to its logical end: but society and art had
already rebelled against it; and we shall see that, whilst
in the fifties Boucher had lost none of his vogue, the success of Chardin and Greuze heralded a different spirit.

CHAPTER III

"PHILOSOPHY"

I. "Philosophy," destructive and constructive. Active Humanism. Practical sense.

II. English Influence at every turn. Montesquieu and the British Constitution.

III. Voltaire. Many-sided activity. Conservatism. Fight against "L'Infâme"; i. e., fanaticism.

IV. Science. Buffon. The Encyclopædia. Diderot.

V. Primitivism vs. Progressivism: Rousseau.

I

THE eighteenth century is known as the age of "Philosophy," "Enlightenment," or "Reason." Every one of these terms has to be used with a capital and with inverted commas. The one most current at the time, "Philosophy," is also the most ambiguous. If by philosophy we mean metaphysical speculation, then few epochs were more devoid of the philosophical spirit than the time of Voltaire. No Frenchman of note, in the eighteenth century, cared to rear one of those somber dreamfabrics, or to write one of those obscure symbolical poems that go by the name of "philosophies." Voltaire and Hegel are at the very antipodes of human thought. If the word "philosopher" evokes in our minds a picture of simplicity and austerity, a Stoic proudly draped in his cloak, a Cynic casting away the last vestige of luxury, then Rousseau might deserve the name: but what about the witty, sociable, pleasure-loving contemporaries and protégés of Madame de Pompadour? If philosophy connotes an amused or lofty detachment from mundane affairs, the sensitive, combative, hard-working Encyclopædists, as well as Rousseau and Voltaire, must be ruled out.

An eighteenth century "Philosopher" was essentially a critic of abuses and a promoter of reforms. G. B. Shaw and H. G. Wells would be recognized by Voltaire as fellow "philosophers," and the ghost of the *Encyclopædia* can be seen vaguely flitting through such American periodicals as *The New Republic* and *The Nation*.

The philosophy of the eighteenth century is not a system, but a spirit. The essence of that spirit had been clearly expressed by two immediate forerunners of the age, Bayle and Fontenelle: "Errors are none the better for being old"; "Authority has ceased to have more weight than reason." The "Enlightenment" therefore is not simply "modern"—every period was modern once; it is "modernistic." It refuses to accept blindly the dictates of tradition. Thoughts, beliefs, institutions, must stand on their own merits in terms of to-day: if they seek to elude the test, they are ruled out as prejudices, superstitions and abuses. The eighteenth century is frankly iconoclastic: not only does it freely indulge in destructive criticism, but it revels in it. The absurd contrast between obsolete claims and actual values is the source of ironical amusement rather than righteous indignation. Louis XV, who was not wholly impervious to the spirit of his reign, chuckled at the thought that he was "the Lord's Anointed."

It is obvious, however, that the spirit of the eighteenth century was not sheer nihilism with a gay mask of flippancy. Much had to be blasted, no doubt, and the débris had to be cleared away: not always an easy task, and frequently a dangerous one. But the Enlightenment, on the whole, is positive, and without paradox may be defined as "Faith, Hope, and Charity": faith in human reason, hope in human progress, charity—in the Pauline sense—under the name of "philanthropy" and *"bienfaisance."* The age, which is so frequently labeled cynical, and which was to end in blood, was thoroughly humane, much more humane than the Renaissance or the century of Louis XIV. Its first exponent, the Regent, was not the best of men by any means, but he was among the most kindly. Marivaux, the delicate trifler, could find such a phrase as this: "In this world, we have to be too kind in order to be kind

enough." Montesquieu said: "I never could see tears without being moved"; and there was in sardonic Voltaire
himself a quivering horror of cruelty.

The *Reason* whose advent was hailed by Fontenelle was
no longer the reasonableness of the preceding period:
Cartesianism had done its work, and the age of self-satis-
fied intellectual compromise was past. But neither was it
the cult of abstract thought and of the geometric method.
Taine, a rigid logician himself, has given the caricature
rather than the formula of the classical spirit, when he
denounced it as the love of generalities divorced from
practical realities. Taine, like all honest and consistent
thinkers, has done the world a great service: he has ex-
plored a blind alley to the very end, and it is unlikely that
his error will be repeated.

We have already noted the evident aversion of the
eighteenth century for metaphysical systems. Montesquieu, Buffon, Diderot, had as good minds as the Germans who, half a century or a century later, were so dex-
terously to juggle with the Absolute: they were restrained,
not by mediocrity, but by common sense. The French
"Philosophers," up to Rousseau at any rate, were always
exposing definite evils and proposing definite remedies:
Voltaire's programme was intensely practical. We shall
see that all "philosophers" also took intelligent interest in
science, and not exclusively in the abstract science of
mathematics; they were fonder of observation and experimentation than of mere reasoning; their master was Bacon
at least as much as Descartes. Finally, they did not live
in the artificial solitude of their library: they haunted
courts, drawing-rooms, academies, coffee-houses. They
were in constant touch with the general public, with men
of affairs, with magistrates, with ministers, even with
rulers: would to God the "Radicals" of to-day had as
good a chance! Such contact would prove fatal to empty
theories. Contemporary America is still living on the
heritage of the Enlightenment: and no one has ever accused her of lacking practical sense.

II

"Philosophy" is England's gift to France. No doubt
the movement could be explained without taking foreign
influences into account: Emile Faguet, for instance, managed to write a brilliant chapter on Montesquieu with
only the most casual references to Great Britain. The
Renaissance would have come, even though Italy had disappeared from the map; the Enlightenment was on its
way, and could not have been denied, even though France
had continued to ignore the culture of her northern neigh-
bour. But the Renaissance did assume a strong Italian
tinge, and the Enlightenment is almost inseparable from
Anglomania.

Strangely enough, that age in which the two nations
borrowed most freely from each other was also one of
bitterest political hostility between them. From 1688 to
1815, there raged an almost uninterrupted series of
Anglo-French conflicts, which has aptly been called "the
Third Hundred-Years'-War." Between campaigns—nay,
during campaigns—English gentlemen hastened to the
Paris salons, where they found the most courteous welcome. It is hard to realize that Horace Walpole or Gib-
bon, in France, were "enemies." Fashions in clothes, car-
riages, sports, gardens, literature, science, politics, constantly crossed and re-crossed the Channel. On the whole,
France received more than she gave. Politically and economically, England was rising fast. Material ascendancy
is not sufficient to ensure cultural prestige: but, if deserved and prolonged, it greatly contributes even to spiritual influence. It may be added that, in so borrowing,
France was getting back her own: for England had never
been so classical as she was then, nor, since the Middle
Ages, so Frenchified. London and Paris in the eighteenth
century were close enough to be mutually intelligible, different enough to be stimulating. The masters of French
thought were no longer Montaigne, Descartes and Pascal,
but Bacon, Locke, Newton, and the "Deists," Toland,

Collins, Woolston, Tindal, Shaftesbury. Similarly, a
hundred years later, the models of the French poets are
not to be sought in the French tradition, but in the works
of Shakespeare, Byron, Walter Scott and "Ossian."

Marivaux wrote a French *Spectator;* Montesquieu discovered the British Constitution; Voltaire was not Voltaire until he had breathed the air of London; Abbé
Prévost, the author of *Manon Lescaut,* translated,
adapted and imitated abundantly the British novels of
the time. Buffon traveled with the young Duke of Kings-
ton; his favourite authors were Milton and Richardson;
and a portrait of Newton adorned his study. Diderot,
the most original of the French Philosophers, borrowed
from Chambers the idea of his *Encyclopædic Dictionary,*
and from Lillo his theory of the middle class tragedy.
The thought of Rousseau is steeped in English deism; his
love for nature found sympathetic echoes in the French
public, because English influences had already made that
sentiment popular; the epistolary form and the moraliz-
ing spirit of his most successful work, *Julie or the New
Heloise,* were taken from Richardson. In the face of such
patent facts—we have quoted only a few of the most obvious—it seems almost incredible that eighteenth-century
France should have been accused of self-complacency, of
unwillingness to learn from others.

The sprightly daring and the occasional riskiness of the
Persian Letters (1721) hardly indicated that their anonymous author was a provincial magistrate, already Chief
Justice at the Parliament of Bordeaux. Montesquieu
found himself famous overnight. We are never allowed to
forget, even in his gravest studies, that he made his débuts
as a wit, and remained in close touch with the most delightful salons in Paris. But he was much more than a
clever satirist. He gave up the details of procedure, for
which he had little taste; sold his office, and devoted himself to his *magnum opus,* a treatise on comparative legislation, *The Spirit of Laws.* First of all, he traveled for

three years, visiting Austria, Hungary, the different cities
and states of Italy, the Netherlands and England (1728–
1731); then he returned to his country estate, and laboured for seventeen years at his gigantic task: such were
the methods of the "hasty," "shallow" and "flippant"
eighteenth century. When the work appeared in 1748,[1]
its triumph was immediate: twenty editions were absorbed
in as many months. Voltaire said nobly: "Mankind had
lost its titles: M. de Montesquieu has restored them." His
singularly even, full and happy career came to an end in
1755.

Montesquieu was no *a priori* theorist: his work was
based on a long and patient investigation of Europe as it
was in his day, and of all available history. He had no
tendency unduly to simplify the problem: his very title
recognized its complexity: *On the Spirit of Laws, or On
the Relations which must exist between the Laws and the
Constitution of each Government, the Manners, Climate,
Religion, Commerce, etc.* He was no radical: despotism,
the rule of fear, he abhors; but, for a true republic, he
sets such a hard condition (it must be founded on "virtue") that democracy should be ruled out also. His ideal
is a monarchical but not despotic government, based on
the sentiment of honour, and limited by the privileges of
intermediate powers. Like Fénelon and Saint-Simon,
Montesquieu regrets the growth of absolutism under the
Bourbons: in former times, there were checks on the excessive preponderance of the crown. But he is too much
of a historian to indulge in retrospective dreams. He
points to a living ideal: in England, a happy balance has
been attained. This result was reached through the separation and proper adjustment of the three "Powers,"
executive, legislative, and judiciary. It was Montesquieu
who first extracted for the rest of the world an intelligible
scheme out of that chaos of precedents vaguely known as
the British Constitution. If, later, too mechanical a copy

---

[1] The *Considerations on the Grandeur of the Romans and their Decadence,* which may be considered as a detached chapter, came out in
1734.

of the British system was forced upon the French, Montesquieu was not wholly to blame. Had his free and cautious spirit been followed, the elements of a new régime might have been sought in the purely French tradition.

III

Voltaire lived at least nine lives, all full to the brim. He was a keen business man, and amassed a large fortune through numberless speculations. He was an official personage, admitted to the Court of Louis XV and to that of Stanislaus Leczynski, entrusted with semi-official diplomatic missions, a chamberlain of Frederick the Great. He was acknowledged as the greatest writer of his time in the noble and academic branches of literature: his *Henriad* was the most successful approach to a national epic that classical France had known; on the tragic stage, he was acclaimed as the worthy successor of Corneille and Racine. He was, however, infinitely greater in non-academic literature, in madrigals, epigrams, satires, philosophical tales, pamphlets, and especially familiar letters. He was, wherever he went, a brilliant society light, at the Temple or at Sceaux, in London, at Cirey, at Lunéville, at Sans-Souci, at Ferney. He was more than an amateur scientist: his experiments in physics may be of trifling value, but he understood and translated Newton at a time when official savants were still demurring. He was the founder of modern history: the all-embracing history of a civilization in his *Century of Louis XIV*, world history in his *Essay on Manners*, and he did enough serious work in that single line to make his fame secure. He turned into the ideal country squire, the village Providence, the enlightened despot, a Frederick II in miniature. And, at the same time, he had become King Voltaire, the Patriarch, the supreme court of appeal for all victims of injustice and intolerance. In the intervals, he found leisure to squabble meanly about a few cords of wood, to be quarrelsome, absurdly vainglorious, mendacious, scurrilous, indecent—the epitome of an age which could read with delight his unspeakable and tedious *Pucelle*, and, the next moment, shed the noblest tears. When he returned to Paris at eighty-four, dying of course, as he had been all his life, he galvanized even the drowsy Academy; blessed young America in the person of Franklin's grandson and in the name of "God and Liberty"; and was finally killed by a surfeit of popular adoration.

Voltaire was even less of an abstract theorist than Montesquieu: indeed he called Montesquieu sharply to task for venturesome affirmations. He too was a painstaking investigator: his *Charles XII* was not superseded for at least a hundred years; his *Louis XIV* remains a monument of scholarship; and even his *Essay on Manners*, which, of its very nature, could only be a compilation, is at least a very diligent critical abstract of the best secondary authorities. He was singularly conservative: he wanted to destroy abuses, not to overthrow the existing régime. He would have spared the abuses rather than hack blindly at the roots of society: his tolerant philosophy is admirably summed up in his charming apologue: *Babouc, or the World as it goes*. Even in religion, he was no mere scoffer. His theism, somewhat trite to be sure, was undoubtedly sincere. He knew the Bible, appreciated its beauties, and recommended it to Madame du Deffand. "It would be a mistake to consider him as a consistent anti-Christian, anti-Catholic or even anti-clerical. He would probably have risen high in the Anglican hierarchy—and deserved it better than Swift. Although the very obstreperous child of Holy Mother Church, he remained within the fold. He lived and died a Catholic, and his worst pranks are those of a son of the house, not of a stranger. He preserved a curious fondness for his old masters the Jesuits; he corresponded with the Pope and received his blessing; he was made, for some neighbourly service, an honorary member of the Capuchin order, and for a time liked to sign himself: *Friar François, unworthy Capuchin*. He built a Church: *Deo erexit Voltaire*. He took his hat off to processions: 'We are not on

speaking terms, but we salute each other.' He compelled
his vicar by legal means to hear his confession and give
him Easter communion. He desired Christian burial; and
it is said that Madame de Pompadour took it into her
head that he should become a Cardinal—like Dubois and
de Bernis—which would have added a supreme touch to
the whole eighteenth century. Voltaire is an inseparable
part of Catholicism, the *gracioso* of the great Miracle
play, the grinning gargoyle of the eternal cathedral."

What he hated, what he wanted to crush, was *l'Infâme*,
Fanaticism, Protestant fanaticism as well as Catholic
fanaticism. The Rousseauistic fanaticism of Robespierre
would have been abhorrent to him, as it was to his disciple
Anatole France. Virtue he respected, even under the
monk's cowl: pretence and cruelty he could not bear. He
was a fighter, and no fighting can be done without atrocities; he is scarred and battle-stained, but we have profited
by his toils. His work is done: too completely for his
fame, for it takes an effort now to realize how bitterly it
was needed. But even to-day, Voltairian irony remains
a useful weapon to keep in reserve, in case "*l'Infâme*,"
Intolerance, should raise its head again.

IV

Science was then inseparable from "Philosophy." Fontenelle was the first notable example of such an alliance;
Montesquieu read before the Academy of Bordeaux
papers on sundry questions of physics and natural history. Voltaire wrote memoirs for the Academy of Sciences and carried on experiments in collaboration with
Madame du Châtelet. Even Rousseau, whose education
was deplorably haphazard, was a botanist of some distinction, and his disciple Bernardin de Saint-Pierre had some
share in the reorganization of the Paris Botanical Garden.
The living symbol of the place that science had assumed
in French society was Buffon. There had been great scientists in France before him: but their position was, in

a sense, eccentric. For the first time, with Buffon, a scientist conquered a leading place in literature, purely as a scientist.

His life was even simpler, fuller, nobler, than that of Montesquieu. He divided his time between two gardens: his own at Montbard, and the King's Garden—the present Museum of Natural History—of which he was the director. In Paris and in Burgundy, he worked with the same unhasting diligence. Legend chooses to remember him, majestically seated in his study, with elaborate lace cuffs that seem inseparable from his personality, inditing eloquent and somewhat stilted descriptions: "The noblest conquest that man has ever made is that of this proud and superb animal. . . ." This starched and periwigged element does exist in Buffon: Voltaire was not wholly wrong when he said of his *Natural History:* "Not so very natural!" But it is a minor aspect. Buffon was a genuine scientist, a patient observer, an indefatigable experimenter, and, apart from a few purple patches, scrupulously simple and direct in expression. The majesty of his style, in his *Epochs of Nature* for instance, is the majesty of the theme, to which he was not unequal. He reminds us of his fellow Burgundian Bossuet, and, like Bossuet himself, of Biblical grandeur. In spite of a few artificial ornaments, he is a great scientific poet in prose, the modern Lucretius.

Buffon remained aloof from the quarrels of his time: not out of prudent selfishness, but because he was genuinely above the strife, and dwelt in the temples serene. Aloof, not isolated: he was a true representative of the eighteenth century, in which he found himself perfectly at home, and which recognized ungrudgingly his tranquil greatness. He was loaded with official, academic and social honours, which he bore with ease. In his case again, the legend that the eighteenth century was an age of frivolous scoffers breaks down completely. A hard worker like Montesquieu and Voltaire, he was, no less than they, a cautious thinker. He used classifications and hypotheses, without which the accumulation of details could never be transmuted into science: but he used them only as instruments, not as idols. He too was impatient of vague generalities. We may add that among his hypotheses some have proved strangely prophetic. He adumbrated transformism and evolution long before Lamarck and Darwin, and the microbian theory a hundred years before Pasteur.

The extraordinary position acquired by science may also be exemplified by the career of Lavoisier, contractor general of taxes, and founder of modern chemistry; or by the reverend admiration with which Franklin, as a physicist, was received in Paris. This golden age of science was to last until the end of the Empire: the immediate successors of Buffon formed a splendid galaxy round the ruler who himself had sought membership in the Scientific Section of the Institute. Later, the Romantic reaction against the Enlightenment caused a partial eclipse of science as a main factor in national culture. The realistic era, in the eighteen-fifties, brought back the scientific ideal, but in harsher and far less humane form than in the days of Buffon.

In the *Encyclopædia*, all the elements of "Philosophy" are combined: English influences, criticism of abuses and superstitions, desire for reform, love of science, faith in progress. The starting-point was the *Cyclopædia, or Universal Dictionary of Art and Sciences*, of Ephraim Chambers (1728): here again, England was in the lead. A publisher, Lebreton, conducted complicated and not over-scrupulous negotiations for a French adaptation of the work. Finally, a hack-writer, Diderot, who had successfully completed the translation of a *Medical Dictionary*, remained chief editor, and, in 1750, sent out his prospectus. But that bohemian happened to be a man of genius, well acquainted in the "Philosophical" world, and, thanks to him, the *Encyclopædia* assumed a significance not found in its prototype, or in any of its successors.

Merely from the material point of view, Diderot's responsibilities were extremely heavy, and he faced them with matchless courage, industry and success. He contributed many valuable articles himself, on Philosophy and on the Arts and Crafts. He recruited, organized, inspired a notable team of workers. He had to contend with the timidity, and even with the dishonesty, of the publishers. He was constantly exposed to the hostility of the conservatives, and particularly of the Jesuits. Twice the work was condemned: but Diderot's tenacity was never shaken for long. He actually profited by the enmity of the Jesuits, who had powerful enemies at Court: "*Les ennemis de nos ennemis sont nos amis.*" Choiseul and Madame de Pompadour protected the work. Malesherbes, who was entrusted with the official supervision of the book trade, was a powerful friend and even an accomplice. The huge fabric finally reached completion, after more than twenty years (1772): a "monster," a hotchpotch, a veritable harlequin's coat: but the epitome of a singularly active and brilliant civilization.

D'Alembert was at first associated with Diderot as editor-in-chief. His scientific fame, his official standing, the unblemished regularity of his life, lent to the enterprise a tone of respectability which Diderot's bohemianism could not have conferred. D'Alembert wrote the opening *Discourse,* a classification of sciences which expressed with cool lucidity the philosophy of the Enlightenment in its more constructive and more austere aspects. Tired with the profitless worries of his position, he soon left the sole editorship to Diderot.

Among Diderot's other collaborators should be mentioned Marmontel for literature; Quesnay and Turgot for political economy; d'Holbach for chemistry; Daubenton for natural history. The very greatest were enrolled: Montesquieu gave an article on Taste; Voltaire wrote many contributions, which he afterwards collected in his delightful miscellany, *The Philosophical Dictionary.* But above all, Voltaire, with unselfish devotion to the cause, made himself the press-agent, the lobbyist, the "office boy," as he put it, of the *Encyclopædia.* To Rousseau was entrusted the article on Music. Buffon had promised

to write on Nature: but, absorbed in an even larger encyclopædia of his own, his vast *Natural History*, he could
not redeem his pledge. Others, without being active collaborators, were known to be in sympathy with the work,
and are usually counted among the Encyclopædists: Condillac the psychologist, Grimm the cosmopolitan journal-
ist, Helvetius, whose difficulties with the censorship created
trouble for his personal friend Diderot and indirectly for
the *Encyclopædia*. Condorcet had a share in the supple-
mentary volumes. He elaborated a great plan for public
education; and, rising superior to the horrors of the time,
he gave in 1793 his *Sketch of the Progress of the Human Mind*—a noble confession of faith when faith was
indeed the evidence of things unseen.

It is the fate of scientific works to be superseded in less
than a generation; the criticism of abuses is obliterated
by its very success. So the *Encyclopædia* was obsolete
before the end of the ancient régime. Of all the passions,
the learning, the wit that went into its composition, we
find to-day nought but the cold ashes. Carlyle may triumph: the *Encyclopædia* is dead. The figure of Diderot,
however, still stands, of truly heroic size, and unquench-
ably alive. In addition to his formidable labour as book-
seller's drudge, editor, compiler, he managed to scatter
his coarse, cheerful, honest vitality in all possible fields:
in dramatic theory—and practice, alas!—in art-criticism,
in licentious writing, in science, and above all, in philosophy. In all realms of thought, he was as much at
home as when he met Catherine of Russia: in the history
and discussion of ancient doctrines, in the threshing out
of contemporary problems, in the rashest flights of Utopian fancy.

With him again, as with Montesquieu, Voltaire, Buffon,
we are struck with the keen sense of the eighteenth century for practical realities. Diderot, the son of an artisan, studied the trades and crafts with indefatigable
curiosity and care. The plates which illustrate his articles in the *Encyclopædia* are models of usefulness as well

as elegance. They prove once more, against all the clever theorizing of Taine, that the "Philosophers" did not live in a world of abstractions, with their heads in the clouds.

V

In Fontenelle, Montesquieu, Voltaire, faith in science and progress was accompanied by faith in the condition of progress, i. e., society, and in its material sign, i. e., luxury. They were intensely modern men, men of the study and of the drawing-room, exquisitely nurtured and cultured, and not without sophistication. But Nature, primitive Nature, which they were forgetting in their refinement, was to have its revenge.

The germ of this reaction is to be found in the "sophisticates" themselves. They had fearlessly denounced abuses in the name of common sense: but their criticism had struck deeper than they meant to go. Many of the forms of society were manifestly, absurdly wrong: but how many? and how wrong? Montesquieu and Voltaire, among others, had indulged in satires of our civilization from the point of view of a civilization totally different—Persia or Sirius. No doubt their conclusion would have been, not to destroy, but to accept "the world as it goes," a world which they found amusing and comfortable. But the scepticism they had turned against certain traditional aspects of civilization could be turned against civilization as a whole. To the "superstitions" of established religions was opposed the universal simplicity of *natural* religion; to the chaos of customs and arbitrary legislation, the eternal majesty of *natural* law. The appeal to "Nature" against the vagaries of traditions was a commonplace of eighteenth-century philosophy.

In a very literal sense, the life-work and the success of Buffon were signs of this "return to nature." In a more philosophical sense, the movement is best exemplified by Diderot. In Diderot we find again the "Naturalism" of Rabelais, his pantheistic faith in Physis, good Mother Nature, his hatred of Antiphysis. Diderot was a nature-lover in every way. He took interest in the natural sciences, like most of his contemporaries; he had a genuine sense, almost romantic in its intensity, for natural beauty; above all, he trusted, like Rabelais, in the essential goodness of human nature.

There were therefore in the middle of the eighteenth century two streams of thought: PROGRESSIVISM, faith in science, industry, civilization; and PRIMITIV-ISM, faith in unchangeable Nature. They coincided for a long time without conflict. Naturalism was used as a battering-ram against artificial survivals, abuses, superstitions; the destruction of these obstacles would open the way for genuine progress, for a civilization no longer out of harmony with "Nature." Both Progressivism and Primitivism were aspects of "Reason" or "Philosophy"; both had the same enemies: the worship of tradition, Christian orthodoxy.

But the alliance between the two tendencies was precarious, and the possibility of conflict became apparent. Hence the subject proposed, for a prize contest, by the Academy of Dijon in 1749: "*Whether the Restoration of Sciences and Arts* (i. e. civilization, intellectual and material progress) *has tended to corrupt or to purify Manners?*" The theme was stated as a question: this is significant, although we may well believe that the judges would have been satisfied with the standard hymn of praise to Civilization. And Rousseau sprang into fame.

The author was practically unknown—a vagabond who was barely beginning to make his mark as a musician; the Academy of Dijon was a provincial body without any great prestige; the prize-winning discourse was not remarkable for wealth of information, or cogency of thought; and many passages were written with a fulsome eloquence that was at the same time juvenile and antiquated. Yet the response was immediate. It seemed as though a liberating word, long expected, had been uttered at last. Evidently Rousseauism was ready when Rousseau appeared: his success registered a widely spread state of mind. Of the two aspects of "Philosophy," Primitivism, once merely the auxiliary of Progressivism, was coming into its own.

The Philosophers, who were still considering Rousseau as one of themselves, were at the same time delighted with his triumph and vaguely anxious. The wildest paradoxes were welcome, provided they would lead to intelligent compromise: but this bear from Switzerland was too consistent for Parisian comfort. Voltaire, more committed than any one to Progressivism (his *Mondain* is an outspoken defence, not only of civilization, but of the most refined and frailest flower of civilization, luxury), was also the one to recognize the danger most clearly. In his irreconcilable hostility to Rousseau, Voltaire was not urged primarily by his wounded vanity: he felt he was defending the one true Philosophical Church against a heresiarch more dangerous than unbelievers.

Rousseau was conscious that he had struck a mine. The attitude which his success forced upon him was doubly welcome: it conferred glory, and it released him from uncongenial trammels. His irregular education, his spiritual solitude, perhaps some physiological weakness, had made him unsociable. He was both insanely proud, and morbidly aware of his limitations. Society had not been unkind to him: but he had not taken it by storm; he never was absolutely at ease in it; and he had often felt an intense desire to run away. It was a great relief to discover that Society was evil, and to be shunned; running away then was not a weakness, but a virtue. Self-taught, and in many fields wholly untaught, a dreamer, he was glad to give up the painful study of facts, as practiced by Bayle, Montesquieu, Voltaire, Diderot. It was so much easier to sweep away the facts (*"Commençons par écarter les faits!"*—*Discourse on Inequality*), and to strike one's heart! The other philosophers had a heart too, but they thought with their heads. Rousseau's was a philosophy of short-cuts: an admirable method, as long as there are no precipices in the way. In all this, the sincerity of Rousseau is not impugned: he adopted in good

faith the doctrines that put his talent and his weaknesses
in the best possible light.

The success of Rousseau was due to a double contradiction: the rationalization of unreason, and the codification
of anarchy. Consistent primitivism would tear civilization down along with its abuses: property, without which
there could be no theft; language, without which there
could be no lies; morality, without which there could be
no sin. Then we would be restored to the happy state of
animal innocence which is called the Earthly Paradise.
This is Rousseau's logical conclusion: as Voltaire said:
"No one could display more ingenuity in urging us to
become beasts." Such a paradox would be amusing in
two brief discourses: it could not be prolonged through
several serious books. Rousseau had to compromise and
to equivocate. He saved and destroyed in the same breath.
In *Emile*, he gave us his idea of a *natural* education
which still would be an education, that is to say a directed
process. In *Julie*, he deals with the problem of a *natural*
love-life, at the same time free and disciplined. In *The
Social Contract*, he defines a state based upon Nature, yet
more efficiently ordered than the present one. In no case
is the result convincing. Emile's natural education is carried on under the most abnormal circumstances, and proceeds through a series of comedies and "fakes." Julie dies
just in time to be saved from adultery; and the Utopia
outlined in the *Social Contract* was to be realized by
Robespierre.

"Philosophy," before Rousseau, had respected science,
kept in touch with the immediate needs of society, enjoyed the amenities of civilization: all these were valuable
elements, which made for sanity, caution, urbanity.
Rousseau's triumph marked the advent of muddle-headed
radicalism, the confusion of false simplicity. For this the
man Rousseau was not responsible: he was but an instrument and a symptom. The trouble was due to the fact
that general education had not kept pace with the ideas
of Montesquieu, Voltaire, Diderot. "Philosophy," in untrained minds, became coarser and more passionate. Hy-

potheses hardened into affirmations, paradoxes into dogmas, subtle speculation into rough logic; until, as an argument, the epigram was superseded by the guillotine.

Coarseness, however, is not an all-sufficient explanation for the triumph of Rousseauism. Illogically perhaps, the new creed was moralistic. Montesquieu and Voltaire, earnest workers though they were, had dallied with the elegant depravity of their time; they had sunk to the level of Crébillon Fils. It was a weakness, and they had to atone for it. Diderot had been as licentious as they, with less restraint in taste; in addition, his "Naturalism" ignored some of the conventions that the world was not willing to discard. These critics of a corrupt society were not free from corruption. Rousseau turned the tables against them. He appealed to the vast number of men who hated at the same time prejudices and looseness. He showed that morality could be preached in the name of Nature as well as in the name of traditional authority. Intoxicated with their battle for intellectual freedom, the Philosophers had neglected moral discipline. A new Renaissance had to be followed by another Reformation. Calvin against Rabelais, Rousseau against Diderot: the comparison is far from perfect, but, as an indication, it will serve.

There was therefore a wholesome side to Primitivism, a breaking away from sophistication and perfumed perversity. It was a rough blast from the open, which destroyed and purified. It did blow down the fabric of the ancient régime, with immense losses to civilization. Had the rotten timber been replaced in time, Rousseauism would have created no peril.

The history of civilization must consider Rousseauism as a collective phenomenon, of which Rousseau himself was but the representative. But the personality of the representative is not without influence. Had Perrault been a man of genius, the Quarrel of the Ancients and the Moderns might have saved France a whole century of pseudo-classicism. Had Auguste Comte or Littré been a Lucretius, Positivism might be a living force to-day, in-

stead of a museum piece.   Rousseau had the essential virtue of a genius: he abandoned himself to his destiny, like
Napoleon; he identified his message with his person; he
attempted, haltingly enough, to live his creed, and his
Confessions were a justification, not of the individual
Rousseau, but of his faith. So Primitivism was not merely
a paradox, and not merely a tendency: it became flesh,
struggled, suffered, and conquered death. We find it exceedingly difficult to entertain any great reverence for
the man Rousseau, for his thought, and even for much of
his art: yet he can not be eliminated from the world's history any more than Napoleon. We find him at the head
of all the great tendencies in the nineteenth century: religious revival, democracy, romanticism, socialism. He is
as ardently combated to-day, in France as in America, as
when he was alive: and we do not fight the dead.

"Philosophy" had to accept Rousseau by the side of
Voltaire, just as the Christian tradition admitted the Old
Testament and the New, the Synoptics and St. John, St.
Paul and St. Peter. The Revolution brought the remains
of both to the Pantheon, where they lie unto this day.
This syncresis, which may not be a reconciliation, has to
be accepted as "the verdict of history."

CHAPTER IV

I

THE Quarrel of the Ancients and the Moderns had
died out without a decisive conclusion. To be sure,
Boileau, the watchdog of Parnassus, had saved the
sacred mountain from desecration; but his was a Pyrrhic
victory, for no age could be more uncompromisingly "modern" than the first half of the eighteenth century. To be
"enlightened" consisted chiefly in condemning the past as
a heap of abuses and superstitions, and in hailing the
dawn of Reason. Voltaire, the most complete representative of his time, exclaimed: "Oh! how happy is this century of iron!" Such a trend of thought would lead French
culture far away from the classical tradition, rooted in
reverence for the past. It announced a freer art, joy-
ously confident in the creative power of living men, in the
growing forces of science and industry. Of such an emancipated art, partly realistic, partly romantic, we find the
promises and even the first fruit in Diderot.

Yet the second half of the eighteenth century was
marked by a deliberate return to antiquity, by a more
rigid classicism than that of Boileau. This tendency cul-
minated under the Empire, in monuments which were al-

most slavish reproductions of Roman models. But it had
its beginning as early as the days of Madame de Pompadour.

Architecture, because it entails long and costly collective efforts, is less affected by purely individual fancy
than the other arts; and thus it affords the clearest symbol of large and durable tendencies. The delightful
frivolity of the Rococo style lost favour; a chaster taste
prevailed. If we compare the ornate and somewhat tormented elevation first projected for the West front of St.
Sulpice in Paris with the majestic portal built by Ser-
vandoni, the change in temper becomes immediately apparent. In the work of Gabriel, the new seriousness entails no sacrifice of elegance. The colonnades of the Place
de la Concorde, with their perfect balance of dignity and
grace, remain the witness of a unique moment in French
culture. The same fortunate blend is found in the interior of St. Genevieve (the Pantheon) by Soufflot: but
already chastity of design is almost verging on frigidity.
Perfection was reached under Louis XVI, in small palaces
and princely residences. Nothing could be simpler than
the Petit Trianon: a cube of masonry with a balustrade
on top, four Corinthian columns or pilasters separating
square or rectangular windows. Yet there is no stiffness
in all these straight lines, no bareness in those plain walls:
it is the triumph of faultless proportion and delicacy in
treatment. The Salm residence in Paris, now the Palace
of the Legion of Honour, is more definitely antique, but
likewise without severity. The forecourt is surrounded
by an Ionic colonnade, which is open on the street side; a
small triumphal arch serves as gateway. The exquisite
charm of this little edifice has survived the hardest trials.
In Paris, crushed between tall apartment houses and an
overwhelming railway terminal, it smiles on, refined, un-
dismayed, as the nobility knew how to smile on the steps
of the guillotine; in San Francisco, its replica in cold-
hued artificial stone, simplified, stiffened, windowless, lost
in a magnificent site for which it never was intended, still
manages to convey the same message of gracious restraint.

Unfortunately, the "antiquising" tendency did not stop there. Already the outside of the Pantheon had revealed the dangers of the new spirit: formality, artificiality. Simplicity in this case is not due to lack of affectation: it is a bid for theatrical impressiveness. The walls, rising unbroken and unadorned to the cornice, are meant to be tremendous in their cyclopean nakedness. But we know they are an architectural deception, and we know that windows are concealed behind their screen. At any rate, the Pantheon, for all its sophisticated ruggedness, has not utterly lost the amenity of the age. The austerity of the neo-antique soon became less amiable. The forty-three guard houses erected by Le Doux at the gates of Paris were frequently redeemed by a sort of weird picturesqueness; but the Odeon, for instance, is decidedly morose. It heralds the self-conscious stoicism which was to impoverish social life during the Revolution. It was a mercy that the First Republic had no time and no money to spare for permanent architecture: the temporary decorations for public festivals reveal the pomposity, the straining for the heroic and the grandiose, that marred the eloquence of the period. With Napoleon, the antique reigned supreme; everything was Roman, with touches of the Egyptian.[1] The logical consequence of the whole movement was reached when French architects sought in Rome not an inspiration merely, but models to be actually reproduced. The very pretty triumphal arch in the Place du Carrousel, by Percier and Fontaine, is a copy of the arch of Septimus Severus. The Vendôme Column repeats that of Trajan. The Madeleine is a huge pastiche of a Greco-Roman temple: an incongruity as a Christian church on the ultra-modern Boulevard, but undeniably an impressive one.

The tendency was no less pronounced in painting. About 1750, Boucher was still the leading master. He retained his supremacy until his death, and his gracefully erotic tradition was kept up by Fragonard. But these

---

[1] Egyptian influences, particularly felt after Bonaparte's expedition into that country, were already noticeable under Louis XVI.

dimpled and rosy nymphs, smiling so coquettishly in their mythological négligés, were no longer in tune with the growing earnestness. Already in 1745, Count de Caylus, an antiquarian as well as a lover of art, was preaching a sterner doctrine. Strangely enough, the influence of Madame de Pompadour herself, and that of her brother Marigny, were working in the same direction. Hubert Robert was brilliantly successful in his spirited paintings of classical ruins; and the splendid prints of Piranesi catered to the same taste and have retained the same appeal.

Ultra-classicism found its perfect exponent in David. It is important to bear in mind that this truly great painter had found his way before the Revolution, and that he, the future Jacobin, had enjoyed the patronage of royalty. *Belisarius, Andromache, the Horatii, Brutus and his Sons,* all these resolutely classical scenes were produced before the storm. He was—in anticipation—a Robespierre of the brush; and when the crisis came, he embraced Jacobinism as the political expression of his artistic temperament. Under the Convention, he became the dictator of Republican art, and the organizer of civic festivals. He admired Marat, directed his impressive funeral, and painted a tragic portrait of "the Friend of the People," stabbed in his bath-tub. It was he who designed the sacred Ark of the Covenant in which the still-born constitution of the new democracy was deposited. Like many other Jacobins, he rallied to Bonaparte, and painted for him vast official canvases, such as the *Coronation* and the *Presentation of the Eagles.* There were in David qualities of realism, which were especially manifested in his portraits; and a vein of romanticism, which revealed itself, almost reluctantly, in the splendour of his historical pieces. But, in theory, and, with excessive consistency, in his practice as well, he was committed to the narrowest neo-classical orthodoxy.[1]

[1] The last great classical sculptors, Pigalle, Falconet, Houdon, Pajou, are free from antiquising neo-classicism. The tendency is represented in other countries, by Flaxman, Thorwaldsen, Canova, Bosio, who had many admirers and disciples in France.

K

In literature, many were carried by the same stream. Most of them are now mere names except for the professional scholar. Who cares at present that a professor by the name of Thomas was considered, until his death in 1785, as a French Cicero? Yet it was Thomas who struck the keynote for the eloquence of the Revolutionary assemblies; and there is much "Thomas" in the addresses and proclamations of Napoleon himself. Who cares that Ecouchard Lebrun (1729–1807) dubbed himself the modern Pindar, and was accepted as such by his contemporaries? Lebrun, like David, was a Republican in his artistic principles even under the old monarchy. With a Cicero and a Pindar, France also had a Vergil in Abbé Delille (1738–1813), the translator of the *Georgics* and the *Æneid*, the faultless versifier who could describe anything from a Miltonic scene to a game of backgammon without ever using an unclassical term. Under the Empire, this brood of pseudo-classicists flourished exceedingly; and no school perhaps has ever equalled the frigid inanity of theirs. Baour-Lormian, Luce de Lancival, have remained by-words; and malignant traces of pseudo-classical influences are found in Chateaubriand, Lamartine and Vigny.

Yet even in this field pseudo-classicism was not wholly barren. Architecture had Soufflot, who is not negligible; painting had David, who is genuinely great; poetry had André Chénier. But Chénier, although the return to antiquity is best exemplified in him, remains an exception. The Chénier whom his contemporaries knew was the author of stiff political odes, just as artificial as those of Ecouchard Lebrun, and considerably more ponderous. There was also in him an erotic poet of no great depth, and a would-be philosophical poet who, if he had lived, would in all likelihood have been a Condorcet in rhyme rather than a French Lucretius. Only in 1819 were his *Idyls*, *Elegies* and classical fragments published. To originality these graceful pieces have no claim; they are antique reminiscences strung together by an artist not yet in full possession of his technique. But Chénier, for one thing, knew Greek infinitely better than Lebrun-Pindar.

Alexandrian culture was his spiritual home; and his Grecian mosaics are no antiquarian pastimes, but genuine modes of self-expression.

There was still a third Chénier, as far above the Hellenistic minor poet as the latter was above Lebrun. Just as the death of Marat had, for the moment, torn David away from his pseudo-classical prejudices, and inspired him to paint a masterpiece of passionate realism, so the spectacle of the Terror roused in Chénier an indignation that flamed forth in his *Iambics*. With Agrippa d'Aubigné, Auguste Barbier and Victor Hugo, he could redeem the meanest of all passions, political animosity, through his lyrical fervor.

Archeology had its place in this "antiquising" movement; but that austere science, reserved for the few, never leads fashion. When it becomes popular, we may be sure that the key of its success is to be found elsewhere. Some of the men who were most influential in fostering the return to antiquity, like Rousseau himself, were totally unaffected by archeology: Rousseau loved antiquity, not out of knowledge, but out of ignorance. But scientific research, vitalized by public interest, added precision and depth to a movement which might have remained purely sentimental. The ancient world, so long merely a rational ideal, if not a pure convention, became a concrete reality.

Nothing contributed more to this change than the discoveries at Herculaneum and Pompeii. The existence of buried ruins at the foot of Vesuvius had been suspected for a long time. But systematic exploration began only in 1738, and its results did not reach the educated general public in France until ten years later. Count de Caylus acted as *liaison* between archeologists and artists; the Academy of Inscriptions served as a meeting-ground for scholars and literary men. Thanks to these agencies, to many missions, and to a wealth of handsome publications, the material side of Greco-Roman life became familiar to modern Paris, as it had never been even in the days of the Renaissance.

The conjunction of scientific research and popular in-

terest is best exemplified in the works of Abbé J. J.
Barthélémy. This excellent archeologist, whose special
field was numismatics, was also in touch with the aristocratic society of his time, a protégé of Choiseul's, a personal friend of Madame du Deffand's. He spent thirty
years in the preparation of a book which was to make the
results of science available for the general reader. An
archeological treatise with a very thin veil of fiction, and
freely interspersed with unadorned disquisitions on technical points, would hardly be expected to become a best-
seller: but the *Voyage of Young Anacharsis in Greece,
About the Middle of the Fourth Century B. C.* (1787)
was immensely successful. In spite of his aristocratic connections, Barthélémy did not suffer at the hands of the
Revolutionists, who left him in charge of the Department
of Medals in the National Library.

As a sign of the same general interest in antiquity, we
may note that even industrial arts and the decoration of
daily life under Louis XVI showed very clearly the influence of Pompeii and its Hellenistic culture. After 1789,
the tendency was more noticeable still. Greco-Roman
names grew in favour. Baron von Cloots, "the Spokesman
of Mankind," chose to call himself Anacharsis. Babeuf,
the communist, became Caius Gracchus. If virtue affected
an antique garb, so did frivolity. The ladies fair and frail
of the Thermidorian reaction and of the Directoire, such
as Teresia Cabarrus (Madame Tallien), adopted the
graceful fashions of classical antiquity—a mode which
Napoleon's sister, Pauline Borghese, was to carry to an
extreme in her statue by Canova.

II

What accounts for this last flaring up of the classical
spirit in its strictest form, almost on the eve of its extinction? First of all, the weakening of obstacles that had
long opposed it. The Renaissance had introduced the cult

of antiquity: but that cult was hampered by the strong survival of feudalism and Christianity. For that reason, sixteenth-century culture is not purely antique, but a delightful hybrid. This compromise had been consolidated in the seventeenth century: Boileau, for instance, was a pure Pagan in literature, but an orthodox Christian in his private life. As a consequence of the Enlightenment, feudalism and Christianity had lost much of their prestige, and the worship of antiquity was left without a check. Antiquity had been called to the rescue against medieval ignorance and superstition, "Gothic night"; its usefulness would not end until medievalism had been finally extirpated; and as France was nearing the goal, the purpose of the movement was becoming clearer. But the worship of antiquity depended to a large extent upon that opposition to medievalism. Allies seldom remain good friends after their common enemy is out of the way. No sooner had classical Reason triumphed but the cry was heard: "Who will deliver us from the Greeks and the Romans?" and Romanticism was ready to follow.

The return to antiquity was accelerated by the "Primitivism" of which Rousseau became the apostle. For a time, antiquity, simplicity, Nature, were held to be one and the same. The extreme sophistication of decadent Hellenism, the corruption of imperial Rome, were ignored. It was the heroic and frugal times of the Republic that were extolled. Rousseau's apostrophe to Fabricius, in his first *Discourse*, was a call to a simpler life, and above all a denunciation of the exquisite luxury in which Voltaire, Madame de Pompadour and their friends revelled so ingenuously. Rousseau's antiquity, inspired by Plutarch, was very different from Chénier's and Madame Tallien's: it was the stoic, sententious and morose antiquity of David and Robespierre. Fabricius, in his *Discourse*, played the same part as *The Peasant from the Banks of the Danube* in Lafontaine's eloquent fable. The "virtuous" Roman is akin to the "virtuous barbarian" of Tacitus, and to the "virtuous savage" so dear to the whole eighteenth century. The uncritical Primitivism which was to cause the

vogue of a spurious Ossian also caused the revival of
Plutarch.

Another element has to be distinguished in this return
to antiquity, an element which is romantic rather than
classical. Antiquity was now looked upon, not exclusively
as the perfect pattern of a rational culture, nor solely as
a model of heroic virtue, but as a source of picturesqueness. The same thirst for colour and movement which was
seeking satisfaction in Orientalism, in exoticism, and in
the Middle Ages, led artists back to antiquity, and particularly to the ruins of antiquity. Whilst archeologists
were dreaming of restorations, the poets enjoyed "ruins
for ruins' sake." A fondness for ruins, since the days of
Joachim du Bellay, had never disappeared from the
French mind; but in the second half of the eighteenth century it reached the delightful absurdity of a craze. Artificial ruins were built; and we remember the time when the
ruined colonnade in the Parc Monceau, a charming relic
of that period, was falling into genuine ruins and had
carefully to be restored to its original ruinous condition.
Ruined temples preceded ruined monasteries, in the favour
of the French public. Hubert Robert was so successful,
not because he was an archeologist, but because he was a
pre-Romanticist as well. The great series of Roman Antiquities by Piranesi reveal the same spirit. The scale of
the buildings is made gigantic; the architecture is at the
same time more massive and more crumbling than in reality; as much attention is given to bushes clinging to a
wall as to the carving of frieze or capital; the contrast
between the magnificence of these remains and the modern
life of beggars and shepherds is almost invariably emphasized with conscious eloquence. It is significant that the
same Piranesi, whose *Albums of Classical Ornaments* had
such an influence on domestic decoration, also etched his
Dungeons (*Carceri*), a gorgeous collection of architectural nightmares, in which the very spirit of Mrs. Rad-
cliffe and of "Monk" Lewis flutters amid cyclopean vaults.
The vigorous and original guard houses of Le Doux, so
unfortunately sacrificed in the nineteenth century, show

the direct influence of Pæstum, but even more those of Hubert Robert and Piranesi. The writer happened to be familiar, in his childhood, with the most elaborate of them, the Rotunda of La Villette; and that mysterious building, most prosaically used for offices and stores, always evoked in his young imagination the romantic vision of a vanished world, grand and terrible.

III

Thus ultra-classicism of the most rigid kind was not free from the spirit that was to supersede it: the new was in germ within the old. With Pre-Romanticism we do not propose to deal at length: it concerns the origins of the nineteenth century rather than the evolution of the classical age. But it is important to note how gradual the change was, and how early it began. We have seen that the essence of Romanticism was found in Rousseau; but in his works, the form remains classical on the whole, with an eloquence not radically different from Thomas's and a reverence for antiquity akin to David's. In Voltaire, on the contrary, whilst his thought never transgressed the clear and narrow circle defined by the Enlightenment, the material elements of Romanticism are not lacking. In dramatic theory, Voltaire was more conservative than in politics or in religion. Yet it was he who actually revealed Shakespeare to the French, although he lived to repent the diffusion of a taste that he had inaugurated. He adapted Shakespearian subjects to his own needs—*Othello* in *Zaïre*, *Hamlet* in *Sémiramis*. He had early in his career delivered himself from the tyrannical exclusiveness of Greco-Roman subjects. Du Belloy's *Siege of Calais* in 1765, M.-J. Chénier's *Charles IX* in 1789, plays on national themes, were hailed with enthusiasm: but it was Voltaire who had opened the way, with his *Zaïre* in 1732 and, in 1734, with his *Adélaïde du Guesclin*. In *Tancrède* or *The Knights*, in 1760, we find already a model of that pale and conventional Romanticism which was later to be known as "Troubadour Style." On the stage as in his

Essay on Manners, he is not satisfied with the familiar Mediterranean tradition: he wants to go farther afield, to embrace the whole world, America in *Alzire,* the Far East in *The Chinese Orphan.* He went so far as to require his actors to wear Chinese and Manchu costumes: the resulting compromise was one of the quaintest masquerades that ever enlivened the stage.

The taste for the Orient was not new, even in the early part of the eighteenth century: already under Louis XIV, Galland had given of the *Arabian Nights* a version which was long to remain unchallenged. There had been a brief Turkish craze, of which the end of Molière's *Bourgeois Gentilhomme* (1670) and Racine's *Bajazet* (1672) are the most notable traces. Throughout the eighteenth century, the Oriental tale had been a favourite. Montesquieu spiced with Oriental ingredients his satirical *Persian Letters.* Voltaire himself, so cool and reasonable, gave his imagination freer rein in his Arabian and Babylonian stories. Chinese art enjoyed a great vogue: Choiseul had his Pagoda at Chanteloup; Eastern lacquer was prized and imitated; and some of the most entrancing designs of the period profess to set forth Chinese patterns and Chinese scenes. Just as archeology was giving a new precision to the old-established taste for classical antiquity, geographical discovery gradually deepened the meaning of exoticism. The public who followed so eagerly the voyages of La Condamine, Bougainville, La Pérouse and d'Entrecasteaux would soon accept less uncritically the fanciful picturesqueness of exotic romance. The taste came first, and created a demand for authentic information. Finally, with Bernardin de Saint-Pierre and with Chateaubriand, actual travelers who were also artists, we find a convincing blend of poetry and observation, with which Romanticism declared itself satisfied.

Nothing could be more symptomatic of a new spirit than the extraordinary vogue of Macpherson's *Ossian,* which Letourneur translated in 1776. Many causes contributed to its immediate and prolonged success. First of all, the eighteenth century, as we have seen, was marked

by Anglomania throughout, even in the long years of warfare between the two countries. Everything that came
from over the channel was sure of a sympathetic reception,
and Macpherson profited by the same favour that was
shown to Thomson and Young, to Richardson and Sterne.
But it was not Anglomania alone that made Ossianism so
catching. That charming French society was eager to escape from itself, from the gilded and scented bondage of
its own cleverness, luxury and sophistication. Never was
there a clearer case of *"toujours perdrix."* Paris sighed
for simplicity: the Quaker-like simplicity of Franklin, the
insipid simplicity of Gessner's Idyls, the theatrical simplicity of David's antique paintings, the comic-opera simplicity of Marie-Antoinette's dairy at Trianon. Especially did France yearn for the simplicity of remote ages
under unfamiliar skies. What could be more different
from Paris under Louis XVI than nebulous Gaelic clans
in the third century? Ossian was declared more primitive
than Homer. The age of Voltaire, wearied with its own
keenness of sight, craved strangely for the vague. The
cult of pleasure had created a longing for melancholy, as
a last untapped spring of interest. So we find in the imagination of the time the characters of Macpherson float-
ing dim and gigantic in a somber mist, by the side of an
antiquity more sharply defined than ever. The hoax became a world-classic. "Ossian" ranks with Shakespeare,
Byron and Walter Scott among the masters of French
Romanticism; and it seems almost incredible that the arch-
realist, the supreme classicist, the Latin *par excellence*,
Napoleon, should have been a fervent reader of Ossian. A
syncretic age if ever there was one, in which all ideals co-
existed, frequently in the same minds, without actually
blending. The one thing this groping in all directions
proved beyond doubt was that the exclusive faith in the
classical doctrine, after ruling for nearly three centuries,
was approaching exhaustion.

IV

So far no great leader had dared openly to blaspheme Reason. Rousseau might wage war on the Enlightenment, proclaim himself the apostle of intuition and sentiment, inaugurate a new mysticism: still he professed to be a rationalist. It was his logic, combined with his passion, that carried away his contemporaries. Yet Reason, although still enthroned, was turning into a constitutional sovereign, who reigns but does not govern. It is curious to watch, at the very moment when the hoariest superstitions were tumbling down, an extraordinary outcropping of new-fangled superstitions, a wild "will to believe" in that era of professed unbelief, a mysticism which accepted, almost consciously, the assistance of mystification. The great Carnival of Faith, so characteristic of the Romantic period, had its beginning in the Age of Reason.

The resistance of the ancient order to inevitable change had compelled the Philosophers to over-emphasize destructive criticism. They had ruined faith in existing institutions: more accurately, they had, not created, but expressed, the scepticism which was growing in almost every mind. But they had not been able to build up a new world, for the débris of the old were still cumbering the ground. Hence a void which was filled in the most curiously haphazard fashion. This thirst for illusion was particularly noticeable among men who, whilst they felt the hopeless absurdity of the régime, were still attached to it by ties of tradition or self-interest. They feared and hoped, and did not know exactly what to hope or fear. Many aristocrats, in a spirit of irresponsible opposition, protested against the ban which had been placed on Beaumarchais's *Marriage of Figaro;* when that daring satire was at last put on the stage, they recklessly applauded its most destructive epigrams; yet many of them had no intention of giving up the privileged position which Figaro had made so plainly ridiculous. Men in that ambiguous frame of mind, credulous and sceptical, dissatisfied with

the present, yet afraid of actual change, enjoying
"abuses" whilst toying with free thought and philanthropy, were the easiest prey for charlatans. It was not
the common people who took up the strangest creeds or
rites, and followed the most outrageous impostors: it was
men who belonged to the aristocracy of wealth and wit.
A cynic would say that they had lost their heads long before the reign of Terror. The years immediately preceding the Revolution were a golden age for adventurers,
especially if they could give to their nostrums a theosoph-
ical flavour. *Schwärmer und Schwindler*, as Sierke appropriately describes that ilk: enthusiasts and rogues.
Paris in 1774, when Louis XVI ascended the throne, was
not very different in this respect from Los Angeles a hundred and fifty years later.

It may seem disrespectful to an ancient and respectable
institution such as Freemasonry to mention its name in
such a connection. Yet it is manifest that, in eighteenth
century France, its spirit was not entirely guided by the
most critical common sense. Its spread was another sign
of Anglomania. The reorganization of the craft in London in 1717 was the signal of a great revival of activity:
indeed it might be called a new birth. A French lodge
was instituted in 1732. Masonry was then one of the
channels of the Enlightenment, and its deistic creed long
bore the imprint of that period. But it acquired also at
that time the anticlerical bias which in France has survived its pristine deism: it has remained a counter militia
mobilized against the Jesuits. Lafayette was a member,
like George Washington, with whom he liked his name to
be linked. The Duke of Orleans, Philip, not yet *Egalité*,
was a master of the craft. But liberal principles in politics and philosophy were not the sole attraction: the Mysteries of Freemasonry proved a great temptation for the
mystagogues, and shady characters like Cagliostro attempted to give a Masonic tinge to their wildest schemes.

By the side of Freemasonry, and at times attempting
to merge with it we find the different groups and move-
ments vaguely described as *Illuminati*. Some might be

the direct heirs of the Spanish *Alumbrados,* with whom Saint Ignatius had been accused of consorting. Others claimed affiliation with the German Rosicrucians; others still went back to the old Knights Templars. Some, like Saint-Martin, disciple of Martinez de Pasquales, were mystics and cabalists as well as theurgists, and came under the influence of Boehme and Swedenborg. The very title of one of Saint-Martin's books, *The Man of Desire,* is significant of the time. But no less significant is the fact that the "Unknown Philosopher," as he chose to sign himself, was very popular in Parisian society.

The clearest connection between "Enlightenment," "Illumination" and Freemasonry is found in the Order of Perfectibilists, organized in 1776 by a German Professor, Weishaupt. Weishaupt, let it be noted, was an ex-Jesuit: the secret character of that great militant congregation has constantly impressed the world and encouraged imitation. The Perfectibilists, also known as *Illuminati,* copied to some extent the hierarchy of the Masons and established relations with their lodges. It is not surprising that Herder should have become interested: but Goethe himself, Olympian though he was destined to be, was attracted by that turbid mixture. The Perfectibilists professed advanced opinions. They were represented in France, but as a mere eddy in the great turmoil that preceded the Revolution.

Mesmer was a portent. In him, science, mysticism and charlatanism blended most convincingly. He came to Paris in 1778, and created a furore with his "animal magnetism" and his "baquet" or vat, a modernized version of the witches' caldron. The government offered him a large sum for his "secret": possibly as a last resort against impending bankruptcy, for Mesmer was an alchemist as well as a forerunner of our medical fakers. A committee of which Franklin was a member examined his scientific claims: his "mesmerism," however, baffled their investigation. He founded a *Society of Harmony,* which was joined by such men as d'Esprémesnil, a power at the time in the uncontrollable Parliament of Paris; by Lafayette,

whose excellent intentions led him to nibble at every bait,
and even by a chemist of note, Berthollet.

From 1748 to 1760, Count de Saint-Germain was a
figure at the Court of Louis XV. He was a cosmopolitan
adventurer of mysterious origin—possibly the illegitimate son of a Spanish queen. Speaking all European languages, endowed with an imperturbable memory, a musician, a chemist, he was, according to Grimm's report,
the most brilliant man he had ever come across: and it was
Grimm's business to meet all the celebrities of his time.
Saint-Germain affords an excellent test of the gullibility
of the age: he did not actually profess that he was in possession of the philosopher's stone and of the elixir of life,
but he gave out hints which were taken up with eagerness.
He served in many ways as a pattern for Cagliostro, whom
he is said to have initiated into Freemasonry.

With Cagliostro we have the perfect example of the
impostor. The fecund imagination of Alexandre Dumas,
in *Joseph Balsamo*, can hardly keep pace with the extravagant adventures of his hero. Cagliostro, like Saint-
Germain, hinted that he had been living for untold centuries; he too was an alchemist, and in addition a con-
cocter of love philters; like Mesmer, he was a miracle-
worker. He also had his pseudo-mystic side; he was in
touch with the Rosicrucians; and he started a Freemasonry of his own, an Egyptian brand of which he proclaimed himself the Grand Copht. Such was his magnificent self-assurance that legitimate lodges sought affiliation with his Order; but, as they refused to destroy their
archives and make a totally new start, their application
was denied. He came to Paris in 1785, and played a part
in the tangled and unsavoury affair of the Diamond Neck-
lace. On that particular score he managed to bluff his
judges out of countenance; but he was condemned on
other counts, had to leave France, and died obscurely in
1795 in a Papal prison.

Such was French society on the eve of the great catastrophe: a welter of ideals and superstitions, the noblest

by the side of the most foolish. We have seen the growth
of an "antiquising" spirit which was to become ever stiffer
and more pedantic until it yawned itself to death under
the Empire. We have seen the favour enjoyed, in the
highest circles, by the rankest charlatans. The clear light
of eighteenth century thought seemed to be losing both in
power and in purity. It is only when the lamps are
dimmed, and to the strain of soft music, that a Mesmer
or a Cagliostro can operate. The same elements of gran-
diloquent fraud are ever with us: but the danger, at the
end of the Ancient Régime, was that such elements were
able to impose upon the social elite. A society that was
no longer able to believe in itself was ready to believe in
anything.

However, if the symptoms of danger have to be noted,
they should not be unduly magnified. Classical France
was herself still. The wit and commonsense of the Voltairian era had survived, in Voltaire himself and in his
admirers. Science was loved and served, as well as "Liberty" and "Philosophy." Reforms were intelligently discussed, and, with Turgot, courageously attempted. The
artificiality of Rococo culture had been tempered by a
new taste for simplicity. "Virtue," not immorality, was
now "The Prejudice in Fashion."[1] It would be naïve to
praise the reign of Louis XVI as an Arcadia of courtly
philosophy: the sardonic grin of Talleyrand should suffice
as a warning. But it was, on the whole, a cheerful, kindly,
sensible age. So it seemed to the contemporaries; and so
it seems all the more to us, with the tragic contrast provided by the Revolution.

---

[1] As a sign of this vogue of virtue, we may note the popularity of a third-rater,
Berquin (1747–1791), "The Friend of Children," whose name has become
synonymous with vacuous innocence. (*Berquinades.*) The Montyon Prizes
for Virtue, still awarded by the French Academy, were created at that time
(1782). An admirable example of "virtue" in the sense of active philanthropy
is found in La Rochefoucauld-Liancourt (1747–1827).

CHAPTER V

CAUSES OF THE REVOLUTION

Ubi nec mala nec remedia pati possumus

I. The Revolution "inevitable": why?—Revolutionary Temper of the French people a fallacy.

II. The French goaded by despair? France on the up-grade under Louis XVI: King, foreign affairs, home government, economic progress.

III. The "Philosophers": responsibility of Montesquieu, Voltaire, Rousseau.

IV. Blind conservatism: among peasants and craftsmen. Rôle of the Parliaments.

V. Selfish privilege. Clergy. Nobility. Nobiliary reaction under Louis XVI. The King's brothers. The Queen. The King's hesitancy.

I

THERE is about the French Revolution an impressive air of cataclysmic inevitability. No event was more clearly prophesied. Even more definite than the utterances of Voltaire and d'Argenson were the cynical epigrams ascribed to Louis XV himself: "After us, the deluge!"—"Pshaw! The old machine will last at least as long as we!" Except in that nihilistic old sinner, the consciousness of an impending crisis did not paralyze effort: but as every move of a man caught in quicksand only accelerates his doom, it seemed as though reform and reaction alike hastened the fateful hour. This dramatic simile, however, is delusive, after the wont of similes, and a little worse than the average. For there was no sense of horror amid the charming and enlightened society so soon to be engulfed. Existence had never been so delicately enjoyable, and the signs of change only added to its zest. "Whoever has not lived before the Revolution, said Talleyrand, has not truly tasted the sweetness of life." Part of that sweetness was due to the very fact that the Revolution was in the air.

"Inevitability" is the last refuge of the lazy-minded. If we ask: "*Why* was the Revolution inevitable?" agreement ceases by magic. We are frequently told that the Revolution broke out in France because the French are a revolutionary people. It may be a compliment or the reverse to be called "Revolutionary": the Daughters of the American Revolution would shudder at the thought that they might become the Mothers of a new A nerican Revolution. A "revolutionary people" may be one that is not amenable to discipline; or it may be one that will not brook tyranny. What Tennyson spurns as "the red fool-fury of the Seine" or "the blind hysterics of the Celt" is revered by Michelet as a Messianic sign. But, whichever way you take it, to explain the French Revolution through the revolutionary character of the French is to tell us that "opium causes sleep because of its dormitive virtue." Few among the pseudo-sciences are quite so dangerous as the psychology of nations. In their long history, the French had shown exactly the reverse of a revolutionary temperament. For eight hundred years, they had faithfully served the same dynasty. They had been obstinately loyal under the most tragic circumstances: when the King was a child, and when he was a prisoner; when he was a wastrel and when he was a madman. They had remained attached to institutions of slow and unconscious growth. It was England, on the contrary, that had given glaring examples of religious instability in the sixteenth century, and of political fickleness in the seventeenth; it was English-speaking countries, on both sides of the Atlantic, that had first revealed a radical turn of mind, and rudely shattered the majesty that doth hedge round a king. It is true that, from 1789 to 1871, France has gone through at least half a dozen major convulsions —hardly a record of political stability. But these were the recurring fits of the same fever, symptoms of a prolonged disease, rather than permanent characteristics. In the last quarter of a century, we have begun to recog-

nize, if not to appreciate, the sturdy conservativeness of
the French. France has long since joined us in the ranks
of retired revolutionists, of all people the most stubbornly
averse to sudden change. Halo or stigma, France's revolutionary reputation is a thing of the past.

An explanation which rises naturally to our minds is
that the Revolution broke out because conditions were bad
beyond human endurance. Even the meekest peasant will
turn. This is a very popular theory, for it is obvious,
dramatic, picturesque. It was long official in the schools
of the Republic. It remains embodied in the significance
attached to the national holiday: on the 14th of July, the
people rose in their wrath and destroyed that symbol of
intolerable oppression, the Bastille.[1] Nowhere do we find
it more vigorously expressed than in the *Tale of Two
Cities*, the only primer of the French Revolution with
which the English-speaking world is thoroughly familiar.
The romancer need not have strained his imagination for
instances of brutal callousness above and incredible degradation below. There are facts aplenty that the apologists of the ancient régime cannot brush aside. La
Bruyère, a hundred years before the Revolution, had
etched his tragic vision of the starved peasantry under
Louis XIV. In spite of what we might call the comic-
opera tradition of French history, there were famines in
the fair and fruitful land; men were actually maimed for
life because they attempted to evade the preposterous salt-
tax; torture was used to wring out the confession of imaginary crimes; serfhood still lingered; feudal rights,
onerous or humiliating, could still be enforced; a man
could be arrested without warrant, kept in jail without
judgment, and there allowed to waste away, if the Powers
did not choose to remember. When such tales are told,
one marvels at the infinite longanimity of the French
people.

---

[1] It is claimed that, strictly speaking, the 14th of July commemorates
the "Federation" of 1790, not the insurrection of 1789: civil concord,
not civil war. But the popular interpretation is at least a short cut to
the essential truth.

Yet we feel that this obvious and all-sufficient explanation does not fully explain. Why was it, for one thing, that the Revolution broke out *in France*, whilst conditions were fully as bad, and in most cases considerably worse, in the other countries of the continent? Why was it that the poorest peasantry in the West took up arms in defence of the ancient régime, whilst the Revolution found its leaders and many of its most enthusiastic supporters among the educated and comfortable middle class?

There is no such things as "the energy of despair": despair is depressing. A pessimistic nation will sullenly accept its incurable ills: it will even cling to them, for fear any change might be for the worse. Sudden and sharp suffering may lash a country into fury, as was the case with the Paris Commune in 1871: but prolonged oppression degrades men into numb acquiescence. A riot may be an explosion of mad despair: a revolution is an act of faith, and a proof of intense vitality. Revolutions break out when nations are on the up-grade, not when they are going down.

II

There is little doubt but France, under Louis XVI, was on the up-grade. Conditions were bad enough, worse, we have every reason to believe, than they are to-day; and even to-day, we could, with unimpeachable documents, draw a very somber picture of our own times! Every scene that Dickens related might be as true as it is lurid, yet the implication would be false. The essential fact was that, in practically all domains, things were improving, and improving fast. The French themselves were clearly conscious that the worst was over. Instead of a profligate, absentee King, watching with Mephistophelian irony the dissolution of his own realm, France had a young sovereign, timid no doubt and slow-witted, but decent, kindly, conscientious, and by no means stupid. During the Seven Years' War, the French jeered bitterly at the disgraceful futility of their government, which cost them two empires:

but twenty years later, their shame had been wiped away. Corsica had been acquired, chiefly as a sign that France had not abdicated. The American War was popular among all classes; the diplomacy of the crisis was ably conducted; the naval and military operations, whilst not sensational, were creditable. There was no taint of decadence, no shadow of national humiliation, about the France of Vergennes, Rochambeau, Lafayette, de Grasse and Suffren.

In home affairs also, there was no reason to despair. The ancient régime, it is true, was capable of entrusting its destinies to a dilapidated embodiment of frivolous wit like Maurepas: but public opinion could force upon that very Maurepas men like Turgot and Malesherbes, and keep them in power for two years. Nor was it a mere accident, a desperate remedy: Turgot was the representative of the old and sound tradition in the French bureaucracy. He was not an untrained adventurer, a radical visionary, although he was something of a *doctrinaire:* he had for twenty years done excellent practical work as Administrator (*Intendant*) of Limoges. A monarchy supported by such dynasties of public servants could face the future. And a régime bold enough, in 1777, to make Necker a minister, was far from hopeless. Necker, a foreigner, a Protestant, a Republican, was called upon to straighten the finances of an aristocratic and Catholic monarchy. Indeed it would be hard to imagine, in any of the leading countries to-day, a parallel to such liberalism. Even if a Soviet Commissar should display marvelous efficiency, England and America would hardly think of offering him a Cabinet position. The France of Louis XVI had a trained administrative personnel, and felt free to supplement it with experts from abroad: it would not therefore perish for lack of able servants.

Turgot's reforms failed, and public opinion was tempted to repeat with Abbé Galiani: "We have reached the time when we can bear neither our ills, nor the needed remedies." Yet, in spite of all opposition, there was progress throughout the reign in the spheres of legislation and government. The judges, as might be expected, had no sympathy with "sentimental" and "doctrinaire" changes that would destroy the traditions of their order and weaken the hands of Themis. But, in spite of their reluctance, the "preliminary" torture administered to the accused on the chance that he might prove guilty was abolished in 1780; and the other forms of that venerable institution were finally suppressed in 1788. The clergy were at least as conservative as the judges: but against their protest, most of the civil disabilities of the Huguenots were removed in 1787. Much of the ancient régime thus disappeared before the outbreak of the Revolution: the last traces of serfhood were abolished in the royal domain in 1779. It was universally felt to be an anomaly that, in spite of Voltaire's denunciation, the obdurate Abbey of St. Claude should still own serfs in 1789. And the other abuses were doomed.

From the economic point of view, the country was booming. It lagged far behind England, and the report of Arthur Young is the reverse of rosy: but in every field, progress was made. Foreign trade nearly doubled between the middle of the century and the Revolution, whilst the figures for 1825 were barely superior to those for 1788. We think of the "ancient régime" exclusively in terms of the old guilds and handicrafts, with their eternal squabbles, their meticulous regulations, their fossilized traditions. But that ancient régime, so reluctant to alter its statutes, was in reality changing fast. We are apt to forget that, before 1789, there were already in France powerful enterprises, operating on a large scale, and with the aid of modern machinery. The Creusot Company was founded in 1787; in 1789, the collieries at Anzin had twelve steam engines; tracks were laid in the vast iron works of Montcenis. Annonay was using machinery in the manufacture of paper. The inventions of John Kay, Arkwright, Cartwright, Crompton, had been brought from over the Channel, renovating the cotton industry. Nor was France satisfied with the importation of English improvements: she contributed actively to the new tech-

nical development. It is hard to realize that as early as
1765, Cugnot was experimenting with an automobile: his
steam truck (1770 model), a crude but convincing affair,
now reposes in the Technical Museum (*Conservatoire des
Arts et Métiers*) in Paris. Jouffroy d'Abbans, translat-
ing into practical terms the early attempts of Denis
Papin, had a steamboat paddling on the Saône, and, in
1783, repeated the experiment on the Seine: Fulton
frankly recognized the priority of the French nobleman.
In 1783 also, the brothers Montgolfier, of Annonay, inflated a balloon with hot air; and Charles, in Paris, sub-
stituting hydrogen for smoke, opened a new path to
human skill and daring.

That early dawn of the industrial era was soon to be
obscured—by the Revolution. For ten years, the French
were too busy tearing each other to pieces to develop their
industry: we may use as a symbol the fact that both
Cugnot and Jouffroy died in poverty and oblivion, their
inventions neglected. When material order was fully restored by Bonaparte, the first task was reconstruction
rather than expansion. And one essential element of
progress was still lacking: cooperation and friendly rivalry with England. So even during the years of prosperity of the Napoleonic Empire, we miss the vigorous,
self-confident spirit of pre-Revolutionary France. Peace
came at last in 1815: but England had taken such a lead
in commerce and industry that competition seemed practically impossible; and the returned émigrés, the men who
had "learnt nothing and forgotten nothing" were not the
men to nerve the nation to bolder efforts. So the auspi-
cious start of the seventeen-eighties was not followed up:
its very traces disappeared in the fickle memory of men.
Most historians place the beginning of the industrial era
in France in the latter part of Louis-Philippe's reign,
after 1840; and the joy in progress which characterized
the time of Louis XVI did not fully return until the Second Empire, in 1852.[1]

---

[1] Louis XVI, like Napoleon III, had enough reliance in French energy
and enough faith in liberal ideas to sign a treaty for freer trade with

III

So it was neither an inborn trait of the French people, nor the sheer excess of their sufferings, that made the Revolution "inevitable." Was it the influence of "Philosophy," of Montesquieu and Voltaire, of Diderot and his crew of Encyclopædists, and, last but most dangerous of all, of Jean-Jacques Rousseau? Materialistic historians are inclined to deny the potency of abstract ideas, for good or evil: but, outside Soviet Russia, no one is bound to accept the materialistic orthodoxy in all its rigour.

The theory, at any rate, is not a new-fangled one. It was proclaimed by the Revolution itself, when, by decree of the National Assembly, the remains of Voltaire and Rousseau were solemnly transferred to St. Genevieve's, turned into a Pantheon. It has this strong point in its favour that it is supported by the enemies of the Revolution as well as by its friends. Victor Hugo places on the lips of Gavroche, as the heroic gamin was sporting among whizzing bullets, a mocking song: *"C'est la faute à Voltaire, c'est la faute à Rousseau."* The burden of this song was repeated in good earnest by the French reactionaries throughout the nineteenth century. The most uncompromising statement of this idea is found in Taine's *Origins of Contemporary France.* Taine diagnosed the disease from which his country found it so hard to recover as "Jacobinism"; and Jacobinism, in his opinion, was but the attempt to translate into facts the doctrines of the Enlightenment. If you are a democrat like Michelet or Victor Hugo, you will say that the Philosophers guided the people out of the house of bondage; if you are Taine, Maurras or Léon Daudet, the story will run: unpractical logicians made the people drunk with their heady doctrines, dissolved the historic bonds of society, and let

England. The agreement of 1786 was working to the greater advantage of England than of France: but active economic cooperation between the two countries, after nearly a century of commercial warfare, was bound to be profitable to both.

loose the uncontrollable fury of the rabble. In both cases,
it is Voltaire's fault, unless it be Rousseau's.

It is not certain that the French are guided by abstract
principles more docilely than other people; but they seem
to require, more imperiously than others, a theoretical
justification for what they actually want to do. They are
rationalizers rather than rationalists. Whilst feudalism
served their purpose, they reduced that living chaos to
the neatest formulæ of which it was capable (Beauma-
noir). When absolutism was in the ascendant, they
turned it into a well-knit system (Bossuet). The facts
preceded the theory. Similarly, in the eighteenth century, it was the desire for reforms—a very practical desire—that created its philosophy, and not an abstract
philosophy that engendered a desire for reform. La
Bruyère, Fénelon, Vauban, later Montesquieu and Voltaire, had pointed out the glaring abuses of the régime,
long before any political radicalism had been evolved.
The "abstract" character of eighteenth century thought,
as we tried to show in our survey of "Philosophy," has
been grossly overemphasized. Montesquieu, unquestionably, was a trained magistrate, a historian, a careful observer, not a callow radical. It was he who first taught
definitely the relativity of human laws, and their dependence upon "climate," i. e., environment. Voltaire, a very
practical man in the conduct of his own affairs, was also
a conscientious investigator. His *Century of Louis XIV*
is a monument, not of eloquence or formal logic, but of
scholarship. He was always ready to expose the absurdity of *a priori* systems, like Leibniz's optimism; and he
was more impatient than Montesquieu himself of fine spun
theories without sufficient support in fact. Neither Montesquieu nor Voltaire desired an upheaval: they belonged,
on different levels, to that administrative and judicial
middle class (*bourgeoisie et noblesse de robe*) which was
the natural ally and indeed the mainstay of the monarchy.
This leaves us with Rousseau as the chief, and almost the
sole, offender, Rousseau, who began magnificently a survey of world-history with the words: "First of all, let us

brush the facts aside!" Curiously enough, Rousseau himself is not such a deep-dyed radical as he has been painted. Voltaire and Montesquieu never dreamt of a democratic republic for France: neither did Rousseau. He tells us unequivocally that his ideal of pure democracy is applicable only in small states. When he was consulted about constitutions for Corsica and Poland, he began, not by brushing the facts aside, but by insisting that the facts should be collected and taken into consideration.

"Philosophy" did not desire to destroy anything except "abuses": that these abuses were real, no one, at the time or since, could honestly deny. The one fault we have to find with the "Philosophers" is that they expressed themselves in rational terms, that they appealed to principles, instead of arguing solely from precedents. France also had tried "muddling through somehow," in accordance with immemorial custom, and in the most approved British fashion. But muddle-headedness is not a thoroughly French virtue. For this regrettable insistence upon definiteness and cogency, Montesquieu, Voltaire and Rousseau are not exclusively to blame: the germs of the disease existed long before their time. Back of them, we find Boileau, voicing the creed of Classicism, and proclaiming that Reason should be served and loved. We find Descartes, refusing to accept anything as true, unless it appeared to his mind clearly and evidently to be such. Shall we say then: "C'est la faute à Boileau, c'est la faute à Descartes"? Hardly, for earlier still, we find the constant efforts of the King's servants to reduce to intelligibility the chaos of customs. The eighteenth century is accused of inventing the dangerous doctrine of general human rights: but if we go back to the middle ages, we read in a Charter of 1147: "A decree of divine Providence has ordained that all men, being of the same origin, be endowed at their birth with a sort of natural liberty. . . . It belongs to Our Royal Majesty to raise them again to liberty. . . ." Or we might find in the famous Ordinance of Louis X, "le Hutin," in 1315: "As, according to the law of nature, every man should be born free . . . we,

considering that our Kingdom is called the Kingdom of
the Franks (*i. e.*, of the Free), and that reality should be
in agreement with the name, have ordered, etc. . . ."
The Rights of Man, natural liberty, natural equality,
were therefore commonplaces of ancient standing, and traditional principles of the Capetian monarchy.[1] Finally,
we may add that the social philosophy of the French Enlightenment was based upon English doctrines and English examples, and that in its turn it influenced the
political thought of America: if our Anglo-Saxon com-
placency has any justification, the French "Philosophers"
can hardly be condemned.

None of these explanations, therefore, carries conviction. The French are not a revolutionary people, much
as they love to jeer and grumble at those in authority.
Their sufferings, very real, tragic indeed, were not growing intolerable: on the contrary, definite improvements
were taking place. The "Philosophers" were not preaching disloyalty, violence, anarchy: they were voicing unquestioned grievances, and their ideal was, not mob-rule,
but the firm government of an enlightened despot—a
Frederick II, a Catherine II; failing this, an enlightened
minister, a Pombal, a Turgot. Reforms were inevitable:
the Revolution was not.

IV

A loyal and patient people was forced into a career of
violence by the uncompromising attitude of the privilege-
holders. The most dangerous form of radicalism is the
radicalism of conservation. Conservation is a misnomer:
as there is no conservation but in progress, so-called conservatism is in most cases reaction pure and simple. England and France have frequently been contrasted in this
respect: England is blessed with conservatives who before
the alternative: "To mend or to end," know how to make

---

[1] Cf. A. Gasquet: *Précis des Institutions Politiques et Sociales de
l'Ancienne France,* Paris, Hachette, 1885. Vol. II, pp. 281-282. Also Lu-
chaire, *Histoire des Institutions Monarchiques,* Livre IV, Ch. III.

the right choice at the proper time. This contrast, however, is not due to any racial difference. England has always had her "die-hards," and her "bitter-enders": and fine, typical English gentlemen they are held to be. There have always been Frenchmen with a genius for compromise, from Michel de l'Hospital and Henry of Navarre to Gambetta, Jean Jaurès and Aristide Briand; and Englishmen with a genius for "Thoroughness," from Strafford to Edward Carson. But England learned her political lesson—imperfectly and with the assistance of three revolutions—a century or so before France.

In that blind resistance to progress, the King was by no means the chief offender, and the Court was not alone. Members of all classes evinced the narrow-mindedness and narrow-heartedness that precipitated the disaster. The worst blow to the monarchy was the failure of Turgot's reforms: but the frivolous scepticism of Maurepas and the selfishness of the clique which he represented were not the only causes of that failure. No reform was closer to Turgot's heart than free trade within the limits of the nation, and particularly the unhampered circulation of cereals. At the first crisis caused by the new liberty, the peasants of Ile-de-France rose in insurrection, besieged Versailles, entered Paris, uttering revolutionary threats. They may have been secretly abetted by the Court and the profiteers, but they distrusted and resented change as bitterly as any feudal lord. The industrial and commercial classes were little better: the abolition of the obsolete and oppressive trade guilds was stubbornly resisted by the masters. Every Frenchman, high or low, was clamouring against "abuses," but was eager to maintain his "rights." And, as England found out in Ireland, one man's rights easily turn into another man's wrongs.

The worst obstacle to orderly progress was probably offered by the Parliaments. Their reactionary attitude was all the more dangerous because it was magnificently camouflaged as respect for the law and resistance to oppression. Even sceptical Paris applauded "the old Romans" when they went into exile in 1771. In the great crisis, the Parliaments, servants of the monarchy and flower of the Third Estate, managed to thwart the efforts of both King and bourgeoisie. We have seen how these Courts of Justice had, through a long tradition, made themselves quasi-independent of the crown, and usurped a semi-political character. There were fine old Parliamentary dynasties, Molé, Séguier, Lamoignon, d'Aguesseau, d'Aligre, forming a "nobility of the gown" as proud and as exclusive as the "nobility of the sword." Their prerogatives, in their eyes, were as essential a part of the "ancient constitution of the realm" as the authority of the King himself. They claimed to be the judges of the moment "when loyalty is no longer compatible with obedience." The old spirit of the Fronde had never died in their midst. It had been kept up by their Jansenist sympathies and their opposition to Ultramontanism. Their establishment was not free from abuses: as their offices were, in practice, hereditary, a young fop or an old rake might sit on the bench. But, on the whole, they were independent, educated, and moral far above the general level.

Their damning fault was that they had become a caste, and therefore the sworn defenders of privilege. For another reason, they were also committed to reaction. Sincerely pious, they strove to atone for their hostility against the Jesuits through their rigour against free thought. The Philosophers had no worse opponents, although some members of the Parliamentary caste were among their best friends. Diderot and Rousseau felt the weight of their enmity; and Voltaire, as a part of his "philosophical" campaign, wrote a *History of the Parliament of Paris* (1769), which was a long arraignment.

In 1771, Maupeou succeeded in effecting a radical reform, which would have reduced the Courts of Justice to their proper rôle. Unfortunately, the circumstances were so tangled that public opinion did not unequivocally endorse the new organization. The right thing had been done through the wrong means, and to support Maupeou meant condoning Jeanne Bécu, Countess du Barry, a favourite from the gutter. In 1774, with the new reign, the Maupeou Courts disappeared, and the old order was practically restored. The Parliaments again used their power to frustrate every attempt at reform. Even more than the Court camarilla, they were the soul of resistance: they opposed Turgot and they opposed Necker. They constantly thwarted the King, who was the only source of their authority. In the struggle, their motives became more involved and more unaccountable. They courted popularity through their resistance to "despotism," although their resistance was most stubborn when despotism was most enlightened. The absurdity of their position led them to the advocacy of desperate remedies. They, who in former ages had feared the States General as a possible rival, called for the revival of that half-forgotten institution. Thus their antiquarianism oddly coincided with the enthusiasm for representative government, which was part of the Anglomania and Americanomania of the time. And these fossils were hailed as prophets when in July 1787, they voted that: "The Nation, represented by the States General, alone has the right of granting to the King the resources which might prove indispensable." But their paradoxical popularity could not last. In their eagerness to oppose, they had over-reached themselves. When the States General assembled, the Parliaments vanished like a ghost at cock crow: "They are on their vacation," said Mirabeau; "let them remain on their vacation for ever. Thus they will pass unnoticed from life to death." And so it happened: a quiet, inglorious end for such an ancient and turbulent body.

V

The opposition of the clergy and of the nobility to every proposed reform was to be expected. But it was neither unanimous nor consistent, and its illogical character made it at the same time weak and irritating. The clergy was open to severe criticism, which did not orig-

inate exclusively from professed Voltairians. Exceedingly wealthy, it refused to contribute its proper share to
the support of the state. Its General Assembly periodically voted, in lieu of taxes, a "gratuitous gift" to the
King: but good care was taken that the burden be light.
This wealth was scandalously ill-divided. To the priests
in actual charge of parish duties went a bare pittance,
called with unintentional irony their "congruous portion"; whilst absentee beneficiaries and aristocratic prelates enjoyed to the full the luxury and laxity allowed by
the time. By the side of a scandalous Prince of the
Church like Rohan at Strasbourg, there was—we could
hardly say a *prolétariat*—but a *plebs* of ecclesiastics, who
were sons of the people, suffered like the people, and,
early in the career of the States General, cast in their lot
with the people. Rent by social and economic grievances,
the clergy was far from united in matters of the spirit.
"Philosophy," the arch enemy, had penetrated deep
among its members. Indeed the "philosophical" group
was well sprinkled with ambiguous ecclesiastics, who retained the title of *Abbé*, and whose orthodoxy was as
paradoxical as Jérôme Coignard's. Without mentioning
Fouché the Oratorian, and Talleyrand the Mephistophelian Bishop of Autun, whom both Church and Revolution would be glad to disown, we find among those curious
characters Raynal, Mably, his brother Condillac, Siéyès.
Even the village priests had caught some of the same
spirit. "Natural Religion" and "Common Sense" had
made many converts. Rousseau's Savoyard Vicar had a
prototype and many congeners. The "Curé Meslier" was
not wholly invented by Voltaire and d'Holbach. According to Voltaire's own testimony, there were still numberless ecclesiastics who were above reproach, and the masses
of the population were still attached to their traditional
religion: yet the position of the clergy, weakened by so
many abuses, had become less secure. But, blind to this
insecurity, the clergy *as a body* remained defiantly intolerant to the very last. It denounced and persecuted
the "philosophical" ideas which were current among its

own members; and it resisted tooth and nail the emancipation of the Protestants.

The nobility had not remained impervious to the new spirit: the "Philosophers" had found friends and protectors in its ranks. Condorcet, the purest embodiment perhaps of the Enlightenment, was a Marquis. Another Marquis, the stormy Mirabeau, incessantly at war with his wife and his son, offered shelter to Rousseau, posed sincerely enough as "the Friend of Man," and, as a leader of liberal political economy, enjoyed a wide influence. So we are not surprised when we find his no less stormy and far more illustrious son marshal the forces of the Third Estate in the early decisive moments of its struggle for power. A Marquis again was Lafayette, a well-meaning and somewhat colourless personage, whose honorable mediocrity makes him more typical than if he had been a genius. La Rochefoucauld-Liancourt, of the highest nobility, was a true liberal, an active philanthropist, and a practical reformer in agriculture. In sharp contrast with this blameless figure, but illustrating the same tendency, we find the Duke of Orleans, a disreputable prince, but at any rate a thoroughly modern one. He had a keen eye for business, and was so mortally afraid of being left behind by the tide of liberal ideas that he plunged headlong into demagoguery.

But it was not easy for the nobility to follow this liberal movement. The nobles were in a difficult plight. The extravagance of court life had become an excessive burden; the new rich, the financiers, were setting a standard to which the old families could no longer conform without undue strain. Their country estates, neglected, mismanaged, brought no adequate returns. From the new sources of wealth, commerce and industry, they were cut off by ancient prejudices: only a few of the highest aristocrats, Chaulnes, Conti, Croÿ, Orleans, actually dared to make money. Had the lesser nobility wanted to engage in gainful occupations, they would have had to face the hostility, and even the legal resistance, of the Third Estate: the "anti-economic prejudice" worked both

ways. The nobles were thus compelled, amid fast changing circumstances, to cling to their ancient privileges and
to extract all they could from the bounty of the King.
So an attempt was made to collect feudal dues from the
peasants more rigorously than before, at the very moment
when these dues had been universally condemned by public opinion. The nobles tightened their monopoly of profitable sinecures in the civil service, of the richest benefices
in the Church, of the higher ranks in the army. Especially did the jeweled paupers of the Court rely upon
royal alms: direct gifts, payments of debts, pensions.
The King was open-handed with his friends, his wife's
friends, and the friends of their friends.

These privileges alone stood between the aristocracy
and ruin: no wonder the old nobility hated to share them
with parvenu families, who had bought a title along with
some office or estate. So the ancient régime stiffened at
the last moment. Access to Court was made more difficult; the list of noble families was carefully revised; by
the notorious Ordinance of 1781, nobles of recent creation,
as well as commoners, were debarred from reaching even
a captaincy. The nobility, like the Parliaments, like the
Clergy as an Order in the State, had shown itself in-
adaptable. It had of its own accord ruled out one of
the alternatives: Mend or End.

A large degree of personal responsibility attaches to
some exalted personages, and particularly to the brothers
of Louis XVI. The Count of Provence and the Count of
Artois were extravagant when extravagance was a public
crime. Their frivolity did not have even the excuse of
good nature: for they were venomous in their hostility to
the Queen. They did their best to force a crisis: when
it came, they were among the first to leave France before
they were in actual danger. They intrigued with foreign
nations against their own. They steadily declined to run
the slightest risk in the defence of their cause; and they
returned from exile unchanged except for an added touch
of religious bigotry, making Bourbonism a by-word.

Heavier still is the responsibility of the Queen. Her

recklessness constantly added to the difficulties of the
Treasury, and would not be curbed. Her thirst for pleasure, interpreted as immorality, weakened the authority
of the crown: it was a sinister omen when a large part of
public opinion believed, with the Cardinal de Rohan, that
the Queen of France could be bribed with a diamond neck-
lace. Her capricious and haughty temper destroyed the
favourable effect that her beauty might produce. On the
French throne, she remained a loyal Austrian: thus dem-
onstrating to the people that a sovereign might be her
nation's enemy. She possessed that obstinacy which, divorced from intelligence and generosity, can hardly be
called strength of mind. Yet the glamour that Burke,
among others, has cast upon her figure still dazzles our
eyes.

The chief cause of the catastrophe, however, is that the
monarchy, in the hour of decision, was untrue to its essential tradition. This was not the fault of the kindly, sensible and conscientious Louis XVI: he hesitated and
shuffled, not simply because his mind and his will were
none of the strongest, but because the ambiguity lay deep
in the history of the Capetian line. The secret of its
power had been its national character, the tacit alliance
of King and people against the selfish, arrogant and
turbulent nobles; but the form of its rule had been aristocratic: in all externals, the King was the first nobleman
in the land. Under Louis XIV, some kind of equilibrium
had been preserved between those conflicting elements;
under Louis XV, the king had lost contact with the people. It would have taken a man of unusual strength and
vision, well advised, well supported, to break loose from
the circle of his immediate friends, and resume his place
at the head of the nation. Louis XVI could not escape.
He felt himself in duty bound to defend those parasites
who posed as his defenders. He spoke of "my nobility,
my clergy": he, the hereditary enemy of privileges, deliberately cast in his lot with the privilege-holders. It is
what a conservative historian, Louis Madelin, calls "*le
faux-bond du Roi*": the King failed his people. Reforms

could have been effected *through* the King: he did not understand. Even then, they might have been carried out *with* the King: he missed his chance again. So the movement swept on, *without* him, and, as he struggled, *against* him: and it was the Revolution.

CHAPTER VI

THE REVOLUTION

The three essential factors: deficit, conflict with the Church, foreign intervention.

I. The immediate cause: *impending bankruptcy*. Prodigality. Wasteful method of tax collection. Unequal distribution. Last efforts: Necker, Calonne. The first Revolution: May-August 1789.

II. *Ecclesiastical Problem.* Financial reorganization of the Church. Administrative reconstruction. Extreme Gallicanism. Opposition of the Pope. Louis XVI, out of piety, commits himself to counter-Revolution. Second Revolution (Aug. 1792): fall of the monarchy.

III. *Foreign intervention.* War. Equivocal position of Louis XVI. Brunswick's manifesto. Exasperation and resulting Terrorism. Victory: national as much as Republican.

IV. *The alleged benefits of the Revolution.* Reorganization of France under the Convention: grandiose projects. Conservative in social-economic matters: sacredness of private property. One grand achievement: vast transfer of real property. Bankruptcy not averted.

V. The "Verdict of History"? Michelet the greatest historian of the Revolution. Spiritual havoc wrought by Revolution.

THE second half of the eighteenth century was filled with a confused struggle between reform and privilege. Reform suffered many a check, privilege scored more than one Pyrrhic victory: yet the trend was unmistakable. The King vacillated: but he had not fully committed himself to the defence of the ancient order, and the people's faith in him as their natural leader had not been completely shattered. This prolonged battle might have proceeded for another generation, in the same manner as the interminable contest between capitalism and labour in twentieth century England. Three factors in succession turned desultory agitation into sharply defined crises. The financial situation brought matters to a head, and the Revolution opened. The reorganization of the

Church completely estranged the King from the reformers, and the monarchy was doomed. Foreign intervention roused passion to a white heat: non-conformity became 3 treason, and Terrorism was urged as the sole means of public salvation.

I

The ancient régime perished through its finances. It was not the "hydra of radicalism" that portended its fall, but, in Mirabeau's words, "hideous Bankruptcy." All its sins of omission and commission finally translated themselves into accusing figures on the balance-sheet. The financial system—if anarchy may be called a system— was wrong at every turn. The expenditure of the Court literally knew no bounds, for it was controlled by no budget, and no adequate records were kept. The irony of it is that Louis XVI was a man of simple tastes; as a master locksmith, he would have been perfectly happy. He was a voracious eater and a mighty hunter: but these pleasures would not have ruined the state. Even Marie-Antoinette toyed with the new ideal of simplicity, which came in with Rousseau-worship and American sympathies. Yet never had the outlay at Versailles mounted higher. The Court was swarming with sinecurists, great and small, proliferating like germs in a diseased tissue. Waste was not an incident, but a principle. Minor establishments like those of the King's aunts devoured the revenue of a province. The Queen's friends, the Polignacs, the Lamballes, were yawning gulfs. We may add that the gigantic parasitism of Versailles was not the only cause of heavy expenditure. A spirited foreign policy is a costly luxury. The American War depleted the French treasury even worse than the insane prodigality of Marie-Antoinette.

This revenue, so freely dissipated, was collected in a most wasteful fashion. Yet how can we find words to condemn the ancient régime in this respect? It believed in the very sound principle that private enterprise will invariably prove more efficient than direct administration by the State. So the collection of taxes was farmed out to great contractors (*Fermiers Généraux*), who made it their business to exact from the people as much as they could, and to yield to the King no more than they had to. These great *concessionnaires* have left a sinister name in history, and the Revolution sentenced to death all the survivors of that hated order. Yet we have seen that this world of finance formed on the whole an intelligent society, which encouraged art and sympathized with "philosophy." Among them was Lavoisier: the scientist in him could not save the financier from the guillotine.

Worst of all was the unequal distribution of the burden. The clergy and the nobility did contribute in cash to the support of the State: but they had never completely overcome the prejudice that taxpaying was in itself something servile. The priest prayed for the State—and faith it needed it!; the noble was ready to shed his blood in its defence; both resented the degrading idea of paying vulgar money. The trouble was that these idealistic orders detained a large proportion of the country's material wealth. The clergy was insolently rich; and, if the old nobility was in financial trouble, it was only on account of its recklessness: it still held an enormous amount of landed property. Furthermore, the richest bourgeois sought to buy themselves titles, and claimed exemption in their turn. Logically, the poor alone were to pay. Whenever an effort was made to submit all sorts and conditions of men and of land to equitable taxation, the upper classes protested against such an insult to their dignity. It looked as though they had faith in but one scriptural passage: From him that hath not shall be taken away even that which he hath.

Necker did his best, from 1777 to 1781. He attempted to shed some light on the chaos of state finances, and to pare down sinecures and pensions. Riddled with epigrams, accused of destroying "the ancient edifice of the monarchy," he had to resign. Calonne tried a method much pleasanter than retrenchment: his panacea was lav-

ishness, which would quicken the economic rhythm and
encourage activity, by restoring optimism. On the
strength of this renewed confidence, more money could be
borrowed, and so *ad infinitum*. No wonder Marie-Antoinette considered Calonne as a wizard. This wild gamble
might have succeeded, had the wealth of the country been
expanding at a faster rate, and had the bulk of the expenditure been of a productive kind: thus did the Second
Empire create genuine wealth through display and borrowing. But under Calonne, the proceeds of taxes and
loans were squandered in sheer extravagance, and bankruptcy drew threateningly near. Calonne was forced back
to the ideas of Necker; and as he knew that the Parliaments would never endorse the sweeping reforms that had
become necessary, he suggested an Assembly of Notables,
which met in 1787. The Assembly turned down his proposals, and he fell. His opponent and successor Loménie
de Brienne had ultimately nothing to offer but the inevitable sacrifices: Notables and Parliaments balked
again. Every attempt at patching up the old machine
had been blocked. In a curious mood of defiance and
desperation, the arch-reactionaries, the Parliaments, endorsed the most hazardous of all remedies, the States
General.

With the meeting of that Assembly (May 5, 1789), the
first Revolution actually begins. Within three months, it
was completed. On June 17, the Third Estate, claiming
to represent the vast majority of the nation, transformed
the States General into a National Assembly; on the 20th,
the deputies swore never to separate until they had given
France a constitution; on the 23rd, they refused to obey
the King's command that they meet as three separate
bodies; on the 27th, the King gives in, and the two upper
orders, Clergy and Nobility, joined the Third Estate.
On the 11th of July, signs of counter-revolutionary activities excited the fear and anger of the Parisian population; on the 14th, the storming of the Bastille was a sharp
reminder that the people would brook no reaction. The
agitation gained the whole of France; the peasants joined

at last the bourgeoisie and the city workers. On the night of August 4th, in a lucid frenzy compounded of logic, generosity and fear, the privilege-holders bowed to their fate. In ninety days, with very little shedding of blood, the abuses had been swept away. The King's popularity was still unimpaired: at that time, Danton, Robespierre, and even Marat were royalists. All that had perished was the last vestige of Feudalism: and the suppression of Feudalism had been the goal of the Kings for three hundred years.

II

Had all Frenchmen worked harmoniously together, the task of reconstruction would still have been formidable: and the quasi-unanimity achieved on the night of August 4th did not survive the sober dawn. Errors, wrangles, crises, were to be expected: still, the worst was over, and no difficulty seemed insuperable. It was the religion question which made a smooth transition between the old régime and the new an impossibility.

The confiscation of Church property was proposed in a spirit, not of vengeance, but of justice. It was hardly safe for the clergy to be absurdly rich in the midst of a bankrupt kingdom; it was even less safe for it to starve its hardest workers in order to pamper a few aristocrats. The necessity of a redistribution was felt by all, and not least by loyal Catholics. Legally, the Clergy, as well as the nobility, had ceased to exist as a separate order in the State: its property was placed at the disposal of the nation. The first use to be made of this property was to assure the adequate support of all priests who were actually ministering to the religious needs of the people. This done, a vast surplus was left, which could be applied to the reduction, or even the extinction of the national deficit. So far, the plan was statesmanlike; and, much as certain conservative elements may have disliked it, they found downright opposition a very unpopular attitude.

The financial readjustment was dangerous, but feasible: unfortunately, there went with it an administrative reorganization of the most sweeping character. The Church had always been so intimately connected with the monarchy that the reform of the one seemed to carry with it the reform of the other. There was nothing spiritual, for instance, about the boundaries of the bishoprics: they followed closely those of the ancient Gallo-Roman cities. Why such an anachronism, and what would be more natural than to have the dioceses coincide with the newly created "departments"? Election, in the new France, had everywhere taken the place of appointment from above: but this method had been used by the primitive Church, and could be restored without interfering with any dogma. The Gallican Church had, for untold centuries, enjoyed a large measure of autonomy under the purely spiritual authority of the Pope. The Declaration of the Four Articles, in 1682, was the most emphatic statement of these claims, which King and Parliament had endorsed, if not dictated. Why should not the State, therefore, enact that the newly elected Bishops should merely notify the Pope of their elevation, without seeking his confirmation of their title? It was extreme Gallicanism no doubt, but still it was Gallicanism, a policy rooted in venerable traditions.

Each of these contentions, separately, would have been defensible, although each would have created bitter difficulties. Coming as they did all together, they proved inacceptable. The Church might grumblingly have jettisoned much of her wealth, if in other respects her ancient customs had not been disturbed. Rome had found it possible before to compromise, albeit reluctantly, with some degree of Gallican independence: the King was His Most Christian Majesty, the Lord's Anointed, the Eldest Son of the Church. But the Gallicanism of an Assembly was a totally different affair: an Assembly did not place its soul, like the King, in the keeping of a confessor; an Assembly was capable of turning the Abbey of St. Genevieve into a Pantheon for Voltaire and Rousseau. It would have been hard enough for the Church to retrace her steps after so many centuries, and to accept the principle of popular election, if the faithful alone had been entitled to a vote: but according to the Constitution, all the *political* electors, including Jews, Protestants and infidels, could take part in the choice of priests. With so many difficulties in its path, we may wonder, not that the Constitutional Church failed, but that its start was not absolutely discouraging, that its personnel was far from despicable, and that it managed to survive, through many trials, until the Concordat.

The Assembly had no thought of religious schism, and professed loyalty to the Pope. But the Pope was injured and affronted at every turn. The King's Ambassador at Rome, Bernis, did nothing to allay his indignation or his fears. On the contrary, it served the purpose of the aristocratic group with which Bernis was in sympathy that the Pope should condemn the Revolution. An unfortunate side issue envenomed the situation: the Pope still held Avignon and the surrounding County, as an enclave in French territory. Some at least of the inhabitants desired union with France; and the annexation of the little district was decided upon without due regard for the legitimate sovereign. Not without deliberation, the Pope condemned at last the ecclesiastical legislation of France, and forbade priests taking the "civic oath." This was the formal declaration of war between the factions. Clerics and nobles now had a religious justification for their struggle. They felt they were fighting, no longer for pride or privilege, but for their faith. And in many provinces the devout peasantry stood with them, whilst even in Paris, the middle class began to waver. Resistance drew persecution, and persecution intensified resistance.

The result of this breach was particularly fateful in the case of the King. Louis XVI had shilly-shallied. He felt obscurely that much good might come out of the movement, and repeatedly, he seemed more than half-reconciled with the change. He was both too kindly and too torpid to offer much of a fight when his own privileges or even those of his closest friends were clipped.

But when Rome had spoken, he obeyed. He obeyed, not only with the passivity of a good Catholic, but with inner alacrity, because the words of the Pope crystallized his latent misgivings. From that time, he might yield to the Revolution, under duress, and with mental reservations: but he was at heart irreconcilable. When the Constitution was at last inaugurated, France beheld the strange and sorry spectacle of a King enthroned who, a few weeks before, had run away in disguise from his capital, and attempted to join the enemies of his own government. It was a miracle that such a situation endured fourteen months. The monarchy collapsed on the 10th of August 1792 at the touch of the populace: but it had received its death wound on the 20th of June 1791, when the royal family started on the pitiful adventure that was to end at Varennes.

III

The last disturbing element was foreign intervention. England and America enjoy an enormous advantage over France: they are allowed to have their civil wars in peace. A nation with artificial frontiers and jealous neighbours can not always follow Napoleon's homely bit of advice: *"Il faut laver son linge sale en famille."*

The irreconcilable French nobles, following the Count of Artois in voluntary emigration, formed a little anti-Revolutionary army at Coblenz: that this army should be tolerated was in itself a *casus belli*. The German princes who held feudal property in Alsace protested against the suppression of their "rights" with as much determination as certain oil companies protest against the Mexican constitution. The Austrian Queen of France was appealing for support to her brother the Emperor. The Pope was denouncing the policy of the Revolution. Apart from these definite causes of conflict, more general factors were at work. It was soon felt that the French Revolution was a European problem. The example of France, the oldest monarchy, and the center of the most brilliant culture, was likely to be contagious. Even liberal princes began to feel uneasy. In addition, they might want to take advantage of France's troubles: France had profited frequently enough by their divisions.

Whilst difficulties were thus accumulating, all parties in France seemed to welcome the idea of war—each hoping that it would strengthen its hands. Marat was among the few publicists who resolutely advocated peace.

When war was finally declared, against the Emperor and his ally the King of Prussia, Louis XVI was placed at a terrible disadvantage. His popularity, for the last time, could have been restored, if, in the hour of national danger, he had resumed his rightful place at the head of his people. But it was felt, and ultimately it was proved, that the royal circle considered the enemies as deliverers. The King was thenceforward a traitor in spirit; the Queen was accused of being a traitor in fact, betraying to her Austrian friends the plans of the French. The manifesto of the Prussian commander, Brunswick, with a tactlessness so enormous that it seems intentional, emphasized the solidarity between the royal family and the enemies of France. *Salus populi suprema lex esto:* no nation engaged in a life-and-death struggle has ever shown much mercy to traitors. And the fact that "treason" was ubiquitous did not dilute its venom: it only made the plight of the country more appalling, and more implacable the resulting mood. England had a short way with Sir Roger Casement: had there been ten thousand such, repression would have been, not more lenient, but swifter still.

The situation of France early in 1793 was unexampled. Half Europe was now in coalition against her; her aristocratic officers had deserted almost in a body; those who remained were hardly to be trusted; no priest could remain faithful to the Pope without being in flagrant rebellion against the Constitution. More than one fourth of France, in the South and in the West, had risen against Paris. Republican France was a besieged fortress, torn by strife within. The result was a state of exasperation

verging upon madness. Of this "preternatural suspicion," as Carlyle called it, of this "obsidional fever,"
Marat is the sinister symptom. The "Friend of the People," as he liked to style himself, had for a long time
found comparatively few sympathizers. But as his worst
predictions came to pass, he seemed to incarnate the sombre resolve of a people at bay. He may not have urged
the massacre of prisoners in September 1792: the ferocity
of many had slowly risen to the pitch of his own. When
Charlotte Corday stabbed him, he was worshipped as a
martyr.

Terror feeds upon itself, and can not compromise. A
cowed adversary remains under suspicion: the very wrongs
inflicted upon his friends make it more likely that he is
nursing plans of vengeance. So the circle of victims
widened endlessly. When actual traitors had met their
fate, open sympathizers, half-hearted sympathizers, possible sympathizers, had their turn. Neutrals followed,
moderate republicans, Terrorists nauseated at last by
the reek of blood. Camille Desmoulins and Danton had
to expiate on the guillotine the crime of "indulgence."
Robespierre alone, unflinching, incorruptible, was restoring the reign of virtue by cutting down all those who
were less pure than himself. As an omen of the millennium which he hoped to establish, he rededicated France
to the worship of a purified deity, the "Supreme Being."
The tragic irony of it all is that Robespierre did not perish through a rebellion of the sane and humane elements:
he was ignobly tumbled down from his throne by a coalition of the vilest, men who had terrorized out of cowardice, and who felt the approaching cold of his accusing
glance. Ill fares the nation that is "saved" by Tallien
and Barras.

The Convention, at any rate, had prevented the armies
from being stabbed in the back. This, and only this, affords a shadow of justification for the Terror. The warfare that raged on the Paris front was of secondary importance: the guillotine made fewer victims than a single
battle. The course of French history at that time can

not be understood if we do not turn our back on the capital and watch the conflict at the frontiers. There the fate of France and the Revolution was being decided. There was the soul of the country and the best of her sons. And, within three years, the ragged hosts of the Republic, with their boyish impromptu generals, had defeated Europe.

The victory was a clear fact: it was registered in the treaties of Basel. Its causes are multifarious and obscure. Whilst Goethe saw at Valmy the dawn of a new era in the history of the world, cynics assert that the unripe grapes of Champagne had much to do with the prompt discouragement of the Prussian troops. A coalition is ever at a disadvantage against a united enemy: especially a coalition of such inveterate rivals as Austria and Prussia were in those days, each mortally afraid lest the other leave her in the lurch on the Western front, and steal a march in the partition of Poland. The loss of her superior officers had not been for France an unmitigated evil: many were mere courtiers without technical knowledge, experience or authority. However, although it was Republican France that fought and triumphed, that France, in all essentials, was one with the France of the kings. Enthusiasm alone does not win battles: the first volunteers fled in a panic. Legions do not spring from the soil, officered, drilled and equipped, when the Country in danger stamps her foot. The revolutionary recruits were not steadied into genuine soldiers until they were "amalgamated" with veterans. The ordnance used by Carnot and by Napoleon was that of Gribeauval, created under the ancient régime. In the more scientific and less aristocratic branches of the service, the artillery and the engineers' corps, many officers had remained loyal to the Revolution. And a man was found who evolved a strategy adequate to the resources and the needs of the time. To the small, carefully drilled armies of the Frederician type, Carnot opposed masses of unprecedented magnitude: twelve hundred thousand men. To the learned chess game of their manœuvres and counter-manœuvres, he substituted a war of swift motion. But Carnot's genius, so unjustly eclipsed in our eyes by the fame of Bonaparte, was not the one decisive element. He was only the "Organizer of Victory." It was the whole momentum of France's tradition that carried her through the desperate struggle. The new liberty fired the enthusiasm of the fighters: but no less ardent was their pride in the ancient fame of France. The nation and the Republic were one: but victory was national, even more than it was republican. This is felt to the present day, when conservatives and even royalists, full of hatred and contempt for the politicians of the Convention, can not repress a thrill of joy at the names of Valmy, Jemmapes, Wattignies and Fleurus.

IV

According to orthodox Republican history, the Convention, torn by factional strife, engrossed in civil and foreign war, harassed by an acute economic and financial crisis, found time and energy to continue the reorganization of France. An impressive list of creations is adduced: the Polytechnic School, the Institute of France, and the introduction of the metric system are among the most famous.[1] Had the Convention achieved much of permanent value under such tragic circumstances, it would indeed be a miracle. Much more probably, it is a myth. No doubt the "Plain" and the "Marsh," as the moderate parties were contemptuously called, had leisure enough to legislate, and to legislate wisely, in the lulls of the storm. Much of their time was wasted in entertaining grotesque delegations, but not all their time. After a century of teeming "philosophy," it was to be expected that innumerable proposals for reform should be ready, and that

[1] The Revolutionary Calendar was discarded at the end of a few years (Jan. 1, 1806); but it remains perennially attractive with the poetical names of its months: Vendémiaire, Brumaire, Frimaire; Nivôse, Pluviôse, Ventôse; Germinal, Floréal, Prairial; Messidor, Thermidor, Fructidor. The minor poet Fabre d'Eglantine worked more durably than Robespierre.

some of them should be elaborate and sensible enough. The great plan for public education drawn up by La-kanal would do credit even to a modern democracy. But the mere endorsement of such a scheme means surprizingly little. As was to be expected, much was voted that remained on paper. A new name tagged on to an ancient institution—the "King's Garden," for instance, a great scientific center under Buffon, became the "Museum of Natural History"—is rather a shadowy victory for progress. With all the palingenesis bluff eliminated, the record of the Convention is creditable enough: but superhuman it is not.

After strange vagaries in the religious field, the Convention came very near undoing the worst blunder of the Constituent Assembly: in 1794, it voted the complete separation of Church and State. Unfortunately this victory for common sense remained a purely negative one: it was not followed by its corollary: free churches in a free state. The ecclesiastical problem remained unsolved, thus enabling Bonaparte, with his patched-up Concordat, to restore a union which could never again be whole-hearted.

The social legislation of the Revolution was, in principle, purely conservative. Whilst feudalism was abolished, private property was declared an inalienable and sacred right. This faith in the sacredness of property was not weakened under the Convention. Individualism remained the official philosophy: the Revolutionists did not foresee the industrial transformation, already well on its way in England, which was to make economic individualism obsolete. It was natural that the great upheaval, and the condemnation of political inequality, should create a demand for economic equality: such a demand the great radical assembly considered with virtuous horror. Death was to be the punishment of any one who should propose a communistic measure, or, as it was called in memory of the Gracchi, "an agrarian law." At the height of the crisis, price-fixing by the state (the "maximum") was adopted as a desperate remedy: but it was abandoned at the fall of Robespierre, and profiteering knew no bounds.

The Thermidorian reaction and the Directoire were the paradise of the *nouveaux riches*.

Blood and destruction had been of no avail. In 1794, or in 1799, the Revolution had not gone a single step beyond its one great achievement, the abolition of feudal privileges on the night of August 4th 1789. The one thing that it had sought to avert came to pass, inexorably. It was the fear of bankruptcy that forced the King to call the States General; the property of the clergy and that of the emigrating nobles were thrown into the gulf, and, in 1795, France was more hopelessly bankrupt than in 1789. The confiscated estates had served as security for paper money, the *assignats*. With the absurd multiplication of these *assignats*, genuine and counterfeited, and with the total loss of confidence in the revolutionary governments, their value had fallen to practically nothing. The treasury was in a more desperate condition under the Directoire than it had been under Calonne and Loménie de Brienne. The ancient régime had perished, but the finances were not saved.

Was the Revolution wholly futile then, a prolonged nightmare that left the country weak and aching? Something substantial had been done: a vast transfer of real property. Not only were the peasants liberated from all feudal dues; but they had a chance of appeasing their land-hunger in purchasing the confiscated estates of nobles and clergy. In payment for these estates, the fast depreciating *assignats* were accepted at their face value, whilst the farmers sold their produce at ever mounting prices. In this way, they got the land for a song. Not all of it went to the tillers of the soil. Many nobles were shrewd or popular enough to keep their estates; others managed to repurchase them secretly through agents: the landed aristocracy is still a power in France, especially in the West. The urban middle class was not likely to let such a splendid opportunity go by, and the bourgeois too secured their share of nationalized property. But on the whole, the impregnable class of peasant proprietors, which existed before the Revolution, was enormously strengthened. This gave the new régime the broadest basis: henceforth, no sweeping counter-revolution was conceivable, for the most conservative class, the peasantry, had been given something tangible to conserve.

V

If time, if discussion, if scholarship could settle anything, we should by this time be in possession of "the truth about the French Revolution." Yet such a verdict seems as far from our reach as ever. The great epic writers, Carlyle, Michelet, Taine, endure, on account of their literary splendour: but in this respect, they do not stand apart from the fictionists, Dickens, Victor Hugo, Anatole France. The most careful modern investigators, Aulard, Mathiez, and their peers, scientific enough in establishing details, are manifestly partisan. Perhaps the one who most nearly carries conviction is Michelet. A much more thorough scholar than Carlyle or Taine, a greater poet, a more generous soul, he alone communicates to us the flame of enthusiasm without which the Revolution proves unintelligible. No movement in history can be understood through the accumulation of material facts alone: a movement is a spirit; or, if a more pedantic term be more acceptable, "a phenomenon of collective psychology." The spirit of Michelet, projected on the chaos of the Revolution, gives it a meaning. The spirit of Taine gives none: men do not fight and work as the French did in those years in a mere fit of national insanity.

With Michelet, we feel impatient at the selfishness and pride of the few incorrigible privilege-holders who goaded a loyal nation into ways of violence. We can not withhold our sympathy from a people fighting in the name of Liberty, Equality, Fraternity; and fighting, not for themselves alone, but for all mankind. If the end could have been achieved in no other way, and especially if it had actually been achieved, we might be inclined not to count the cost.

But the spiritual havoc wrought by the Revolution was

more permanent than mere loss of goods, or even of lives. The mystic faith in violence created by the apparent victory of the Revolution is a poison which, after a century of turmoil, has not been fully eliminated. The great crisis made the majority of Frenchmen unjust toward their own past: in order to justify the massacres of September, the death of the Royal Family and the rule of Terror, the ancient régime had to be maligned. Napoleon I and Louis-Philippe tried to reconcile past and present: but their eclecticism was not wholly successful. Generations were brought up in the belief that, before 1789, everything was wrong, except the denunciations of a few "Philosophers." This mutilation of history—in this we agree with the most conservative historians, Dimier, Bainville, Maurras—is a mutilation of the national soul.

If we compare France in the middle of the nineteenth century with France in the middle of the eighteenth, we can not suppress a feeling of loss. It ought not to be so: material progress is undeniable; knowledge as well as comfort were more widely diffused, poetical sources long sealed had been reopened, science was assuming profounder meaning. Yet, with it all, we are conscious of a vulgarisation, a rebarbarisation. We do not wish to idealize the ancient régime: but it offered at its best a combination of grace and seriousness, of wit and generosity, a smiling and active confidence in human nature, in reason, in progress, which we do not find in the spiritually shrunken elites of the succeeding age. The wisdom of prejudice, the sacredness of loose thinking, the beauty of make-believe, the worship of mere wealth, the legitimacy of force, all these ideas were obsolete among "Philosophers" long before 1789; and the nobles themselves were fast catching "philosophy." In what Léon Daudet not inaptly calls "the Stupid Nineteenth Century," every crude and brutal fallacy took a new lease of life; nor was it any less crude or brutal because it assumed romantic glamour or pseudo-scientific rigour. This regression of the governing classes is well marked throughout Europe, and not merely in France: a Catherine II, a Frederick

II, even a Joseph II, were incomparably more "enlightened" than their successors, and Spain, Portugal, Naples, could tell the same tale. For this new darkness that overspread European culture, the Revolution is responsible: because the light became a torch, it had to be extinguished. We are barely rediscovering at present our true leaders, and restoring contact with them over the reactionary abyss created, in recoil, by the Terror. When our thought is again as clear, as free, as generous as Voltaire's, the wounds inflicted by the Revolution will at last be healed. We can hardly forgive the great cataclysm for setting back, indefinitely, the promises of the Enlightenment; least of all can we forgive the blind conservatism which forced the irrepressible spirit of reform into the catastrophic channel of revolution.

CHAPTER VII

THE SUPREME CLASSICIST: NAPOLEON

Career, Personality, Legend.

I. *Napoleon's career as a conqueror.* Policy determined by treaties of Basel. No permanent result. Heavy cost. Glory not unalloyed. Heritage of hatred. Conquests detrimental to diffusion of French ideas.

II. *Napoleon's career as a civil ruler.* Constitutions. Codes. Prefects. Legion of Honour. University of France. Concordat. Friend or foe of the Revolution?

III. *Napoleon's personality.* Morality and taste not above mediocrity. Efficiency in swift decision. Ambition unchecked by tradition or scruple. Touch of madness.

IV. *The Napoleonic Legend:* a creation of Romanticism. Napoleon the supreme classicist, and the Romantic ideal incarnate.

THREE elements are mingled in Napoleon's marvelous destiny: his career, his personality, his legend. They blend so intimately that it is almost impossible to tell them apart. Yet the attempt should be made. Historians too often ascribe to the man what in truth belongs to the epoch; and they mistake for the cold light of science what in fact is the afterglow of romance.

By "career," we mean the facts of Napoleon's public life, the historical events of which he was the center—battles, treaties, *coups d'état*, institutions. It is obvious that these were not purely and simply the extension of his personality, but rather its colourful setting. The man Napoleon would have had very much the same temper, and, potentially, the same genius, if, born fifty years earlier, he had lived and died in obscurity, a fractious petty noble in wild Corsica. He needed the storm to rise, and he did not create the storm. He used it, he gave it a dramatic focus: but we are not certain whether he deflected it at all. Much that happened during his reign, much that was done in his name or even by his express command, neither originated with him, nor even was fashioned by him. A necessity deeper than the power of a single man was at work. Napoleon was no King Log: but, like all leaders, he was driven; like all autocrats, he was a figure-head; like all gods, he was a symbol.

By "legend," we do not mean a fabrication or a myth: Napoleon, we firmly believe, actually did exist in the flesh, and performed most of the things that are related of him. A "legend" is the epic amplification of reality that takes place, spontaneously, half-consciously, in the popular mind, and is further elaborated by the poets. A legend is much more difficult to detect than a lie: it is a magic light which plays upon reality, reveals it and transmutes it. You may spend a lifetime investigating the facts that fit into the legend, without ever questioning its fundamental delusion. Some of the most scholarly among the biographers of Napoleon are as uncritical in this respect as medieval hagiographers.

Between these vast collective forces—the anonymous, uncontrollable logic of events, and the poetic imagination of the people—the personality of Napoleon, definite and intense though it was, almost disappears. Emil Ludwig promised us a study of Napoleon the Man: but on every page of his book, we find instead Napoleon the Ruler or Napoleon the Hero of Romance. And it is the supreme triumph of Napoleon's genius that his personality should thus be absorbed. There may be men who are greater than their fate: Napoleon was not one of them. Neither did he prove unequal to his opportunity. He embraced his career so ardently, he identified himself with it so consciously, that men could reasonably doubt whether Napoleon shaped the events, or the events Napoleon.

I

A paradox reduced to an epigram is mere flippancy; expanded into seven learned volumes, it becomes a corner stone of history. Albert Sorel, in his *Europe and the French Revolution*, demonstrated, to the satisfaction of most scholars, that Napoleon's flamboyant career hardly

affected the essential course of events. For the constant
wars which marked his reign, his "insatiable ambition"
was not solely responsible; the ultimate day of reckoning,
all his genius could not avert. The settlement at Waterloo
and Vienna in 1815 was the consequence of the treaties of
Basel twenty years before; and the treaties of Basel
themselves were dictated, not by the spirit of the Revolution, but by the ghosts of Henry II, Richelieu, Mazarin
and Louis XIV.

The Convention, as we have seen, had defeated her enemies abroad and was in possession of the left bank of the
Rhine. The new principle of democracy was: No more
conquests! But when, after so many hundreds of years,
the goal of the monarchy had been reached at last, great
was the temptation not to let it slip away. A Revolutionist might say: Perish the colonies rather than a principle!: the colonies were rather shadowy in his mind, the
Rhine was a reality. Some kind of a compromise could
be effected. Conquest? No: but liberation: did not the
tricolour bring freedom in its folds? Annexation? By
no means: but the willing reunion of free peoples. There
were enough sympathizers with France in the Rhineland
to lend colour to such a plea; there was as yet too little
national feeling in Germany to make a protest irresistible. The educated classes knew French: the common people had not taken the habit of expressing themselves.
Thus the whole left bank of the Rhine became French,
with surprizingly little opposition.

There were a few men in 1795 who foresaw the dangers
of such a policy. Carnot was among them: he would have
been satisfied with a mere rectification of the frontiers.
But the momentum of the monarchical tradition was too
great: it seemed as though the hour of "manifest destiny"
had come. Now every moderate conquest in the past had
cost at least one war to confirm it. Even if the treaties
of Basel had been signed by Austria and England, they
would only have marked a truce. But the sudden extension of France to the Rhine was no ordinary conquest:
it was of such magnitude as to destroy the equilibrium of

Western Europe. And although the Rhinelanders did not rebel against France, although they remained loyal to their new country until 1813, although they did not welcome the Germans as liberators even then, although they became Prussians with the greatest reluctance, still it was almost inconceivable that they should ever be thoroughly assimilated by France. The case of Alsace is an exception. Alsace had become French a hundred and fifty years before, at the time of Germany's deepest humiliation and of France's most unquestioned supremacy; and yet, even in 1870, Alsace was not fully Frenchified. The Rhineland in French hands would have been a constant provocation to war.

We hate the word "inevitable": yet it seems hard to imagine how events could have taken a different turn. There was nothing permanent about the treaties of 1795: ultimately France had to be reduced to her true "natural" frontiers. "Natural" frontiers are the result of a complex compromise between physical geography, linguistic boundaries and national tradition. Such frontiers may change and do change: but, in old countries, they can not change suddenly. Dynasties may at a stroke widely expand their nominal domain: a Flemish Spaniard may control Austria. But as dynastic states become more truly national, their boundaries solidify.

We are therefore led to the conclusion that the most sensational aspect of Napoleon's career, his military conquests, was a brave show and nothing more. He left France smaller than he had found it: in 1815, she returned to her frontiers of 1792. In the meantime, French armies had entered Cairo, Vienna, Berlin, Madrid and Moscow; and foreign troops had bivouacked on the Champs-Elysées. But the result was scrupulously the same as if the government of Louis XVI had not declared war in 1792, or as if Carnot's wiser counsels had prevailed in 1795. Had no commander of genius been found, not even a Moreau or a Masséna, the settlement might have taken place in 1797 instead of 1815. Had a wiser diplomat or a still greater war leader than Napoleon stepped on the scene, the day of reckoning might have been postponed by a few years, and France might have permanently retained a few more square miles of German land, such as the Saar valley. Napoleon himself was fond of alluding to "the nature of things": here the nature of things was against him. He was a great gambler: but with the cards he had in his hand he could not win. This he ought to have known, had he possessed the infallible practical sense with which he is credited.

The gigantic adventure failed in its essential purpose: to keep in French hands the leadership of Europe. The cost in human lives was real enough; the spiritual cost, in the perpetuation of diffidence, hatred and brutality, was greater still. What do we find on the credit sid˃?

First of all, Glory: and who will be so craven as to count the deaths that go to the making of a great epic? This belongs to the "Legend," which we shall examine in its place. In sober historical terms, the military career of Napoleon justifies no such unqualified pride. According to General Ballard (who considers the Emperor as "the greatest man that ever lived"), Napoleon waged twelve wars, won six and lost six.[1] Four times his armies were lost or shattered altogether: in Egypt, abandoned by him, his forces had to capitulate; in Russia, they melted away; after Leipzig and after Waterloo, they became a mob. He entered the capitals of all his enemies, except England: but, for the first time in four centuries, Paris was captured by foreign troops. When a nation pays as dear for "glory" as France did in those days, it should be entitled to less equivocal and more durable results.

It is said that Napoleon the Conqueror, disastrous to France, proved in the end a good European. As the "booted missionary" of the Revolution, he shattered

---

[1] Gen. C. R. Ballard: *Napoleon, an Outline*. Probably Gen. Ballard had these in mind: won: Italy 1796-97; 2nd Italian Campaign (Marengo), 1800; Austro-Russian War (Austerlitz) 1805; Prussian War (Iena) 1806; Russia (Friedland) 1807; Austria (Wagram) 1809. Lost: Egypt; Spain; Russia 1812; Germany (Leipzig) 1813; France 1814; Belgium (Waterloo) 1815.

wherever he went the survivals of feudalism; he introduced
modern principles, modern methods of administration,
which were not lost when he fell; he hammered Germany
and Italy into nations. Are we sure that these benefits
could have been imparted only by the brutal means of
military conquest? Europe before 1789—much more so
than in 1815—was culturally one. No nation, even if it
had been so minded, could have kept its progress within
its own boundaries. The Enlightenment, from England,
had gained France, and from France, the whole continent, not through wars, but in spite of wars. King Voltaire needed no armies. The Encyclopædia forced its way
alone. The ideas of Beccaria spread without military
force. Not Marlborough, Clive or Wolfe, but Montesquieu and Voltaire, were the best apostles of England's
political principles. Rousseau affected American thought
without the assistance of a single soldier. It might rather
be maintained that armed intervention checked the natural
spread of liberal ideas. Napoleon controlled Naples and
Spain: both countries, in the eighteenth century, had
shown at least interesting velleities of reform; both, in the
early nineteenth, were noted for their blind love of reaction. A healthy national consciousness, on the basis of a
common culture, was dawning in Germany at the end of
the ancient régime. What Napoleon did was to warp
such a growth, to give a tremendous impetus to Prussian-
ism, to create to some extent a Germany in his own image,
"through blood and iron."

II

It is impossible to tell the story of modern Europe
without Napoleon: yet Napoleon's strategy and his diplomacy were not creative forces. They were the form,
not the substance of history. To a smaller extent, this
holds true of Napoleon's career as a civil ruler. In this
field also, he was a sign rather than a power. His purely
political institutions have not survived. They were a thin
mask for his autocracy; and, with much verbiage, his con-

stitutions contained but a single word: Napoleon. His
imperial nobility never was taken very seriously. On the
other hand, many of his reforms and institutions have
proved lasting, and it may be said that he provided the
framework of France's national life for a hundred years.

But, just as the essential conditions of his military career were laid down for him as early as 1795, the lines of
his civil activities were determined long before he came to
power. What he attempted, what he partly achieved, was
a compromise between traditions and principles. Such a
compromise was under way, and was bound to come about
as soon as the great crisis of 1793–94 was well over. Much
that the Revolution had destroyed was destined never to
rise again, because, even before 1789, it had a mere semblance of life. The revolution completed on August 4th
1789 was final, because it registered a fact: Feudalism
was dead. Had Louis XVIII come to the throne in 1799,
he could not have restored that corpse to life; moreover,
with all his limitations, he was too sensible even to desire
the resurrection of his ancient enemy. On the other hand,
radical democracy never existed in France. If it prevailed
in name under the Convention, it was in fact sacrificed to
the most ruthless oligarchical dictatorship, a dictatorship
justified by desperate need. When the need disappeared,
democracy remained in abeyance. Had Robespierre himself survived, he could have retained power only through
compromise: a compromise that would sacrifice phantoms
and recognize reality, *i. e.*, the enormous preponderance
of the middle class, *mesocracy*.

This compromise took place under Napoleon, and bears
the imprint of Napoleon's personality in the same way as
the coinage of the time bears his imperial profile. The destruction of ancient customs made new legislation necessary; this new legislation was elaborated by the Revolutionary Assemblies; the compilation of these new laws in
convenient form—were it only by some enterprising publisher—would have formed a Code; and the Code would
in essentials have been the same, whether the ruler's name
be Napoleon or Louis XVIII, Louis-Philippe of Orleans

or Lafayette, Carnot or even Barras. The First Consul
hastened the work of compilation, an obvious advantage,
yet not invariably an unqualified advantage. He took active part in its composition, but chiefly in order to inject
into it as much of his autocratic temper as he could. No
King would have dared to be as frankly reactionary as
Bonaparte.

Napoleon restored the "intendants" of the ancient
régime, under the name of prefects, as the representatives of the central government; but he did not restore
the local franchises which to some extent held in check—
and justified—the power of the Intendants. Those French
reformers who are now attempting to revive provincial
autonomy under the new label of Regionalism might well
curse Napoleon for his ruthless policy of centralization.
But in this case again, Napoleon is not so much to praise
and not so much to blame. He continued the Convention,
which continued the Bourbons. "One faith, one law, one
king" was the goal of the ancient régime; that France
should be "one and indivisible" was a cardinal article of
faith with the Revolutionists; "Federalism," as it was
called in 1793, tending to weaken this unity and indivisibility, was detested as a crime against the nation.

No institution created by Napoleon has been so immediately and so smoothly successful as the Legion of
Honour: but the Legion of Honour was not a novel idea.
It was the Order of St. Louis, founded by Louis XIV,
and abolished in 1793, restored under a modern name.
The monopolistic system of public education which he
called the "University of France," on the contrary, was
more original; but it never worked as Napoleon had
planned, and was destined to remain an imposing façade.

We find in his compromise with the Church, the Concordat, the most typical example of his method. His desire in all things was to obtain material results, and to obtain them quickly; about the means, he was not over-
scrupulous; about distant consequences, he was indifferent or blind. The transformation wrought by him in the
Church situation was little short of magical: on the eve

of the *Coup d'Etat*, disorder and diffidence; a few months
later, discipline restored, persecution ended, good will established. But out of the chaos that prevailed under the
Directoire, sheer weariness was already pointing the
proper way out: liberty, tolerance. Napoleon artificially
linked a non-sectarian State with the Churches, hoping
thereby to turn the clergy into a spiritual police. He
made free use of his favourite weapons: coercion, bribery,
equivocation and deceit. The result was that the Concordat led to open conflict under his own reign, and to
a century of petty wrangling thereafter. We can not forget that, within ten years of this solemn covenant, the
Pope was a prisoner and the Emperor excommunicated.
He called the Concordat his worst mistake: yet, in the very
notion of a Concordat, he was following Francis I; in the
Gallicanism of the "Organic Articles" which, of his own
authority, he tagged on to the agreement, he was following Louis XIV and Bossuet; in believing that Church and
State could not be separated, he was following the Constituent Assembly. His lack of originality was his excuse. Perhaps a weak, anonymous government alone
could have adopted the negative solution which we now
feel to be the wisest.

At times Napoleon claimed that his mission was to consolidate the Revolution; to trusted friends like Molé, he
professed that his task was to curb and destroy that same
Revolution. The latter is more in accordance with his
temperament and training. His ideal was that of Louis
XIV: but his method was that of the Convention. He was
a Revolution—or more strictly a Counter-Revolution—
in one person, an Anti-Jacobin in as great a hurry as
the Jacobins themselves. Swiftness of decision and of action is admirable in the war game; in the normal life of
a nation, haste can destroy, but not create. The abolition of feudalism could be done in a few moments, like a
long-delayed surgical operation: the reconstruction of the
country needed a patience which Napoleon did not possess. He regretted quaintly enough that he was not his
own grandson: generations will not be skipped. His de-

sire to create conservative institutions by a sudden *Fiat* is of the same kind as the action of a brand-new American college, framing "traditions" which "would go into effect next Monday at eight o'clock." His mushroom nobility, his parvenu dynasty, were not even hot-house products: they were plants made out of wax and paper. In so far as he exerted his sovereign will against "the nature of things," his work was but splendid make-believe; and the "nature of things" did not need a Bonaparte.

We can not repeat too emphatically that this view of Napoleon's career as in all essentials predetermined is neither hostile nor favourable to the hero. If it robs him of credit for miraculous achievements, it absolves him also of many heavy responsibilities. Constant wars, excessive centralization, autocracy, are the worst charges against him: but in these respects, he acted only like the Committee of Public Safety—a Committee of One; and the Committee of Public Safety had acted like a collective Louis XIV. These considerations are not a criticism of his personal ability: he was the most efficient dictator in history, until Mussolini appeared. They are not even a condemnation of dictatorship: if it remains true to its original spirit in ancient Rome, it may be a precious instrument in a sudden and desperate emergency. What we condemn is dictatorship as a permanent method of government, dictatorship attempting to turn itself into a régime and a tradition.

III

If we examine without partizanship Napoleon the man, we find him neither lovable nor execrable. He was ruthless: a professional soldier, and in times of revolution, can not be expected to be squeamish; and, in his own words, a hundred thousand lives meant little to him, so long as he had his steady "income" of cannon fodder. Yet he never was gratuitously, fiendishly cruel. The judicial murder of the Duke of Enghien was "worse than a crime:

a blunder": but he honestly thought that such an act of intimidation was needed. He was not truthful: in all his negotiations, and particularly in those with the Spanish Bourbons and with Alexander of Russia, he stooped to equivocation and prevarication. But in those days—so radically different from ours—every statesman was expected to lie for his country. He was not sincere: even when he did not lie, he loved to pose. Alfred de Vigny ascribed to Pope Pius VII the words that sum up so much of Napoleon's character: *"Commediante! Tragediante!"*; and a British historian bluntly calls him "a play actor, and a vulgar one at that." But his great predecessor Louis XIV was not free from theatricality, and a popular idol can not afford to despise his own histrionic gifts.

He shared the common feelings of mankind: he was a good son, a fairly good brother, a tolerable husband—as crowned husbands go—and as good a father as the average man. He sacrificed public interests to his Corsican clannishness, when he distributed Kingdoms among his relatives. But he hoped thereby to buttress his throne, and he showed very little brotherly tenderness for Lucien, Louis or Jérôme, when their desires or interests did not coincide with his own. The love of the iron man for his infant son has brought tears to many sympathetic eyes: as a matter of fact, it was the heir to the Empire rather than the little human soul that he cherished in the King of Rome. He did not, as Louis XV had done, allow his lust to interfere with the business of the State: but there was in some of his affairs a trooper-like brutality which pertained to the soldier of fortune rather than to the national hero. In business matters, he was honest, so long as honesty seemed the best policy. He did not like to be robbed beyond reason; and when he "became the State," he saw to it that the State was getting good value for its money. In his very first campaign, he curbed the acquisitive propensities of the army contractors. He allowed his generals, like Masséna, to loot only in the measure in which it placed them at his mercy. He went to Italy penniless: on his pay as a Republican general, he managed to buy a house in the rue Chantereine, a château at Malmaison, and to keep extravagant Josephine in a semi-regal state.

But a superman is not supposed to be a copybook moralist; he need not even be supremely intelligent in fields not his own. In many realms, Napoleon's mind was on a level with his heart. Whenever he speaks of religion, —whether with a touch of Oriental fatalism, or with a dab of Italian superstition, or like a pure Voltairean, half theist, half sceptic, or again like a disciple of Rousseau's *Savoyard Vicar*,—his thoughts are second-hand, slightly soiled and frayed. They are the thoughts that a busy adventurer would pick up here and there, in the lull of serious business. His one contribution to philosophy is his—soldierly—dread of independent thought, which he was pleased to dub "Ideology." Ideologists ought to be shot! In science, he was able to appreciate practical contributions like Humphry Davy's miners' lamp; but he did not understand Fulton. He encouraged studies which could not conceivably create a danger for the established order: but he publicly insulted Lamarck, the most original thinker of the time. In art, his taste inclined to the richly substantial. If the Empire Style still possesses undeniable merits, it is because its ultra-classical stiffness was relieved by a delicacy of execution inherited from the age of Louis XVI. When the Louis-Seize influence finally vanished, whilst Empire heaviness survived, we had the mahogany abominations of the Louis-Philippe era. And indeed there is a closer kinship than is commonly imagined between the tastes and principles of the two eclectic sovereigns, the two monarchs issued out of the Revolution, the two "Best of Republics," the Soldier-Emperor and the Citizen-King.

In literature, he was able to appreciate Corneille, the most obvious of the classics; he was taken in—with the whole continent—by the vogue of "Ossian"; and he liked Chateaubriand, because his *Spirit of Christianity* served the same cause as the Concordat. But he also shared the common admiration for the inane versifier Delille.

In offering these obvious remarks, we are not attempting to belittle Napoleon, but only to define him. We do not expect our modern Kings, Presidents or Generals to be arbiters in matters of culture: indeed the most notable "artistic" Emperors, Nero and William II, made the world yearn for sovereigns who knew their proper place in the realm of the spirit. Why should Napoleon be judged by an absurdly exacting standard? Culture was not his business. But it is of some importance to dispose of the superstition that he was a miracle of nature, a universal genius, a Leonardo da Vinci on the throne. We wonder how Leonardo would have fared as an Emperor?

In all these respects, therefore, Napoleon, as was to be expected, was not above mediocrity; and it was because he was substantially the Average Man that he has been idolized by the average man. Mediocrity is not incompatible with success; indeed, it is a necessary ingredient in success; but it will not create success. There were points in which Napoleon was supreme, and perhaps unique; and we thoroughly agree with M. de la Palisse that these points were his efficiency and his ambition.

Napoleon was trained as a soldier, and never was anything else. His efficiency is that of the military commander, who constantly has to meet life-and-death emergencies. The means may be rough, brutal, unphilosophical, costly in the end: but they must work. For detecting the pressing need and devising in a flash the immediate remedy, Napoleon's intellect was preternaturally keen. In a crisis—war, revolution, cataclysm—the military or dictatorial method is indispensable. If a building in the path of a conflagration has to be dynamited, you can not have it condemned by due process of law. In days of "normalcy," the army régime is singularly depressing. Of the larger efficiency that will allow for experiments, initiative and growth, Napoleon I had a lesser share than his nephew Napoleon III.

Napoleon's ambition inevitably calls for the hackneyed adjective "boundless." But the literal truth of this commonplace is worth emphasizing. Every other leader in the Revolution had his ambition checked at some point by some loyalty, some diffidence or some fear: it might be a principle, a prejudice, a tradition, or simply common-sense. Napoleon alone was absolutely free. He was not a Frenchman; between him and the King, there was no immemorial and sacred tie; the French nobles had scoffed at him, and he was not in honour bound to their cause. But he was not a man of the people. He was not a believer, and he was not a "philosopher." Hoche or Carnot might hesitate: there was nothing to halt him.

His self-confidence increased with achievement, and with the confidence of others. It was his greatest asset never to doubt his own ability: he silenced self-criticism as successfully as the Hamlets and the Amiels of this world cultivate it. He could never have uttered the sacramental words: *Domine, non sum dignus!*

No inner check: the word *impossible*, which is very French, does not exist in the Napoleonic vocabulary. No outer check: a military commander expects passive obedience. The result is magnificent, but neither safe nor sane. In practical details, the matchless realism of Napoleon's mind acted as a guide for his imagination. When he dreamed of vast schemes, he was literally unbalanced. In this respect, he differed widely from Louis XIV and from Bismarck, who, like himself, succeeded in imposing their supremacy upon Europe. Both the Grand Monarch and the Iron Chancellor had some sense of limitations, of possibilities. They knew that *"trop est trop."* Their ambitions were wrong, and in time had to be atoned for: still there was in their plans some degree of plausibility. The Empire, on the contrary, was a mad venture. Contemporaries knew it, both in France and abroad. The huge machine made itself tragically felt at times: but it never was accepted in good earnest. England and Metternich did not believe in that phantasmagory; neither did Talleyrand, who knew it from within; neither did Madame Letizia, Napoleon's mother, who expressed the feelings of his best friends when she said: "If only it would last!"

It is that element of Oriental mirage, of romanticism,

of actual insanity, that gives the Imperial gamble its
magic glamour.   Not Napoleon's efficiency: no one is
truly fascinated by a perfect bureaucrat or a martinet.
His efficiency merely added a touch of realism to a wild
fairy tale, and made it almost credible. This is an artistic device which is invariably effective: we find that kind
of appeal in Balzac's *Peau de Chagrin*, or in Wells's *War
of the Worlds*.

IV

Thus we are led from Napoleon's career and from his
personality to his Legend. Upon that great theme we
shall touch very briefly, for it goes beyond the scope of
this book. The "Legend" did not actually begin until
Napoleon's second exile, perhaps not until his death. And
it was the product, not of the classical spirit, which is our
subject, but of Romanticism. Napoleon became a Myth,
like Faust, Don Juan and Prometheus. Pérès and
Whately, in their clever skits casting "historic doubts"
on the actual existence of Napoleon, were nearer the truth
than they knew. A fabulous Napoleon was born in their
days.

It may seem strange that the man whom we called the
Supreme Classicist should become the hero of Romanticism. The two elements were blended in his career, in
his style and in his character. He was a Latin and a man
of the eighteenth century: his culture was classical. He
carried the classical spirit to its logical consequences. The
Renaissance had been the re-discovery of antiquity: the
Empire was a complete return to antiquity. There were
still feudal elements in the monarchy of Louis XIV: Napoleon goes back to Cæsar and Augustus. In the buildings of the sixteenth and even of the seventeenth centuries,
traces of medieval traditions may be found: Napoleon's
monuments are Roman pastiches pure and simple. He
was the representative of the essential classical quality,
discipline. He wanted society to form in proper ranks
and files, like the couplets of Boileau. The logical, stand-

M

ardized, hierarchical world that he wanted to shape was a classical world.

But in this disciplined Europe, he alone was free. All other personalities repressed, his own was unchecked. Whilst every one had to perform his task at his appointed place, Napoleon could gamble his soul against fate. So the solitary figure at the apex of this classical edifice was the Romantic ideal incarnate: adventure, gigantic dreams, the Ego challenging destiny, and the world well lost.

APPENDIX

BIBLIOGRAPHY

The aim of these notes, as of the whole book, is not to be exhaustive, but to point out the next step—the most easily available and clearest account of the subject, and especially the bibliographic instruments for further investigation.

Works provided with bibliographies are marked: Bibl.

Illustrated works are marked: Ill.

As readers interested in French civilization may be presumed to have a reading knowledge of French, the works listed in the first eleven divisions are all in French. A brief list of works in English is appended as Section XII.

I. BIBLIOGRAPHIES

H. Hauser, E. Bourgeois, L. André: *Les Sources de l'Histoire de France*, XVI–XVIIème Siècles, 9 vols. Paris, Picard, 1906–1926.

G. Lanson: *Manuel Bibliographique de la Littérature française moderne*, 5 vols. Paris, Hachette, 1921.

Cf. Bibliographical note to each chapter in Lavisse: *Histoire de France*, listed under III.

II. ICONOGRAPHY

Armand Dayot: series of illustrative albums: Flammarion, Paris. *Louis XIV*, 1909; *De la Régence à la Révolution*, 1906; *La Révolution Française*, 1896; *Napoléon*, 1908.

III.   GENERAL HISTORY OF CIVILIZATION

A. Rambaud: *Histoire de la Civilisation Française*, 2 vols. Paris, A. Colin, "édition révisée" (?). Bibl. A lucid and compact compilation.

G. Hanotaux (editor): *Histoire de la Nation Française*, 15 vols. Paris, Plon Nourrit, in course of publication. Ill. All the different aspects of French civilization are presented in separate volumes, most of which will be found listed below.

E. Lavisse (editor): *Histoire de France Illustrée*, Tomes V to IX (2 vols. to a tome). Paris, Hachette, 1903 seq. Bibl., Ill. All aspects of French civilization are also presented; division in *periods*, not in special histories. Cf. particularly E. Lavisse's own contribution, *Louis XIV*, in VII, i; VII, ii; and VIII, i.

Histoire de France Contemporaine, Vols. I, II, III, Revolution and Empire. Paris, Hachette, 1920–1921. Bibl., Ill. A continuation of the above.

E. Levasseur: *Histoire des Classes ouvrières*, etc., listed under Economic History, is almost a complete history of civilization.

IV.   GEOGRAPHY

P. Vidal de Lablache: *Tableau de la Géographie de la France*, in E. Lavisse, Histoire de France, I, i. Paris, Hachette, 1903–1920. Ill.

Jean Brunhes: *Géographie Humaine de la France*. Paris, Plon, 1920. Ill.

Jean Brunhes et P. Deffontaines: *Géographie Politique et Economique*. Paris, Plon, 1926. Ill. These form Vols. I and II of Hanotaux's *Nation Française*.

P. Jousset: *La France, Géographie Illustrée*, 2 vols. Paris, Larousse, 1912–1920. Profusely illustrated.

V.   POLITICAL HISTORY

E. Lavisse (editor): *Histoire de France Illustrée*. Cf. under I. The best general work of reference. Bibl., Ill.

Louis Madelin: *Histoire Politique*, 1515–1804. Paris, Plon, 1924. Ill. In Hanotaux: *Nation Française*. Thoughtful and scholarly.

Jacques Bainville: *Histoire de France* (separately and in *Heur et Malheur des Français*). Paris, Nouvelle Librairie Nationale, 1924. Royalist, but moderate. Phenomenally successful in France.

VI.   ECONOMIC HISTORY

E. Levasseur: *Histoire des Classes Ouvrières et de l'Industrie en France avant 1789*, 2 vols. Paris, Rousseau, 1900–1901. Remains important. *Bibliography* separately, 1903.

E. Levasseur: *Histoire du Commerce de la France*, Tome I: Avant 1789. Paris, Rousseau, 1911.

G. d'Avenel: *Histoire Economique de la Propriété, des Salaires, des Denrées et de tous les Prix en général*, 6 vols. Paris, Leroux. (Vicomte d'Avenel has published a number of popular works based on his *Histoire Economique.*)

H. Sée: *L'Evolution Commerciale et Industrielle de la France sous l'Ancien Régime*. Paris, Giard, 1925. Important Bibl.

Germain Martin: *Histoire Economique et Financière*. Paris, Plon, 1927. In Hanotaux: *Nation Française*. Ill.

VII. HISTORY OF SOCIETY

V. du Bled: *La Société Française du XVIème Siècle au XXème Siècle*, 9 series. Paris, Perrin, 1903; 1913.

P. Bonnefon: *La Société Française du XVIIème Siècle*. Paris, Colin, 1907.
La Société Française du XVIIIème Siècle. Paris, Colin, 1914. (Lectures extraites des Mémoires et Correspondances.)

Louis Ducros: *La Société Française au XVIIIème Siècle*, d'après les Mémoires et Correspondances du Temps. Paris, Hatier, 1922. Ill.

H. Sée: *La Vie Economique et les Classes Sociales en France au XVIIIème Siècle*. Paris, Alcan, 1924. Bibl.

H. Sée: *La France Economique et Sociale au XVIIIème Siècle*. (A model of condensation.) Paris, Colin, 1925. Bibl.

M. Magendie: *La Politesse Mondaine*, etc., *au XVIIème Siècle*, 2 vols. Paris, Alcan, 1925. Important Bibl., Ill.

H. Carré: *La France sous Louis XV*. Paris, Quantin, 1891. Bibl., Ill.

F. Funck-Brentano: *L'Ancien Régime*. Paris, Arthème Fayard, 1926. Bibl. (A very readable and substantial survey.)

(Edmond and Jules de Goncourt were among the pioneers of Social History, and their numerous works on the eighteenth century still provide fascinating reading.)

VIII. HISTORY OF RELIGION

Georges Goyau: *Histoire Religieuse*. Paris, Plon, 1922. Ill. In Hanotaux: *Nation Française*. (Catholic.)

Henri Brémond: *Histoire Littéraire du Sentiment Religieux en France depuis la fin des Guerres de Religion jusqu'à nos jours*. (Catholic.) 6 vols. Paris, Bloud et Gay, 1924–1926.

Sainte-Beuve: *Port-Royal* (1840–1848; revised 1867), 7 vols. Paris, Hachette, 1912. (Remains essential.)

On the Church and the Revolution, cf. principally:

A. Debidour: *Histoire des Rapports de l'Eglise et de l'Etat en France de 1789 à 1870*. Paris, Alcan, 1898. (Anticlerical.)

P. de la Gorce: *Histoire Religieuse de la Révolution Française.* Paris,
3 vols., 1909–1921. (Catholic.)
Also A. Aulard and Mathiez.

(Religious History is attracting much attention in modern France,
principally Pascal (V. Giraud), Bossuet (A. Rébelliau), and J. J. Rousseau (Masson).

IX. HISTORY OF ART

Louis Hourticq: *Histoire Générale de l'Art : France.* Paris, Hachette,
1914. Bibl., Ill. (A perfect introduction; admirably written, pro-
fusely illustrated, useful bibliographies.)
André Michel (editor): *Histoire de l'Art,* 17 vols. (8 tomes). Paris,
Colin, 1906 seq. (A general history; long chapters devoted to
French art, particularly IV, ii; V, ii; VI, ii; VII, i, ii.) Ill.
L. Gillet: *Histoire des Arts.* Paris, Plon, 1922. Ill. In Hanotaux:
Nation Française.
S. Rocheblave: *L'Art et le Goût en France de 1600 à 1900.* Paris, Colin,
1923. Ill. (A brief, but illuminating survey.)

X. HISTORY OF LITERATURE, SCIENCE, AND PHILOSOPHY

J. Bédier et P. Hazard (editors): *Histoire de la Littérature Française Il-
lustrée,* 2 vols. Paris, Larousse, 1923. Bibl., Ill.
F. Brunetière: *Histoire de la Littérature Française Classique,* 4 vols.
Paris, Delagrave, 1904–1917. (Completed by Brunetière's friends.
Classicism expounded by its most thorough-going modern cham-
pion.)
E. Faguet: *Etudes Littéraires, XVI-XVII-XVIIIèmes Siècles,* 3 vols.
Paris, Lecène Oudin; frequently reprinted. (Stimulating.
Hostile to eighteenth century.)
G. Lanson: *Histoire Illustrée de la Littérature Française,* 2 vols. Paris,
Hachette, 1923. Bibl., Ill. (The one-volume edition, Hachette,
has been an indispensable *vade-mecum* to students since 1894.)
L. Petit de Julleville (editor): *Histoire de la Langue et de la Littérature
Française des Origines à 1900,* 8 vols. Paris, Colin (Vols. III, IV,
V, VI, VII: 1897–1899). Bibl., Ill.
Picavet, Bédier, Jeanroy: *Histoire des Lettres,* Vol. I (jusqu'à Ronsard).
F. Strowski: Vol. II (De Ronsard à nos Jours), 2 vols. Paris, Plon,
1921–1923. Ill. In Hanotaux: *Nation Française.*

LANGUAGE

Ferdinand Brunot: *Histoire de la Langue Française des Origines à 1900,*
t. I–IX. Paris, Colin, 1905–1927 (in course of publication). Bibl.
(A monumental History of Civilization through language.)

SCIENCES AND PHILOSOPHY

E. Picard, H. Andoyer, Ch. Fabry, A. Colson: *Histoire des Sciences*, Vol. I.

M. Caullery, R. Lote: Vol. II, 2 vols. Paris, Plon, 1924. Ill. In Hanotaux: *Nation Française.*

XI. MISCELLANEOUS

Works referred or alluded to in this volume on account of their doctrinal importance.

Louis Bertrand: *Louis XIV.* Paris, Arthème Fayard, 1923. (Louis the Great as the national hero; sensational success.) (New Illustrated Edition.)

Louis Dimier: *Les Préjugés Ennemis de l'Histoire de France.* Paris, Nouvelle Librairie Nationale, 1917. (Conservative, paradoxical, penetrating.)

Charles Maurras: *Enquête sur la Monarchie.* Paris, Nouvelle Librairie Nationale, 1909. (The intellectual leader of Neo-Royalism, Positivistic Catholicism, and Classicism.)

Jules Michelet: *Histoire de France : Révolution*, 1847–53, 7 vols.
Renaissance et Temps Modernes, 1855–67, 11 vols. New Edition. Paris, Flammarion, 1893–99.

A. Sorel: *L'Europe et la Révolution Française*, 8 vols. Paris, Plon, 1885–1904. (Vol. I, *Les Mœurs Politiques et les Traditions*, a remarkable picture of the diplomatic Ancient Régime. Thesis: continuity of tradition reasserting itself through Revolution and Empire.)

H. Taine: *Les Origines de la France Contemporaine*, 6 vols. (New edition, 11 vols.) Paris, Hachette, 1876–1893. (Systematic, passionate, powerful.)

A. de Tocqueville: *L'Ancien Régime et la Révolution.* Paris, Lévy, 1856. (A classic of philosophical history.)

XII. A FEW WORKS IN ENGLISH

Section III. Arthur Tilley, editor: *Modern France*, a Companion to French Studies. Cambridge, University Press, 1922. Bibl., Ill. (Only the chapter on Architecture is illustrated.) (A massive compendium by excellent authorities.)

Section V. G.W. Kitchin: *A History of France*, 3 vols. Oxford, Clarendon Press, 1896–1906. (Revised edition.) Bibl. Vol. II: 1453–1624; Vol. III: 1624–1793. (Solid.)

V. W. Stearns Davis: *A History of France.* New York, Boston, Houghton Mifflin, 1919. Bibl., Ill. (A workable adaptation of a good French manual.)

V. The National History of France. London, Heinemann.
  1. Louis Batiffol: *The Century of the Renaissance*, 1921. Bibl.
  2. Jacques Boulenger: *The Seventeenth Century*, 1920. Bibl.
  3. Casimir Stryienski: *The Eighteenth Century*, 1916 (dry). Bibl.
  4. Louis Madelin: *The French Revolution*, 1916 (notable).
  (A good series; sponsored by J. C. Bodley; the French versions
  were awarded prizes by two academies.)

V. Paul Wiriath: Article *France* (Political History) in *Britannica*.
  (By one of the best disciples of E. Lavisse.)

Section VII. Emile Bourgeois, tr. by Mrs. Cashel Hoey: *France under Louis XIV : its art and its ideas*. New York, Scribner, 1897.
  Ill. (A very handsome volume.)

VII. Cécile Hugon: *Social France in the XVIIth century*. London
  and New York, Macmillan, 1911. Brief. Bibl., Ill.

VII. Paul Lacroix: *The XVIIIth Century*. New York, Scribner, 1876.
  Ill. (By the well-known polygraph "Bibliophile Jacob.")

VII. Hélène Clergue: *The Salon :* a study of French Society and Personalities in the XVIIIth century. New York, Putnam, 1907.
  Ill. (A very readable introduction.)

Section VIII. A. H. Galton: *Church and State in France*. London,
  Arnold, 1907. Bibl. (Very brief on pre-revolutionary period.
  Moderate.)

VIII. A. Aulard: *Christianity and the French Revolution*. Boston, Little, Brown, 1927. (Rather disappointing from "the greatest living
  authority" on the Revolution.)

Section X. C. H. C. Wright: *A History of French Literature*. Oxford
  University Press, new edition, 1925. Bibl. (Thorough.)

X. W. A. Nitze and E. P. Dargan: *A History of French Literature*.
  New York, H. Holt, 1927 (revised edition). Bibl., Ill. (Excellent.)

X. L. Lévy-Bruhl: *History of Modern Philosophy in France*. Chicago,
  Open Court, 1899. Bibl.

X. G. Saintsbury's *French Literature* is emphatically not recommended.

Section XI. Arthur Young: *Travels in France*, etc., 1787–88–89. Bibl.
  (Conveniently in Everyman's Library, 1915.)

XI. Edmund Burke: *Reflections on the Revolution in France*. Oxford,
  Clarendon Press, 1898.

XI. Thomas Carlyle: *The French Revolution* (1837), edited by J. Holland Rose, 3 vols. London, Bell, 1913. (Bohn's Popular Library.)

XI. G. Lytton Strachey: *Books and Characters* (Racine, Mme. du
  Deffand, Voltaire, Rousseau). London, Chatto, 1922. (The di-
  vinely appointed interpreter of classical France to the English-
  reading world.)

XI. Mary Duclaux (Mary Robinson): *A Short History of France*.
  (Tenuous as history, but full of sympathy and charm.)

CHRONOLOGICAL SUMMARY

I. SIXTEENTH CENTURY

(CHARLES VIII, 1483–1498)

1491.   Marries Anne, Duchess of Brittany.
1494.   *ITALIAN EXPEDITIONS* begin.
1495.   Rapid conquest and immediate loss of Kingdom of Naples.
1498.   Charles VIII dies of accident at Amboise, and is succeeded by distant cousin, Louis of Orleans.

HOUSE OF VALOIS–ORLEANS

1498–1515.   LOUIS XII, "Father of the People," marries Anne of Brittany; Italian expeditions; claims to Milan and Naples. Checked by Holy League (Pope, Aragon, Venice, joined later by England and Maximilian, Emperor).
1513.   Peace with the Pope, Spain,
1514.   The Emperor and England.

HOUSE OF VALOIS–ANGOULEME

1515–1547.   FRANCIS I.
1515.   Reconquers Milan by brilliant victory of Marignano over the Swiss.
1516.   Perpetual peace (Fribourg) with the Swiss, in force until the Revolution.
1516.   Concordat with the Pope, in force until the Revolution; supersedes the Pragmatic Sanction of Bourges, 1438.
1517.   Luther nails his ninety-five propositions at Wittenberg.
1519.   Charles V elected German Emperor against Francis I.
1520.   Luther burns Papal Bull and is excommunicated.
1520.   Meeting of Francis I and Henry VIII of England near Calais (Camp of the Cloth of Gold).

RIVALRY BETWEEN FRANCIS I AND CHARLES V

1521–1526.   First War; treason of Charles of Bourbon, Constable.
1525.   Francis I defeated and captured at Pavia.
1526.   Treaty of Madrid, renouncing Italian claims, overlordship of Flanders and Artois, and ceding Burgundy.
1527–1529.   Treaty of Madrid broken, war renewed. Peace of Cambrai; cession of Burgundy withdrawn.
1529.   Definite beginning of religious persecution; Louis de Berquin executed.

1530.	Beginnings of Collège de France.
1532.	Clement Marot: *Adolescence Clémentine*.
1532.	Rabelais: *Chroniques Gargantuines*.
1531–1536.	Robert Estienne: *Thesaurus Linguæ Latinæ*.
1533.	Rabelais: *Pantagruel* (later, Book II).
1533–1534.	Sharp religious crisis (Affair of the Placards; Cop).
1534.	Jesuits founded by Ignatius Loyola.
1535.	Rabelais: *Gargantua* (later becomes Book I).
1535–1536.	Calvin: *Christian Institute* (in Latin).
1536–1538.	Claims to Milan renewed; Third War; Francis I allied with Soliman; truce of Nice, on the basis of possession.
1539.	Great Ordinance of Villers-Cotterets (almost a code).
1539–1540.	Charles V, on his way to Ghent, which had rebelled, crosses France and is received with great honours.
1540.	Jesuits approved by Pope.
1541.	Calvin: *Christian Institute* (in French).
1542–1544.	Fourth War; France allied with Clèves and Soliman; Charles V with Henry VIII.
1544.	Peace of Crespy-en-Valois; Italy given up, Burgundy retained.
1545–1563.	Council of Trent; Catholic Reformation.
1546.	Rabelais: Book III.
1547.	Francis I succeeded by his son.
1547–1559.	HENRY II. (Diana of Poictiers—Growing influence of the Lorraine-Guise family.)
1548.	Prohibition of mystery and miracle plays.
1548 (?).	La Boétie: *Discourse on Voluntary Servitude*.
1549.	Du Bellay: *Defence and Illustration of the French Language*.
1549–1550.	Du Bellay and Ronsard begin their careers as poets.
1552.	Taking advantage of religious difficulties in Germany, France annexes the three Bishoprics, Metz, Toul, and Verdun. Provisional confirmation of conquest by truce of Vaucelles.
1552.	Jodelle: *Cléopâtre*, classical tragedy.
1556.	Charles V abdicates. War continues with Spain and England.
1557.	French sharply defeated at St. Quentin.
1558.	François de Guise reconquers Calais.
1559.	Peace of Cateau-Cambrésis; Italy lost, three Bishoprics and Calais retained.
1559.	Amyot: translation of *Plutarch*.
1559.	Henry II wounded to death in a tournament.
RELIGIOUS WARS, 1560–1598.	
1559–1560.	FRANCIS II, sixteen years old, son of Henry II and Catherine de' Medici; husband of Mary Stuart. Rivalry between Guises and Montmorency; the nephews of Montmorency, Coligny, Châtillon, d'Andelot become leaders of Huguenots, in alliance with Bourbon-Navarre.

1560.	Conspiracy of Amboise; Huguenots try to rescue King from influence of Guises; thwarted and rigorously punished.
1560–1574.	CHARLES IX, ten years old, brother of Francis II.
1562.	Rabelais's *Fifth Book;* largely apocryphal.
1560–1572.	First three religious wars; really a single war with brief and insincere truces. Indecisive. La Rochelle, Cognac, Montauban and La Charité officially turned over to Huguenots; Henry of Navarre to marry Marguerite of Valois, sister of the King.
1572.	Night of St. Bartholomew, August 23; massacre of Protestants.
1572.	Ronsard: *Franciade.*
1572.	Henry Estienne: *Thesaurus Linguæ Grecæ.*
1573.	Fourth War: ends in a compromise.
1574–1589.	HENRY III, brother of Charles IX; a degenerate. Fifth War, led on the Huguenot side by Henry of Navarre; concessions granted to Protestants. The Ultra Catholics, dissatisfied, form the Holy Catholic League,
1576.	under the leadership of the Guises, and in alliance with Spain.
1576–1578.	Bodin: *The Republic.*
1577.	Sixth War; the Huguenots, defeated, again secure favourable terms, the King being afraid of the ascendancy of the Guises.
1577.	d'Aubigné begins his *Tragics,* published 1616.
1578.	H. Estienne: *Dialogue of the New Italianized French Language.*
1579.	Du Bartas: *The Week,* religious epic.
1580.	Seventh War.
1580–1588.	Montaigne's *Essays* (Gournay edition, 1595).
1585–1589.	Eighth War, or War of the Three Henrys: Henry III, Henry of Navarre, Henry of Guise. Paris controlled by the League, *i. e.*, by H. de Guise; King flees to Blois.
1588.	States General at Blois; Henry of Guise and his brother the Cardinal murdered; Mayenne, their brother, becomes leader of the League.
1589.	Henry III and Henry of Navarre jointly before Paris (St. Cloud); Henry III assassinated by a monk.
1589–1789–1830.	HOUSE OF BOURBON.
1589–1610.	HENRY IV (Henry of Navarre) not recognized by the Catholics.
1589.	Henry IV victorious at Arques and Ivry; besieges Paris,
1590.	which is relieved by the Duke of Parma; the Moderates or Politiques rally to him.
1593.	He abjures Protestantism at St. Denis.
1594.	*Satire Ménippée* against League and Spain, works for Henry IV; the King crowned at Chartres; Paris sur-

rendered to him; he is recognized by the League leaders, particularly by Mayenne.

1598.   Religious wars ended by Edict of Nantes.

1598.   Treaty of Vervins with Spain; conquests restored to France.

II. SEVENTEENTH CENTURY (1598–1715)

Henry IV, aided by Sully, devotes himself to the economic reconstruction of France.

1601.   Charron: *On Wisdom.*

1608.   St. François de Sales: *Introduction to Devout Life.*

1608–1627. Honoré d'Urfé: *Astrée.* Malherbe, Régnier.

1610.   Alleged "Grand Design" of Henry IV for the reconstruction of Europe; extensive preparations for war in Germany. Henry IV assassinated; succeeded by his son,

1610–1643. LOUIS XIII, nine years old.

1610–1617. Regency of the Queen-Mother, Marie de' Medici. Influence of Concini and his wife. Rebellion of the nobles.

1614.   States General (last before 1789); abortive.

1617.   Concini arrested and killed; d'Albert de Luynes in power; Queen Marie banished.

1618.   Hotel de Rambouillet rebuilt; assumes social and literary leadership.

1621.   Rebellion of the Huguenots; death of de Luynes. Return to power of Queen Marie; she quarrels with Richelieu, hitherto her protégé.

1624–1642. Unbroken rule of Cardinal Richelieu.

1627–1628. Rebellion of Protestants. Siege of La Rochelle; political
1629.   privileges taken away from Protestants by Peace of Alais, or Edict of Grace.

1630.   Day of Dupes (November 11); last effort of Queen Marie's faction. Gaston, brother of the King, conspires; Mont-
1632.   morency in open rebellion; defeated; executed.

1631–1648. Participation of France in *THIRTY YEARS' WAR,* against Spain and Austria. Richelieu at first subsidizes Gustavus-Adolphus of Sweden; who dies in 1632; uses also Bernard of Saxe-Weimar (d. 1639).

1634–1637. Academy founded.

1636.   Spaniards take Corbie in Picardy; panic; victorious effort.

1636.   Corneille: *The Cid,* tragedy.

1637.   Descartes: *Discourse on Method.*

1640.   Corneille: *Horace, Cinna,* tragedies.

1640.   Jansenius: *Augustinus.* JANSENISM.

1641.   Conspiracy of Cinq-Mars against Richelieu.

1642.   December 4, death of Richelieu.

1643.   Corneille, *Polyeucte,* tragedy.

1643. May 14, Louis XIII dies; succeeded by his son,
 LOUIS XIV, 1643–1715
 then five years old.
 Regency of the Queen Mother, Anne of Austria; Cardinal Mazarin, Queen's favourite, all powerful. War in Germany and war with Spain continue.

1643. Condé victorious over Spaniards at Rocroy.

1644. Corneille: *The Liar*, first masterpiece of classical comedy.

1647. Vaugelas: *Remarks on the French Language*.

1648. Scarron: *Burlesque Æneid*.

1648–1653. The *FRONDE;* last attempt at armed resistance to monarchy.

1648–1649. Old Fronde, or Parliamentary; treaty of Rueil.

1649–1653. New Fronde (Princes), in alliance with Spain. Principal characters: Cardinal de Retz, Condé, Turenne (shift positions); and romantic heroines: Melle de Montpensier, Mme. de Chevreuse, Mme. de Longueville, etc. Ruin of the country. Mazarin returns in triumph.

1649 seq. Melle de Scudéry; pseudo-antique society romances, *Cyrus, Clélie*.

1656–1657. Pascal: *Provincial Letters;* high point in conflict between Jansenists and Jesuits.

1657. Alliance with Cromwell against Spain.

1659. Peace of the Pyrenees with Spain (seed of future war).

1659. Molière: *Les Précieuses Ridicules*, first masterpiece; rebellion of commonsense against affectation.

1661. Death of Mazarin.

PERSONAL REIGN OF LOUIS XIV (1661–1715)

The King his own Prime Minister. Policy of magnificence. Served by Colbert, Louvois, Turenne, Condé. New generation of great classical writers.

1662. Bossuet preaches at the Louvre.

1662. Molière: *School for Wives*.

1664. Molière: *Tartuffe* (first version).

1665. La Rochefoucauld: *Maxims*.

1666. Molière: *The Misanthropist*.

1666. Boileau: *Satires*.

1667. Racine: *Andromaque*.

1668. La Fontaine: *Fables*.

1667–1668. First War of Conquest: *WAR OF DEVOLUTION*, or of the Queen's Rights. Conquest of parts of Flanders and Franche-Comté. A Triple Alliance (England, Holland, Sweden) compels Louis to sign

1668. Peace of Aix-la-Chapelle, retaining only twelve fortified towns in Spanish Netherlands, particularly Lille.

1669–1679. "Peace of the Church"; persecution of Jansenism mitigated.

1671. First letters of Mme. de Sévigné to Mme. de Grignan.

1673. Molière's last play: *The Imaginary Invalid.*

1674. Boileau: *Poetic Art.*

1674. Corneille's last play: *Suréna.*

1677. Racine retires after failure of *Phèdre.*

1678. Mme. de Lafayette: *Princess of Cleves.*

1678. Lafontaine: *Fables,* second series.

1672–1678. Second War of Conquest. (*WAR OF HOLLAND.*) Prepared by disruption of Triple Alliance.

1672. Crossing of the Rhine; easy conquest of Southern Holland. The brothers de Witt, leaders of the aristocratic republican party in Holland, are killed, and superseded by William III of Orange, henceforth the soul of European resistance to Louis XIV. Sluices opened, Amsterdam saved; Holland allied with Empire and Spain. Louis in person conquers Franche-Comté again. Last campaigns of Condé and Turenne.

1678–1679. Series of treaties at Nymwegen. Holland restored. France keeps Franche-Comté. Louis at the height of his power, "nee pluribus impar."

1679. Recrudescence of intolerance against Protestants and Jansenists. Difficulties with the Pope.

1680–1683. Chambers of Reunion; French courts of claims deciding what territories had once belonged to France's recent conquests. Decisions enforced by French troops.

1681. Strasbourg thus "united" with France.

1682. Gallican attitude of the King in his conflict with the Pope supported by French Assembly of the Clergy. Declaration of Four Articles, drawn up by Bossuet (clearest statement of traditional Gallicanism).

1683. Death of Colbert.

1685. Revocation of the Edict of Nantes. Large exodus, although emigration was prohibited. Huguenots in Holland, England, Brandenburg. Lutherans in Alsace preserve their religious liberties.

1686. Fontenelle: *Plurality of Inhabited Worlds.*

1687. Ch. Perrault: *Century of Louis the Great:* salient episode in Quarrel of the Ancients and the Moderns.

1687. Bossuet: *Funeral Oration of Condé;* knell of the Golden Age.

1688. La Bruyère: *Characters.*

1691. Racine's last tragedy: *Athalie.*

1689–1697. Third Great War of Louis XIV: *WAR OF THE AUGSBURG LEAGUE.* William of Orange, king of England since 1688, the center of the League.

1688.   The Palatinate (cause or pretext of the conflict) ravaged
          by the French.
1689.   Grand Alliance: Augsburg League (Emperor, Sweden,
          Spain, Bavaria, Saxony, Palatinate), plus Savoy, Eng-
          land, and Holland. Catinat and Luxembourg, French
          generals, more than a match for William III and Eu-
          gene of Savoy. Naval disaster at Cape La Hogue.
1697.   Treaties of Ryswick; France acknowledges William III
          as king of England; restores some "reunions"; barrier
          of fortresses in Spanish Netherlands garrisoned by
          Dutch troops as a protection against France. Posses-
          sion of Alsace with Strasbourg confirmed to France.
          A draw.
1697.   Fénelon: *Maxims of the Saints;* Quietism controversy
          with Bossuet.
1697.   Bayle: *Critical Dictionary,* the arsenal of "Philosophy."
1699.   Fénelon: *Télémaque,* pedagogical romance and aristo-
          cratic Utopia.
1701–1714. *WAR OF THE SPANISH SUCCESSION.*
1700.   Charles II of Spain dies, leaving his dominions to Duke
          of Anjou (Philip V), grandson of Louis XIV. Louis ac-
          cepts, in spite of previous agreements; "No more
          Pyrenees." Grand Alliance, England, Holland, the
          Emperor against France; Eugene of Savoy, Marlbor-
          ough, and Heinsius leaders of the Coalition, after the
          death of William III.
1704.   French defeated at Blenheim,
1706.   at Ramillies and Turin,
1708.   at Oudenarde.
1708.   Lille surrenders; severe winter; great distress; rise of the
1709.   financiers (Samuel Bernard); cf. Lesage: *Turcaret.*
          France humbled, sues for peace. Terms too harsh,
          revulsion. Louis appeals to the nation.
1709.   Eugene and Marlborough win costly and indecisive bat-
          tle of Malplaquet over Villars. Vendôme successful in
          Spain, the Spanish people supporting Philip V.
1711.   Marlborough removed from command on account of
          political changes; Grand Alliance disrupted by death of
          Emperor.
1712.   Victory of Villars at Denain.
1713.   Series of treaties at Utrecht. France loses Acadia, New-
          foundland; Philip V keeps Spain and colonies, but loses
          European possessions of Spain; Spanish Netherlands to
          go to Austria.
1713.   Papal Bull *Unigenitus* condemning Jansenism.
          War with Empire continues. Eugene of Savoy unsuc-
          cessful.

| 1714. | Treaty of Rastadt, confirming peace of Ryswick. |
| 1715. | Louis XIV dies, succeeded by his great-grandson, five years old. |

III. THE EIGHTEENTH CENTURY (TO THE REVOLUTION)

1715–1774.	LOUIS XV,
1715–1723.	THE REGENCY. Philip of Orleans, regent. General tone of immorality. Louis XIV's policies abandoned. Religious toleration.
1717. 1720.	Alliance with England against Spain (Alberoni); treaty of London.
1718–1720.	Financial "System" of John Law; Royal Bank, Mississippi scheme. Wild speculation. Collapse.
1715–1735.	Lesage: *Gil Blas*.
1718.	Arouet assumes name Voltaire. First tragedy, *Œdipus*.
1721.	Montesquieu: *Persian Letters*.
1721.	Dubois, with the favour of the Regent, becomes Cardinal,
1722–1723.	Prime Minister. Dubois and Regent die, 1723.
1723–1726.	Duke of Bourbon, prime minister.
1725.	King married to Marie Leczynska.
1726–1743.	Fleury (soon Cardinal), tutor of Louis XV, overthrows Duke of Bourbon. Quietly successful government.
1726–1729.	Voltaire in England; great formative period.
1730.	Bull *Unigenitus* the law of the State and the Church; Jansenism persecuted. Miracles at St. Médard's Cemetery.
1732.	Cemetery closed.
1733–1735.	*WAR OF THE POLISH SUCCESSION;* by treaty of Vienna (1738), Stanislaus Leczynski receives Lorraine for life, with reversion to France (d. 1766).
1734.	Voltaire: *Philosophical Letters* (manifesto of Anglicized "Enlightenment").
1734.	Montesquieu: *Greatness and Decadence of the Romans.*
1735.	Prévost: *Manon Lescaut.*
1736.	Voltaire: *The Wordling (Le Mondain)*, poem.
1741–1748.	*WAR OF THE AUSTRIAN SUCCESSION,* France and Prussia against Austria and England. Dupleix in India.
1744.	Beginning of Mme. de Pompadour's influence.
1744.	King falls sick at Metz; manifestations of popular affection—Louis the Well-Beloved.
1745.	Victory of Maurice de Saxe (Louis present) at Fontenoy.
1748.	Peace of Aix-la-Chapelle; no gain. "A King's, not a merchant's peace."
1748.	Montesquieu: *Spirit of Laws.*
1749.	Buffon's *Natural History* begins to appear.

1749–1750. Rousseau: *Discourse on Sciences and Arts.*
1751–1753. Voltaire at Potsdam with Frederick II.
1751. Voltaire: *Century of Louis XIV.*
1751–1780. Publication of the *Encyclopædia* (Diderot, editor).
1753–1758. Voltaire: *Essay on Manners.*
1755. Rousseau: *Discourse on Inequality.*
1756–1763. *SEVEN YEARS' WAR.* Partly through Mme. de Pompadour, continental alliances reversed. France, Austria, and Russia against Prussia and England. Fighting in Europe; French defeated at Rossbach by
1757. Frederick II; in India: Clive victor at Plassey; in
1759. America: death of Wolfe and Montcalm at Quebec.
1763. Treaties of Paris and Hubertsbourg; England's colonial supremacy firmly established.
1757. Damiens's attempt of King's life.
1758. Voltaire: *Candide* (against optimism).
1758–1760. CHOISEUL, minister of foreign affairs.
1760. Voltaire: *Tancrède*, tragedy (pre-romanticism).
1761–1762. Rousseau: *New Heloise; Emile; Social Contract.*
1761–1762. Jesuits condemned and expelled from France.
1762–1765. Calas, unjustly executed, declared innocent through Voltaire's efforts.
1764. Death of Mme. de Pompadour.
1764. Voltaire: *Philosophical Dictionary.*
1765. Du Belloy: *Siege of Calais*, national tragedy.
1765. Sedaine: *Philosopher without Knowing it*, drama.
1768. Corsica bought. (1769: Napoleon born.)
1769. Voltaire: *History of the Parliament of Paris.*
1769–1774. Mme. du Barry, favourite.
1770. Choiseul falls. Retires to Chanteloup; great popularity.
1771. Maupeou reforms Parliaments.
1772. First partition of Poland.
1774. Death of Louis XV; succeeded by his grandson
1774–1792. LOUIS XVI.
1774. Maupeou Courts abolished; old Parliaments restored.
1774–1781. Maurepas most trusted minister.
1774–1776. TURGOT, minister of navy and finances.
1776. *Werther* and *Ossian* translated.
1776. American Independence.
1777–1781. Necker, minister of finances.
1778. Alliance between France and United States. Vergennes minister.
1778. Deaths of Voltaire and J. J. Rousseau.
1778. Buffon: *Epochs of Nature.*
1778–1783. *AMERICAN WAR;* Lafayette, d'Estaing, Rochambeau; Suffren, de Grasse.
1783. Treaties of Paris and Versailles.

1783–1787.	Calonne minister; prodigality a system.
1784.	Beaumarchais: *Marriage of Figaro* (revolutionary spirit).
1785.	Scandal of the Diamond Necklace; supposed to have been given to Queen Marie-Antoinette by Cardinal de Rohan. Queen unpopular.
1787.	Assembly of Notables at Versailles refuse support to Calonne.
1787–1788.	Loménie de Brienne succeeds Calonne.
1788.	Increasing difficulties with Parliament.
1788.	Barthélémy: *Young Anacharsis* (revived interest in antiquity).
1788.	Loménie resigns. Necker returns. States General summoned.

IV. THE REVOLUTION AND THE EMPIRE

1789.	May 5. Meeting of the States General.
	June 17. The Third Estate votes itself a NATIONAL CONSTITUENT ASSEMBLY. Joined later by the other orders.
	July 14. Fall of the Bastille.
	Sporadic, spontaneous uprisings in the country; "The Great Fear." Tricolour adopted. First émigrés.
	Aug. 4. Renunciation to feudal rights.
	Oct. 5–6. Mob (mostly women) brings Royal Family from Versailles to Paris.
1790.	Constitution and Civil Organization of the Clergy voted.
1791.	June 20. Flight of King; arrested at Varennes; reinstated.
	Oct. 1. LEGISLATIVE ASSEMBLY.
	Feuillants (Royalists) and Girondists.
1792.	April 20. War declared against Austria.

FIRST COALITION AGAINST FRANCE (Prussia, Austria)

	July 11. Manifesto of Brunswick. "The Country in Danger."
	Aug. 10. Tuileries stormed. King seeks refuge in Assembly. Suspended.
	Sept. 2–7. Massacre in the prisons.
	Sept. 20. Victory over Prussians at Valmy.
	Sept. 21. CONVENTION meets. First Republic proclaimed. Victory of Jemmapes.
1793.	Jan. 21. Louis XVI executed.
	Feb. 1. War with Great Britain, Holland, Spain (Sardinia had already joined coalition).
	April 6. Committee of Public Safety. The Mountain (radicals) in control. Girondists eliminated.

1793.	Marat assassinated. Vendée, whole West and South in revolt. Catholic Church in rebellion. Reign of Terror. Carnot "organizer of victory."
1794.	Recrudescence of Terror with absolute supremacy of Robespierre. Danton executed. Condorcet: *Sketch of the Progress of the Human Mind.* A. Chénier: *Iambics.*
	June 8. Ceremony in honour of "Supreme Being"; Robespierre high priest.
	June 26. Victory of Fleurus.
	July 27. IX THERMIDOR; Fall of Robespierre. Convention henceforth dominated by **THERMIDORIAN REACTION** (Barras, Tallien).
1795.	Treaties of Basel, with Prussia and Spain. Left bank of the Rhine in French hands.
	Oct. 5–13. Vendémiaire: Bonaparte crushes Royalist uprising in Paris (the "whiff of grapeshot").
1795–1799.	**DIRECTORY**; bourgeois régime, corrupt, vacillating, weak, and violent.
1796.	War continues with England and Austria. Great plan of Carnot. Failure of Jourdan compels Moreau to retreat. Brilliant campaign of Bonaparte in **ITALY**; leads to
1797.	Peace of Campo Formio with Austria. Creation of satellite republics.
1798–1799.	Bonaparte's **EGYPTIAN CAMPAIGN**. Fleet destroyed at Aboukir; fails before St. Jean d'Acre. Abandons his army, which capitulates.
1799–1801.	*SECOND COALITION AGAINST FRANCE;* England, Austria, Russia, Portugal, Naples, Turkey. Masséna at Zurich and Brune in Holland defeat the Allies.
1799.	Nov. 9. (XVIII BRUMAIRE), Coup d'état; Bonaparte seizes power.
1799–1804.	CONSULATE.
1800.	Victories of Marengo (Desaix, Bonaparte) and Hohenlinden (Moreau) lead to the
1801.	Peace of Lunéville with Austria.
1801–1802.	Concordat with the Pope.
1801–1802.	Chateaubriand: *Atala; Spirit of Christianity.* ('04, *René.*)
1802.	Peace of Amiens with England.
1803.	War resumed.
1804.	Conspiracy of Pichegru; Moreau exiled; Enghien executed.
1804–1814.	NAPOLEON I, EMPEROR OF THE FRENCH.
1805.	*THIRD COALITION AGAINST FRANCE* (England, Austria, Russia).
	Oct. 21. Trafalgar.
	Dec. 2. Austerlitz. Peace of Presbourg with Austria.

1806. Confederacy of the Rhine established. Holy Roman Empire officially at an end.
FOURTH COALITION (England, Russia, Prussia). Prussia destroyed at Jena and Auerstaedt; Berlin entered. Berlin Decree; Continental Blockade against England.

1807. War with Russia continues; Eylau, Friedland. Peace of Tilsitt with Russia and Prussia.

1807. Madame de Stael: *Corinne.*

1808–1814. Intervention in Spain and Portugal. *PENINSULAR WAR* (Wellington).

1809. Chateaubriand: *The Martyrs.*

1809. *FIFTH WAR AGAINST ENGLAND AND AUSTRIA.* Wagram; peace of Vienna.

1810. Napoleon divorces Josephine and marries Marie-Louise of Austria. Greatest extent of French Empire; 130 departments under immediate control. Spain, Naples, Northern Italy as feudatory states; whole of Germany and Grand-Duchy of Warsaw "protected" or "allied."

1810. Mme. de Stael: *Germany* (suppressed).

1811. Birth of King of Rome.

1812. *RUSSIAN WAR.* Grand Army, 600,000 men, less than half of them French; Austria, Prussia, Spain officially allied with Napoleon. Borodino. Moscow. Retreat from Moscow. Total loss of Grand Army. Malet conspiracy in Paris.

1813. *CAMPAIGN OF GERMANY;* one enforced "ally" after another joins the crusade of liberation.
Oct. 16–19. Leipzig, "Battle of the Nations," French routed.

1814. Renewal of opposition in French Chambers, long silent. *CAMPAIGN OF FRANCE;* Napoleon at his best. Minor victories. Paris capitulates. Napoleon abdicates and is sent to Elba.

1814–1815. FIRST RESTORATION OF THE BOURBONS. Very moderate terms of peace. Tactless methods of returning émigrés.

1815. March 1. Napoleon lands at Cannes; THE HUNDRED DAYS.
March 20. Paris; Additional Act to the Constitution. War renewed.
June 18. Waterloo.
June 22. Second abdication, in favour of his son, Napoleon II. Paris entered a second time by the Allies.
SECOND RESTORATION OF THE BOURBONS.
Napoleon sent to St. Helena (d. 1821).
Harsher terms of peace (Treaties of Vienna).

INDEX

INDEX

Names and Topics treated in the book are indicated in capitals and small capitals.

Names and Topics alluded to are indicated in small Roman.

Titles of books, plays, pictures in *Italics*.

"Characters in works of fiction" between inverted commas.

Unless otherwise indicated, dates after name are birth and death. In the case of sovereigns, the first and last dates stand for birth and death; the second and third, for dates of reign. *E. g.*, Napoleon: 1769–1804–1814–15–1821: born 1769, Emperor 1804, abdicates 1814 and again 1815, dies 1821.

A

Abbeville, city in Picardy, 183

Abélard, philosopher (1079–1142), 55

ACADEMY: French (Académie Française), 54, 139–142, 148, 200, 212, 213, 219, 248–249, 266
of Sciences, 219, 222, 267
of Inscriptions, 219, 283
of Bordeaux, 267
of Dijon, 254, 273

Adélaïde du Guesclin, tragedy by Voltaire (1734), 287

Adone, Italian poem by Marini, 1623, 143

Adrets, Baron des, Protestant leader, 1513–1587, 13, 106

Africa, epic, Petrarch, 44

Aguesseau, d', great Parliamentary family, 73, 307

Aigues-Mortes, city in Languedoc, 165

Aiguillon, duke d', minister under Louis XV, 1720–1782, 231

À'Kempis, Thomas (*Imitation*), 29

Alais, peace granted to Protestants, 1629, 125, 199

Alanus de Insulis, poet, ca. 1128–1202, 43

Alarcón, Spanish dramatist, d. 1639, 143

Alary, Abbé (Club de l'Entresol), 1689–1770, 244

ALEMBERT, d', mathematician and encyclopædist, 1717–1783, 250, 251, 252, 253, 270

Alexandre, Battles of, painted by Lebrun, 159

Alexander I, Emperor of Russia, 1777–1825, 341

Alexandrian poetry, 47, 283

Aligre: great Parliamentary family, 307

Alsace, 36, 94, 178, 180, 321, 334

Alumbrados: mystic sect, sixteenth century, 292

Alzire, or the Americans, tragedy by Voltaire, 1736, 288

Amboise, conspiracy, 1560, 107

America: influx of precious metals, 91

American War (War of Independence), 1778–1783, 299, 315

Amerigo Vespucci, navigator, 1451–1512, 26

Amyot, bishop, translator of Plutarch, 1513–1593, 47

Ancien Régime, by Funck-Brentano, 1926, 7.

Ancien Régime (*Origines de la France Contemporaine*), Taine, 1876, cf. Taine.

Ancien Régime et la Révolution, de Tocqueville, 1856, 8.

Ancre, Marshal d', cf. Concini.

Andelot, d', Protestant leader, 1521–1569, 108

Andromache, painting by L. David, 281

Angélique, Mother, cf. Arnauld

Anglomania, cf. England: influence

Anjou, Province, 51, 58

Anne of Austria, queen, 1601–1666, 122, 128, 151

Anne of Brittany, duchess and queen, 1477–1514, 61

Annonay, town, 300, 301

Anti-Bigot, or the Deist's Quatrains, 1622, 203

Anticlaudianus, poem by Alanus de Insulis, 43

"Antiphysis," in Rabelais, 41, 106, 273